Discovering
Philosophy

Discovering Philosophy

Fourth Edition

Thomas I. White

Hackett Publishing Company, Inc.
Indianapolis/Cambridge

Copyright © 2022 by Hackett Publishing Company, Inc.

25 24 23 22   1 2 3 4 5 6 7

For further information, please address
    Hackett Publishing Company, Inc.
    P.O. Box 44937
    Indianapolis, Indiana 46244-0937

    www.hackettpublishing.com

Cover and interior designs by E. L. Wilson
Composition by Aptara, Inc.

Cataloging-in-Publication data can be accessed via the Library of Congress Online Catalog. Library of Congress Control Number: 2022930808

ISBN-13: 978-1-64792-069-2 (pbk.)
ISBN-13: 978-1-64792-070-8 (PDF ebook)

The paper used in this publication meets the minimum requirements of American National Standard for Information Sciences—Permanence of Paper for Printed Library Materials, ANSI Z39.48–1984.

∞

CONTENTS

PREFACE

This book aims to be a comprehensive and challenging introduction to philosophy for the student who is more comfortable with secondary than with primary sources. Although philosophers do speak in their own words in this text when appropriate, this book consists primarily of summary, explication, and discussion of the major arguments on the issues involved. The writing style is relatively informal. The text is organized in a conventional and straightforward way. It begins with an overview of philosophy (Chapter 1) and an introduction to logical thinking (Chapter 2). It then explores a series of basic issues related to human action and our dealings with each other: determinism and freedom (Chapters 3 and 4), ethics, and its ultimate justification (Chapters 5 and 6). Next, it proceeds to more theoretical issues: the nature of reality and knowledge (Chapters 7 and 8) and the existence of God (Chapter 9). The book concludes with three chapters that examine nontraditional questions or perspectives: whether a dolphin is a "person" (Chapter 10), the different claims by Karl Marx and Albert Einstein that things aren't the way they appear to be (Chapter 11), and the way that Buddhism and Native American thought see the world very differently from a traditional Western perspective.

Spirit of the Book

My first goal in writing this book was to produce a text that students would actually read. Thus, the style, tone, and content aim to make the text easy to read, unintimidating, and intellectually engaging. In the same spirit, I have also included a fair amount of material from other disciplines. One of the most difficult aspects of teaching introductory philosophy is students' limited prior exposure to it. They usually know something about the natural and social sciences, however, so certain chapters may help some students feel more comfortable. The treatment of determinism and freedom (Chapters 3 and 4) employs arguments from psychologists B. F. Skinner and Sigmund Freud and neuroscientist Benjamin Libet. The chapter on dolphins draws from marine biology. Albert Einstein is central to Chapter 11. This book also makes a concerted effort to recognize the important contributions of female thinkers: Carol Gilligan, Virginia Held, Janice Moulton, and Martha Nussbaum.

More than anything else, however, I have tried to write a book that helps students become adept and comfortable with doing philosophy—and doing it at an intellectually respectable level. Central to this book, therefore, is the activity of argumentation and consideration of the intricacies of the arguments we explore.

In the exploration of an argument, you will find that I sometimes hazard my own opinion about the strengths or weaknesses of certain positions. (Whenever I do this, however, I try to make it plain that my opinion is just that—my opinion, not the "correct answer," and not something with which you or your students will necessarily agree.) I do this primarily to demonstrate that after understanding a philosopher's position we are supposed to react to it, not memorize it. I also do this to stimulate students' thinking and to help generate class discussion. My opinion is usually offered simply in passing comments, but I have also included one extended interpretation of some of the philosophical literature discussed. In Chapter 6, I offer a speculative reading of Socrates's idea that vice harms the doer. Chapter 10 reflects my own research on the question of dolphins and personhood.

I hope that this book achieves these aims, helps you in working with your students, and helps them reach the goals you set for them in your course. I will be grateful for any reactions, positive or negative, that you or your students have to this text and particularly for any suggestions for improving it.

Every book is the product of many hands, so I would like to express my thanks to those who helped with the revision and production of this book: B. Patrick Williams of Chemeketa Community College; Raymond Watkins of Central Carolina Technical College; Jeff Herman, my agent; Jeff Dean, my editor; Liz Wilson, production director; and Lori Rider, copy editor. Of course, any weaknesses in the final product are my responsibility.

Thomas I. White
Amherst, Massachusetts

TO THE STUDENT

Western philosophy emerged centuries ago on the shores of the Aegean and in the dusty streets of Athens. To the thinkers of ancient Greece, doing philosophy was a natural part of being human. "What is the nature of the world around us?" they asked. "How do our minds work?" "What is the path to happiness?"

The spirit of philosophy has not changed in the two thousand years that have followed. Philosophy is still devoted to understanding the world around us and within us. It requires that we use our minds to explore reality in general and the human experience in particular. Despite the stereotyped image of the philosopher as someone out of touch with everyday experience, philosophy has the most practical of aims: to understand the basic issues of life. This book is written with the original spirit of philosophy in mind. Its first aim is to show you how natural a part of life philosophy is and that, without knowing it, you have already wrestled with many philosophical problems.

The methodology of philosophy does not come as naturally, however. Accordingly, this book also hopes to introduce you to philosophical argumentation and to skills of analytical and critical thought needed for practicing philosophy. Its second aim, then, is to get you comfortable doing philosophy.

Ultimately, I hope that this book will help you experience firsthand the value, pleasure, and adventure of philosophy. Philosophy enriches our lives in ways that nothing else does. It expands our sense of the nature of our world and of ourselves. It gives us a new universe to explore. It helps us clarify our life's goals and choose the means by which we hope to achieve them. Philosophy strengthens our control over our own lives and thus helps us remain the "captain of our souls." As you experience this for yourself, I hope you will make philosophy an integral part of your life.

Part One: Introduction

Chapter 1

What Is Philosophy?

Most of us have either the wrong idea, or no idea at all, of what studying philosophy is all about. If you're feeling uncomfortable about the prospect of taking a philosophy course, perhaps the following will help ease your mind.

First off, you're probably feeling uncertain because you don't know what to expect from a philosophy course. You've already studied subjects like mathematics, history, English, foreign languages, biology, and chemistry. You may have also done a little anthropology, sociology, or political science. You have worked with computers. You know what art and music are, whether you studied them or not. Your previous experience, then, gives you some idea of what's coming in college courses on these subjects.

But philosophy? That's different. You've heard about philosophy and philosophers, but it's probably not something you immediately relate to. There is something about philosophy and philosophers that's alien to the way average people see themselves. After you graduate, you probably expect to be a lawyer, computer programmer, sales manager, teacher, or corporate executive. But who aspires to be a philosopher? You know the image most of us have—someone impractical, unrealistic, and absentminded, some character with hair flying in every direction, lost in thought while pondering "great ideas."[1]

This image of a philosopher being "out of touch" is even suggested by the very word "philosophy." Literally, the word means "love of wisdom." (It derives from two ancient Greek words: *philia*, "love," and *sophia*, "wisdom.") And who's going to go around saying that they "love wisdom" except somebody who's a little strange?

You will find, however, that philosophy is a natural activity. In one way or another most people either already think like philosophers or can do so with just a little help. That's because when it comes down to it, as you're about to see, philosophy is a way of thinking that comes naturally.

What Is Philosophy About?

What is **philosophy** about?[2] And how is philosophy such a natural thing to do that you're probably already doing it without knowing it?

---

1. One of the first caricatures we have of a philosopher is that of the Greek thinker Socrates. In the comedy titled *The Clouds*, Aristophanes portrays the philosopher as someone absolutely useless and ridiculous. When we first meet Socrates in the play, he's sitting in a basket suspended in midair and staring at the sky.
2. The first time a word listed in the glossary appears in each chapter, it will be in boldface type.

More than anything else, philosophy is *thinking*. The main instrument that philosophers use in conducting their investigations is the human mind. They don't try to solve philosophical problems by conducting scientific, empirical research. They *think*. So do you. You think just because you're human.

Of course, philosophers don't just think about whatever crosses their minds. They think about *life's most basic questions*:

- Are our actions free or determined?
- How do we know the difference between right and wrong?
- What is the purpose of life?
- Is there a God?

Who doesn't think about some very basic questions every now and then? You may not make a career out of it, but you have done it.

Philosophers also try to come up with answers to these questions, to explain them to other people, and to defend them against criticism and opposing answers. And you've also done some of that.

> **philosophy** Philosophy is an active, intellectual enterprise dedicated to exploring the most fundamental questions of life.

Philosophy even tries to get something positive out of uncertainty, confusion, and argument. If philosophers who disagree can't prove whose answer is right, they believe that discussion can still produce a greater understanding of the issues at stake. And you have probably had that experience as well.

"Doing" Philosophy in Real Life

Imagine, for example, that your friend asks you to help him cheat on an assignment. You're torn between loyalty to a friend and uneasiness about doing something dishonest. You tell him you would rather not help him cheat. He tries to get you to change your mind, explaining that he doesn't see anything wrong with what he's asking. But you don't see it that way. The two of you get into a long discussion of cheating—why you think it is wrong, why he doesn't, why he thinks friendship is more important, and why you do not. It may surprise you to hear that this fairly typical event in the life of a college student contains all the basic elements of doing philosophy.

How you determine the difference between right and wrong is certainly a basic issue. We base all our actions on our sense of right and wrong. So the subject of your disagreement with your friend is philosophical. In your discussion with him you're forced to explain your decision, so you have to think seriously about your assumptions. In order to handle his objections, you have to think further about the issues and defend your position against his arguments. Let's say that ultimately neither one of you convinces the other. Has the discussion produced anything? Sure—a better understanding of the issue and of each other.

This is what philosophers do too. They think about basic questions and come up with answers, explain why they think that way, and defend their positions against people who disagree. Philosophers do this in the hope of either settling the matter or at least producing a greater understanding of the issues involved.

Now consider all the times you think about fundamental questions. You wonder whether God exists and if there is any way of proving it. Your best friend discovers she's pregnant and the two of you talk about whether she should have an abortion. You consider taking a drug that's illegal in your state but legal in many others. In all these cases, you're thinking about standard philosophical questions, coming to some personal answers, and growing in your understanding. The only difference between you and a professional philosopher is that he or she thinks about the same questions in a more technical, disciplined, and informed way.

Doing philosophy, then, is one of the most common activities of life, something natural, normal, and, best of all, familiar.

Philosophy—Activity, Not Content

Note in particular that philosophy is an activity. Philosophy is active, not passive. It's a way of thinking, something you do, a skill you get better at as you practice, not a body of facts that you memorize. And there is a good and bad side to that. The good news is that once you get the hang of it, philosophical thinking expands your ability to see things. It also encourages you to think independently. You can entertain all kinds of ideas or theories about an issue then make up your own mind. No philosophy teacher will ever say to you, "I don't care what you think, just give me the correct answer to my question." How you think about the questions and about other philosophers' answers and how you explain and defend what you think are what it's all about.

Moreover, philosophers are not "authorities." They are only as good as their arguments. If their arguments are not convincing, forget it. The ancient Greek thinker Socrates may have been a great philosopher, but you don't just take his word for it. He still must convince you.

The bad news, however, is that since you probably haven't studied anything like this before, you're going to have to learn new ways of handling things. In a philosophy course, you start by understanding a philosopher's ideas. But then you need to come up with your own judgment.

Philosophy is a dynamic process. That is one of the things that makes it so interesting—and hard to get used to. It isn't just learning the answers that earlier philosophers have come up with. It's also coming up with your own. So get used to the idea that you are about to embark on an active enterprise.

The Basic Issues

Because the subject of philosophy is the "basic issues" of life, it's not surprising that we encounter a wide range of topics and problems when we study philosophy. Over time, philosophy has been divided into several branches, each devoted to different, but still basic, questions. What are these issues and what are the parts of philosophy?

The Most Fundamental Issues

Every philosophical question is basic. But some questions are more basic than others, and philosophy starts with those.

Reality

What's the most elementary thing you can say about yourself? That you're tall? Short? White? Black? No. That you are male or female? Simpler than that. That you are human? Still simpler. Just that you are. What's the most fundamental characteristic of any object you can describe? Distinguishing characteristics? No. Simply that it is real. It exists. Now we've hit bedrock, because the nature of reality, or of existence, is the most basic issue we can talk about. The most fundamental philosophical question, then, is: what is the nature of *reality*?

What do we mean when we say something is "real"? What's the difference between "real" and "not real" or "imaginary"? Does something have to exist physically to be real? Or is it enough that it exists in our minds? Which are more real? Chairs and tables that present themselves to our eyes but that will eventually wear out, break up, and be thrown out precisely because they're material objects? Or the circles and triangles that we see only with our mind's eye, which are "perfect" and haven't changed or decayed a bit since humans discovered the abstract world of mathematics thousands of years ago?

Free Will

Consider another basic aspect of life. Think again about the most fundamental things you can say about yourself. You exist. You're alive. You control your actions. That is, your deeds are not merely automatic products of instinct. You have what philosophers call free will.

But do you really? Sure, we all *feel* free. Yet aren't our choices influenced by our upbringing, the values we're taught, the norms provided by our culture? Perhaps some of our behavior is determined by our genetic makeup. What about the impact of our worst, irrational fears? What about the power of the unconscious mind? Perhaps you believe that God has people's lives all planned out. Perhaps you believe in fate. And if the future is somehow already determined, what room is left for choice? These problems lead us to yet another basic philosophical question: how "free" are we?

Knowledge

Another basic feature you have is intelligence. You can think and know things. Intellectual activity is such a basic part of human life that our species is named for this ability—*Homo sapiens* ("the thinking hominid"). This brings us to another philosophical issue: what is involved in *knowing* something?

At first this might look like a simple question. We say we know something when we have acceptable reasons or proof for what we claim. I can say that I know that my computer is sitting in front of me because I can see it. I also know that the great English humanist Sir Thomas More died in 1535 because I've done research on More for years, and that is what the historical records show. I even know that the sum of the interior angles of every triangle that ever has or ever will exist is 180 degrees. Have I measured them all? Not very likely. How do I know it? Because this is, in fact, the definition of a triangle.

Each of these three examples involves knowledge, but each example is different. I claim to know something in each case, but the reasons I give keep changing. My first claim is based on direct sense experience. The second involves secondhand evidence, ultimately based on someone else's firsthand experience. And the third doesn't rely on sense experience at all. If they're so different, do all these examples involve knowledge? The same kind of knowledge?

Right and Wrong

So far, we've identified basic philosophical issues raised by the simple fact that we exist (reality), that we do things (free will), and that we know (knowledge). Let's move on to something a little less abstract.

When we choose what to do, we use certain standards or values to guide us. We also use these values to evaluate what other people do. Our society, like all societies, suggests some standards for our behavior, the most important of which are laws and customs. Organizations we belong to, schools we go to, religious groups we belong to, and companies we work for also have their rules, regulations, and policies.

But sometimes those are not enough, or they may conflict with each other. For example, even though it is illegal, many underage students use false IDs to buy liquor. Do you think they're doing something wrong? The traffic laws say you should stop at red lights and stop signs. But what should you do if you are rushing a sick friend to the hospital? Your religion tells you that sex before marriage is wrong, but you are deeply in love with someone and you don't feel that anything you do would be wrong. These ethical dilemmas lead us to yet another philosophical question: how do we separate *right* from *wrong*?

Questions about right and wrong can get as complicated as those about reality or knowledge. We need an ultimate standard of conduct. But where do we find something like that? How do you choose between two actions, both of which seem wrong to you? How would you explain the basis of your standard of right and wrong to someone who disagrees with you? Maybe your standard is influenced by your personal religious beliefs. Yet how could you convince an atheist that you were right? Even if you do have some standard for separating right from wrong, why should you act on it? Why should you do right and not do wrong? What if you don't have enough money for books and you can steal it from somebody who's rich? Is there any good reason not to, especially if you can get away with it?

Many questions come up when we look at the everyday problem of evaluating human actions against some fundamental standard. And, it will come as no surprise, these are philosophical questions.

How Do We Organize Our Communities?

Questions of right and wrong come up because we live with other people and need some standard for judging their conduct as well as our own. But the fact that we live in communities also creates some issues on a larger scale—and still more philosophical questions. How should decisions be made that affect the common good? Does everybody vote about every little thing? Or do you assign some of these decisions to others—that is, do you create a government? What kind of government do you want? Who gets to make the rules that everybody in the group must live by? What if the group's rules force some people to do things they find wrong according to their personal standards? Are they entitled to disobey those rules? How do you decide if a law is "just" or not?

"Big" Issues: The Meaning of Life

Philosophers are nothing if not curious, so it shouldn't surprise you that they can't resist tackling the really "big" questions.

We didn't create our universe, so how did it get here? Is it the result of natural processes operating over billions or trillions of years? Or did someone create it? Are we alone in this universe, or is there a *God* as well? Not surprisingly, proofs for the existence of God have been debated by philosophers for thousands of years.

These sorts of questions raise still more. If there is a spiritual dimension to reality, does that mean that we have "souls" or "spirits" that continue to exist after our bodies wear out? Is there life after death? For that matter, have we lived other lives before this one? More people on this planet believe in reincarnation than reject the idea. Who is right?

Also, what is the *purpose of life*? Is it a test of some sort? If so, what counts as "passing"? Making a lot of money and becoming rich and famous? Doing some kind of important work? Devoting our lives to helping people less fortunate than ourselves? Growing personally or spiritually as much as possible? Questions of the ultimate purpose of life, then, are also common grist for the philosopher's mill.

The Subject Matter of Philosophy

This quick survey of a few basic questions should give you a decent idea of what philosophy is all about. It is not some arcane study that has nothing to do with real life. It is an intellectual activity devoted to understanding the most basic dimensions of what it means to exist as a human being alone and in community with others. As such, it has everything to do with real life.

Philosophical Questions

The questions that philosophers ask are obviously varied. One thing they have in common is that all these questions arise from thinking about the fundamental aspects of life. But they also share something else that is distinctive of a philosophical question—their *conceptual* nature.

If I ask you if it's raining, how do you find out the answer? You look outside. And if I ask you how many students are in a particular classroom at noon on Monday? You go and count the people. In each case, you get the facts. Many questions are like this. They're answered by doing some empirical investigation.

Or what if you want to know if you can leave your car somewhere overnight without getting a ticket? You call the police. What if you want to know if you can take a particular deduction on your taxes? Contact the IRS. In these cases, you're still getting facts, but they're facts of a different kind. There are specific answers that will settle your questions, but you must find the right person, book, or body of law that tells you what they are. You must seek the judgment of an authority.

Philosophical questions, by contrast, involve conceptual issues. Think about the account of the philosophical topics you just read. All those philosophical questions boil down to basic concepts or principles. And that is the defining feature of a philosophical question. Reality, knowledge, right, wrong, justice, and the like are all concepts. The challenge of a philosophical investigation is exploring the principles and concepts at issue and applying the results to situations that involve those ideas.

Philosophical "Answers"

Similarly, the "answers" to these questions share an important property that also characterizes philosophy. Because of the conceptual nature of the fundamental issues philosophy considers, philosophers can never give absolute proof that they are right.

Philosophical questions do not get "solved" as empirical questions do. The empirical question "How many inches are in a foot?" has a single, correct answer; all others are wrong. But a philosophical question like "Is abortion wrong?" has more than one plausible answer. Depending on the positions taken on such debatable issues as "life," "personhood," and "rights," we can find even completely opposing arguments that are reasonable and believable. Similarly, we can make a plausible case for saying that we're free to choose anything we want whenever we want to. On the other hand, we can also make an intelligent case for saying that our sense of freedom is an illusion—that we fool ourselves into thinking we're free when our behavior is actually determined. It is simply a characteristic of philosophical issues that we fall short of absolute certainty. And this means that philosophical thinking generally deals more in probability and plausibility than absolute truth and falsehood.

The Parts of Philosophy

You now have an understanding of the subjects that philosophy discusses and something of the nature of philosophy. However, without realizing it, you also have acquired a sense of the primary branches of philosophy.

Very fundamental and abstract issues relating to existence in general (like the nature of reality) and human existence in particular (such as free will) are taken up in the part of philosophy called **metaphysics**. The ancient Greek philosopher Aristotle called this branch of philosophy "first philosophy," and that's a good way to think about it. Metaphysics concentrates on the first or most fundamental questions we encounter when we begin studying the most basic issues of life.[3]

> **metaphysics** Metaphysics is the part of philosophy concerned with the most basic issues, for example, reality, existence, personhood, and freedom versus determinism. Metaphysics was originally referred to by Aristotle as "first philosophy."
>
> **epistemology** Epistemology, also called "theory of knowledge," is the part of philosophy concerned with "knowledge" and related concepts.
>
> **ethics** Ethics, also called "moral philosophy," is the part of philosophy concerned with right, wrong, and other issues related to evaluating human conduct.
>
> **political philosophy** Political philosophy is the part of philosophy that addresses the philosophical issues that arise from the fact that we live together in communities. These issues include the nature of political authority, justice, and the problem of harmonizing freedom and obligation.

Another fundamental part of philosophy is theory of knowledge, or **epistemology**, which takes up the questions we saw earlier related to the nature of knowledge. "Epistemology" combines two Greek words, *epistéme* and *logos*, and literally means "the study of knowledge." *Epistéme* means "knowledge." *Logos* has many meanings, but in this context it means "the study of." The suffix "-logy" can be found at the end of many English words: "biology" (the study of life), "geology" (the study of the earth), and so on.

When we encounter the practical issues of philosophy, we move into **ethics**, or *moral philosophy*, and **political philosophy**. "Ethics" is the part of philosophy that discusses right and wrong, and the word is derived from the Greek word for "custom, habit, or character," *ethikos*. ("Moral" comes from the Latin word for "character," *mores*.) "Political philosophy" takes up the wider issues that arise from our living together, such as legitimate authority, justice, and speculation about the ideal society. Its root is *polis*, another Greek word, which means "city."

---

3. "Metaphysics" comes from two ancient Greek words, *meta* "after," and *physika* "physics." In light of contemporary usage, where "metaphysical" usually means "abstract" or "abstruse," you might think that "metaphysics" takes its name from the fact that it studies highly abstract issues "beyond the physical realm." While such questions are "metaphysical," the word is actually a historical accident. The Greek philosopher Aristotle gave a series of lectures dealing with the most basic questions in philosophy; as I mentioned, he called this "first philosophy." The treatise containing these lectures was never given a title, but after Aristotle's death his students traditionally filed it after Aristotle's lectures on nature, which the philosopher called "the physics." Thus, *METAPHYSICS* meant something more like "the scroll filed after *The Physics*" than "lectures on transcendental questions." That is why the best way to understand metaphysics is to remember that Aristotle called it "first philosophy." That is, think of it as the part of philosophy that asks the "first" or most basic questions.

Aristotle (384–322 BCE) was born in the small town of Stagira in Macedonia, just to the north of Greece proper, into a family with a strong medical tradition. His father was the court physician to the king of Macedonia, and this medical heritage strongly influenced Aristotle's intellectual development. Aristotle's philosophical investigations covered an extraordinary range of topics and were characterized by a largely empirical approach, but he also did work in such natural sciences as biology and astronomy.

Aristotle arrived in Athens at the age of eighteen and studied at Plato's Academy until the death of his teacher some twenty years later. Leaving Athens, Aristotle traveled to Asia Minor, where he seems to have spent a few years studying marine biology. He was then recalled to the Macedonian court in order to tutor the son of King Philip. The boy was Alexander, whose military conquests subsequently left him remembered as "Alexander the Great." Aristotle returned to Athens in 334 BCE and established his own school, the Lyceum, where he taught for the next eleven years. The death of Alexander in 323 BCE, however, unleashed a wave of anti-Macedonian sentiment in Athens, and a charge of impiety, a capital offense, was leveled against Aristotle. Rather than allow Athens to "sin twice against philosophy," as Aristotle put it (the philosopher Socrates had been executed on the same charge in 399 BCE), Aristotle left Athens for an island north of the city, where he died the following year.

Metaphysics, epistemology, ethics, and political philosophy are the main divisions of philosophy. But given the wide range of topics that philosophers study, it should come as no surprise that there are also many important but more narrowly focused branches of philosophy, like philosophy of art, philosophy of science, and philosophy of language. Finally, in a class by itself, there is **logic**, the part of philosophy devoted to studying reason itself and the structure of arguments. Logic is the foundation on which any philosophical investigation is built, and modern philosophy of logic explores some highly technical philosophical questions.

Why Studying Philosophy Is Valuable

So far you have seen that philosophy stems quite naturally from thinking about life's basic questions. And you have been introduced to some of those questions and to the different branches of philosophy. You should now be ready for what we're going to study in the chapters ahead.

Before we move on, however, we should address one more issue—why studying philosophy is worthwhile. Whatever you imagine you will get out of a philosophy course, let me assure you that if you work hard through this course, you will develop skills, abilities, and insights that will help you for the rest of your life.

Analytical Abilities

The skills you will pick up are easy to describe. You will develop stronger analytical abilities. You will handle abstract problems better. You will learn how to argue more effectively.

And you will have a stronger imagination. Philosophy helps to shape in a positive way what we might call the "general cut of your mind." This is invaluable in whatever career you choose to follow. The most successful people use analysis and argument all the time. Successful people make their mark by solving difficult problems and convincing other people they're right.

In preparing this book, I asked several successful executives to tell me what they thought students should study if they wanted to succeed in business. They listed only a few technical subjects—accounting and finance, for example. (The technical end of business, they said, you learn mainly on the job.) Otherwise, they suggested courses that help develop your ability to think about problems analytically and to communicate your analysis and recommendations to other people. Time and again, these executives identified philosophy as one of the most important areas you can study for learning how to think in a disciplined, analytical, and imaginative way.

Vision and Insight

The way that philosophy helps you see the world is no less real than its practical benefits to your career. Studying philosophy exposes you to a wide range of problems that you wouldn't meet otherwise. It simply lets you see more of the world. It stretches your imagination. It challenges you to come up with your own answers to tough issues that do not have ready-made solutions. If you take it seriously, philosophy teaches you different ways of looking at the world.

Studying philosophy helps you develop insight into some of life's great puzzles and fashion your own vision of what life is all about. As you go through life, you will be challenged all along the way to make decisions about who you are and what's important to you. What will you do with your life? What career will you pursue? Will you marry? And if so, what kind of person? Will you have children? How will you rear them? What will you tell them is important? What are you willing to do for money and success? How will you cope with the crises you will encounter in your own life or in the lives of those you love—illness, accidents, problems on the job or at home, death? Philosophy helps you develop a sense of what life is all about and where you're going.

In fact, Socrates, one of the first great philosophers, thought that philosophy is the single most important element in making our lives worthwhile. "The unexamined life," he said, "is not worth living." The habit of thinking philosophically lets us scrutinize our values, our goals, and the means we've chosen to achieve them, and it helps us keep our lives on course. In Socrates's mind, at least, philosophy makes it possible for us to control our own destiny. And that's no small matter.

As you now know, philosophy is simply thinking systematically about life's most basic issues. When it comes down to it, there is no way that thinking about these questions cannot make you better prepared to live your life.

Previews of Coming Chapters

Now that you have a sense of what philosophy is, you're ready to plunge in yourself. What's coming up in the rest of this book? We cannot cover every important aspect of such a large subject in an introductory text. We will, however, talk about most of philosophy's basic topics and a few specialized ones.

We'll start preparing ourselves by "tuning the instrument," that is, the mind. Since we do philosophy by thinking, the best place to begin is by studying some of the "rules of reason" alluded to earlier. Chapter 2, "Thinking Like a Philosopher," will introduce you to the ground rules regarding logic and critical thinking.

In the next section, "Exploring the Basics of Who We Are and Dealing with Others," we look at some of the most fundamental characteristics of our existence. We start with two chapters that consider opposing points of view about the issue of human freedom. In "The Case for Determinism" (Chapter 3), we look at the arguments in favor of determinism, and we explore the case for free will in Chapter 4 ("The Case for Freedom"). Then we examine basic issues related to our living with other people. We look at how philosophers talk about "right" and "wrong" in Chapter 5. In Chapter 6, "Why Be Ethical?", we ask why we should make the effort to do what's right.

In the chapters that make up "Fundamental Theoretical Issues," we explore basic philosophical problems of a more abstract nature. We start with absolute bedrock—"What Is Real and How Do We Know It?" Chapters 7 and 8 give us competing answers, the former emphasizing the physical senses (empiricism) and the latter the mind (rationalism). In Chapter 9, "Does God Exist?", we examine the main "proofs" for the existence of God.

We'll conclude with "Perhaps Things Aren't Really the Way They Appear": three chapters that question a variety of claims most people think are too obvious to doubt. Chapter 10 ("Dolphins—Personhood, Rights, and Flourishing") argues that humans aren't the only animal on the planet with advanced intellectual and emotional abilities. Chapter 11 looks at the provocative but very different ways in which Marx and Einstein argue that things aren't what they appear to be. Our final chapter ("Alternative Perspectives") examines two serious challenges to a traditional, Western perspective—Buddhism and Native American thought.

This book, then, will give you a basic but solid understanding of what philosophy is all about. It will serve as a road map for what many of us think is one of life's most exciting, enriching, and engaging adventures—discovering philosophy. You will see new sights, explore new worlds, expand your horizons, and, most importantly, learn much about yourself. As with any journey, what you get out of it is mainly up to you. But if you give philosophy half a chance, it just might take you to a place you never want to leave.

Discussion Questions

1. Have you already thought about any of the philosophical questions identified in this chapter? What spurred this? Another course? A debate about a controversial issue? A dramatic or life-changing experience? Your own proclivity to think deeply?

2. Later chapters of this book will explore in depth the main philosophical issues identified previously. But try your hand at taking a position and fashioning an argument on any of the following questions: How free are our actions? What makes an action morally wrong? Does God exist?

3. What do you expect to get out of studying philosophy? What will make it worth all the time and effort you will put in? Will just a good grade do it? If philosophy doesn't help you become more successful in your career, does that mean it has no value?

Selected Readings

A superb source for detailed information about almost every philosopher and philosophical issue is *The Encyclopedia of Philosophy*, edited by Paul Edwards, 8 vols. (New York: Collier-Macmillan / Free Press, 1967, reprinted 1972). An excellent online source is the Stanford *Encyclopedia of Philosophy* (https://plato.stanford.edu/). Also see *The Philosopher's Index* (https://philindex.org/).

Chapter 2

Thinking Like a Philosopher

The preceding chapter described philosophy as thinking about the basic issues of life. But philosophy is not just any kind of thinking. Scientists and religious or political authorities, for example, think in the process of their inquiries, but they direct their attention to empirical data, sacred texts, or legal records. The grist for the philosopher's mill, however, is neither scientific facts nor the conclusions of authorities. Rather, it is ideas—"reality," "free will," "determinism," "knowledge," "right," "wrong," and the like. Philosophers try to sort out the abstract issues using a special kind of thinking that is methodical, logical, and critical.[1]

Critical Thinking

The idea that philosophical thinking is critical may at first suggest to you that it aims to find fault or criticize. "Critical," however, is derived from the ancient Greek word *kritikos*, which means "skilled in judging." To think critically, then, simply means to judge whether or not some claim is believable and convincing, that is, whether it's based on solid facts or good reasons. All intellectual disciplines that deal with evidence and proof are based on **critical thinking**, so to this extent philosophy is similar to other areas.

Critical thinking combines healthy skepticism and analytical skills in a way that lets you determine for yourself the truth or legitimacy of the claims someone is making. Accepting without question the statements of someone in authority is not thinking critically. For example, if you said, "Abortion is morally acceptable because it is legal" or "Abortion is wrong because my religion says so," you would not be thinking critically. You want to look behind the positions of these authorities (law, on the one hand, and a religious

---

1. The fact that philosophy is so conceptual, that the results of philosophical thinking are ultimately judged by rules of reason, and that arguments are evaluated for how "reasonable," "convincing," or "plausible" they are reveals another and perhaps the most general hallmark of philosophy. This is difficult to put simply, but we might say that unlike enterprises like science, law, or religion, the ultimate point of reference in philosophy is the mind itself. Scientific thinking, for example, can be critical, analytical, and conceptual, and can lead to arguments that are no more than probable. But in the end its final focus is on the physical world. Not so with philosophy. In philosophy we do think about issues related to the world of science, religion, law, medicine, and so on, but philosophical thinking focuses on the theoretical and conceptual dimensions of these disciplines. Simply put, philosophical thinking is a product of the ideas we find in or create with our minds. We think about simple ideas (concepts), put our conclusions into larger ideas (arguments), and evaluate those arguments by still other ideas (the rules of reason). Philosophy is ultimately and essentially a mental enterprise.

> **critical thinking** To think critically is to judge whether some claim is believable and convincing, that is, whether it is based on solid facts or good reasons. All intellectual disciplines that deal with evidence and proof are based on critical thinking.

official, on the other) and judge whether they have good reasons for their conclusions.

Considering how often someone tries to persuade you of something, critical thinking should be a constant feature of your life. Your parents try to convince you to aspire to medical school, to choose a particular major, or to study harder. Your friends might challenge some of your parents' arguments, encouraging you to major in music and trying to persuade you that studying too hard will ruin your social life. Advertisements try to induce you to buy a new product; political speeches, to vote for a particular candidate. We are barraged by other people's explanations for why we should act or think in a particular way. Furthermore, we just as often attempt to convince other people of things. You try to get a coworker to trade hours with you so that you can go to a special concert. You attempt to talk your teacher into excusing you from the final exam because you have a straight A average. You design the publicity for a webinar with an eye to getting as many people as possible to attend. Our lives—what we do, what we experience from others—sometimes seem like endless rounds of persuasion.

What Is Argumentation?

Philosophical thinking is essentially critical thinking. Philosophers are not "authorities" making pronouncements that you are simply supposed to accept. Philosophers make claims backed up by reasons and arguments, and they offer them for public scrutiny. Philosophers judge other thinkers' arguments, and they expect their own words to be treated the same way. As a type of critical thinking, then, philosophy is an active, intellectual process that sifts and sorts through whatever facts, concepts, theories, and speculations can be used to argue in support of competing positions in a philosophical controversy. Philosophical thinking is critical thinking in that its primary focus is on arguments.

The term **argument** does not mean the emotional fights you have with your friends, roommate, parents, siblings, spouse, or significant loved one. Instead, an argument is a rational attempt to prove a point by offering reasons or evidence and drawing some conclusion from it. Unlike the angry, one-sided, emotional blowout, a good philosophical argument is reasoned, orderly, logical, and convincing—or at least plausible. And it's not as dull as it sounds. People develop strong feelings about positions they hold, and discussions often get spirited. But if you start an evening talking calmly about an important issue and later find yourself looking around for something to throw at your opponent, you've probably stopped arguing and started fighting. Just keep the difference between the two clear.

In the same vein, remember that critical, philosophical thinking appeals to the intellect. A philosophical argument does not use language the way advertisers, courtroom attorneys, and politicians do—as a device to sway people's emotions. If it does, it is no longer properly philosophy. What, then, is the hallmark of good critical thinking? What are the characteristics of strong and weak arguments?

What Is Logic?

In much the same way that we have building codes to ensure that a house is built well, there is also a "thinking code," that is, guidelines and rules for what makes an argument pass "philosophical inspection." We find this code in that part of philosophy called **logic**.

Logic is the branch of philosophy devoted to determining what counts as solid, disciplined, reasoned thinking. In fact, the ancient Greek philosopher Aristotle sees it as so basic that he calls it not so much a part of philosophy as the "instrument" we use to do philosophy. Logic is both a process of reasoning and the rules that govern the process, and we use those rules to distinguish between correct and incorrect conclusions when we engage in an intellectual investigation of a question.

It's difficult to learn much about logic in just one chapter of a textbook because it usually takes at least a full semester to start getting comfortable with this part of philosophy. So we're going to look only at some basic issues related to good, logical thinking (on the one hand) and poor, illogical thinking (on the other).

Logic and Wizards

We're going to start our study of logic where you'd probably least expect it—talking not about some philosopher but about an interesting challenge faced by some wizards-in-training that happens to be a good introduction to logic. In the first book of J. K. Rowling's classic series of novels, *Harry Potter and the Philosopher's Stone*,[2] Harry Potter, Ron Weasley, and Hermione Granger discover that hidden somewhere in Hogwarts is the Philosopher's Stone, a magical object that can guarantee immortality. Fearing that it might be used to bring the dark wizard Lord Voldemort back to power, the young wizards decide to find it before one of Voldemort's supporters does. The three friends get past a variety of enchantments designed to protect the stone, but then Harry and Hermione find themselves trapped by walls of fire. In front of them, however, is a table with seven bottles and a piece of paper containing a poem that gives clues for getting through the

---

2. You may be more familiar with this book being referred to as *Harry Potter and the Sorcerer's Stone*, not *Harry Potter and the Philosopher's Stone*, the title which British author J.K. Rowling gave to the book when originally published in the UK. However, as Brynna Cole explains, "Scholastic publishing head Arthur A. Levine was concerned that American readers wouldn't be drawn to that title. Philip W. Errington explained in his biography of series author J.K. Rowling that the publisher wanted 'a title that said "magic" more overtly to American readers.' Levine suggested titles like *Harry Potter and the School of Magic*, but Rowling refused them. The issue proved to be with the word 'philosopher,' which isn't inherently mystical. Rowling eventually suggested changing the title to *Harry Potter and the Sorcerer's Stone*, and that's what Scholastic went with." https://www.cbr.com/harry-potter-why-philosophers-stone-changed-title/. Out of respect for the author, we're going to use her original title, especially since there's no reason to avoid "philosopher" in a philosophy text.

fire. After reading the poem, Hermione points out that it's actually a riddle. She solves it by logic, not magic.

Here are the seven bottles on the table.[3]

The poem says that one of the seven bottles lets you go through the room, one takes you back where you came from, two contain nettle wine, and three hold poison. Poison is always to the left of wine but isn't in either the biggest ("giant") or smallest ("dwarf") bottle, the bottles on either end are different but don't contain the potion to go forward, and the bottles that are second from the left and second from the right contain the same thing.

Which of the bottles will let you go through the fire and thwart Voldemort? Let's figure it out.

Step 1. Here are the bottles.

STEP ONE: Information from the poem

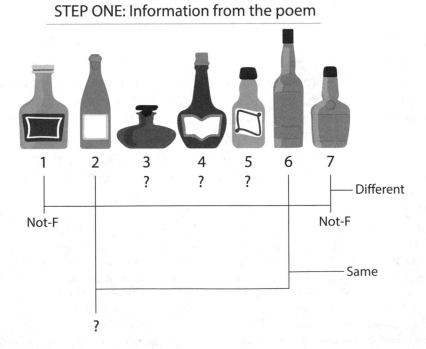

As a shorthand, let's label the different contents P (poison), W (wine), B (the potion that will let us go back), and F (the potion that we want, that is, the one that will let us go forward). The poem gives us four clues:

Clue 1: Poison will always be on the left side of the nettle wine.

Clue 2: Bottles 1 and 7 contain different substances but not the potion that will let us go forward.

Clue 3: The bottles are different sizes, and neither the "dwarf" nor the "giant" bottle contains poison.

Clue 4: Bottles 2 and 6 contain the same substance.

Step 2. Because we're told there are three bottles of poison on the table, it's probably a good idea to start by seeing if we can figure out which bottles to avoid. Clue 3 tells us that neither the "dwarf" nor the "giant" contains poison. If we examine the size of the bottles, we can see that bottle 3 is the smallest and bottle 6 is the largest. So we can conclude that neither bottle 3 nor bottle 6 has poison.

STEP TWO: Comparing the size of the bottles and using Clue 3

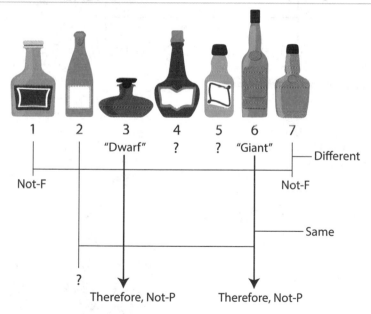

Step 3. What can we figure out next? If we put together what we just learned (that bottles 3 and 6 aren't poison) with Clue 4 (that bottles 2 and 6 contain the same substance), we can conclude that bottle 2 isn't poison either.

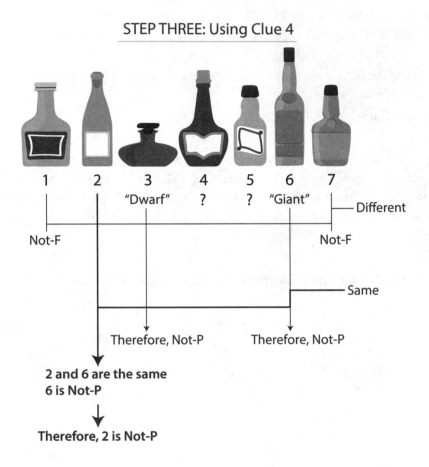

STEP THREE: Using Clue 4

Step 4. Let's keep our focus on avoiding the poison. We now know that the poison isn't in bottles 2, 3, and 6. That leaves four bottles to worry about because we've been told that there are three bottles of poison. Clue 2 tells us that bottles 1 and 7 are different. Since bottles 1 and 7, then, can't both be poison, that means that the poison is in either bottles 1, 4, and 5 or 4, 5, and 7. And because bottles 4 and 5 are there under both possible combinations, we know that both bottles 4 and 5 are definitely poison.

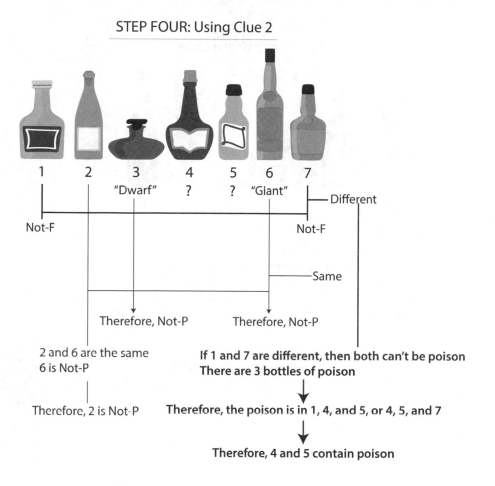

STEP FOUR: Using Clue 2

1   2   3   4   5   6   7
          "Dwarf" ?   ?   "Giant"

— Different

Not-F   Not-F

— Same

Therefore, Not-P   Therefore, Not-P

2 and 6 are the same   **If 1 and 7 are different, then both can't be poison**
6 is Not-P   **There are 3 bottles of poison**

Therefore, 2 is Not-P   **Therefore, the poison is in 1, 4, and 5, or 4, 5, and 7**

Therefore, 4 and 5 contain poison

Step 5. Let's take stock for a minute. We know that bottles 4 and 5 are poison. That leaves the third bottle of poison unaccounted for. We're also still looking for the two bottles of wine, the potion that will let us go forward, and the potion that will let us go back. It may not look like we've gotten very far, but remember that Clue 4 tells us that bottles 2 and 6 contain the same substance. And that means that bottles 2 and 6 must be wine. Only one bottle of poison, one forward potion, and one backward potion are left to locate. Wine is the only thing that's in two of the bottles.

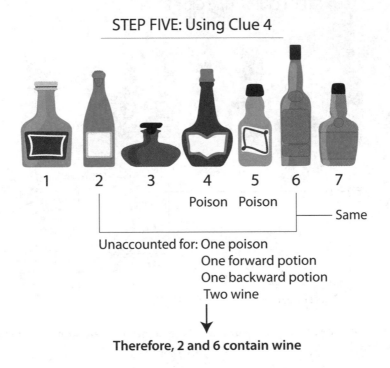

STEP FIVE: Using Clue 4

1   2   3   4   5   6   7

Poison   Poison

—— Same

Unaccounted for: One poison
One forward potion
One backward potion
Two wine

↓

Therefore, 2 and 6 contain wine

Step 6. Now that we know where the two bottles of wine are, we can locate the missing bottle of poison. Clue 1 tells us that the poison will always be on the left side of the nettle wine. We already know that bottles 4 and 5 are poison, and they're to the left of the nettle wine in bottle 6. Because we now know that bottle 2 is nettle wine, this means that bottle 1 is the third bottle of poison.

STEP SIX: Using Clue 1

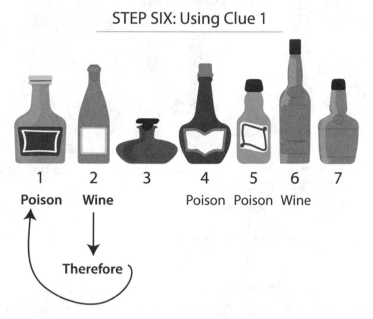

Step 7. We're down to the final two bottles: 3 and 7. One has the magic potion that will let us go through the flames in front of us; the other has the potion that gets us through the flames behind us. Because Clue 2 tells us that bottle 7 won't let us go forward, that one must have the potion that will let us go back.

STEP SEVEN: Using Clue 2

Step 8. Since we've accounted for six bottles, that just leaves bottle 3. So that must be the potion we've been looking for the whole time—the one that will let us go through the fire ahead of us.

You should be able to see that we figured out which bottle contained the correct magic potion simply by applying the information from the poem to the facts at hand in a careful and methodical way. Now let's examine the steps we took and see how they demonstrate good, logical thinking.

Hermione's Solution and Logic: Constructing Arguments

While in commonsense terms we can say that we have a puzzle here that we want to solve, from a philosophical perspective we'd say that we're faced with constructing an argument that shows us what we want to know. An argument is simply a series of statements that gives us good *reasons* to think that the argument's conclusion is true (or at least very likely to be true). In our case, we're looking to construct an argument that reveals which bottle we should drink. That is, we're looking to be able to say: "On the basis of clues and facts A, B, C, D, and so forth, bottle X will get us through the fire ahead of us." Think of it this way. As much as you might trust Hermione, wouldn't you feel more comfortable drinking the bottle she hands you if she explained the *reasons* she's so sure it's the right bottle? Her explanation to you would be an argument. As a general rule in philosophy, we're expected to offer good arguments that explain why we think as we do. Arguments have two parts: the **conclusion** (the ultimate claim that we're making) and the **premises** (the reasons for accepting our conclusion). In ordinary

> **conclusion** The technical label for the argument's claim, point, or result is the conclusion.
>
> **premises** The reasons that allegedly lead to the conclusion of an argument are called premises.

conversation, people in effect "signal" that they're giving you the premises of an argument when they use words or phrases like "because," "since," "in light of the fact that," and "the reason being that." Words or phrases that signal a conclusion include "therefore," "so," "as a result," "it must be the case that," and the like.

We start by identifying what we are sure about—the initial *premises* of our argument. In this case, our premises are the information and clues that come from the poem and from the way the bottles are placed on the table.

Our initial premise—the information we're given—is:

1. There are seven bottles standing in the following order. (We know this because we can see it.)

Three contain poison, two nettle wine, one a potion for going forward, and one a potion for going back. (The first few lines of the poem tell us this.)

2. Poison will always be on the left side of the nettle wine. (Clue 1)

3. Bottles 1 and 7 contain different substances but not the potion that will let us go forward. (Clue 2)

4. The bottles are different sizes, and neither the "dwarf" nor the "giant" bottle contains poison. (Clue 3)

5. Bottles 2 and 6 contain the same substance. (Clue 4)

Once we had the basic information, we could get rolling. In Step 2, we combined Clue 3 (neither the "dwarf" nor the "giant" contains poison) with what we could see—that bottle 3 is the smallest and bottle 6 is the largest—to conclude that neither bottle 3 nor 6 contained poison.

Notice that while it's absolutely common sense to conclude that bottles 3 and 6 don't have the poison if we're told that neither the smallest nor the largest has the poison, from the perspective of logic, we actually have two short arguments. Notice how the conclusion follows from the premises in each argument.

A. 1. Neither the "dwarf" nor the "giant" contains poison. (Clue 3) **[Initial Premise]**

2. Bottle 3 is the "dwarf." (Looking at the bottles) **[Initial Premise]**

3. Therefore, bottle 3 doesn't contain poison. **[Conclusion]**

B. **1.** Neither the "dwarf" nor the "giant" contains poison. (Clue 3)   **[New Premise]**

  2. Bottle 6 is the "giant." (Looking at the bottles)   **[Initial Premise]**

  3. Therefore, bottle 6 doesn't contain poison.   **[Conclusion]**

In Step 3, we put together another short argument. And notice how both conclusions that we just arrived at now serve as new facts or reasons (that is, premises) that we can use to draw new conclusions.

  1. Bottles 2 and 6 contain the same substance. (Clue 4)   **[Initial Premise]**

  2. Bottle 6 doesn't contain poison. (Our conclusion from the arguments in Step 1)   **[New Premise]**

  3. Therefore, bottle 2 doesn't contain poison.   **[Conclusion]**

With Step 4, we came up with another argument. But this one is a little more involved because it's like a chain of small arguments with conclusions that we immediately use to keep going.

  1. Of the seven bottles, bottles 2, 3, and 6 don't contain poison. (What we concluded in our arguments from Steps 2 and 3)   **[New Premise]**

  2. Therefore, there could still be poison in bottles 1, 4, 5, and 7.
  [Preliminary Conclusion]

  3. However, of the seven bottles, only three contain poison. (Information from the first part of the poem)   **[Initial Premise]**

  4. Therefore, the poison is in:

   a. 1, 4, 5

   b. 1, 4, 7

   c. 1, 5, 7 *or*

   d. 4, 5, 7   **[Preliminary Conclusion]**

  5. But bottles 1 and 7 are different; that is, they can't both be poison. (Clue 2)   **[Initial Premise]**

  6. Therefore, there are only two possibilities for where the poison is:

   a. 1, 4, 5 *or*

   b. 4, 5, 7   **[Preliminary Conclusion]**

  7. And since bottles 4 and 5 are part of both possibilities, we know that bottles 4 and 5 contain poison.   **[Conclusion]**

Step 5 shows the benefit of simply stopping and thinking. Instead of continuing to ask, "Where's the poison?" we took a different tack and ended up finding the two bottles of nettle wine.

1. Bottles 2 and 6 contain the same substance. (Clue 4)   **[Initial Premise]**

2. Because bottles 4 and 5 contain poison and because there are three bottles of poison, only *one* more bottle of poison needs to be accounted for. (Conclusion from Step 4 argument, combined with information from the poem)   **[New Premise]**

3. Similarly, only *one* of the remaining bottles contains the potion that will let us go forward and only *one* contains the potion that will let us go back. (Information from the poem)   **[Initial Premise]**

4. There are *two* bottles of nettle wine to be identified. (Information from the poem)   **[Initial Premise]**

5. Therefore, bottles 2 and 6 must be nettle wine.   **[Conclusion]**

Once we determined the location of the wine, we were on our way to our final conclusion. Step 6 identified the last bottle of poison.

1. Bottle 2 is wine. (Conclusion from argument in Step 5)   **[New Premise]**

2. Poison is always on the left side of the nettle wine. (Clue 1)   **[Initial Premise]**

3. Therefore, bottle 1 contains poison.   **[Conclusion]**

Once we knew the contents of five of the seven bottles, Step 7 gave us the location of one magic potion—the one that will let us go back.

1. Bottles 3 and 7 contain the two magic potions. (Information from the poem combined with the conclusions of the arguments from Steps 4, 5, and 6)   **[New Premise]**

2. Bottle 7 doesn't contain the potion for going forward. (Clue 2)   **[Initial Premise]**

3. Therefore, bottle 7 contains the potion for going back.   **[Conclusion]**

Once we can identify six of the bottles, Step 8 leaves just the one we're looking for.

1. The contents of six of the seven bottles are as follows: 1—poison, 2—nettle wine, 4—poison, 5—poison, 6—nettle wine, 7—potion for going back. (Conclusions from arguments in Steps 4 through 7)   **[New Premise]**

2. The only substance unaccounted for is the potion for going forward. (Information from the poem)   **[Initial Premise]**

3. Therefore, bottle 3 contains the potion for going forward.   **[Conclusion]**

So the first thing that the process of using logic to find the correct magic potion shows us about logic is primarily about putting together good *arguments*—where the conclusions follow from the premises.

Hermione and Logic: Allowable and Forbidden "Moves"

The second thing that we can learn about logic from Hermione's solution is the *structure* of good arguments. Despite the variety of facts that we took into account in solving our problem, each of the small arguments we constructed along the way had a similar structure. For clarity, we're going to rephrase the arguments a little. But they're still the same as what we did previously. For example:

> Step 2. IF a particular bottle is the "dwarf," THEN it doesn't contain poison.
>
> Bottle 3 is the "dwarf."
>
> THEREFORE, bottle 3 doesn't contain poison.

> Step 2. IF a particular bottle is the "giant," THEN it doesn't contain poison.
>
> Bottle 6 is the "giant."
>
> THEREFORE, bottle 6 doesn't contain poison.

> Step 3. IF a particular substance is in bottle 6, THEN that same substance is in bottle 2.
>
> The substance in bottle 6 is something other than poison.
>
> THEREFORE, the substance in bottle 2 is something other than poison.

> Step 5. IF we can identify which substance can be in two bottles, THEN we know what's in bottles 2 and 6.
>
> The only substance that can be in two bottles is nettle wine.
>
> THEREFORE, bottles 2 and 6 contain wine.

All four of these arguments have the same structure:

1. We know that IF (one particular thing) were true, THEN (a second particular thing) would also be true.

2. We know that (the first particular thing) is in fact true.

3. THEREFORE, we know that (the second particular thing) is also true.

In fact, this (IF A, THEN B; A; THEREFORE, B) structure for an argument reflects one of the most basic rules of logic. And if we took the time, we could reconstruct every argument in our solution so that it had a similar step-by-step, premise(s)-conclusion structure.

Good, Logical Thinking, and Rules

Thinking like a philosopher, however, isn't just being as careful and methodical as Hermione. Logic actually has "rules." Good arguments follow them. Bad arguments break them.

Here's another useful example from *Philosopher's Stone*. One of the challenges that came before Harry and Hermione encountered the seven bottles was a chess game. Harry, Ron, and Hermione found themselves on a huge chessboard, and the only way they could continue their search was to play their way across. The three take their places as chess pieces and Ron masterminds a victory. Chess, like every game, has particular rules. There are two players and each has sixteen pieces: eight pawns, two rooks, two knights, two bishops, one queen, and one king. Each piece is allowed to move only in specific ways. For example,

> Rook—as many spaces as you want (without jumping another piece), straight ahead, straight back, left, or right
>
> Bishop—as many spaces as you want (without jumping another piece) but only diagonally
>
> Queen—what applies to both a rook and bishop combined
>
> Knight—something of an L-shaped move in which you can jump over other pieces

Every time it was Ron's turn, he had to make sure that the move he had in mind was allowed by the rule that governs what each piece can do. In essence, he had to be able to say, "I can move this piece diagonally because it's a bishop, and the rule that describes how a bishop can move allows it."

Logic is the same. That is, there are rules that govern good, logical thinking. And the only way we can, as it were, make "moves" that take us through an argument and to a conclusion is if they're allowed by those rules.

Let's take a simple example. The most basic structure for an argument starts with an "IF. . . , THEN. . ." statement. If we can say that the IF part is true, then we're entitled to conclude that the THEN part is also true. For example,

> IF someone is a student at Hogwarts, THEN he or she is studying witchcraft and wizardry.
>
> Neville Longbottom is a student at Hogwarts.
>
> THEREFORE, Neville Longbottom is studying witchcraft and wizardry.

Logicians have a Latin name for this rule: *modus ponens*. Loosely translated, we can simply call it the Asserting Rule—which says something like, "If you have an IF A, THEN B statement that you know to be true; and if you can assert that A is true; then you can conclude that B is true." (IF A, THEN B; A; THEREFORE, B.) It doesn't matter what the subject matter of our argument is. Any argument that follows that rule gives us a conclusion that we can believe.

If someone was born in London, then he was born in England.

Neville was born in London.

Therefore, he was born in England.

If today is Tuesday, then tomorrow is Wednesday.

Today is Tuesday.

Therefore, tomorrow is Wednesday.

If a bottle contains poison, then it stands to the left of nettle wine.

Bottle 5 contains poison.

Therefore, bottle 5 stands to the left of nettle wine.

Or, if you want to keep thinking about the parallel with chess, we can "move" through the premises of an argument to the conclusion as long as we meet the conditions laid down in this rule.

But what about this argument?

IF someone is a student at Hogwarts, THEN he or she is studying witchcraft and wizardry.

Dudley Dursley is NOT studying witchcraft and wizardry.

THEREFORE, Dudley Dursley is NOT a student at Hogwarts.

From a commonsense viewpoint, the conclusion seems right. We're told that Dudley isn't studying witchcraft and wizardry, and that if you're a student at Hogwarts, that's exactly what you're studying. So Dudley can't be at Hogwarts. But this conclusion isn't covered by our Asserting Rule (IF A, THEN B; A; THEREFORE, B), so what do we do? Fortunately, this "move" is covered by another rule for precisely such circumstances. Logicians call it *modus tollens*, and we can call it the Denying Rule. That is, "If you have an IF A, THEN B statement that you know to be true; and if you can deny that B is true; then you can also deny that A is true." (IF A, THEN B; NOT-B; THEREFORE, NOT-A.) As with our Asserting Rule, it doesn't matter what the subject matter of our argument is. Any argument that follows this rule gives us a legitimate conclusion—only, strictly speaking, it's about what isn't the case, not what is the case.

If someone was born in Paris, then she was born in France.

Xijuan was not born in France.

Therefore, Xijuan was not born in Paris.

If today is Tuesday, then tomorrow is Wednesday.

Tomorrow is not Wednesday.

Therefore, today is not Tuesday.

If a bottle contains poison, then it stands to the left of nettle wine.

Bottle 7 does not stand to the left of nettle wine.

Therefore, bottle 7 does not contain poison.

We've discovered two rules so far—our Asserting Rule (IF A, THEN B; A; THERE-FORE, B) and our Denying Rule (IF A, THEN B; NOT-B; THEREFORE, NOT-A). Can we uncover a third one from another argument with a NOT in it—only in a different part of the argument?

IF someone is a student at Hogwarts, THEN he or she is studying witchcraft and wizardry.

Dudley Dursley is NOT a student at Hogwarts.

THEREFORE, Dudley Dursley is NOT studying witchcraft and wizardry.

At first, you might think that the conclusion follows from the premises and that this points to another kind of Denying Rule—one in which we deny that the IF part of the first premise is true (IF A, THEN B; NOT-A; THEREFORE, NOT-B). But before you draw that conclusion, look at this version of the argument—only this time applied to Fleur Delacour, a student at Beauxbatons Academy of Magic, the French school for witchcraft and wizardry.

IF someone is a student at Hogwarts, THEN he or she is studying witchcraft and wizardry.

Fleur Delacour is NOT a student at Hogwarts.

THEREFORE, Fleur Delacour is NOT studying witchcraft and wizardry.

Since we know that Fleur Delacour is studying witchcraft and wizardry—only at a different school—the conclusion to this argument can't be true. And yet the argument seemed logical when we applied it to Dudley Dursley a moment ago. What's going on?

Poor, Illogical Thinking: Structural (or Formal) Fallacies

The problem with our arguments about Dudley and Fleur is that we've now gone from good, logical thinking to poor, illogical thinking. How do we identify bad thinking? Fortunately, we do so in a way that's similar to how we recognize good thinking. That is, in the same way that following specific rules guarantees that we'll have a logical argument, there are standard ways of breaking the rules that guarantee that we'll end up with an illogical argument. No matter how much it looks like the conclusion follows from the premises, it doesn't.

Offering illogical arguments of this sort is like cheating in a game. Imagine that you're playing chess with a friend, and you decide to move your bishop a few squares—but you jump over other pieces to do it. And if your friend challenges the move, you say: "The rules say that bishops can move diagonally. I moved my bishop diagonally. So the move's OK." Unless your friend truly knows the rules of chess, she may go along with your explanation. But the fact is that you cheated. The rule describing what a bishop can do doesn't really authorize the move you just made.

It's the same in the case of the Dudley and Fleur arguments that we've just been looking at. To "move" from the premises in those two arguments to the conclusions may seem logical, but it actually breaks a rule of logic. It's like cheating. Any argument with this form (IF A, THEN B; NOT-A; THEREFORE, NOT-B) is actually illogical. In fact, this classic bit of rule breaking has a specific name in logic: Denying the Antecedent. (Logicians call the IF part of a sentence the "antecedent," and the THEN part the "consequent"—hence, "denying the antecedent.") The poor logic here is obvious in these examples:

> IF someone was born in Paris, THEN he or she was born in France.
>
> Madeleine was NOT born in Paris. (Madeleine was born in Tours.)
>
> THEREFORE, Madeleine was NOT born in France.
>
> (The error revealed: If Madeleine was born in Tours, then she obviously was born in France.)

> IF it's July, THEN it must be after June.
>
> It is NOT July. (It is September.)
>
> THEREFORE, it is NOT after June.
>
> (The error revealed: September is NOT July but obviously is after June.)

In the hands of clever manipulators, it is surprisingly easy to be taken in by bad logic. So it's important to be on guard against this sort of trickery and deception. For example, imagine that a political candidate says, "For the entire time that Senator Smith has been in office, the crime rate in our state has been increasing. And you can count on that continuing as long as he's in Washington because Senator Smith is soft on crime. But if you elect me, my tough, anti-crime plan will make that crime rate plummet." It's possible, of course, that this candidate has a good plan for combating crime. However, what he's offered us at this point is nothing more than the following bad argument:

> IF Senator Smith remains in office, THEN the crime rate will continue to increase.
>
> Elect me and Senator Smith will NOT be in office.
>
> THEREFORE, elect me and the crime rate will NOT continue to increase.

So unless this candidate gives us a more convincing argument for why his approach to crime is better than Senator Smith's, not only does he not deserve our vote, he also deserves to be exposed as a manipulator.

Poor, Illogical Thinking: Informal Fallacies

Logicians call logical mistakes **fallacies**. The fallacy we've just been looking at (Denying the Antecedent) is considered to be a structural or *formal fallacy* because the mistake is in the structure or the form of the argument. If you take a logic course at some point, you'll learn more structural fallacies. But for the purposes of this textbook, it makes more sense for us to move on to fallacies that we're more likely to run into in everyday life. These are called *informal fallacies*, and they're logical mistakes that appear in the language used or the kind of claims that are made in an argument rather than the formal structure of the argument. If you want to find examples of informal fallacies in the real world, you will unfortunately have no trouble. The homes of the worst examples are probably politics, advertising, social media posts, fringe websites, and online comment sections.

> **Fallacies** are weaknesses or mistakes in argumentation. Fallacies concerned with an argument's "form" or logical structure are formal fallacies. Subject matter fallacies are called informal fallacies.

Illogical Thinking: An Example

While there are specific labels for informal fallacies (you'll find a list at the end of this chapter), start by seeing which errors you can find in the following fictional dialogue. (Most of the fallacies are informal, but a couple of structural fallacies also appear.) Unfortunately, both the number of examples of illogical thinking and the harsh tone are representative of too many political discussions.

The Dialogue

Laura sat in the corner of Campus Coffee with books and notes spread across the dark wood table. She stared intently at a page of formulas she was trying to master for organic chemistry.

Her friend's voice startled her. "I should have known this is where you'd be hiding. It was pretty clear last night you were out of your depth when it came to discussing politics, and you'd want to avoid me." Rick sat down opposite her in the booth and placed a mug of fresh coffee in front of her. "Call it a peace offering. I shouldn't have been so hard on you. After all, how can a chem major keep up with a philosophy major in that kind of conversation? My father's a chemist, and he's rubbish when it comes to discussing politics."

She poured some cream into the cup, stirred it, and took a long drink of the warm liquid. She shook her head and laughed. "*I* couldn't keep up? I major in something that deals with *facts*. You, Plato, Aristotle, and the other guys in the band *just make things up*." She closed her eyes and pretended to go into a trance. "I see it! The Platonic Form of. . . of. . ." Her face tightened in concentration and she pointed her finger in her friend's direction. "Silliness!" She flicked her hand dismissively. "You were too enamored with the sound of your own voice to realize how ridiculous you sounded. I guess being that clueless explains why you plan to throw your vote away and cast it for Benson."

Rick frowned. "Hey! I'm trying to make peace here. And Benson's a good guy. He's been Mayor for a few years now. Downtown is finally starting to come back. Everyone feels really optimistic about the future. You don't change horses in the middle of a stream."

"Stream? We're talking furious white water that's going to devastate the town with a raging torrent of leftist anarchy! We need to elect Sylvius before this scourge takes hold and makes it impossible for any of us to feel safe in our beds at night! She's a strong champion of the ways we've always done things. She knows what's worked in the past and will make sure we don't stray from that. Her family has been devoted to this area since they first came over on the *Mayflower*, brought civilization with them, and tamed the wilderness. The only reason Benson is running is because he wants to destroy all the things that have made this city great."

Rick shook his head. "I genuinely feel sorry that you're blind to the complexities of economic and political forces. If Sylvius had won in the last election instead of Benson, downtown would have no Mom-and-Pop businesses. One name-brand store after another would have forced out the locals. She would have unleashed the heartless forces of greedy corporate capitalism. I did some research on her and discovered that her brother once got investigated for fraud. It's all about money with her. First, it will be letting some company run the municipal parking lots. Next, if your house is burning down, a privately owned fire department won't do anything for you until you give them your credit card. She's part of a secret group of aspiring politicians across the country who have agreed to privatize as many parts of government as possible."

"Don't tell me you believe everything you read on the internet?"

"Of course not. Do I look stupid? My information came from a research-driven, public interest nonprofit." He pulled his tablet out of his backpack and read. "Here's what they say. 'This organization is devoted solely to research that will enhance the public good. All funds support that endeavor.' Like I said, Sylvius wants to grind us under the heels of the banks who will rig the deck and fill the pockets of the rich."

She balled up a piece of paper and threw it at his forehead. "You really don't know the first thing about how the economy works, do you? The banks don't control things, the 'invisible hand' does. Normal people freely making decisions. I remember enough from Econ 101 to know how the free market works. *Wealth of Nations*? Adam Smith? Professor of *Moral Philosophy* Adam Smith? There's someone *you in particular* should defer to."

He scoffed. "The only reason he had that post was because there weren't business schools at the time. No *genuine* professor of moral philosophy would have said that you should be selfish and ignore what's good for your neighbors."

"Go ahead. Sidestep the issue. Sylvius just wants to protect a system that gives everyone the opportunity to be happy by getting what they want." She wagged her finger at him. "That's what *freedom* means. Your guy wants to impose godless socialism on us. No freedom. No choices. No churches. The same kind of car, clothes, entertainment for everyone. Where I can go. What I can do. All controlled by the state! Is that what you want? It's Sylvius and freedom, or Benson and servitude. It's not a hard choice for me!"

He threw his hands up in exasperation. "Laura! All Benson is suggesting is that the city provide free high-speed internet downtown. He's not talking about blowing up the economy!"

"Public internet is just the beginning. It's a short step from that to tracking every website I visit when I'm logged in and turning on my laptop's camera to spy on me after I come out of the shower."

"Wait a minute. Didn't Sylvius suggest public internet when she ran last time?"

"Yes. But she didn't do it to undermine everything we stand for. She did it to promote businesses downtown by making it a more attractive place for people to hang out. And you seem to forget that Benson opposed the idea last time. But he clearly figured out a way to use the idea to advance his scheme."

"Do you see conspiracies everywhere with Benson? I'm sure he just thought about it some more and changed his mind."

She laughed. "You mean like the way he also reversed himself on the Mayor's salary, the City Advisors' salaries, allowing the public to attend the Council's weekly meetings? Do I need to go on? He railed against these things when the other party ran the city. Do you honestly think he changed his positions on all of them just because he 'thought about it some more'?" She punctuated with air quotes for effect. "You're so naive."

Rick put his hands up. "Look. I didn't come to fight but to make peace. I may prefer Benson, but there's actually a lot I like about Sylvius. A stint of feminine leadership would make the Mayor's office less aggressive. And in the last debate, she made a couple of interesting comments challenging climate change."

She raised her eyebrows. "A philosophy major wading into the world of science? I'm impressed. Which comments?"

"How this past winter was much colder than normal. And that there's a Nobel prize–winning scientist who's a climate skeptic. I guess this is all more debatable as a scientific issue. Sylvius really made me think twice."

She groaned, grabbed her backpack, and pulled out a large, green paperback—*Global Climate Change: A Primer for Poets and Philosophers*. Handing it to Rick, she packed up her backpack and stood up. "Your assignment, young man, is to read this before tomorrow and tell me what was wrong with what you just said."

A Thicket of Faulty Thinking

Political discussions are among the best examples of *very* bad thinking. The passion people bring to such conversations is admirable, but it regularly shuts off the rational part of their brains. It also—as we see in Laura and Rick's case—makes them less likely to be civil. Garden variety insults and plain meanness have become as much a hallmark of political discourse as bad thinking.

Most of the mistakes that these two friends make involve subject matter rather than logical structure, and this is the kind of weakness we find most often in everyday conversations, in speeches, and in advertisements. This dialogue, then, is a fair place to practice judging how convincing the arguments we encounter are.

> Laura sat in the corner of Campus Coffee with books and notes spread across the dark wood table. She stared intently at a page of formulas she was trying to master for organic chemistry.
>
> Her friend's voice startled her. "I should have known this is where you'd be hiding. It was pretty clear last night you were out of your depth when it came to discussing politics, and you'd want to avoid me." Rick sat down opposite her in the booth and placed a mug of fresh coffee in front of her. "Call it a peace offering. I shouldn't have been so hard on you. After all, how can a chem major keep up with a philosophy major in that kind of conversation? My father's a chemist, and he's rubbish when it comes to discussing politics."
>
> She poured some cream into the cup, stirred it and took a long drink of the warm liquid. She shook her head and laughed. "*I* couldn't keep up? I major in something that deals with *facts*. You, Plato, Aristotle, and the other guys in the band *just make things up*. She closed her eyes and pretended to go into a trance. "I see it! The Platonic Form of. . . of. . ." Her face tightened in concentration and she pointed her finger in her friend's direction. "Silliness!" She flicked her hand dismissively. "You were too enamored with the sound of your own voice to realize how ridiculous you sounded. I guess being that clueless explains why you plan to throw your vote away and cast it for Benson."

Ad hominem: Rick and Laura start off with personal insults.

Unwarranted inference/sweeping generalization: Just because Rick's chemist father isn't adept at political discussions doesn't mean that's true about any other chemist.

> Rick frowned. "Hey! I'm trying to make peace here. And Benson's a good guy. He's been Mayor for a few years now. Downtown is finally starting to come back. Everyone feels really optimistic about the future. You don't change horses in the middle of a stream."
>
> "Stream? We're talking furious white water that's going to devastate the town with a raging torrent of leftist anarchy! We need to elect Sylvius before

> this scourge takes hold and makes it impossible for any of us to feel safe in our beds at night! She's a strong champion of the ways we've always done things. She knows what's worked in the past and will make sure we don't stray from that. Her family has been devoted to this area since they first came over on the *Mayflower*, brought civilization with them, and tamed the wilderness.

Post hoc: Rick claims that just because good things happened *after* Benson was elected, he gets to say the Mayor *caused* them. He needs to back up this claim with evidence.

False analogy; exaggerated, emotional language; appeal to emotions: Both Rick and Laura are guilty here. Changing horses in the middle of a stream is not analogous to changing Mayors in a community where that regularly happens. Unfortunately, Laura compounds her mistake by piling on with unsubstantiated accusations and an appeal to fear ("raging torrent of leftist anarchy").

Appeal to tradition/incomplete evidence: Laura goes on to make two other mistakes. Just because a practice has persisted through time is no guarantee that it's good to continue. Also, as proud as she may be of her ancestors, they did not arrive in a "wilderness" that had to be tamed. There was a robust Native American civilization.

> Rick shook his head. "I genuinely feel sorry that you're blind to the complexities of economic and political forces. If Sylvius had won in the last election instead of Benson, downtown would have no Mom-and-Pop businesses. One name-brand store after another would have forced out the locals. She would have unleashed the heartless forces of greedy corporate capitalism. I did some research on her and discovered that her brother once got investigated for fraud. It's all about money with her. First, it will be letting some company run the municipal parking lots. Next, if your house is burning down, a privately owned fire department won't do anything for you until you give them your credit card. She's part of a secret group of aspiring politicians across the country who have agreed to privatize as many parts of government as possible."
>
> "Don't tell me you believe everything you read on the internet?"
>
> "Of course not. Do I look stupid? My information came from a research-driven, public interest nonprofit." He pulled his tablet out of his backpack and read. "Here's what they say. 'This organization is devoted solely to research that will enhance the public good. All funds support that endeavor.' Like I said, Sylvius wants to grind us under the heels of the banks who will rig the deck and fill the pockets of the rich."

Contrary-to-fact conditional: Rick cannot know what *would* have happened if Sylvius had won.

Insulting, emotional language: "Heartless forces of greedy corporate capitalism."

Incomplete evidence/guilt by association: First, Sylvius's brother was *investigated* for fraud, not charged and/or convicted. Even if he's dishonest, we can't say his sister is as well just because they're related.

Questionable claim: Secret group? Trying to stoke fear by referring to some dark conspiracy is increasingly popular—and completely baseless and manipulative. (Have you ever noticed how all the "secret conspiracies" are dark and evil?)

Slippery slope: Rick goes from parking lots to an unlikely disaster scenario with no reasonable explanation.

Incomplete evidence: There's a good chance the organization Rick is referring to isn't being fully candid. "Public interest nonprofit" does not mean it's been certified as such by a state agency or the IRS and therefore neutral when it comes to politics. It might be set up so that it doesn't aim to generate a profit. But it may be closer to a special interest lobbying organization.

Insulting, emotional language: "Grind us under the heels. . ."

> She balled up a piece of paper and threw it at his forehead. "You really don't know the first thing about how the economy works, do you? The banks don't control things, the 'invisible hand' does. Normal people freely making decisions. I remember enough from Econ 101 to know how the free market works. *Wealth of Nations*? Adam Smith? Professor of *Moral Philosophy* Adam Smith? There's someone *you in particular* should defer to."
>
> He scoffed. "The only reason he had that post was because there weren't business schools at the time. No *genuine* professor of moral philosophy would have said that you should be selfish and ignore what's good for your neighbors."
>
> "Go ahead. Sidestep the issue. Sylvius just wants to protect a system that gives everyone the opportunity to be happy by getting what they want." She wagged her finger at him. "That's what *freedom* means. Your guy wants to impose godless socialism on us. No freedom. No choices. No churches. The same kind of car, clothes, entertainment for everyone. Where I can go. What I can do. All controlled by the state! Is that what you want? It's Sylvius and freedom, or Benson and servitude. It's not a hard choice for me!"

Appeal to authority: Laura is suggesting that Rick should defer to her on Adam Smith's authority based on him being a professor of moral philosophy.

Irrelevant reason/false statement/exaggeration: Whether or not there were business schools in Smith's time is irrelevant. And he does not endorse selfishly ignoring the welfare of others. What he really wrote in *Wealth of Nations* was: "Every individual is continually exerting himself to find out the most advantageous employment for whatever capital he can command. It is his own advantage, indeed, and not that of the society, which he has in view. But the study of his own advantage naturally, or rather necessarily, leads him to prefer that employment which is most advantageous to the society."

False statement/exaggeration: Laura is as guilty as Rick of distorting facts. Socialism is an economic system that does not rely on the free market, but it does not aim at oppressing the population. Her characterization, very common in the United States, is simply false.

False dilemma/straw man: Laura unreasonably paints the options as "good" versus "bad."

> He threw his hands up in exasperation. "Laura! All Benson is suggesting is that the city provide free high-speed internet downtown. He's not talking about blowing up the economy!"
>
> "Public internet is just the beginning. It's a short step from that to tracking every website I visit when I'm logged in and turning on my laptop's camera to spy on me after I come out of the shower."
>
> "Wait a minute. Didn't Sylvius suggest public internet when she ran last time?"
>
> "Yes. But she didn't do it to undermine everything we stand for. She did it to promote businesses downtown by making it a more attractive place for people to hang out. And you seem to forget that Benson opposed the idea last time. But he clearly figured out a way to use the idea to advance his scheme."
>
> "Do you see conspiracies everywhere with Benson? I'm sure he just thought about it some more and changed his mind."
>
> She laughed. "You mean like the way he also reversed himself on the Mayor's salary, the City Advisors' salaries, allowing the public to attend the Council's weekly meetings? Do I need to go on? He railed against these things when the other party ran the city. Do you honestly think he changed his positions on all of them just because he 'thought about it some more'?" She punctuated with air quotes for effect. "You're so naive."

Slippery slope: Laura offers her own version of one event leading to disaster.

Unknowable fact: Laura cannot know why Benson changed his mind.

Inconsistency: On the surface, Laura's criticism of Benson seems reasonable. Inconsistency (some would call it "hypocrisy") is a common fault in politics. Party A uses tactics or advances positions that they condemn when Party B does exactly the same thing.

Questionable claim: Rick's explanation for Benson's changes in positions is suspect—particularly given Laura's additional detail.

> Rick put his hands up. "Look. I didn't come to fight but to make peace. I may prefer Benson, but there's actually a lot I like about Sylvius. A stint of feminine leadership would make the Mayor's office less aggressive. And in the last debate, she made a couple of interesting comments challenging climate change."
>
> She raised her eyebrows. "A philosophy major wading into the world of science? I'm impressed. Which comments?"

> "How this past winter was much colder than normal. And that there's a Nobel prize–winning scientist who's a climate skeptic. I guess this is all more debatable as a scientific issue. Sylvius really made me think twice."
>
> She groaned, grabbed her backpack and pulled out a large, green paperback— *Global Climate Change: A Primer for Poets and Philosophers*. Handing it to Rick, she stood up. "Your assignment, young man, is to read this before tomorrow and tell me what was wrong with what you just said."

Circular reasoning: Because gentleness is a standard part of the definition of "feminine," Rick is going in a circle—not to mention that not all females are "feminine" in this sense.

Irrelevant reason: "Weather" and "climate" are two different things. Rick's reference to the former in a discussion of the latter is largely irrelevant.

Incomplete evidence: Rick apparently does not know that the scientist he's referring to is a physicist, not a climate scientist (97 percent of whom consider global climate change to be real, serious, and human-caused). By this scientist's own account, he spent no more than a day looking into the issue before making his famous denial.

Weak Thinking: A More Sophisticated Diagnosis

The formal and informal fallacies we've seen in this chapter so far are actually relatively easy to discover—as long as we take our time and carefully scrutinize the claims people make. However, the philosopher Janice Moulton argues that even some examples of thinking that *on the surface* seem perfectly reasonable can have a serious weakness because of an important feature of the history of philosophy. That is, she argues that because most major philosophers over the last two thousand years have been men, philosophy itself has been distorted by the fact that it has been dominated by a methodology largely connected to the "masculine experience."[4]

Moulton bases her analysis on the idea that aggression has traditionally been seen as natural and desirable in men and unnatural and offensive in women. Nonphysical aggression is taken in Western society to indicate power, ambition, energy, authority, competence, and effectiveness. Considered as a positive trait, claims Moulton, aggression has been incorporated as a basic aspect of philosophical methodology. Hence, Moulton sees the basic procedure of philosophy as an expression of a masculine trait. She calls this methodology the "Adversary Paradigm." "Under the Adversary Paradigm," she explains,

> it is assumed that the only, or at any rate, the best, way of evaluating work in philosophy is to subject it to the strongest or most extreme opposition. And it is

---

4. Janice Moulton, "A Paradigm of Philosophy: The Adversary Method," in *Discovering Reality: Feminist Perspectives on Epistemology, Metaphysics, Methodology, and Philosophy of Science*, ed. Sandra Harding and Merrill B. Hintikka (Dordrecht, Netherlands: D. Reidel, 1983), 149–64.

assumed that the best way of presenting work in philosophy is to address it to an imagined opponent and muster all the evidence one can to support it. The justification for this method is that a position ought to be defended from, and subjected to, the criticism of the strongest opposition; that this method is the only way to get the best of both sides; that a thesis which survives this method of evaluation is more likely to be correct than one that has not; and that a thesis subjected to the Adversary Method will have passed an "objective" test, the most extreme test possible, whereas any weaker criticism or evaluation will, by comparison, give an advantage to the claim to be evaluated and therefore not be as objective as it could be. Of course, it will be admitted that the Adversary Method does not guarantee that all and only sound philosophical claims will survive, but that is only because even an adversary does not always think of all the things which ought to be criticized about a position, and even a proponent does not always think of all the possible responses to criticism. However, since there is no way to determine with certainty what is good and what is bad philosophy, the Adversary Method is the best there is. If one wants philosophy to be objective, one should prefer the Adversary Method to other, more subjective, forms of evaluation which would give preferential treatment to some claims by not submitting them to extreme adversarial tests.

Moulton claims that such a methodology in reality "restricts and misrepresents what philosophic reasoning is," and she engages in a far-reaching account of the problems of the Adversary Paradigm: defects in the paradigm itself, misinterpreting the history of philosophy, restricting what is considered a philosophical issue, and bad reasoning. In short, Moulton implies that what *should* be the goal of philosophical inquiry—the search for truth—has given way to the honing of debating skills. This, she argues, results when a historically masculine trait is made into an intellectual virtue.

Unfortunately, if we revisit Laura and Rick's conversation, we see that both speakers give us reason to take Moulton's criticism seriously. They automatically think the object of their conversation is to defeat the other. They take adversarial stances from the outset, never considering that if they're actually looking to uncover the truth about which candidate will help the city the most, their all-or-nothing, zero-sum approach gets in the way. They're blind to the fact that the debate isn't who is the angel and who the demon. Sylvius and Benson likely have both strengths and weaknesses. There may even be a third, different candidate who would be even better.

Final Thoughts About Philosophical Thinking

You have now been exposed to a daunting variety of common errors in thinking. Whenever you encounter any of them, know that the speaker's conclusion rests on shaky ground. Also, know that anyone using faulty thinking on you is looking to undermine your freedom and your ability to control your own life by tricking you into doing what they want you to do.

Why do people argue this way? These fallacies are not difficult to understand, so why is there so much uncritical thinking going on?

One reason is probably that weak thinking results from the force of habit, inertia, or laziness. We simply do not want to change, and critical thinking requires hard work, energy, and discipline. The ideas we're familiar with make us feel secure, and we see no reason to change things.

Negative emotions like fear probably have more to do with it, however. What's at stake in the outcome of the election that Rick and Laura debate? Power. What's the risk? Watching someone else put through laws and policies that may be to your disadvantage. How does that make you feel? Probably threatened and a little afraid. Again, with those feelings inside you, the desire to win by any means, say, by attacking the character of the other candidate, can easily be stronger than wanting to argue logically.

Emotions like worry and fear also underlie the ordinary selfishness that seems to drive our use of fallacies. We want what we want, and we don't care about other people. We use our persuasive powers to get our way. Whether we realize it or not, we treat other people as competitors or out-and-out enemies, and we probably feel we can't trust them. They may keep us from getting what we need. They are a threat.

Or consider prejudice. Prejudiced people may be angry and hateful to those they discriminate against, but they may also be afraid of them. People whose skin color, gender, sexual orientation, or ethnic background differs from ours can make us uncomfortable. We may feel uneasy about people unlike ourselves. We don't know what they'll do or how they'll treat us. At best, we keep our distance until we find out what they're like. When we learn they're no different from us, we're no longer afraid of them. But until we know that, we try to keep them from getting enough power to threaten us, and part of that is indulging in biased, faulty thinking. In other words, we give in to our fear and let it cloud our minds. One of the strongest barriers to good thinking, then, is fear. Fear may show itself as anger, envy, selfishness, hatred, or wild conspiracy theories. But these are just expressions of our fear. And don't underrate the power of such emotions. History has shown what devastation fear and hatred among nations can wreak. Our personal fears can be just as damaging to our inner world, blinding our critical faculties with their dark energies. When we argue, then, we must be aware of what we feel as well as what we think. A good critical thinker may have to scrutinize not only the intellectual character of an argument but its emotional temperature as well.

Appendix: An Overview of the Fallacies

Structural ("Formal") Fallacies

Affirming the consequent: Claiming that if the consequent (then-part) of a particular if-then statement is true, then so is the antecedent (if-part).

Contradiction: Asserting or implying directly opposite statements "A" and "not-A."

Denying the antecedent: Claiming that if the antecedent (if-part) of a particular if-then statement is not true, then neither is the consequent (then-part).

Subject Matter ("Informal") Fallacies

Accent: Implying something (rather than arguing for it) by the way a speaker states a point. This can be done by emphasizing words in certain ways or by quoting someone out of context.

Ad hominem: Latin for arguing "against the person." Trying to undermine an argument by attacking the arguer rather than the reasons he or she cites.

Appeal to authority: The flip side of ad hominem—trying to prove a point by relying on the authority of its source. The authority can be of an individual, the majority, traditional wisdom, a religion, or the like.

Appeal to emotions: Trying to sway or persuade people by appealing to their feelings, not their minds.

Appeal to ignorance: Claiming that something is true because it cannot be shown to be false.

Begging the question (circular reasoning): Assuming to be true what the argument is supposed to prove as true.

Contrary-to-fact conditional: Claiming that if past events had been different, the outcome would also have been different.

False analogy: Using a comparison that does not fit the case at hand.

False dilemma: Misrepresenting a situation by claiming there are fewer options than is actually the case.

False statement: The claim is simply false.

Guilt by association: Trying to undermine someone by linking him or her with unsavory friends or associates.

Hasty conclusion: Trying to prove too much from your evidence. The evidence is relevant; it just is not strong enough to let you draw the conclusion you want.

Incomplete evidence: Ignoring relevant evidence.

Insulting, exaggerated, inflammatory language: Closely related to appeal to emotions. Describing a situation with emotionally loaded words that slant and distort the account. Hurling personal insults.

Irrelevant reason: Just what it suggests. Facts or theories that do not bear on the matter under discussion.

Questionable cause: Drawing an unwarranted conclusion about the cause of something.

Questionable cause: *post hoc:* Assumption that just because one event preceded another, it must have caused it. *Post hoc ergo propter hoc* is Latin for "After this, therefore because of this."

Questionable claim: An assertion that, for one reason or another, is problematic.

Slippery slope: A special version of hasty conclusion, claiming that one event will trigger a devastating chain reaction.

Statistical fallacies: Using questionable statistics to reach unwarranted conclusions. Mistakes can involve everything from research design to the method of collecting data, to the sample polled, to the conclusions drawn from the data.

Straw man: Exaggerating or distorting a position to make it easier to refute.

Unknowable fact: Citing a fact that cannot be known and objectively confirmed.

Unwarranted inference or sweeping generalization: Having insufficient grounds to generalize, arguing from stereotypes, or assuming that what is true of some members of a group is true of all members.

Discussion Questions

1. Take a newspaper editorial or online opinion piece and identify the argument: the premises and the conclusion. How good an argument is it?

2. Is it fair to label *ad hominem* a fallacy? Why should we treat everyone's arguments alike? If someone is a manipulator, or in some other way dishonest or disreputable, isn't he or she probably up to no good? Why shouldn't we be able to discount his or her arguments because of that? By the same token, aren't there some authorities whom we should simply believe?

3. What is your reaction to the fallacious thinking and appeals to emotion used in advertising? Does it really convince people? Is there anything wrong with it?

4. Considering how much the public good is determined by the outcome of our elections, would you support a law requiring that no candidate may make false, unwarranted, illogical claims in his or her speeches, advertisements, and campaign literature? Is there any reasonable way that anyone could *not* support such a law? Wouldn't opposing such a law amount to supporting intellectual dishonesty and trickery? How could that be consistent with democracy?

5. What does the pervasiveness of weak thinking say about our society? Is good thinking too tough? Are we simply too selfish to be intellectually honest?

6. Look at your own attempts to convince other people. When are you most likely to "finesse" things with faulty thinking? What lies behind it?

Selected Readings

For a standard introduction to formal logic, see Irving Copi, Carl Cohen, and Kenneth McMahon, *Introduction to Logic*, 14th ed. (Taylor & Francis, 2013). For an introduction to informal logic, see Morris S. Engel, *With Good Reason: An Introduction to Informal Fallacies*, 6th ed. (Bedford/St. Martin's, 2014).

Part Two: Exploring the Basics of Who We Are and Dealing with Others

Chapter 3

The Case for Determinism

One of the features of life is what philosophers refer to as the problem of *appearance versus reality*. Things very clearly look one way but turn out to be different. It certainly seems like the sun goes around the earth. It's the other way around. If you sit quietly, it feels like you aren't moving. But you are. Not only is the earth moving through space, it's spinning on its axis. This tension even extends to our inner experience. If you're superstitious, you may think that wearing your "lucky [sweater, socks, underwear, cap, etc.]" is responsible for making good things happen. You have a track record that convinces you. However, we live in a physical world of cause and effect, so your clothing doesn't have any magical powers. When confronted with a question of appearance versus reality, we can typically determine the reality by using reason, logic, and science.

But sometimes it's not so easy to determine which is which. We *feel* as though we're completely free in choosing our actions. At the same time, however, we know—in sharp contrast to the sense that we can do whatever we choose—that we live in a physical world constrained by laws of cause and effect. Everything that happens is the product of prior causes. This is the classic philosophical problem of **free will** versus **determinism**. We control our actions. Yet our actions are no different from everything else around us—they're the end result of a causal chain. Both can't be true. Which is it?

We'll explore this conundrum in the next two chapters. You've probably always assumed you have free will, so let's start with the best arguments for the other side, determinism.

Freedom Versus Determinism

Obvious Limits to Our Freedom

The subjective experience of freedom is so strong, you may be tempted to reject determinism out of hand. But consider how many ordinary ways your actions are limited.

Imagine you're walking along with your significant other when you find a wallet filled with cash. When you pocket the money, your companion objects. "That's stealing! I'm not going to be involved with somebody who's dishonest. Do what you like but forget about me forever." This can feel like very strong pressure. You're still free to choose, but you surely don't feel as free as if you had been alone when you found the wallet.

A variation on feeling direct pressure might be if you find the wallet when you're alone, but say to yourself, "My parents would be disappointed if they knew I kept it. I can't do it."

The very structure of our personalities—the fact that our inner, emotional reactions to certain things influence our behavior so profoundly—seems to set limits to our freedom.

Take fear, for example. Most of us have enough fear of high places, falling off ladders, and the like that hang gliding is about the last thing that appeals to us. Imagine that a friend invites you to go hang gliding with her. Are you *free* to join her, strap yourself into the harness, and throw yourself off the side of a mountain with only a sheet of nylon between you and eternity? Yes and no. No one is stopping you, so you are free. But it's possible you would be so afraid that you *could not* do it. Not just "preferred not to" but *could not* under any normal circumstances.

Guilt is another feeling that limits our freedom. If you know that guilt will plague you if you take something that belongs to someone else, the anticipation of those feelings can be so strong that you cannot steal. Maybe you were severely punished as a child for stealing. The memories are so vivid that you know that guilt will torment you if you take the money out of the wallet. You may even think your feelings are irrational, but you feel them anyway. In any event, you don't feel totally free. As with the previous example, in one way we are free, but in another way we're not.

The Contradiction: Freedom and Determinism

The more we look at the issue of how free we are, the more complex, confusing, and full of contradictions it becomes.

On the one hand, if I ask you, "Are you free and in control of your actions?" you might say, "Absolutely!" And you probably believe that other people are just as free as you are. If your friend Lori is doing badly in class because she's not studying, you don't feel much sympathy when she complains that her low grades will hurt her future. You figure that all she has to do is sit down and work. It's her choice. If someone steals a car, we want the thief punished. "He knows what he's doing," we say, "and he deserves the full penalty of the law. Give him something to think about the next time he considers taking somebody's car." We assume the car thief is free and in control of his actions. He is the cause of the theft, and he is responsible for it.

Yet as often as we talk about how free people are, we're just as ready to act as though they're puppets. If you learned that the car thief's friends and family were also criminals, and that crime was all he was ever taught, you'd probably concede that his environment had much to do with his current behavior. His upbringing led him to crime. You might then think that the criminal does not need punishment as much as rehabilitation in a better, more law-abiding environment. That is, most of us seem to think that in one way or another, the actions people take are determined by something other than their own dispassionate assessment of a situation and their free choice among possible options.

Even the staunchest believer in freedom must concede that forces—external and internal—can at least limit our actions. This means that determinism must be taken seriously.

Determinism, Science, and Materialism

Although deterministic theories may differ in their details, they all contain a common thread: the idea that free choice is impossible because anything that exists is physical and material, and physical, material objects are subject to laws of nature like cause and effect.

While modern science obviously sees things this way, the much older philosophical outlook known as **materialism** argues basically the same thing.

Materialism is a theory about the nature of reality that claims that if something exists, it must be physical. Materialism has a long history in philosophy. The ancient Greek philosophers Leucippus (c. 450 BCE) and Democritus (460–371 BCE) argued that the building blocks of absolutely everything that existed were tiny material particles too small for us to see. Foreshadowing the modern atomic theory of matter, Democritus called these particles "atoms." (*Atomoi* in Greek means "uncuttable.") The great early modern English philosopher Thomas Hobbes (1588–1679) echoes the Greeks with his belief that all that exists are atoms in motion.

> **materialism** Materialism is a theory about the nature of reality. It claims that if something exists, it must be physical and subject to natural laws like cause and effect. Materialism logically implies determinism.

According to materialist thinkers, nothing immaterial exists—not souls, spirits, minds, or the like. We may *think* our "minds" are qualitatively different from our bodies and that our immaterial minds decide what we want to do and then make our material bodies act accordingly. But the materialist says we're wrong. Anything we attribute to an immaterial "mind" is a function of something physical—most likely the brain.

Moreover, anything material and physical is subject to natural laws like cause and effect. That is, materialism logically implies determinism. As Leucippus puts it, "No thing happens at random but all things as a result of a reason and by necessity."[1] If everything that exists is material and physical, how could our actions be anything other than the end result of some chain of cause and effect? *Free choice*, then, is an illusion. Our actions are simply the result of some combination of material events or forces. Even when we *feel* free, a materialist thinker would argue that our actions are dictated by something physical.

A materialist explanation of human behavior might even argue that the chain of causes that makes us act in a certain way also produces an electrochemical state in the brain that causes us to feel as though we're choosing an action. In fact, Thomas Hobbes argues that actions that we think are "**voluntary**" are anything but. He explains that when we see something that we like or dislike and then act accordingly (trying to get it or avoiding it), what actually happens is that the impact of the atoms from the object first creates a desire

---

1. *A Presocratics Reader*, ed. Patricia Curd, trans. Richard D. McKirahan and Patricia Curd, second edition. (Indianapolis: Hackett Publishing Co., 2011), 110.

(or aversion) and then produces our action. In other words, our subjective experience that we're "choosing" what to do is a product of material forces.[2]

Given the fact that we don't understand how the brain works well enough to identify all the precise steps that inevitably determine our actions, isn't it possible that something of this sort is going on when we "choose" our actions? After all, not being able to identify a material cause doesn't mean it's not there. When the plague swept through medieval and Renaissance Europe, medicine wasn't advanced enough to identify the precise cause. Some people even thought it was a punishment from God. However, scientists eventually discovered that the illness was caused by being bitten by a flea carrying the plague bacterium or by handling an animal that was infected. Why couldn't the same sort of thing apply to human behavior in general? That is, even though we can't currently identify all the details of the process that determines our actions, maybe research on the brain will ultimately demonstrate that our actions are simply the last step of a material, biological causal chain.

In this chapter we're going to look at four different arguments for determinism. We'll start with a simple approach: **behaviorism**. We'll then move to a more psychological one: **Freudianism**. Then we'll discuss the intriguing work of neuroscientist Benjamin Libet. We'll conclude with the ancient Stoics. You may have already encountered behaviorism and Freudianism if you've studied psychology. It's not unusual for different disciplines to study the same issue, although they look at problems through different lenses. This is a good example of how different intellectual perspectives lead to a richer understanding of a problem. We should also note that many contemporary psychologists and cognitive scientists are more than a little skeptical of behaviorism and Freudianism. However, this does not diminish the usefulness of these perspectives in setting in relief important issues in the debate between freedom and determinism.

Freedom, Determinism, and Responsibility

Before we get into the details of deterministic theories, it's important to realize that the debate over free will and determinism is not just some academic exercise. The free will/determinism debate leads us directly to the crucial concept of responsibility.

Responsibility is at the heart of all our traditions of reward and punishment. When we praise or blame people, we assume they *deserve* it. That is, we presume they're free and in control of their actions. Grades, jobs, salaries, promotions, jail terms, elections, marriages, divorces—these and many other positive and negative experiences in life are based on the idea that each of us is the author of his or her actions and can be held responsible for them. Thus, responsibility makes sense only if we are free. But if determinism is correct, doesn't the notion of responsibility evaporate? And if that happens, what kind of world are we left with—personally, socially, politically?

---

2. Thomas Hobbes, *Leviathan*, chapters 1 and 6.

Take the case of Wyatt, a student in your chemistry class who is caught red-handed sabotaging your final experiment and those of four other top students. Wyatt desperately wanted an A in the class, so he ruined the lab work of his chief competitors. Should he be punished?

If everyone is free and in control of his or her actions, of course Wyatt should be punished. He knew what he was doing, planned his actions, tried to advance himself by hurting others, and broke time-honored rules of academic honesty. There is no reason to let him off the hook. The only issue is how severe the penalty should be.

But what if we ask, "What *caused* Wyatt to do what he did?" Suppose Wyatt's domineering parents try to run all their children's lives. They want him to be a physician like his father, so they chose his college (which they pay for), his major, and even the courses he takes. They insist that he get straight As. But Wyatt does poorly in science and hates medicine—he would rather go into music. When he told his parents this, they said that if he couldn't get into a top medical school, he could go sweep floors. Furthermore, they said, his failure would stress his father's already weak heart. Wyatt was working hard to manage a B+ in the chemistry course, and he figured that his only hope was to sabotage the work of the A students. That way, he would throw off the curve and hope to squeak by.

Years of parental intimidation have made Wyatt a weak and frightened young man. He needs his parents' approval and support. He feels guilty at the prospect of letting them down. He also believes that his father's heart might not stand the disappointment if he cannot get into a good medical school. He is working as hard as he can—but it's just not enough. As he surveys his situation, he feels hopeless and depressed. One night he's alone in the lab, and in a moment of desperation, he tampers with his competitors' experiments. When the opportunity to cheat arose, Wyatt was no more able to resist it than a hungry dog can resist a piece of meat.

What do you think now? Given Wyatt's relationship with his parents and their demands, his action was the predictable result of their pressure and threats. He was desperate to please them, and his cheating was his ultimate response to their insensitivity and domination. Under the circumstances, how much control does Wyatt have over what he did? Doesn't he now seem more like a victim?

If you're at all sympathetic, you can feel for Wyatt. You may not like what he did, but you can understand it. If you were in his shoes, you might even do what he did. Should he be punished? If so, you probably wouldn't suggest as strong a penalty as you did when we assumed that he was totally free. When you know what caused him to act the way he did, you probably feel sorry for him.

The significance of this example, however, is that if you are willing to let Wyatt off the hook, you're saying that he is not fully *responsible* for what he did. He is a product of his circumstances. His upbringing made him weak, but that isn't his fault. You can't punish people for that. And that's very different from our first assessment of this case. In other words, as long as we believe in free will, we have no trouble holding people fully responsible for what they do. As soon as we say that other factors determine our actions, the concept of responsibility is the first casualty. Sometimes it's just diluted. Other times, it's washed away altogether.

From a practical standpoint, this is why the free will/determinism dispute is so important. If behavior is determined, what grounds do we have for holding people responsible for what they do? How can we reward or punish, praise or blame, if our accomplishments and mistakes are the result of causes beyond our immediate control? Yet how can we as individuals or as a society function without some concept of responsibility?

Behaviorism

Now that you understand the main lines and importance of the free will/determinism debate, we can get down to the arguments for determinism. (We'll take up the other side—arguments for freedom—in the next chapter.) Because the foundation of deterministic theories is that we live in a world of cause and effect, we'll look at thinkers who see themselves as scientists, not philosophers.

behaviorism Behaviorism is the school of psychology that focuses exclusively on observable behavior and denies free will. Behavior is seen as an organism's "response" to a "stimulus"; the likelihood of a behavior recurring is increased by "positive reinforcement," and it is decreased by "negative reinforcement."

We start with a straightforward argument for determinism based on the idea that human actions are deceptively easy to explain—behaviorism.

If you have ever heard of "stimulus–response," "operant conditioning," "positive and negative reinforcement," or "programmed learning," then you have already met behaviorism and psychologist B. F. Skinner. As you can guess from their name, "behaviorists" focus solely on observable behavior. They also assume that humans act in *predictable* ways in line with natural laws of *cause* and *effect*. Skinner's outlook is captured well in his statement from *Beyond Freedom and Dignity* that "man is a machine in the sense that he is a complex system behaving in lawful ways."[3]

Behaviorism looks at human behavior in terms of cause and effect or, as behaviorists put it, *stimulus* (cause) and *response* (effect). Our actions do not result from free choice; rather, they are predictable responses to stimuli. Our experience of external events trains, or *conditions,* us so that a specific stimulus always evokes the same response. Skinner maintains that our actions—that is, our responses—are controlled primarily by the consequences that follow what we do. If the consequences are positive, the odds go up that we will act that way again. If the results are negative, the odds go down. Skinner refers to these rewards and punishments as *positive* and *negative reinforcements.*

For example, if you say "Hi" to Vanya and she responds with a warm, friendly smile, what will you do the next time you see her? You will repeat your greeting and hope for the smile again. Why? In Skinner's terms, you got "positively reinforced" in the first exchange because Vanya's smile made you feel good, and people are highly motivated to feel good. Thus, the next time you encounter Vanya (the *stimulus*), the odds are better

---

3. B. F. Skinner, *Beyond Freedom and Dignity* (Indianapolis: Hackett Publishing Co., 1971, 2002), 202.

Burrhus Frederic Skinner (1904–1990) was born in Susquehanna, Pennsylvania, to strict parents. As Skinner put it in his autobiography, "I was taught to fear God, the police, and what people will think." A talented child, Skinner began writing stories while very young, and he published his first poem when only ten. He was interested in gadgets, designing and constructing numerous machines throughout his youth. And he also was strongly interested in music, starting with the piano, moving to the saxophone, and even playing in a jazz band during high school. Skinner graduated from Hamilton College as an English major and, having resolved to be a writer, set up a study in the attic of his parents' home in Scranton. Subsequently moving to New York's Greenwich Village, and then touring Europe for a summer, Skinner gave up on a literary career because he thought he had "nothing important to say." Intensely curious about human behavior, however, Skinner turned from a literary to a scientific approach and enrolled in graduate school at Harvard University in 1928 to study psychology. After receiving his doctorate, Skinner remained at Harvard conducting his classic experiments on the conditioning of rats. He then went to the University of Minnesota and Indiana University before returning to Harvard in 1948. Skinner was a prolific writer, having authored not only scientific works but also popular accounts and defenses of behaviorism, a utopian novel, and his autobiography.

than even that you will say "Hi, Vanya" (the *response*). By contrast, if you say "Good morning" to Bill and he spits on your shoes (*negative reinforcement*), you will be sure to leave him alone tomorrow. Positive reinforcement increases the odds of a behavior being repeated, while negative reinforcement decreases them.

Skinner's explanation of human behavior is clear, simple, and deterministic. "A scientific analysis of behavior must assume," he explains in *About Behaviorism*, "that a person's behavior is controlled by his genetic and environmental histories rather than by the person himself. . . . There is no place in the scientific position for a self as a true originator or initiator of action."[4] As far as Skinner is concerned, once we begin studying human behavior scientifically, "freedom" as it is traditionally understood bites the dust.

Whatever Happened to Freedom?

Note that Skinner is not some kind of fascist or dictator. He does not argue, as the Renaissance political theorist Machiavelli does, that clever manipulation is the best strategy. That would be saying simply that people can be controlled. Skinner's theory holds that it is impossible for us *not* to be controlled. It's just the nature of things. The world is constructed in such a way that there is no freedom or genuine choice. Everything we do is the inevitable result of prior causes, and what we imagine to be "freedom" is just that—imaginary.

Perhaps Skinner's best exposition of his position on freedom can be found in his utopian novel *Walden Two*. Skinner explains his ideas in an interesting bit of dialogue between a behavioral scientist (Frazier) and a philosopher (Castle).

---

4. B. F. Skinner, *About Behaviorism* (New York: Vintage, 1974), 208.

"My answer [to the question of freedom] is simple enough," said Frazier. "I deny that freedom exists at all. . . . You can't have a science about a subject matter which hops capriciously about. Perhaps we can never *prove* that man isn't free; it's an assumption. But the increasing success of a science of behavior makes it more and more plausible."

"On the contrary, a simple personal experience makes it untenable," said Castle. "The experience of freedom. I *know* that I'm free." . . .

"The 'feeling of freedom' should deceive no one," said Frazier. "Give me a concrete case."

Accepting the challenge, the philosopher picks up a book of matches. He tells Frazier that he's free either to hold or to drop them. But Frazier is unconvinced.

"You will, of course, do one or the other," said Frazier. "Linguistically or logically there seem to be two possibilities, but I submit that there's only one in fact. The determining forces may be subtle but they are inexorable. I suggest that as an orderly person you will probably hold—ah! you drop them! Well, you see, that's all part of your behavior with respect to me. You couldn't resist the temptation to prove me wrong. It was all lawful. You had no choice. The deciding factor entered rather late, and naturally you couldn't foresee the result when you first held them up. There was no strong likelihood that you would act in either direction, and so you said you were free."

"That's entirely too glib," said Castle. "It's easy to argue lawfulness after the fact. But let's see you predict what I will do in advance. Then I'll agree there's law."

"I didn't say that behavior is always predictable, any more than the weather is always predictable. There are often too many factors to be taken into account."[5]

Castle's Conditioning. This exchange between Frazier and Castle is worth dwelling on for a minute. Castle wants to refute Frazier's claim that we are not free. Castle *feels* free and assumes that the simple example of holding or dropping a matchbook according to his preference proves Frazier wrong. Castle does not feel that anything compels him to drop the matches. Frazier, of course, sees it differently. First, he believes that everything must have a cause. Here he is convinced that his remark that Castle would hold them caused the philosopher to do just the opposite.

Second, Frazier warns that the feeling of freedom is misleading and that forces can act on us without our noticing it. That Castle does not *feel* that his action was determined by outside forces does not mean that it *wasn't*.

If Frazier is right, we can assume that over the years Castle has received positive reinforcement when he proved people wrong. Like many professional academics, when Castle exposed the weaknesses in other philosophers' arguments, his colleagues probably praised his sharp, analytical mind. Castle is thus conditioned to expect pleasure from proving people wrong, so he automatically does it again. It is virtually a reflex at this point, and Frazier knows this. However, if Castle had been reinforced differently in the

---

5. B. F. Skinner, *Walden Two* (reprinted Indianapolis: Hackett Publishing Co., 2005), 241–42.

past, he would have acted differently. If he had been positively reinforced for showing people that they were right instead of wrong, he would have held the matches.

Human Freedom and the Weather. Skinner's analogy between predicting behavior and predicting the weather is also instructive.

What are the odds that the forecast you hear today for a couple of days from now will be right? About one in three. Many hurricanes that meteorologists say will slam into Florida veer off at the last moment. Why is the weather so hard to predict? Are meteorologists just a bunch of quacks? Of course not. The factors that influence the weather are simply too numerous and complicated for scientists to master. But does our difficulty with predicting the weather mean that a storm system with a mind of its own exercised its free will and decided to arrive over your picnic on Saturday? Hardly. Even though we do not do terribly well predicting it, we do know that the weather is the result of natural forces behaving in accordance with natural laws, whatever they may be.

What is true for the weather is true for human events, thinks Skinner. Just because we miss much in predicting how people will act does not mean that our actions are not determined by outside forces over which we have no control. Like the weather, our behavior is produced by too many factors to be readily understood. Certainly the sources of human behavior are too complex to be understood in every detail by a science very much in its infancy. Nonetheless, Frazier believes, Castle has no more power over his decision to hold or drop the matchbook than a hurricane does over whether it will sock Key West, Boca Raton, or Jacksonville.

Conditioning: An Experiment. You may be getting annoyed at how Skinner could deny something that is so obvious to you—that you are free and in control of your actions. But before you make up your mind, try this experiment in conditioning. Your teacher is your subject.

According to Skinner's theory, our behavior is determined by the consequences that follow our actions. If we perform an action and then something we like happens (positive reinforcement), we will likely repeat what we've done. If something we do not like happens (negative reinforcement), we won't.

To see how this works, you might try to condition one of your instructors to act in a certain way, without him or her knowing it. Here's what you do. First, explain what you're doing to as many people in the class as you can. Second, pick the behavior that you want to reinforce—walking back and forth, standing in a particular spot, gesturing to the class with a marker or piece of chalk, or whatever. The object of the game is to administer positive reinforcement every time your instructor performs the behavior you have chosen. Look interested, nod your head, ask questions, take notes. When he or she stops the behavior, go to negative reinforcement. Look bored, act confused, shuffle your feet, look at your watch, stare out the window. When your teacher goes back to the chosen behavior, respond positively again. After a while, you should find your teacher doing the behavior you selected most of the time. (One class took "being near the radiator" as the behavior they wanted to reinforce. By the end of the semester, their instructor was so well conditioned that he simply sat on the radiator throughout each class.)

If you do this right and have not been too obvious about it, you will see that you have controlled someone's behavior without that person's knowledge. You will have conditioned your instructor to act in a certain way because she or he wants the positive feeling that comes with the interest you show.

One of the most disturbing things about Skinner's ideas is that we can usually find similar examples of conditioning in our own lives. Maybe we've been conditioned to please other people, to take care of them, to be aggressive, or to be dependable. Finding conditioning in our own lives is a much more powerful challenge than some abstract theory. Look for some ways that you've already been conditioned, and *when*— not *if*—you find them, ask yourself what you think of Skinner's position on freedom.

Determinism: Freud and Control by the Unconscious

Skinner's brand of determinism may seem extreme, especially if you have never doubted the freedom of your own choices. But at least Skinner limits himself to observable actions that result from an observable reinforcement process. He doesn't propose anything hidden or mysterious. But what if everything you did was determined by forces located in the depths of your psyche and beyond the reach of your conscious mind? Just such a powerful and intimidating form of determinism has been proposed by Sigmund Freud.

Not merely a giant in the history of psychology, Sigmund Freud is one of the most important figures in the history of Western thought. Freud's theories about the structure of the personality and the power of the unconscious have

Sigmund Freud (1856–1939) was born in what is today the Czech Republic, but he spent most of his life in Vienna, where his family moved when he was four years old. Freud's forty-year-old wool merchant father was strict, but his twenty-four-year-old mother was loving and protective. Freud was a brilliant youth. He had been reading Shakespeare since he was eight years old, he entered high school early, and he mastered Hebrew, German, Latin, Greek, French, English, Italian, and Spanish. Hoping for a career in scientific research, Freud studied medicine at the University of Vienna. Freud took three years longer than normal to graduate, however, and studied enough philosophy to make him consider taking a philosophy degree after finishing medical school. Personal and financial pressures led him to go into the practice of medicine, eventually specializing in nervous disorders. Freud studied hypnosis in Paris with the famous French psychiatrist Jean Charcot and then the new "talking cure" of the Viennese physician Josef Breuer. This method, encouraging patients to talk about their symptoms and feelings, was the basis of Freud's landmark work on the unconscious, the structure of the personality, and his creation of psychoanalysis. Freud reached the peak of his career in the early decades of the twentieth century, but at the same time he began suffering from cancer of the mouth (probably induced by his smoking about twenty cigars each day). He underwent many operations and suffered constant pain. After the Nazis occupied Vienna in 1938, Freud was harassed until he left for London. He died there the following year.

had as dramatic an effect on our thinking as Galileo's claim that the earth moves around the sun. Freud is one of a handful of thinkers whose ideas have fundamentally changed how we understand ourselves. In the last two hundred years, only Darwin and Marx have had as great an impact.

An immensely talented youth, Freud initially pursued physiological research. But he gradually turned to medicine, specializing in what we today call "psychosomatic disorders," those cases in which patients have genuine symptoms without any medical cause. Freud came to see the human mind has an extremely powerful *unconscious* element— drives, memories, and motives of which we are completely unaware. This insight became the foundation on which Freud built a theory of human personality and behavior that has profoundly influenced Western thinking on the subject.[6]

The Conscious, the Preconscious, and the Unconscious

The heart of Freud's thought is his concept of the *unconscious*, that part of our personality of which we are *not* aware (hence, "*un*conscious") but which nonetheless profoundly influences our thoughts and actions. This is by far the biggest and most important part of the personality. Freud uses the image of an iceberg to express this idea. The *conscious*, he says, is like the visible tip of the iceberg. The *unconscious* is all the rest that is under the surface, the larger and, we might also say, the more dangerous part. If you are sailing among icebergs and steering only according to what you can see, you'll find yourself sinking before long. Similarly, if you ignore the unconscious part of the personality, you may find yourself in deep trouble.

Expressions of the Unconscious. Freud believes that the unconscious has a pervasive influence in our lives and surfaces in many ways. The most obvious is in our dreams where the unconscious says things about our lives through a special language of pictures and symbols.

> **Freudianism** Freudianism is the largely deterministic, psychological theory developed by Sigmund Freud that claims that the human personality has both conscious and unconscious dimensions. Behavior is ultimately determined by unconscious primal drives, early childhood experience, and the interplay of the three parts of the personality—the id, ego, and superego.

Another common example directly related to the theme of this chapter is what are called "Freudian slips," when our unconscious controls what we say. Sometimes, for example, when you intend to be polite, you may say what you really mean. "What do you think of my new dress?" asks your best friend. You think it's ugly, but you don't want to hurt her feelings, so you try to say "It's gorgeous!" What comes out of your mouth instead is "It's grotesque!" What you said to your friend, then, was not the product of a

---

6. Freud's theory is both complicated and sophisticated, certainly much more complicated than behaviorism. Rather than attempting a full treatment of Freud in these few pages, we will deal with only a few of his major ideas.

free, conscious will. In fact, your unconscious made you say something you consciously did not want to say.

The Unconscious and Determinism. "Freudian slips" are just one case where the unconscious influences what we do. This example is trivial, however, in comparison to the larger workings of the unconscious.

Just think about how we're bombarded by appeals to our unconscious in everyday life. Advertising uses subliminal messages that are imperceptible to the conscious mind. Status and sex are used so that you'll associate them with particular products—and then buy them. If you ever used a subliminal or self-hypnotic recording to help you stop smoking or relax, you were appealing to the unconscious. Restaurants, stores, hotels, and hospitals carefully select the colors they use because of their unconscious effect on our appetite or sense of well-being. These are all appeals to unconscious processes.

Freud does not believe that the unconscious is merely "important." He thinks the unconscious controls virtually everything we do, usually in ways we are completely unaware of. Once you grant the existence of the unconscious as Freud defines it, you can begin to see just how deterministic Freudian thought is. Once you understand the structure of the personality as Freud sees it and how the unconscious works within it, you can make fairly accurate inferences about the forces at work in someone's personality. You can then explain and even predict human behavior. And you do so without reference to "free will."

The Structure of the Personality

A quick sketch of Freud's view of the personality will show you how powerful Freud's case for determinism is.

Even the most superficial treatment of Freud's theory cannot fail to mention the three components of the personality that he posits: the *id,* the *ego,* and the *superego.*

The id. The *id* is the most deeply buried, unconscious part of the personality, and it is the source of our basic drives and all our psychological energy. Primitive and untamed, the id has only two basic drives—sex and aggression—that are instinctual and biologically determined. The id operates according to what Freud calls the "pleasure principle." It is always seeking pleasure through the immediate satisfaction of its needs. The id is also unrestrained, irrational, and unrealistic—almost "unhuman" in a way. If the id had its way, it would try to satisfy its every impulse whenever and wherever it felt like it, no matter what the circumstances.

The ego. The *ego* is the second component of the personality. The word "ego" means "I," and the concept conveys something close to our ordinary sense of self. The ego operates according to what Freud calls the "reality principle." It is aware of what's possible and impossible and is able to accept limits and to act in a practical way. The ego's job is to figure out appropriate ways to satisfy the id's desires. That means determining an acceptable time, place, and fashion for such satisfactions. According to Freud, the relationship between the ego and id is like that of a rider to a spirited horse. The horse provides the power, but the rider, that is, the ego, controls it.

The superego. But the rider isn't alone on the horse. Your riding instructor, so to speak, is on the horse with you, holding on to you, telling you how to ride and what you should and shouldn't do. This is Freud's third part of the personality, the *superego*. "Superego" is a Latin word that literally means "over" or "above" the "I." In English, the concept that comes closest to the superego is the "conscience," that part of us that stands over us, looking down at what we do and judging whether our actions are right or wrong.

Like the id, the superego is an unconscious mechanism. Generally in place by age five or six, it consists of the internalized prohibitions communicated to us by our parents and our culture. The superego can be a useful guide, but more often it's a pain in the neck. To return to the horse-and-rider image, you can think of the superego as a terribly strict riding master yelling criticism at you all the time. Hardly ever happy with what we do, the superego is as irrational, demanding, and uncompromising as the id. But while the id hungers for immediate gratification, the superego wants moral perfection. Nothing less will do.

Whenever we fall short of perfection, the superego punishes us by making us feel bad. Have you ever felt very guilty about doing something that wasn't really so bad? Have you ever beat yourself up inside for being like everybody else—given to making mistakes, maybe a little selfish now and then? If you ever felt deep shame for being less than a saint, that was your superego at work.

Personality Structure and Determinism

Now that you know something about Freud's idea of how the personality is structured, you can better understand why his theory of human behavior is deterministic. Obviously, the ego is in a no-win situation. It's caught between two insatiable and contradictory desires, one for wanton pleasure, the other for moral perfection. The ego is always under pressure, but sometimes the conflict is unbearable. When this happens, the result is anxiety. The ego that experiences anxiety feels threatened and is compelled to reduce the tension. It looks for the quickest way to restore some sense of equilibrium. As a result, we act in particular ways, or feel specific emotions, or even distort our perception of reality.

Two aspects of this process bear on the free will/determinism debate. First, the ego's move to reduce anxiety is like a *reflex* action. When the ego feels anxiety, it *automatically* reacts to reduce it, much as we instinctively pull our hand off a hot stove.

Second, all this goes on *without our realizing it*. In Freud's theory, the process of reducing anxiety is unconscious and governed by the interplay of the id, ego, and superego. In effect, our unconscious makes a decision and hands it to our conscious mind with orders to carry it out. Our conscious mind, however, experiences all this as coming up with an idea of our own and freely choosing what we do. In reality, the choice was already made, and it wasn't even close to being free.

For example, have you ever wanted to do something you honestly believed was all right to do but didn't because you felt too guilty? Perhaps it was something as simple as wanting to go to a movie but staying home because you felt you should work on a paper. You might feel as though you freely chose peace of mind over the guilt. But Freud would say that your ego resolved an anxiety-producing situation by caving in to the demands of your superego and making you feel so bad that you *couldn't* do what you wanted to do.

Anxiety caused by a dominant superego can even bring on physical symptoms. Most of us know someone like Pearl, who always gets a sore throat the morning she's supposed to give an oral report in class. Or someone like Ravi, who lies to his boss ("I've got a doctor's appointment next Friday") so that he can go to a ball game—but who, when the day comes, wakes up sick and cannot go. Did Ravi choose to get a twenty-four-hour bug? No. His anxiety is so high, and his superego is so strong, that it cuts him down. But at least now that he did nothing wrong, he doesn't feel guilty.

Defense Mechanisms and Determinism

These limits to our freedom are obvious. A more subtle way that the ego tries to reduce anxiety, however, is through what Freud calls "defense mechanisms." They're called that because they are psychological strategies that defend the ego against anxiety. There are numerous defense mechanisms, but they all have three things in common. They distort reality, they are unconscious processes, and they lead us to accept the distorted picture of reality as accurate.[7]

Actions produced by the workings of our defense mechanisms are surely the result of something other than rational, free choice. How can we act freely when we deceive ourselves about the facts of a situation? If someone put a hallucinatory drug in your coffee, would you say that everything you did under the influence of the drug was the result of your free choice? Of course not. So why should it be any different if our faulty perception is caused by something psychological rather than chemical?

We don't need to analyze all the defense mechanisms here. We should look quickly at two of them, however, because their existence reinforces the Freudian idea that the unconscious and not the conscious mind controls what we do. And, if that is so, it presents a major obstacle to human freedom.

Projection is the defense we use when we attribute our own feelings—feelings that are unconsciously troubling—to somebody else. Suppose that you're doing poorly in a course and you think it's because your teacher dislikes you. (Actually, you're not studying very hard and the course is tough.) Let's start with the fact that you're unconsciously feeling angry at your teacher for not being easier. Aggression is one of the id's main impulses, and the id is now pressuring your ego to let your teacher really have it. Your superego, however, won't stand for this, and it threatens your ego with what will happen if you give

---

7. Freud's defense mechanisms are repression, reaction formation, projection, regression, rationalization, displacement, and sublimation.

in to the id. Harassed by real conditions in the outside world, as well as by your id and superego, your ego experiences growing anxiety. In projection, the anxiety is relieved by giving in to the superego, but satisfying the id by taking its hostility and attributing it to the person you're angry at. So instead of consciously feeling that *you hate your teacher,* you unconsciously reverse the roles and believe that *your teacher hates you.* In other words, you *project* your feelings onto the object of your feelings and assign them to him or her.

This relieves your anxiety in lots of ways. You keep your own image of being a "nice" person. You avoid the risks involved in getting angry at someone who might penalize you for it. And by blaming someone else for your problems, you can continue to be lazy. The projection lets you distort reality without knowing you're doing it. And you feel perfectly justified in not working hard.

Reaction formation is another way the ego defends itself against anxiety. The essence of this mechanism is that the ego takes a disturbing impulse and unconsciously converts it into its opposite. Some people, for example, find aggressive impulses deeply disturbing. For any number of reasons, they neither understand their angry feelings nor know what to do with them. Furthermore, being aggressive does not conform to their image of a good person. Again, the ego is caught between the id's primal drives and the superego's moral standard, and anxiety develops. In a case of reaction formation, the ego gives in so much to the superego that it now labels as evil everything to do with aggression. The person in the grip of this mechanism may become incredibly sweet, passive, and accommodating, filled with love for everybody he meets. He may go around preaching to everyone else how bad competition and war are. His anger has been converted to its opposite—love. The superego is satisfied, and the person's unconscious tension is reduced.[8]

Freud's defense mechanisms are especially pertinent to our investigation of free will versus determinism because their basic effect is to *distort reality.* If our unconscious gives us a false picture of reality, how can we ever act freely? In *projection,* we attribute our own feelings to someone else. In *denial,* we unconsciously refuse to see what is right before our eyes and obvious to everyone else. *Repression* totally erases painful memories and feelings, and it can even affect our bodies. It's not unusual to find cases of impotence, frigidity, and even paralysis caused by unconscious reactions to anxiety.

The Unconscious and the Power of the Past

One other part of Freud's thought bears upon his determinism, and that is his belief in the effect of early childhood experiences on our adult personality. Freud claims that who we are as adults is the direct result of what happened to us in our childhood. We *do not choose* to be the way we are; we are made this way by the interplay between our inner psychological world and people and events outside us.

---

8. Be sure you realize that defense mechanisms this extreme are not a part of everybody's life. In other words, you might be right that your teacher dislikes you. And many proponents of nonviolence are healthy and sincere in their convictions.

Our personalities, whom we fall in love with, what kind of careers we choose, what motivates us, even our hobbies, everything about us is supposedly the product of our past. All this significant fashioning is accomplished by the time we are five or six, before we're even aware of what's going on. Here's one example of Freud's basic claim that the core of our being is shaped by our past.

Your friend Melissa is always getting involved with the wrong man. She is a sensitive, emotional person who finds rich, emotionally distant men irresistible. (The men are also usually married.) It never works out. The pattern is always the same—attraction, love, disappointment. Outsiders can easily see what's wrong. Melissa keeps picking the wrong kind of man. She wants a deep emotional connection with lots of intimacy and expression of feeling. But the men she picks are neither emotional nor communicative.

What advice would you give Melissa? Probably to pick someone more like herself. "It's easy," you say. "Choose somebody different."

Freud, however, would see Melissa's unhappiness as the inevitable and predictable result of her emotional history, which has put into place powerful unconscious forces that compel her to choose those whom she does. Even if she dated someone who's "more her type," it wouldn't work. She wouldn't find the relationship satisfying. She is locked into a pattern of poor choices and unhappiness.

For the purposes of this chapter, we can skip over the details of why this is happening to her.[9] All that counts is that Melissa's actions may feel free to her, but they aren't. Unconscious forces determine her fate.[10]

Libet: A Contemporary Challenge to Free Will

Skinner's version is painfully simple. Freud's is complex and convoluted. Both raise significant challenges to the idea that we are in complete control of all our actions. Nonetheless, while both thinkers see themselves as proceeding according to evidence—not abstract theories—it's easy to be skeptical. In terms of our ordinary experience of being human and making our way through life, behaviorism seems too simple and Freudianism seems unnecessarily complex. The challenge to free will by Benjamin Libet is harder to ignore.

Libet is a contemporary neuroscientist who decided to study what goes on in the brain when we activate our free will, that is, when we *freely decide* to perform an action and then carry it out. His findings are stunning. In his experiment, *before* any of his subjects

---

9. If you're interested in an explanation, see Freud's understanding of the stages of human development and what happens when we don't progress through these stages as we should.

10. It may look like Freud's theories condemn us to a life of unhappiness. However, even though Freud thought that we could never totally escape from the power of the unconscious, he did propose a way of at least mitigating its painful tyranny: psychoanalysis.

consciously decided to perform an action, measurable brain activity took place that the subject wasn't aware of.[11]

The design of Libet's experiment is as simple as his findings are striking. Subjects were wired up in a way that measured electrical activity in the brain.[12] They had two tasks. They would flick their wrist. Also, using a special clock Libet devised, they would note *the moment they decided* to flick their wrist before actually doing so. In other words, they were to identify the exact moment when they were *freely choosing* to act—that is, the moment they were engaging their free will. Subjects were in complete control of the experiment. They didn't have to complete the actions according to a particular pattern or time constraint.

In theory, if our actions are the result of our free, self-conscious decisions, activity in the motor area of Libet's subjects' brains should start when they *were consciously aware of their intention to act*, that is, when they, in effect, told the brain to perform the action. What actually happened, however, is that brain activity initiating the movement began about half a second (about 500 milliseconds) *before* subjects consciously made their decisions. Libet explains, "The initiation of the freely voluntary act appears to begin in the brain unconsciously, well before the person consciously knows he wants to act!" The fascinating, but obviously troubling, implication of this fact is that the seemingly very clear and deliberate experience we have of freely forming intentions to engage in actions might simply be, as Libet puts it, "tacked on as epiphenomena with no causal power." That is, his subjects' subjective experience of deciding to move their wrists didn't cause the movement. Rather, it appears to be the product of unconscious brain activity. Simply put, this suggests that free will is an illusion.

However, while Libet's work may make us skeptical of the existence of free will, it nonetheless also makes a clear case for what some thinkers have referred to as "free won't." Libet discovered that after having made the decision to act, subjects were able to refrain from doing so, "stopping or vetoing the final progress of the volitional process, so that no actual muscle action ensues." And, unlike their original decision to act that was preceded by unconscious brain activity, no such activity was recorded before a veto. Seen in this light, he writes,

> The role of conscious free will would be, then, not to initiate a voluntary act, but rather to *control* whether the act takes place. We may view the unconscious initiatives for voluntary actions as 'bubbling up' in the brain. The conscious-will then selects which of these initiatives may go forward to an action or which ones to veto and abort, with no act appearing.[13]

---

11. Benjamin Libet, "Do We Have Free Will?" in *The Volitional Brain: Towards a Neuroscience of Free Will*, ed. Benjamin Libet, Anthony Freeman, and Keith Sutherland (Exeter, UK: Imprint Academic, 1999), 47–57.

12. To be specific, electrodes were placed to record from the left motor cortex, the right motor cortex, and the midline.

13. Libet, 54.

In a causal universe, empirical data about electrical activity in the brain are hard to ignore. And there are important limitations about Libet's findings as they apply to the overarching question of whether his experiments show that the concept of free will is meaningless. His experiment is about one simple activity—flexing a wrist. What about the more complicated decisions we make—especially about difficult ethical dilemmas? Also, Libet himself points out that he hadn't identified all the factors in the process. He noted that the unconscious brain activity he detected probably starts "in an unknown area that then activates the supplementary motor area in the cerebral cortex."[14]

One of the most intriguing questions Libet's experiment raises is, "If the subjects' conscious decision wasn't ultimately responsible for the wrist flexing, what was?" The measurements on all forty subjects were the same. So it's unlikely that patterns of positive reinforcement or deep-seated, unconscious psychological issues were in the mix. Those would be unique to each individual. Instead, we're seeing a phenomenon consistent across members of the same species. What's the ultimate cause of the unconscious process Libet discovered?

Nonetheless, despite the myriad of questions Libet's work raises, when it comes to our experience of freely making decisions about our actions, what *appears* to be the case doesn't match with scientifically verifiable reality.

Determinism and Responsibility

Skinner, Freud, and Libet make a strong case against free will. Skinner says our actions are the result of external rewards and punishments, and that they are products of how we've been reinforced over time. Freud sees our behavior as dictated by personality structure, primitive drives, the need to reduce anxiety, and early childhood experiences. Libet's experiment suggests that what we think are free, conscious decisions are actually the product of unconscious processes in our brains.

What does this do to the concept of responsibility, however? After all, it makes no sense to punish someone for an action that was determined by forces beyond that person's control. Skinner, for example, maintains that "a moral or ethical lapse . . . needs treatment, not punishment." He sees basically no difference between physical and moral illness:

> Compare two people, one of whom has been crippled by an accident, the other by an early environmental history which makes him lazy and, when criticized, mean. Both cause great inconvenience to others, but one dies a martyr, the other a scoundrel. Or compare two children—one crippled by polio, the other by a rejecting family. Both contribute little to others and cause trouble, but only one is blamed. The main difference is that only one kind of disability is correctable by punishment, and even then only occasionally. It is tempting to say that only one person in each case could do something about his condition, but should we not say that we could do something besides blaming him?[15]

---

14. Libet, 51.
15. Skinner, *About Behaviorism*, 215–16.

Skinner rejects punishment as both an inappropriate and inefficient way to change behavior. But punishment at least has a place in behaviorism. It serves as negative reinforcement, and that might change someone's behavior. In Freud's world, however, blame and punishment would seem to have no place at all, especially when we talk about people who are psychotic. For example, insanity is accepted as a legal excuse.

Libet's discovery that we have veto power ("free won't") gives us stronger grounds for responsibility. We may not be responsible for the impulses that bubble up, but we can refuse to act according to them.

What If Determinism Is True? The Stoics

One of the most challenging features of determinism is emotional. How do we handle the fact that our actions are more the product of forces beyond our control than we think they are? Skinner, Freud, and Libet undermine our sense of freedom, but they don't offer advice about how to deal with that in real life. One school of thought, however, does: the ancient Stoics.

In contemporary parlance, to behave "stoically" means something like gritting our teeth and bearing adversity without complaint.[16] That's unquestionably an oversimplification of the ideas these philosophers advanced. But there's a kernel of truth here in that, while **Stoicism** was a genuine school of philosophy, it was more of a practical guide to living. It was very popular in Hellenistic Greece and Rome, and it even included the Roman emperor Marcus Aurelius among its adherents. What's important for our purposes is that the Stoics weren't simply determinists; they advised how we could achieve peace of mind nonetheless.

The Stoics were thoroughgoing materialists who saw everything as the result of cause and effect: "an order and series of causes wherein cause is connected to cause and each cause of itself produces an effect. . . . Therefore, nothing has happened which was not going to happen, and likewise, nothing is going to happen of which nature does not contain the efficient causes."[17] They illustrate this as follows: "It is as though a dog is tied behind a cart. If he wants to follow, he is both dragged and follows, exercising his autonomy in conjunction with necessity. But if he does not want to follow, he will nevertheless be forced to. The same thing happens in the case of men. Even if they do not want to follow, they will nevertheless be forced to go along with what has been destined."[18] What this image shows, however, is that one thing is in our control—our attitude. And that is the key to the Stoic's advice.

---

16. This word comes from the school of thought, although its original meaning was simply "porch"—the spot in the Agora in Athens where the first thinkers of this school gathered.

17. Cicero, *De Divinatione*, SVF II, 921 in *Greek and Roman Philosophy after Aristotle*, ed. Jason Saunders (New York: Free Press, 1966), 101.

18. *Hellenistic Philosophy: Introductory Readings*, second edition, trans. Brad Inwood and L. P. Gerson (Indianapolis: Hackett Publishing Company, 1997), SVF II, 975, pp. 189–90.

One of the most famous Stoic thinkers was Epictetus (55–185 CE), who began life as a slave, but eventually received his freedom and began lecturing. His most famous work is called the *Enchiridion,* or *Handbook.* It is fundamentally a guide to living. Its message is clear and straightforward:

> Of all existing things some are in our power, and others are not in our power. In our power are thought, impulse, will to get and will to avoid, and, in a word, everything which is in our own doing. Things not in our power include the body, property, reputation, office, and, in a word, everything which is not our own doing. . . . What disturbs men's minds is not events but their judgments on events. . . . Ask not that events should happen as you will, but let your will be that events should happen as they do, and you shall have peace.

Paradoxically, Epictetus argues that this is actually the path to *freedom.*

> Exercise yourself then in what lies in your power. Each man's master is the man who has authority over what he wishes or does not wish, to secure the one or to take away the other. Let him then who wishes to be free not wish for anything or avoid anything that depends on others; or else he is bound to be a slave.[19]

Even if our actions are just part of an inevitable causal chain, is it possible that Epictetus points to at least one feature of our existence that is completely within our control? If so, could that be enough to keep the door open to the idea that we actually have free will? Could that give us enough leverage to start pushing back against determinism?

Determinism: A Final Word

Deterministic theories may be unsettling, especially if you have never before questioned the existence of free will. Determinism's strongest argument is probably that it claims to be based on physical laws of cause and effect. And since we live in an age dominated by science, it is hard to resist a no-nonsense approach that explains everything in terms of natural principles backed up by empirical evidence. A universe that consists of an almost infinite chain of causes, which includes effects of previous causes, which stretch back in time to the start of the universe, and which are responsible for each thing being the way it is, seems understandable, at least in theory.

But while this approach is all well and good for physical objects like trees and natural events like the weather, it's unsettling when we apply it to our own actions. Try telling yourself that you are *not* free, that all your actions are causally determined. Most of us will admit that we struggle against internal and external forces when we take action. Sometimes *they* win; sometimes *we* do. But hardly anyone thinks we *never* win. All of us have experiences that make us absolutely certain we are free and can control at least some aspects of our own lives. There are times when we make up our minds to do

19. *Greek and Roman Philosophy after Aristotle,* 133–36.

something and doggedly, sometimes heroically, persist against tough opposition and long odds until we succeed. At such moments, we are positive that our own strength of will, not conditioning or unconscious forces, lets us prevail.

In spite of the deterministic arguments, it still seems as if having control over our destiny is a hallmark of being human. Our sense of this power feels too real to most of us to dismiss it as an illusion, or, as Libet refers to it, an "epiphenomenon." There must be more to it than what we've seen so far. And that is what the next chapter is about.

Discussion Questions

1. Reflect on your own life. To what extent do you find your actions free or determined?

2. "Conditioning" is similar to the process by which we develop habits. How many habits do you have? Are there any you feel you simply could not break—or at least you would have a great deal of trouble breaking? If so, are these examples of your actions being determined?

3. Do you accept the existence of the unconscious? Do you ever feel that you don't know why you act as you do in certain situations? Is it possible your actions are being dictated by unconscious forces? If you reject the unconscious, how do you explain dreams?

4. What do you think about the "insanity defense"? What about "temporary insanity"? What about someone who commits a "crime of passion"? Do you think you could ever get so angry that you would lose control of yourself? If you hurt someone as a result, would it be fair to punish you? Do you believe you should be held responsible for what you do in such a state?

5. Which of these "deterministic" factors do you think limit the amount of responsibility we have for our actions: conditioning, unconscious forces, childhood trauma, being raised by dishonest parents, and social and economic class?

6. Libet's experiment is particularly thought-provoking. What do you make of it?

7. What is your astrological sign? Do you fit your astrological profile? If so, is this evidence for determinism?

8. Christianity claims that God knows everything—past, present, and future. God knows right now, then, everything you will do tomorrow. In that case, do you really have any choice in the matter? Does God's foreknowledge support determinism?

Selected Readings

General discussions of the problem of freedom versus determinism can be found in the *Stanford Encyclopedia of Philosophy* (https://plato.stanford.edu/).

For B. F. Skinner's main ideas, see: *Walden Two* (New York: Macmillan, 1948; Reprinted Indianapolis: Hackett Publishing Co., 2005); *Science and Human Behavior* (New York: Macmillan, 1953); "The Machine That Is Man," *Psychology Today* (April 1969), 20–25, 60–63; *Beyond Freedom and Dignity* (New York: Knopf, 1974; Reprinted Indianapolis: Hackett Publishing Co., 2002); and *About Behaviorism* (New York: Knopf, 1974). For Skinner's life, see: the two volumes of his autobiography, *Particulars of My Life* (New York: Knopf, 1976) and *The Shaping of a Behaviorist* (New York: Knopf, 1979), and also Skinner's contribution to *A History of Psychology in Autobiography*, ed. E. G. Boring and G. Lindzey, vol. 5 (New York: Appleton-Century-Crofts, 1967), 385–413. The primary source for Freud's writings is the twenty-four volumes of *The Standard Edition of the Complete Psychological Works of Sigmund Freud*, ed. and trans. J. Strachey (London: Hogarth Press, 1953–74). Individual works are published by W. W. Norton and Company. See, in particular, *New Introductory Lectures on Psychoanalysis, On Dreams, Civilization and Its Discontents*, and *The Future of an Illusion*.

Libet's experiment has sparked extensive debate among philosophers and neuroscientists. For example, see: the essays in *The Volitional Brain: Towards a Neuroscience of Free Will*, ed. Benjamin Libet, Anthony Freeman, and Keith Sutherland (Exeter, UK: Imprint Academic, 1999); and Josef Seifert, "In Defense of Free Will: A Critique of Benjamin Libet," *The Review of Metaphysics* 65, no. 2 (2011): 377–407, http://www.jstor.org/stable/23055749.

Chapter 4

The Case for Freedom

It's late September and the pennant race in the East is very tight. The Red Sox and the Yankees are neck and neck. The season's final game between these two teams will settle the matter. Richard, an avid Yankee fan, decides to drive up to Boston with some of his buddies. On the way to Fenway Park, they stop off at a bar for a few beers. During the game, Richard, as usual, has a few too many. Feelings run high, Boston wins, and on the way out of the game, Richard bumps into a jubilant Red Sox fan. The guy looks at Richard's Yankee cap, pushes him and says, "Outta my way, loser!" Richard explodes—he has a hair-trigger temper—slugs the guy and is arrested. When he sobers up the next morning, he says to the judge, "I'm sorry. I just lost control. The beer, losing the game, the put-down, and my temper—it was too much for me to handle. That guy pushed my buttons and I lost it."

Did something beyond Richard's control make him do it? Was his brain so impaired by alcohol that he didn't know what he was doing? Richard himself admits that he "lost control." He didn't even *feel* he had any choice in the matter. With the alcohol, the excitement, and his temper, we don't need a sophisticated explanation to see his behavior as determined.

But is that all there is?

It's tempting to let Richard off the hook. Between the beer, the game, and the insult, how could he *not* react as he did? You could have bet on it. Yet if you were on the wrong end of Richard's fist, you surely wouldn't say, "Hey, no problem—behavior's all determined. We're both victims here."

Our dilemma, then, remains. Considering the strong case we've seen that can be made for **determinism**, is there any room for freedom? Can we have it both ways—understanding that human behavior fits into a causal universe but allowing for choice and responsibility?

In this chapter we explore the other side of the free will/determinism question. Thinkers who argue for free will approach the issue in various ways, but they share the conviction that we as human beings are free and in control of what we do. We'll look at the ideas of the Greek philosopher Aristotle, the American philosopher and psychologist William James, and the French thinker Jean-Paul Sartre.

Aristotle: The Commonsense Philosopher

One of the three greatest ancient Greek philosophers, Aristotle emphasized common sense and empirical observation.

Voluntary and Involuntary Acts

The ancient Greeks did not refer to the problem of free will versus determinism in the same terms we use. Aristotle talks instead about **voluntary** versus **involuntary** action. Like many philosophers who argue for free will, Aristotle does not discuss the question in a vacuum. He comes to it through the question of responsibility. Determinists don't talk much about responsibility, as you saw in the previous chapter. But free-will philosophers make much of it because freedom and responsibility are inseparable: each implies the other. Thus, in the *Nicomachean Ethics,* Aristotle raises the question of voluntary versus involuntary action in the process of discussing moral responsibility and how human character is formed.

voluntary Aristotle labels as "voluntary" actions that are under our control. This includes habits or dispositions that seem to be out of our control but nonetheless result from earlier choices made when the matter was in our power. This also includes actions done from culpable ignorance or negligence. Aristotle thinks we are responsible for all voluntary actions.

involuntary Aristotle labels as "involuntary" actions that result from constraint or ignorance. He does not think we are responsible for involuntary actions.

Aristotle is very much a commonsense philosopher, and common sense tells us that people should be held responsible for what they do. He starts from what he takes as a self-evident fact that we can deliberate about our actions and make choices. Basically, he believes that we are responsible for those actions we choose, and that we are not responsible for those we don't choose. If an action results from constraint or ignorance, it is *involuntary.* If we are free from force or pressure and know everything we should know about what we're doing, the action is *voluntary.*

Richard the Yankee fan might think that Aristotle is on his side. "Because I was drunk and all worked up," he says, "I didn't really know what I was doing. I was *ignorant,* see? I didn't really choose what I did or act *voluntarily.*"

Culpable Ignorance and Negligence

But Aristotle is no pushover. In his opinion, if we are responsible for not knowing what we are doing, we are accountable for whatever we do. Showing that this principle is recognized even in the laws of ancient Athens, Aristotle explains that the penalties are twice as high if an offender does something wrong while drunk. A person had the power not to get drunk and is, therefore, responsible for putting himself in a condition in which he doesn't know what he is doing. Obviously, Richard cannot escape on this score.

Aristotle also gets tough with people who simply should have known better. Again referring to the Athenian legal system, he notes that people who are ignorant of the law are punished because they should have known the law, could easily have known the law, or were just plain negligent in not knowing it. In contemporary society this is called *culpable ignorance* or *culpable negligence* because the lapse is so serious that we're willing to find someone at fault for it. (*Culpa* is Latin for "fault" or "blame.")

To this, Richard grumbles, "That doesn't make any sense. *What* should I have known? That the Yankees were going to lose? That some jerk was going to ask for trouble? Get real." But aren't there some things about this situation that Richard should have known better about? Couldn't anyone who knew him have predicted what might happen? Wasn't Richard negligent or careless in giving no thought to what he'd probably do at the game?

Notice that after the dust settles, Richard can explain what happened. He's not saying, "I can't understand it. I've never done anything like that before." He isn't ignorant of what he's apt to do. In fact, it sounds as if Richard often drinks, loses his temper, and punches people out. Maybe once Richard is drunk and wrapped up in the game, he loses control over what he does. But what about beforehand when he's sober and calm? He can think about the situation, realize the risks, and decide not to go to the game. Or if he does go, he doesn't have to drink before or during the game. He can *voluntarily* choose at some point not to put himself in circumstances (a highly emotional game) or a condition (drunk) in which he will probably do something stupid. If he doesn't, can't we say that he is culpably negligent or careless?

Actions or Character: Which Comes First?

Richard still wants to push his case, however. "That might work for somebody with a different personality," he explains, "but not with me. I can't control my temper. It's just the way I am. The least little thing and—bam!—I explode and take a swing at somebody. How can you hold me responsible for something like that?" This is Richard's best defense. He is negligent or careless because of his personality. His actions stem from his character. And who would hold us responsible for the shape of our personalities?

Aristotle would. He thinks that what we do shapes and defines who we are. Our actions determine our character. Aristotle has met the likes of Richard before:

> But presumably his character makes him inattentive. Still, he is himself responsible for having this character, by living carelessly, and similarly for being unjust by cheating, or being intemperate by passing his time in drinking and the like; for *each type of activity produces the corresponding character.* This is clear from those who train for any contest or action, since they continually practice the appropriate activities. Only a totally insensible person would not know that each type of activity is the source of the corresponding state; hence if someone does what he knows will make him unjust, he is willingly unjust. [Emphasis added.][1]

As Aristotle sees it, over the years Richard has developed the habit of giving in to his temper. That is why his temper has become a part of his personality.

The actions we perform while our characters are being shaped, then, determine how we turn out. Aristotle sees the process of character formation as being exactly like that of learning any skill. If you want to be a gymnast or skateboarder, you must start off doing

---

1. Aristotle, *Nicomachean Ethics*, in *Aristotle: Introductory Readings*. Trans. Terence Irwin and Gail Fine (Indianapolis: Hackett Publishing Co., 1996), 1114a, p. 238.

things right from the beginning. You want to develop the right habits so that the proper movements will be second nature to you. If you let yourself do things the wrong way, you will still end up with a set of movements that are second nature, but they will be the *wrong* movements. The same holds for any skill. Whether we are any good at it in the end depends on what habits we develop while learning it.

Aristotle views the development of our personalities in the same way. The traits we end up with result from how we behave and what inner dispositions we develop. He explains:

> For actions in dealings with other human beings make some people just, some unjust; actions in terrifying situations and the acquired habit of fear or confidence make some brave and others cowardly. The same is true of situations involving appetites and anger; for one or another sort of conduct in these situations makes some people temperate and gentle, others intemperate and irascible. To sum up, then, in a single account: A state of character arises from the repetition of similar activities.[2]

So where did Richard's personality traits come from? From what he did in the past, from the bad habits that he allowed himself to develop and for which he is totally responsible. Although Richard's personality and behavior are set in stone now, had he behaved differently earlier, he would have developed different personality traits.

Could Richard have behaved differently? Presumably he wasn't born like this, and he didn't get like this overnight. Aristotle would argue that at some earlier time in Richard's life, it was possible for him to control himself. If he cannot control himself at age twenty-one, it is because he gave in to his anger all along. And even if it has always been hard for him to control his temper, he should have seen this as a problem and found some better ways to express his anger.

Aristotle supports his theory about character development by citing the case of a sick man.

> For neither does a sick person recover his health simply by wishing; nonetheless, he is sick willingly, by living incontinently and disobeying the doctors, if that was how it happened. At that time, then, he was free not to be sick, though no longer free once he has let himself go, just as it was up to us to throw a stone, since the principle was in us, though we can no longer take it back once we have thrown it. Similarly, then, the person who is now unjust or intemperate was originally free not to acquire this character, so that he has it willingly, though once he has acquired the character, he is no longer free not to have it now.[3]

Richard's Last Try: The Perception of Good

Richard has one argument left. And it's a good last shot.

---

2. Aristotle, *Nicomachean Ethics*, 1103b.
3. Aristotle, *Nicomachean Ethics*, 1114a.

"Look," he snarls, "your argument is totally irrational! People are self-interested—we choose what we think will make us happy. Maybe my perception of what's good for me is a little off. I can accept that. I don't like waking up in jail any more than the next guy. But how I see things when they're happening isn't a matter of *choice*. How can you blame me as if I were cold sober when I clobbered that guy? You call that fair?"

Richard seems to have two good points. For one thing, he suggests people naturally choose what they perceive will lead to their own happiness. For another, he claims that it's not his fault that his perception is off. He may be responsible for his character traits, but how could he be responsible for his very perception of reality?

Actually, Aristotle agrees with Richard that we all choose what we perceive to be in our own interest. Even if some action is ultimately to our disadvantage, at the moment we choose, we choose what we think will make us happy. If we give up our life to save somebody else, for example, what we want at that moment is to preserve the other person's life. We can even apply this principle to Aristotle's example of the sick man. Perhaps the person decided he'd feel better by ignoring his physician's orders. Perhaps he foolishly preferred some short-term pleasure instead of long-term health. Such choices still fit the idea that every choice is made in line with our perception of what will bring happiness.

It sounds like Richard is suggesting another variety of determinism in which we all automatically select what we *perceive* will make us happy. If people have no control over their perception of what is good, then is it fair to blame them if they do the wrong thing?

Aristotle gives no ground, however. "If," the philosopher argues back, "each person is in some way responsible for his own state of character, then he is also himself in some way responsible for [what appears to him to be good]."[4] Aristotle thinks that as we choose the actions that eventually define our personalities, we affect the entire inner mechanism that processes data from the outside world. Thus, we create our own understanding of reality, just as we create our own character.

Aristotle might grant that Richard hit the other fellow because, although he was wrong about it, he perceived that that action would make him happy. But he had that perception only because he had given in to his anger for years. The cumulative effect of all his past actions includes everything that contributed to his latest action—his perception of the situation, his feelings, his inclinations, and so on. In other words, if Richard had acted differently in, say, the last ten years, when it was in his power to do so, his perception of reality would have been different today. Aristotle ultimately concedes nothing to Richard. Although Aristotle admits that some actions are the product of bad habits or ignorance, he does not call these acts involuntary. He still holds us accountable for them. In his opinion, we fashion ourselves with every small deed we do when we have the power to make choices. Therefore, we are responsible not only for how our actions turn out but also for the kind of person we become.

---

4. Aristotle, *Nicomachean Ethics*, 1114a–b.

Aristotle and Freedom

Aristotle gives us a solid, commonsense defense of freedom. He thinks most of our actions are voluntary, hence, free choices. Moreover, he suggests that, directly or indirectly, we choose our character, habits, and the very way we perceive reality. Thus, we are responsible for any action that flows from any of those factors. Even when forces overwhelm us, unless it's a case of coercion or ignorance, we cannot escape the responsibility that our freedom brings with it.

Aristotle's ideas are dramatically different from those of the determinists. So if you've been leaning toward determinism, you've certainly got something to contend with now. To Aristotle, it's obvious that we are free. Only the clearest examples of being forced to do something count as "involuntary" for him. Aristotle *is* aware that at certain moments we may *feel* compelled to do something by habits we have developed. But he firmly believes that the factors that shape our personality were in our power in the past. Therefore, we are responsible today for the consequences of our habits or dispositions that we allowed to take root years ago. On this matter, Aristotle is uncompromising. Unless we have irrefutable evidence to the contrary—like a gun to our head—our actions result from our free choice.

William James: The Pragmatic Philosopher

Another philosopher who approaches the free will/determinism debate from a commonsense perspective is the American thinker William James. James was a psychologist as well as a philosopher, and his arguments in favor of free will over determinism put a good deal of weight on inner, subjective states—which seem to argue against determinism. Like Aristotle, James is a thinker with a practical tilt. He is the most important representative of the school of thought known as **pragmatism**.

> **pragmatism** Pragmatism is a school of thought that takes a practical and inclusive approach to solving philosophical problems. In connection with the debate between free will and determinism, William James defends free will with the argument that, when we take everything into account, "indeterminism" is an explanation that simply "works better."

Pragmatism and Freedom

Pragmatism is often misunderstood. We use "pragmatic" in everyday speech to mean not just "practical," but "cynical," even "amoral" and Machiavellian. This does not describe the philosophical school of pragmatism, however.

William James's conception of "pragmatism" recognizes that important questions like "Are our actions determined?" aren't simply interesting intellectual puzzles. They are directly connected with the experience of everyday living. The best answers to these questions, then, should "work" for us in a very practical way. They should let us understand the world better. They should fit with our general understanding of life that combines both objective and subjective elements. As James explains in "The Dilemma of Determinism,"

> When we make theories about the world and discuss them with one another, we do so in order to attain a conception of things which shall give us subjective satisfaction; and if there be two conceptions, and the one seems to us, on the whole, more rational than the other, we are entitled to suppose that the more rational one is truer.[5]

Echoing this approach in "What Pragmatism Means," James remarks that

> [pragmatism's] only test of probable truth is what works best in the way of leading us, what fits every part of life best and combines with the collectivity of experience's demands, nothing being omitted.[6]

William James (1842–1910) was born into an accomplished New York family. He was the son of the religious thinker Henry James, Sr., and the brother of the famous novelist Henry James, Jr. Trained as a physician at the Harvard Medical School, James was nonetheless widely educated and interested in a variety of fields. At one point in his life, he considered a career as a painter, and he spent a year on a scientific field expedition in Brazil. But he ultimately taught philosophy and psychology at Harvard, where he became prominent in both fields. James is best known in philosophy as an exponent of the pragmatic conception of truth and a defender of free will. He also explored the phenomenon of religion in *The Varieties of Religious Experience*. As one of the founders of American psychology, he established one of the world's first experimental psychology laboratories at Harvard, and he wrote *Principles of Psychology*.

On the issue of free will versus determinism, then, James's pragmatic outlook makes him favor freedom because he thinks that the presumption that we are free simply "works" better than determinism does. That is, the idea that there is some element of choice in our actions gives us a more rational and satisfying account of experience than the idea that everything is determined.

Be careful you don't think that because James is both a scientist and a "pragmatic" philosopher—someone who talks about whether explanations "work" in a practical way—all he's interested in is hard facts. Objectivity and scientific ideas of empirical proof are important to James. But in assessing ideas and explanations, he also looks to see whether they have what he calls "moral rationality." That is, does an explanation fit with our inner,

5. William James, "The Dilemma of Determinism," in *The Will to Believe and Other Essays in Popular Philosophy* (New York: Barnes & Noble Books, 2005), 117.
6. William James, "What Pragmatism Means," https://www.gutenberg.org/files/5116/5116-h/5116-h.htm.

subjective experiences? In the case of the debate between free will and determinism, James would allow us to use our "feeling of freedom" in evaluating arguments for the opposing sides. Thus James's "pragmatic" approach to the question of freedom versus determinism lets us reflect on our everyday, subjective experience of life.

Rational and Satisfying Explanations

Before we get into the details of James's argument, note just how different his approach is from that of a hard-nosed scientist for whom the only thing that counts is observable, measurable data. Anything else is subjective, unscientific, and unacceptable. To such a scientist, a rational and satisfying explanation is one that obeys the canons of logic and the demands of scientific proof. A meaningful assertion can be made only on the basis of observable fact. This lets us say only things like "Hahn's sweater is red," "Norbert has brown hair," and "Dolphins have no vocal cords." You can make complicated statements of this sort, but the bottom line is always the same. Someone can say, "Prove it," and you must be able to come up with hard evidence.

James's approach is looser and more inclusive. He uses a fairly broad definition of "rational," one that includes logic and science, of course, but adds some of the more subjective human responses. This is particularly clear in situations involving ethics. Suppose, for example, that someone got out of an important commitment with you by telling a lie. You find out about it and confront the culprit. The liar, however, replies somewhat flippantly, "There's nothing wrong with what I did. There's no law against it. People do it all the time." Can you prove that person wrong? Are there empirical facts to summon in support of your view? No. You were inconvenienced and disappointed, but nothing more than that. Still, the liar's explanation probably doesn't satisfy you. Something about it rubs most of us the wrong way. Maybe it's just your feeling that lying shouldn't be excused so readily. Nonetheless, James would consider your disappointment or disapproval rational and relevant evidence in assessing this situation.

Indeterminism

William James's argument for freedom appears in a famous address called "The Dilemma of Determinism." James's basic strategy is to show that determinism is simply not a very satisfying explanation for human actions. Although he doesn't think that anyone can ultimately prove the issue one way or the other, he thinks that free will, which he calls **indeterminism**, explains human behavior better.

He sets up the two positions in stark opposition:

> **indeterminism** Indeterminism is William James's position that in any circumstance we genuinely have more than one option from which to choose. Accordingly, he argues, our actions are not determined.

[*Determinism*] professes that those parts of the universe already laid down absolutely appoint and decree what the other parts shall be. The future has no ambiguous possibilities hidden in its womb. . . . *Indeterminism*, on the contrary, says that the parts have a certain amount of loose play on one another, so that the laying down of one of them does not necessarily determine what the others shall be. . . . Of two alternative futures which we conceive, both may now be really possible.[7]

Indeterminism and Possibilities

James's first argument for indeterminism is more abstract than anything we have looked at so far in this debate. But it homes in on determinism's central claim that when we have choices to make, we aren't really choosing among genuine options or possibilities. It may look as if there are options, the determinists say, but that is our mistake.

Let's say that you're walking home and come to a fork in the road. Both paths take you where you want to go. They are equally direct, scenic, and flat. You've gone both ways at different times with no pattern of preferring one over the other or of alternating routes. There is no apparent reason for you to choose one or the other now. This time you take the path on the left.

What were the odds of your taking the left fork? One in two. And the right fork? Again, one in two. You would say that, and James would say that. But the determinist says that you're fooling yourself and that it wasn't even *possible* for you to take the right fork. The odds weren't one in two, but zero. The odds for the left fork, on the other hand, were one in one. A situation may look as if it presents more than one possibility. But the determinist says that only one thing can happen.

This, of course, does not square with how we feel about the situation. When presented with a choice of two routes, we feel as though we have two genuine possibilities. Even if we have a strong preference for one, it still feels *possible* for us to select the other. James's first argument for indeterminism, then, is built on this very basic human experience—the feeling that when we make a choice about something, we believe that we have different *possibilities* to pick from. It's no illusion—the choice is real and the outcome genuinely unknown.

Can we prove that these options or possibilities exist? No. But how does it feel to you? Didn't you choose which school to go to? For some people this is a difficult decision. Especially early in the process, you probably felt that several schools were real possibilities. And what about your future? Don't you think there are different paths your life might take? Different careers, different people to fall in love with, different places to live? In every area of life, in fact, you probably sense many different possibilities.

As James points out, the determinist says that an apparent option is either necessary or impossible. According to determinism, then, it was necessary and unavoidable that you attend this school. Despite what you went through in trying to make up your mind, deciding to go to a different school was impossible. The causes of your action were already

---

7. William James, "The Dilemma of Determinism," in *The Will to Believe and Other Essays in Popular Philosophy* (New York: Barnes and Noble Books, 2005), 119.

in place. James, on the other hand, thinks that it was possible for you to have chosen differently.

This idea of possibilities is so important to James because he thinks that it makes his case. To prove that determinism is wrong, James doesn't try to show that a hundred possible options are equally likely every time we're faced with a choice. All it takes is one other genuine possibility:

> "Free-will" does not say that everything that is physically conceivable is also morally possible. It merely says that of alternatives that really tempt our will, more than one is really possible. Of course, the alternatives that do thus tempt us are vastly fewer than the physical possibilities we can coldly fancy.[8]

William James's first argument in favor of free will, or indeterminism, is that if it is at least possible for us to select more than one of the apparent choices, then determinism is wrong. If more than one option is genuinely possible, neither the universe nor our actions are fixed and necessary as determinists claim they are.

Pragmatism and Possibilities

But James does not dismiss determinism just because we feel that possibilities exist. As a pragmatist, he needs to show that indeterminism gives us a more rational and more workable explanation of reality than determinism does.

James goes at this by pointing out that he could take two streets to go home after his lecture—Divinity Avenue or Oxford Street. Imagine that he takes Divinity. Now let's turn back the clock to the point where he makes his choice. This time imagine that he takes Oxford. James writes:

> Now, if you are determinists, you believe one of these universes to have been from eternity impossible. . . . But looking outwardly at these universes, can you say which is the impossible and accidental one, and which the rational and necessary one? I doubt if the most ironclad determinist among you could have the slightest glimmer of light on this point. In other words, either universe *after the fact* and once there would, to our means of observation and understanding, appear just as rational as the other. There would be absolutely no criterion by which we might judge one necessary and the other matter of chance.[9]

We can rationally conceive of James taking either road. If determinism is correct, however, one of these choices is impossible. But why? Nothing suggests that one road should be impossible. That idea simply makes no sense. Seen this way, determinism does not give us a rational and satisfying account of the world. Indeterminism, on the other hand, seems to match our experience and our expectations very well. As an explanation, it is more satisfying and "works" better.

---

8. James, "The Dilemma of Determinism," 289.
9. James, "The Dilemma of Determinism," 123.

James's criticism of determinism is made particularly effective by his comment that when we look at his choice between Divinity and Oxford "after the fact," we fail to discover a causal chain that made it inevitable that he would take the street he did. But that's not always the case with even complicated instances of cause and effect. Take the weather, for example. The behavior of storms and air currents can be difficult to forecast. Meteorologists, however, typically do an excellent job of explaining after the fact why a typhoon veered away from the mainland at the last minute. Once all the facts are in, a close analysis will show how it was all a matter of cause and effect. James's argument is that his selection of street can't be explained as necessary even looking back at it. Therefore, it must have been a function of free choice among more than one genuine possibility.

Feelings of "Regret"

James's other major argument against determinism is, like his first one, based on ordinary human experience. In this case, he refers to our everyday sense of justice and fairness.

James begins with the basic observation that we regularly feel dissatisfied with life. He says that we live in "a world in which we constantly have to make what I shall, with your permission, call judgments of regret. Hardly an hour passes in which we do not wish that something might be otherwise." Some of these regrets are trivial—it is raining, you have a quiz today—and you can put them behind you fairly easily. Other dissatisfactions stick with us, however, and they often involve our sense of right and wrong. James writes,

> Some regrets are pretty obstinate and hard to stifle, regrets for acts of wanton cruelty or treachery, for example, whether performed by others or by ourselves. Hardly anyone can remain entirely optimistic after reading the confession of the murderer at Brockton the other day: how, to get rid of the wife whose continued existence bored him, he inveigled her into a desert spot, shot her four times, and then, as she lay on the ground and said to him, "You didn't do it on purpose, did you, dear?" replied, "No, I didn't do it on purpose," as he raised a rock and smashed her skull. Such an occurrence, with the mild sentence and self-satisfaction of the prisoner, is a field for a crop of regrets, which one need not take up in detail. We feel that, although a perfect mechanical fit to the rest of the universe, it is a bad moral fit, and that something else would really have been better in its place.[10]

Once again, whose explanation of such a terrible event works better and is more satisfying, the determinist's or the indeterminist's? Determinism must maintain that the murder was destined from eternity. "For the deterministic philosophy," explains James, "nothing else for a moment had a ghost of a chance of being put into their place. To admit such a chance, the determinists tell us, would be to make a suicide of reason."

This doesn't sit right with James—or with most of us. James asks, "If this Brockton murder was called for by the rest of the universe, if it had to come at its preappointed

---

10. James, "The Dilemma of Determinism," 127.

hour, and if nothing else would have been consistent with the sense of the whole, what are we to think of the universe?" Determinism, then, gives us a world in which it is irrational to think that such terrible crimes do not have to happen. Isn't there something basically wrong about such a universe? Seen this way, determinism doesn't strike us as either rational or satisfying.

Determinism may be able to account for all the causal forces that impelled this man to murder his wife. That's what James means when he says that this tragedy has "a perfect *mechanical* fit to the rest of the universe." But James thinks that our analysis cannot stop there. The murder, he says, has "a bad moral fit." To understand the event more fully, we must consider more than cause and effect. A crime such as this has another dimension to which we all respond on a deeper, more personal level. No ordinary person can contemplate what the husband did without a deep sense of horror and revulsion. Yet determinism argues that such a feeling is both inappropriate and irrelevant to any discussion of the husband's deed.

The way William James expresses this is to say that determinism "violates my sense of moral reality through and through." There is more to understanding and evaluating an action than looking impersonally at cause and effect, he suggests. We must also use what he calls our "moral rationality" and see what our basic sense of ethics tells us about the situation. Our moral outrage over this murder tells us something important that cannot be ignored. Normal people consistently react to cruelty, unfairness, and injustice in a host of ways: shock, dismay, blame, anger, and so on. That is a fact of human experience. *But we wouldn't react this way unless we believed that people could act differently.* It would be irrational to do so.

In effect, James says that when we pay attention to what our ordinary sense of right and wrong (our "moral rationality") tells us about a situation, we have more reasons to reject determinism. Indeterminism gives us a more rational and satisfying explanation because it maintains that the husband who murders his wife because he was bored with her was in control of his actions, did something wrong, and deserves to be punished severely.

James and Freedom

As we saw earlier, William James doesn't think it's possible to prove beyond any doubt whether determinism or indeterminism is right. He does, however, make two important points that lead him to believe that indeterminism is more rational, more satisfying, and simply "works better" as an account of human action.

First, the human mind is more satisfied with the idea that genuine choices, options, or possibilities are real, not imaginary. It simply makes more sense to us. When you go to a theater showing seven different movies, all of which you would like to see, you feel you have seven genuine alternatives. What if someone walked up to you and said, "No, it's already determined. You have no choice. It is necessary that you see the one you pick and impossible for you to choose any other"? You'd think that this person was more than a little strange. The idea simply does not square with what we take to be an almost self-evident dimension of human life. Similarly, if someone is cruel to you, it seems perfectly sensible and rational for you to feel that the act was wrong, that it never should have happened, and that the person doing it should be punished. Imagine that you and a friend are walking along and someone jumps out of the shadows, flashes a knife, and takes your money. If, after the robber runs off, your friend turned to you and calmly said, "It's too bad that particular chain of causes and effects led us to being mugged," you'd wonder what planet your friend came from. The normal reaction in this circumstance is anger and the certainty that the thief had chosen to do something wrong. And James takes this normal, moral sense as further reason for thinking that our actions are not determined.

There's no great mystery to James's arguments for "indeterminism." Like Aristotle, James relies very much on our everyday sensibilities that people are free and that, from a commonsense standpoint, free will is easier to accept than determinism. Notice that, as was the case with Aristotle's arguments, the idea of responsibility plays a major role here. To accept determinism means that we must give up a very strong belief—one that feels virtually self-evident—that it is rational and fair to hold each other responsible for what we do. Determinists may argue on scientific grounds. But, like virtually every philosopher who argues for freedom of the will, James and Aristotle build much of their case on moral grounds.

In citing the murder case, James in particular implies that one of the most important things at stake in the free will/determinism debate isn't a philosophical issue at all but a civic or moral one. If determinism is correct, we have no rational basis on which to punish even the most heinous crimes because it is wrong to penalize people for actions they did not choose. Yet if we go in that direction, what kind of a society are we left with?

Jean-Paul Sartre: The Existentialist Philosopher

Both Aristotle and William James make commonsense arguments for free will. We feel as if we make real choices. Our conventional moral sense tells us that other people can control their actions and are responsible for them. Not all arguments for free choice rely on our everyday experience, however. Indeed, one of the most extreme defenses of freedom grants us so much freedom that the argument seems to defy common sense.

Think again about the movie theater and imagine that it's on your way home from school. As you drive past it one day, your car, which has been stalling a lot, coughs and dies. Your phone's battery is dead, so you're stuck there. You were rushing home to study for a big test tomorrow, but because it's started to pour, you decide to wait in the lobby until it lets up. Then you'll walk the rest of the way. As you stand there, a stranger walks up to you and says, "I've got a gun. Do as I say, and I won't hurt you. You and I are going to see a movie." You go to the ticket window and find that the only show not sold out is a re-release of a movie that gave you nightmares when you saw it as a kid. You have no choice. The two of you see the movie, and your captor disappears into the night.

Did you have any freedom in this situation? It doesn't look like it. You were stuck someplace you didn't want to be, kidnapped at gunpoint, and forced to watch a movie you didn't want to see. But what if someone told you that you were *totally free* in that situation and that your commonsense perception that you were not free is a serious mistake on your part?

Before you dismiss this suggestion completely, let's consider the movie scenario again. As background, however, we should look at the "big picture." You *chose* to continue your education. You *chose* the school you are in. You *chose* to drive your car in bad shape. You *chose* the course you now have an exam in. The same pattern holds for your immediate predicament. You *chose* to wait at the theater rather than walk in the rain or try to hitch a ride on the road. You *chose* to go along with your kidnapper and not resist. You did that because you *chose* to protect your life.

You've even made choices that determine your emotions. On the one hand, you can *choose* to believe the promise that you will not be hurt; you can *choose* to make the most of the situation and try to enjoy the movie by watching it this time through an adult's eyes. All this will keep you calm. Or you *choose* to *doubt* your kidnapper's word, focus on your bad fortune, and remind yourself how the movie scared you years ago—which will make you miserable and terrified. Clearly, you make choice upon choice in that situation.

You may think it is unrealistic to say that you made choices here. But let's face it—you didn't really *have* to do any of the things you did, did you? You don't even *have* to protect your life. Of course, it is nicer to be alive and healthy than dead, but that is your choice. You are free to endanger your life if you want to.

Just look at all the choices you've made with complete freedom. When we look at the story this way, you become the architect of almost everything about the situation you find yourself in.

Extreme Freedom and Existentialism

The case for absolute freedom is put most persuasively by the twentieth-century school of philosophy called **existentialism**. The existentialists argue for a position directly opposed to the determinists, who claim that everything about us—all our actions and all our feelings—is determined. On the contrary, existentialism argues that we are totally free and that absolutely everything about us is a product of our own choices. We are completely free at every moment, the existentialists insist, and we are responsible for each detail of our lives. The existentialist position on freedom is so extreme that it may seem unbelievable—just as unbelievable, perhaps, as extreme determinism. But give it a chance. Existentialism is built on the belief that we humans are free

> **existentialism** Existentialism is a school of thought based on the idea that "existence precedes essence," that is, that our nature is determined by the actions we choose to do. Existentialism argues that freedom is such an unavoidable, and sometimes uncomfortable, characteristic of life that we are "condemned to be free." We are completely free at every moment, absolutely everything about us is a product of our own choices, and we are responsible for each and every detail of our lives.

and that shaping our lives according to our own plans is the central project of our lives. And this outlook has made existentialism one of the twentieth century's most important contributions to philosophy.

Sartre and Existentialism

One of the best representatives of existentialism is the French philosopher Jean-Paul Sartre. Sartre's basic ideas on freedom are clear and straightforward—hard to accept, perhaps, but nonetheless clear and straightforward.

Sartre's position on human freedom is intimately connected with his overall view of the nature of reality. First, Sartre does not believe God exists. (Not all existentialists are atheists, but Sartre is.) Thus, there is no supreme being who determines the nature of things and the rules of the game. Sartre also rejects the idea that either natural evolutionary forces or inner psychological ones set any direction for human life. Without such forces, absolute freedom is all that is left. To Sartre, freedom is simply a basic fact of human existence—as basic as cause and effect are to determinists.

> Jean-Paul Sartre (1905–1980), the main proponent of existentialism, was a famous novelist and playwright as well as a major philosopher. Educated in Paris, Sartre began his career teaching in France and Germany. He was involved in the Resistance during World War II and was politically active throughout his life. His major philosophical opus is *Being and Nothingness*. Some of his literary works include *Nausea, No Exit*, and *Saint Genet*.

Essence Precedes Existence

When Sartre renounces God and all natural forces, he also rejects what he calls the long-standing philosophical belief that **essence precedes existence**. This is the idea that the basic nature of something—its *essence*—determines the shape, activity, and possibilities of its everyday life—its *existence*. Something's essence "precedes" its existence in that it is logically prior to it. That is, it sets the ground rules or boundaries of what that object or being can do.

For example, the essence, or nature, of a computer is to be a device designed to generate, retain, and manipulate electrical impulses so that it can store data, perform certain operations, and create images on a screen. What it actually does in the course of a day—its existence—is set by the computer's capacities and limits—its essence. Within the specifications and possibilities determined by the computer's components, it will perform certain functions. That's all it can do. It can't make breakfast for you (at least not yet). This and many other things are beyond its essence. Thus its existence will never include them.

To apply the idea that essence determines existence to humans, let's look back at Freud's thinking. There we find that the essence of being human—our nature, what we are—is to be a biological creature with an inner mental and emotional life characterized

> **essence precedes existence** Philosophers have traditionally held that the "nature" of something determines what it is able to do, its limitations, its defining characteristics, and the like, that is, its "existence." This position is rejected by the existential belief that our choices determine our nature ("existence precedes essence").

by two basic drives (sex and aggression) and a three-part personality structure (id, ego, and superego), which develops through various psychosexual stages and which uses various defense mechanisms. Our existence—what we do in our lives—is then completely determined by our essence. Our conscious self primarily tries to arbitrate the insatiable and contradictory demands of our id and superego. Within this frame of reference, it would be ridiculous to say, "I choose to live with no instinct for aggression." It is simply beyond our essence.

Existence Precedes Essence

Sartre sees the situation as completely reversed when it comes to humans. He turns the "essence precedes existence" formula around and says that **existence precedes essence**. (This emphasis on "existence" obviously shows up in the name "existentialism.")

Sartre denies that there is such a thing as a "human nature," or a human "essence," that determines or limits our choices. He claims that what we choose to do (our existence) determines our nature (our essence). The first principle of existentialism, then, is "Man is nothing else but what he makes of himself." If this is so, then people are absolutely free. As he explains in the essay "Existentialism," "If existence really does precede essence, there is no explaining things away by reference to a fixed and given human nature. In other words, there is no determinism, man is free, man is freedom."[11]

The most important thing is what we do with our freedom. Thinking, wanting, or hoping may be important parts of our freedom, but Sartre believes that what is critical is what we *do*. Sartre claims, "There is no reality except in action. . . . Man is nothing else than his plan; he exists only to the extent that he fulfills himself; he is therefore nothing else than the ensemble of his acts, nothing else than his life."[12]

> **existence precedes essence** "Existence precedes essence" is the existentialist rejection of the traditional idea that something's nature determines its abilities and limitations in how it lives. Existentialism maintains instead that our choices ("existence") determine our nature ("essence").

Life gets its meaning and purpose, then, from what we do with it. It is as if each one of us were given a huge mound of clay. We are sculptors who will give the clay life and shape. Each choice we make in our lives is like the movement of our hands as we fashion the clay into a definite form. And if we pause, step back, and decide we don't like how the

---

11. Jean-Paul Sartre, "Existentialism," in *Existentialism and Human Emotions* (New York: Philosophical Library, 1957), 15–16.
12. Sartre, "Existentialism," 32.

sculpture is turning out, we can start all over and try to make something different. Seen this way, life is a totally open enterprise.

Human Imagination and Creativity

When Sartre argues in favor of freedom by denying a fixed human nature, he's not being naive. He does recognize that human beings have certain biological needs and limitations. Who could deny that a human being is a land-based mammal that needs food and water to stay alive? But Sartre regards choices about even these things as somehow within our power. We are, after all, free to choose whether or not to eat and remain alive. And because of our special abilities, we can search for ways to do things that lie beyond our limits. Take flying, for example. Birds can fly; humans cannot. But we found a way to do the impossible and fly, didn't we? So in a way, we can transcend our biological limitations.

Obviously what makes all this possible is human imagination, intellect, will, desire, and the capacity to choose. This is what Sartre means when he says, "Man is freedom."[13] Even if the evidence of your own life leads you to feel that our possibilities are not endless, look at the life of our species. Humans have found ways to do all kinds of "impossible" things: underwater travel, space flight, building roads through mountains, splitting the atom, defeating "incurable" diseases, breaking the four-minute mile, and becoming fast friends with sworn enemies. The list goes on and on. To say that "existence precedes essence," then, is to attest to our enormous creative powers as human beings.

Condemned to Be Free

When you think about it, the tremendous possibilities that come from being as free as Sartre envisions us to be are truly thrilling. Think of that "I-can-accomplish-anything-I-put-my-mind-to" feeling. But Sartre sees freedom as so fundamental and so pervasive that the prospect is not all upbeat. A full awareness of our responsibility for each and every facet of our lives can be troubling. This much freedom ultimately makes us anxious. As Sartre puts it, we are "condemned to be free."[14] That is, we have been thrown into a situation that requires endless, often terrifying decisions about everything in our lives.

The phrase also conveys the idea that we are trapped—sentenced to a situation we can never break out of. Even if we want to avoid freely fashioning our life, we can't. "For I am responsible," he continues, "for my very desire of fleeing responsibilities. To make myself passive in the world, to refuse to act upon things and upon Others is still to choose myself."[15] Whether we go our own way, go along with what everyone else does, or try to do nothing, we choose that course of action. We must accept the responsibility for absolutely everything we do, including ducking out on our responsibilities. We always have

13. Sartre, "Existentialism," 23.
14. Sartre, "Existentialism," 23.
15. Jean-Paul Sartre, "Freedom and Responsibility," in *Existentialism and Human Emotions*, 57.

the choice. We always have an option. We always have control. We can never escape it. As Sartre explains:

> Man is condemned to be free because he did not create himself, yet, in other respects is free; because, once thrown into the world, he is responsible for everything he does. The existentialist does not believe in the power of passion. He will never agree that a sweeping passion is a ravaging torrent which fatally leads a man to certain acts and is therefore an excuse. He thinks that man is responsible for his passion.
>
> The existentialist does not think that man is going to help himself by finding in the world some omen by which to orient himself. Because he thinks that man will interpret the omen to suit himself. Therefore, he thinks that man, with no support and no aid, is condemned every moment to invent man.[16]

Responsibility and "Bad Faith"

Freedom, of course, automatically carries with it the fact of responsibility. If you freely choose to do something, you are responsible for your action and its consequences. In Sartre's scheme, we must feel responsible all the time.

That can be quite a punishment, especially when most of us regularly try to avoid taking full responsibility for our lives. Being responsible for making solid, authentic choices at every juncture is hard to handle. Yet when we choose not to do it, Sartre accuses us of acting in "bad faith"—lying to ourselves about our responsibility.

Sartre illustrates bad faith in *Being and Nothingness* with a story about a woman on a date. The man wants to begin an affair; the woman does not know what she wants to do. She knows she must eventually make a decision, but she tries to put it off. Then the man takes her hand and caresses it. This calls for a decision. The woman now should either take her hand away, indicating her lack of interest, or respond in a way that encourages the man. What happens, however, is that "the young woman leaves her hand there, but she *does not notice* that she's leaving it." She goes on talking about something intellectual, while her hand "rests inert between the warm hands of her companion—neither consenting nor resisting—a thing." Instead of making a decision, she denies that one is called for. She refuses to accept the responsibility for making a choice. For Sartre this is a superb image of how we try to avoid our freedom. This woman acts as though she doesn't even notice that the man has taken her hand.[17]

We all find ways of acting in "bad faith." You don't return a phone call from someone you want to break up with because you don't want to deliver the bad news. When your friend calls back later you say, "I'm sorry. I was so busy I forgot you called." You try out for the soccer team—but only half-heartedly. When you don't make it, you tell yourself,

---

16. Sartre, "Existentialism," 23.
17. Jean-Paul Sartre, *Being and Nothingness*, trans. Hazel Barnes (New York: Washington Square Press, 1966), 67.

"I didn't really want to play soccer anyway." In both cases, you deny reality and avoid a real decision.

Of course, "not to decide is to decide." The woman in Sartre's story decided to do nothing now. You have decided to let your friend think the romance is still on. You decided not to do your best at the tryouts. But Sartre thinks that acting in "bad faith" like this is dishonest. The only good way to live is to accept head on the responsibility that comes with our freedom, make decisions, and face the consequences.

The Extent of Our Responsibility

Sartre is merciless when it comes to our accepting responsibility. No matter what happens in our life, we can never blame anybody else. Our own responsibility is total. "Man being condemned to be free," says Sartre, "carries the weight of the whole world on his shoulders; he is responsible for the world and for himself as a way of being." Responsible for the whole world? "Sartre can't mean it," you say. "Responsible for my small corner? Fine. But more than that's crazy."

Does Sartre actually mean what he says? Absolutely. The most dramatic proof of this lies in a passage from his book *Being and Nothingness,* where he talks about the responsibility of an individual person for a war. Sartre fought with the French underground in World War II, and you'd think he wouldn't hold the citizens of an invaded country in any way responsible for such a misfortune. Yet in Sartre's view:

> Thus there are no accidents in a life; a community event which suddenly bursts forth and involved me in it does not come from the outside. If I am mobilized in a war, this war is my war; it is in my image and I deserve it. I deserve it first because I could always get out of it by suicide or by desertion; these ultimate possibles are those which must always be present for us when there is a question of envisaging a situation. For lack of getting out of it, I have chosen it. This can be due to inertia, to cowardice in the face of public opinion, or because I prefer certain other values to the value of the refusal to join in the war (the good opinion of my relatives, the honor of my family, etc.). Any way you look at it, it is a matter of a choice. This choice will be repeated later on again and again without a break until the end of the war. Therefore we must agree with the statement by J. Romains, "In war there are no innocent victims."[18]

This is certainly one of Sartre's most troubling ideas. Yet it does dramatize just how much freedom and power Sartre thinks we really have. Believing that you are genuinely responsible for everything around you might overwhelm you. But if you could cope with that responsibility, you would also feel extremely powerful. After all, if you really are responsible for something, you must also have the power to change it.

---

18. Sartre, *Being and Nothingness,* 678.

The Extent of Our Power

Most of us feel uneasy about Sartre's extreme claims because we feel relatively powerless in life. Sartre's war example is perfect. We feel that we have about as much control over a war as we do over an earthquake. And if we have no power over something, how can we have any responsibility for it?

We do, however, have more power over things than we think we do. Take the simple example of how other people treat us. By and large, people treat us exactly the way we tell them to. It is almost entirely under our control.

"Not so," you say. "I'm shy, withdrawn, and—if I have to admit it—kind of uninteresting. Nobody ever likes to talk to me. I can't help it. It's just the way I am." But how do people know you're "shy, withdrawn, and uninteresting"? Do you wear a sign? Can they read minds? No, you tell them with your actions. You don't mingle with them. You don't smile. You don't say you're glad to see them. You stay quiet and invisible in a conversation. This is how you choose to act around others, and these are cues that say, "Leave me alone."

But try this experiment sometime. When you're with a group of people who don't know you, consciously decide to be different from how you usually are. If you're shy, act outgoing. If you're usually serious, be fun loving. If you usually play dumb, be serious and intellectual. Don't be phony. Say to yourself, "Tonight I choose to be different. I don't have anything to lose, and I don't have to stay like this for the rest of my life. But tonight I'm someone who's _____." Do you know what will happen? People will respond as though this is how you've been all your life. That's because you're telling them who you are and how to treat you. And who you choose to be inside is the single most important influence on how people treat you.

Now try a bigger exercise in freedom and power. Think of some important issue at your school or in your community, something that bothers you and that should be changed— some example of unfairness, discrimination, dishonesty, harm to the environment, etc. If someone said to you, "So go change it," you would probably reply, "You're crazy. One person can't change things like that. It's up to the _____ (fill in the blank: "the Student Senate," "Administration," "City Council," etc.). I'm just me." Now recall Sartre's conviction that each of us is responsible for everything that goes on in the world and *feel* the weight of that responsibility. Think again about what you want changed and feel responsible for it. Suddenly, "I'm just me" becomes "I'm the person responsible for this." You are as important as anyone else connected with it. If this is so, there must be something you can do to make things better.

Suppose it's a school policy you want changed. People made it and people can change it. Get advice about how to proceed. Talk to your professors, counselors, and administrators. Find out who else thinks the way you do. When someone says, "We simply cannot change things," find a new path to take. Feel complete responsibility for the situation. If you can't convince the right people, it's because you didn't find the right argument. Try again—there's always somebody else to talk to.

But don't complain and don't blame anybody else. Sartre says, "The peculiar character of human-reality is that it is without excuse." Existentialism does not let you shift responsibility. If you blame somebody else, you abdicate your responsibility.

If you truly accept responsibility for the cause you champion, don't give up. Do everything you can, and you will get somewhere. You may not get everything you want, and you may not get it when you want it. But eventually you will change something for the better. Even if that policy stays in place, you will have changed the way some people think. And you may at least have stopped other similar policies from being enacted.

Existentialism maintains that we regularly underestimate how much power we have. If you doubt it, try it.

Sartre and Freedom

Sartre writes about many other philosophical issues, but this is his basic view of freedom. Sartre rejects determinism so completely that he believes that "man is freedom." We choose everything about our lives—even our very essence. Indeed, humans are so free that we are "condemned" to constant choices. Sartre believes that we must feel totally responsible for every facet of our own lives—and even those of others. If we fail to do so, we are acting in "bad faith." As you can see, then, existentialism is the antithesis of determinism.

Freedom Versus Determinism: A Closing Word

We can make strong cases for both determinism and freedom. We do live in a world of cause and effect, and science has given us no reason to think that humans aren't subject to the laws of causality that govern the entire universe. Determinists argue that forces beyond our control shape everything we do. Aristotle, James, and Sartre refuse to dismiss the sense of freedom that is one of the most distinctive and precious dimensions of human life. Each side presents convincing arguments.

We also seem to give credence to both outlooks in different circumstances without even thinking about the contradiction. As friends get to know one another better—as we learn about each other's personal histories, families, personal quirks—we tend to forgive or overlook things that otherwise might bother us. We act as though much is out of our friends' conscious control. Yet if someone hurts us, we usually are not inclined to dismiss the injury as the unfortunate workings of a deterministic world. We believe that people can choose what they do, and we hold them responsible for their actions. We deal with one another and we raise generation after generation on the premise that they can learn how to behave with intelligence, consideration, and responsibility.

Much hangs in the balance. If determinism is true, we cannot reasonably hold people responsible for their actions. How can we blame them for what is beyond their control? Instead, unethical and criminal behavior should be "treated" as if it were an illness. Yet if free will is true, don't we have to give up empathy, understanding, and compassion when we evaluate one another's actions? Why should we consider extenuating circumstances, the impact of someone's background, or the effects of traumatic experiences in childhood if all of us freely control what we do? Wouldn't those factors just be excuses for irresponsible behavior?

The debate over free will and determinism, then, is not simply a theoretical issue. It bears directly on the day-to-day realities of life—personal and social responsibility, praise, blame, reward, punishment, mercy, and understanding.

But both sides can't be right. We cannot have it all. Now comes the hard part. *You* settle the issue.

Discussion Questions

1. Think about the example of Richard the Yankee fan that opened this chapter. Imagine that he's someone about your age. How severely should he be punished? It's not unusual for there to be a lot of drinking at parties on university campuses and for some fights or destruction of property to result. How should the people involved be treated? Should their level of intoxication be taken into account? How? Should it lessen their punishment or make it worse?

2. Do you agree with Aristotle's idea that our actions form our character? If it were true, much of our personalities would be under our control. Think of some of your character traits or habits—particularly ones you are not proud of. Did they develop because you chose to act certain ways when you were younger? How much responsibility do your parents have for how you turned out? Is there any part of your personality or character that you think is completely beyond your control?

3. If you are sympathetic to determinism, how do you counter William James's claim that as long as it's possible for us to do at least one thing other than what we chose in a particular situation, then determinism must be wrong? Maybe we don't have an infinite number of genuine options when we make choices, but don't we generally have at least two?

4. If you think determinism is correct, how do you account for the presence of the ordinary feelings that we have associated with regret, praise, blame, guilt, and responsibility? These have been part of human beings for thousands, if not millions, of years. Why would these feelings—feelings that presume freedom on the part of ourselves and others—persist if they were fictions? Particularly if you think of yourself as a hard-nosed scientist who believes in the evolutionary workings of nature and natural selection, how can you account for their persistence? Wouldn't they have disappeared long ago if they weren't connected to something real—that is, our free will?

5. Sartre claims that "existence precedes essence." Do you agree? How much under your control are fundamental properties of your being? If Sartre is right,

changing our "existence" alters our "essence." How much power do you have to make dramatic changes in yourself? Have you ever done so? Most of us don't feel that we have that kind of power, but what about the many stories of people who have absolutely turned their lives around by sheer force of will? Does Sartre exaggerate our control and freedom, or do we underestimate them?

6. Have you ever acted in "bad faith"? Do you agree with Sartre that it is a dishonest and inauthentic way to behave? Did you thereby weaken your "essence"?

7. What do you think of Sartre's idea that we are "condemned to be free" and the extent to which he takes the idea of responsibility? You probably cannot relate to Sartre's example of being involved in a war, but think about something that happened to you that was unpleasant, disturbing, and none of your doing. Is there any value in acting according to Sartre's recommendations: to lay claim to the event, believe that we deserve it, have choice in the situation, bear responsibility for what happens, and so on?

Selected Readings

Aristotle's main discussion of voluntary and involuntary action can be found in Book Three of his *Nicomachean Ethics*. William James's argument for "indeterminism" is spelled out in "The Dilemma of Determinism," an address that he delivered to students at the Harvard Divinity School in 1884. See William James, *The Will to Believe and Other Essays in Popular Philosophy* (New York: Barnes and Noble Books, 2005). For the fundamental tenets of existentialism, see Sartre's *Existentialism and Human Emotions*, translated by Bernard Frechtman (New York: Philosophical Library, 1957; reprinted Citadel Press, 1987), and *Being and Nothingness*, translated by Hazel E. Barnes (New York: Philosophical Library, 1966; reprinted Washington Square Press, 1993).

Chapter 5

Right and Wrong

Tyson is a talented IT major who also runs cross-country. He makes friends with a few guys in his classes, discovers they all belong to the same fraternity, and expresses an interest in becoming a member himself. Tyson is Black, however, and he would be the first nonwhite member of the fraternity. Tyson's admission is virtually a sure thing, but Jeff, one of the fraternity brothers, is a racist and cannot stand the idea of Tyson being accepted. Jeff decides to make Tyson withdraw his name, so he sends him anonymous letters full of racial slurs and threats. One letter says that if he doesn't withdraw his application he'll have an "accident" and find himself with a broken leg at the start of the running season. Tyson ignores the threats until he finds the tires on his car slashed one day and a racial epithet keyed into his car. He changes his mind and pulls out.

What is your reaction? Any decent person would condemn this. How would you feel if you were on the receiving end? Hurt and angry, of course. Asked to explain your reaction, you'd probably say that what Jeff did was "hurtful," "wrong," "uncaring," "lousy," "cruel," or some such thing. Evaluating behavior is something we do every day. But it's also an important area of philosophy. We call it **ethics**, or *moral philosophy*. Ethics aims to establish reasonable standards for acceptable human conduct and to apply those standards to particular cases.[1]

We'll start by examining the foundation of a philosophical approach to ethics. Then we'll explore four different approaches philosophers have come up with for evaluating the moral character of actions.

Right, Wrong, and Philosophy

You may wonder what right and wrong have to do with philosophy. Doesn't religion determine moral standards? Don't laws specify what we can and can't do? Furthermore, aren't right and wrong relative? Various cultures have different conceptions of morality. Ideas change over time. And, finally, isn't the individual the only legitimate judge of ethics?

These are good questions, but they reveal two common misconceptions about ethics. People either tend to be too rigid, citing laws or religious teachings as the final word on a

---

1. Some people distinguish between the terms "moral" and "ethical," using one term to mean "high standards" and the other to mean "common practice." Others use them to distinguish between "practical" and "theoretical" issues. Because there is no consensus on this matter, however, we use these two terms synonymously in this discussion. The terms "ethics" and "moral" come from Greek and Latin words, respectively, both of which mean "character."

moral question. Or they are too loose, throwing out all objectivity and reducing ethics to a cultural or personal question. A philosophical approach to ethics gives us a way to avoid those extremes and overcome the weaknesses of religious and legal approaches.

Religious and Legal Approaches

You have probably encountered ideas about right and wrong most frequently in the rules and teachings of your religion and the laws of your area. Religions and laws give us standards against which to evaluate our actions. And they back up their judgments with an appeal to some sort of authority. From the standpoint of philosophy, however, determining right and wrong by appealing to religious authority or laws is too rigid an approach.

Religions offer explicit moral evaluations of human conduct. They give us their particular views of virtue and sin. They draw these conclusions from sacred texts or the spoken wisdom of their founders and current leaders. Ultimately, of course, they attribute their ideas about how we should behave to God. Philosophy and religion, then, go at questions differently. Philosophers demand convincing arguments; devout believers must finally give up on proofs, operate on faith, and accept some religious authority. In addition, when we survey all the religions on earth, we find considerable disagreement over right and wrong. Philosophy and religion don't speak the same language or operate by the same rules. Thus, what is acceptable in a religious investigation is generally inappropriate in a philosophical exploration.

Note, however, the qualifying phrase "generally inappropriate." To the extent that religious positions raise issues that we can investigate rationally, they are relevant to philosophy. For example, some religious objections to abortion include the assumption that a fetus is so much a "human life" that preventing its birth is wrong. This assumption is something we can gather data on, discuss, and argue about rationally. We can ask if a fetus is an actual person, and if so, how. If not, we can ask how abortion could be wrong. And so on. Similarly, everything from the Ten Commandments to the teaching of Jesus or the Quran to the Buddhist Eightfold Path raises ethical issues about how we should treat ourselves and others, which we can talk about philosophically. Although religious arguments don't settle philosophical questions, they can suggest important topics that otherwise might not get enough attention.

The same can be said about laws. Laws are precise standards for evaluating human conduct, but they arise out of politics, which is very different from philosophy. Laws can vary dramatically from place to place, and they change over time. They don't have to be just and fair. What's "legal" versus "illegal" and "ethical" versus "unethical" aren't necessarily the same. In the United States, laws that allowed slavery and discrimination were repeatedly judged to be constitutional, even though that's now recognized as a mistake. Some unethical actions are illegal (rape, murder), but some are legal (selfishly manipulating and deceiving your best friend). Some illegal actions are probably morally neutral (crossing against the light in the middle of the night on a deserted street), and some illegal actions can even be morally positive (civil disobedience for the sake of correcting an injustice).

Nonetheless, as with religious positions, even if knowing why an action is legal or illegal may give us some relevant information for a philosophical discussion, to claim that right and wrong are determined by the law is to make an unwarranted appeal to authority.

Differences Among Cultures, Individuals, and Circumstances

Does this mean, then, that ethics is ultimately "relative" to societies or individuals? Different cultures have different norms. Individuals in the same society vehemently disagree about what's right and wrong. Does ethics boil down to the opinions of cultures and individuals, then?

> **ethical relativism** Ethical relativism denies the existence of universal, objective ethical principles and asserts that ethical judgments are simply an expression of the limited perspective of individuals or societies.

As attractive as **ethical relativism** might be at first blush, it has some serious problems. After all, if we claim that "ethics is all relative to the individual," we would have no basis for criticizing Adolf Hitler or a terrorist who kills innocent children to advance a political cause that he or she sincerely believes in. Sincerity is a wonderful virtue, but most of us know in our hearts that it's not an infallible touchstone for moral truth.[2]

Most of us recognize the importance of respecting other cultures, and we want to be able to accept customs different from our own. We recognize that honoring freedom and individuality means that we need to tolerate ideas or behaviors with which we disagree. Particularly on personal moral issues, we want the autonomy to make decisions according to our most sincere beliefs, and we want other people to respect our judgments about what is right and wrong for us. However, although many of us may want to conclude on the basis of these desires that "ethics is relative," what we probably mean is something like "ethics is too complicated for simple, objective solutions." The fact that there can be such difference in ethical judgments among cultures and individuals, then, doesn't automatically mean that it's impossible to find at least some general moral principles on which we can all agree.

Studying cultural and individual variety may help us turn up information that is relevant to a philosophical inquiry. Why are varying practices accepted or condemned in this or that society? If you and I differ, what are our respective arguments? By looking

---

2. It's important to note that a few important philosophers have defended the idea that ethics is subjective and, strictly speaking, doesn't deal in "truth." The eighteenth-century British thinker David Hume, for example, claims that moral judgments are a function of feelings, not reason or facts. The twentieth-century British philosopher A. J. Ayer reduces a statement like "Stealing money is wrong" to "Stealing money—boo!!!" Discussions of theories of this sort take us into the domain philosophers call "meta-ethics," the analysis of the meaning and validity of the concepts we use when we do "normative ethics," that is, when we make ethical judgments about actions. Because this chapter focuses on normative ethics, we don't have the space to pursue this line of inquiry.

into these things, perhaps we can find something relevant to a rational, philosophical approach to understanding and evaluating human conduct.

Many people argue that "ethics is relative" because they see dangerous implications to the belief that there are objective ethical standards. They fear that this can be used as a defense for forcing cultures that are doing things "wrong" to change their ways, punishing people simply because they don't follow a society's norms, or stigmatizing otherwise good and decent individuals just because they think for themselves. Notice, however, how much this position is based on a belief in the fundamental importance of freedom, autonomy, and personal choice. If defenders of ethical relativism say that it's wrong for me to punish someone for his or her beliefs, they're actually—without realizing it—making a case for at least these as objective ethical principles that need to be respected.

The Philosophical Approach: Well-Being and Flourishing

If ethics is not a matter of religious rules, secular laws, cultural traditions, or personal feeling, what does it involve? Is there really a rational, secular, and philosophical standard we can use to evaluate human actions? Can such a standard of right and wrong be firm enough to provide dependability and consistency, yet flexible enough to accommodate differences in individual circumstances?

There is such an ethical standard, and it is surprisingly simple. The most basic standard used in a philosophical approach to ethics is nothing more sophisticated or mysterious than the real-life *well-being* or *flourishing* of the people involved. Philosophical ethics doesn't judge right and wrong in terms of sacred texts, divine will, subjective beliefs, personal feelings, the word of some authority, laws, or the traditions in a particular culture. Instead, it uses a standard that aims to be objective, neutral, rational, public, and secular—whether good or harm is experienced by the people involved, whether they have a reasonable opportunity for a successful and satisfying life, and whether individuals are being treated the way they're entitled to.

Putting this in the most general terms, we can say that from a philosophical perspective, what makes something an *ethical issue* is that it involves important issues of human well-being and flourishing. To the extent that an action advances, is conducive to, or maximizes human flourishing, it's *morally positive*. On the other hand, to the extent that an action prevents, retards, or minimizes the welfare of those involved, it is *morally negative*.

There's much to be said for using an approach based on *human well-being* and *flourishing* for trying to resolve disagreements about ethical issues. It is free of the problems that plague personal, emotional standards that can be neither explained nor defended. If we disagree about whether cheating on an anatomy final in a pre-med class is right or wrong, it's pointless for us to trade statements about how we *feel*. But it would certainly be productive for us to discuss the practical impact on the well-being of those involved and whether anyone involved is treated in a fundamentally disrespectful way.

Basing ethical evaluations on what promotes the well-being and flourishing of those involved has a simple, practical, and commonsense feel to it. However, the next question we need to address is obviously, "How do we know what promotes human *flourishing*?" Fortunately, the contemporary philosopher Martha Nussbaum gives us an excellent answer.

Flourishing is an important feature of Nussbaum's thought. This idea is central to her "capabilities approach" to ethics, which she developed to address critical questions related to social justice in the contemporary world.[3] One of its most important characteristics is that it has a biological basis. As she explains, *flourishing* incorporates a perspective that ultimately comes from Aristotle, the Greek thinker who was not only a philosopher but a competent biologist. As she puts it, "each creature has a characteristic set of capabilities, or capacities for functioning, distinctive of that species, and that those more rudimentary capacities need support from the material and social environment if the animal is to *flourish* in its distinctive way."[4]

If we link this with the scientific ideas of evolution and adaptation, we can say that beings have evolved *specific abilities or capabilities* in order to allow members of a species to have successful and satisfying lives. Therefore, if they are going to be able to develop these abilities and to *flourish*, their environment must provide them with *certain conditions*.

The conditions necessary for flourishing, then, aren't a matter of personal opinion or preference. The conditions necessary for a human being to *flourish* are the result of millions of years of evolution and adaptation. During this time, we developed distinctive traits, abilities, and behaviors that made it possible for our species to survive and prosper. Because *Homo sapiens* is a sophisticated species, each of us now requires a complex set of conditions to be met if we are to grow and develop as fully as possible into individuals who are not only physically and emotionally healthy but equipped with the various skills needed to operate successfully in our societies and to have a satisfying life.

What are those conditions? Nussbaum identifies ten "Central Capabilities." She believes that we need to experience at least a minimal level of each in order "to pursue a dignified and minimally flourishing life."[5] These include: life, physical and emotional health, safety, liberty, education, significant relationships, freedom of thought and conscience, equality, respect for one's dignity, participation in one's government, ownership of property, and rest.[6]

---

3. Martha C. Nussbaum, *Women and Human Development: The Capabilities Approach* (New York: Cambridge University Press, 2000); *Frontiers of Justice: Disability, Nationality, Species Membership* (Cambridge, MA: Harvard University Press, 2006); *Creating Capabilities: The Human Development Approach* (Cambridge, MA: Belknap Press of Harvard University Press, 2011).

4. Martha C. Nussbaum, "The Capabilities Approach and Animal Entitlements," in *The Oxford Handbook of Animal Ethics* (Oxford: Oxford University Press, 2011), 237; emphasis added. Because this approach recognizes that different species have different requirements in order to flourish, one of its great virtues is that it is particularly helpful in discussing interspecies ethics.

5. Nussbaum, *Creating Capabilities*, 33.

6. Nussbaum, *Creating Capabilities*, 33–34. For the sake of simplicity, we've referred so far only to human well-being and human needs as a basic standard in ethics. But don't mistake this as meaning that

Interestingly, Nussbaum's list is very similar to the United Nations' Universal Declaration of Human Rights, which is effectively another list of the conditions humans need to flourish. This document refers to *rights,* but it may just as well say the conditions that must be met if humans are to grow, develop, and flourish in a healthy fashion so as to have a reasonable opportunity for a successful and rudimentarily satisfying life. The document consists of thirty articles, but the main rights include: life itself, freedom, equality, personal security, protection by a just legal system, political rights, a private life, the ability to choose marriage and family, freedom of thought and action, access to the benefits of a society (government, culture, education, and protection against illness), work, and rest.[7]

Note that, like Nussbaum's list, these items can be grouped into two categories. First, there are *material* or *physical* conditions. The Declaration lists: life, liberty, security of person, freedom of movement, freedom of assembly, a certain standard of living, work, education, and rest. It also identifies material conditions that men and women need protection against: slavery, torture, interference with their private lives, and the like.

But the articles also talk about acceptable and unacceptable procedures or *ways of treating people.* We're told we have rights to equality before the law, fairness, a presumption of innocence, impartial tribunals, marriages based only on consent, and equal pay for equal work. And we're entitled to be protected against discrimination, arbitrary arrest, being accused of an offense that wasn't a crime when we did it, being deprived of our property for no reason, and so on.

Understanding flourishing this way, then, lets us make the following claims. *Actions that are ethically positive provide us with the conditions we need if we are to have the opportunity for a successful and rudimentarily satisfying life, because these are the conditions necessary for humans to grow, develop as fully as possible, and flourish. Ethically negative actions make it difficult or impossible for humans to flourish.*

Something for the Skeptics

We should pause at this point because some of you may be skeptical about some of these ideas.

Are these truly <u>needs</u>?

First, let's consider a possible objection that, except for things like food and shelter, we aren't talking about conditions we absolutely, positively *need* in order to flourish.

The simplest way to test whether something is *necessary* for a successful and satisfying life is to imagine what life would be like without it.

One of Nussbaum's detailed descriptions of a necessary condition for flourishing has to do with being treated with appropriate respect: "Having the social bases of self-respect

---

ethics doesn't apply to nonhumans. See Chapter 10, "Dolphins—Personhood, Rights, and Flourishing," where Nussbaum's concept of flourishing is applied to dolphins.

7. "The Universal Declaration of Human Rights of the United Nations," *General Assembly Resolution 217 A(III) of 10 December 1948.*

and nonhumiliation; being able to be treated as a dignified being whose worth is equal to that of others. This entails provisions of nondiscrimination on the basis of race, sex, sexual orientation, ethnicity, caste, religion, national origin."[8]

Because humans are so adaptable, most of us could probably adjust to living in a society where we were regularly disrespected and discriminated against. But how successful could you be at having the life you wanted? How much of your potential could you actually develop? You would constantly be the target of unfair bias. You would be denied opportunities for such critical requirements as a decent place to live and a job of your choice. You would be thwarted at every turn. At the same time, you would see the people who were victimizing you getting benefits they didn't deserve. Human beings—no matter what the traditions or norms of their culture—don't experience frustration, discrimination, and disrespect as satisfying. Being told every day that you are inferior would eat away at your self-respect. These are hardly conditions that would let anyone grow, develop their potential as much as possible, and flourish.

No matter what part of the world people live in, no matter what the traditions of their culture, no ordinary human being is going to experience anything but frustration and dissatisfaction at being deprived of the opportunity to develop his or her abilities.

Admittedly, we can find examples of autocratic societies in which people seem relatively content with circumstances, despite not having many basic human rights respected. This, however, is simply a testimony to human adaptability. To say that people have made peace with this as their lot in life is different from saying they're flourishing. Philippa Foot is particularly eloquent on this point. She writes,

> Granted that it is wrong to assume identity of aim between peoples of different cultures; nevertheless there is a great deal that all men have in common. All need affection, the cooperation of others, a place in a community, and help in trouble. It isn't true to suppose that human beings can flourish without these things—being isolated, despised or embattled, or without courage or hope. We are not, therefore, simply expressing values that we happen to have if we think of some moral systems as good moral systems and others as bad. Communities as well as individuals can live wisely or unwisely, and this is largely the result of their values and the codes of behavior that they teach. Looking at these societies, and critically also at our own, we surely have some idea of how things work out and why they work out as they do. We do not have to suppose it is just as good to promote pride of place and the desire to get an advantage over other men as it is to have an ideal of affection and respect. These things have different harvests, and unmistakably different connections with human good.[9]

---

8. Nussbaum, *Creating Capabilities*, 34.
9. Philippa Foot, "Moral Relativism," in *Relativism, Cognitive and Moral*, ed. Jack Meiland and Michael Krausz (Notre Dame, IN: University of Notre Dame Press, 1982), 164.

Four Approaches to Ethics

If we look carefully at the details of what Nussbaum and the Declaration say we need, we can find four important requirements. We need to be protected from material harm. We need to be treated with appropriate respect. There are times we need the care and assistance of others. Our actions toward others will either be motivated by respect for these facts or not. These requirements actually point to four different perspectives philosophers have developed about how we determine the ethical character of actions.

> **consequentialist** A consequentialist approach to ethics claims that the ethical character of an action depends on whether its consequences are positive or negative.
>
> **utilitarianism** Utilitarianism is a teleological ethical theory advanced by Jeremy Bentham and John Stuart Mill. It uses pleasure and notions like "the greatest good of the greatest number" as standards for judging the morality of actions.

One school of thought claims that the ethical character of an action depends on whether its *consequences* are positive or negative. This **consequentialist** approach focuses on the actual, material conditions of life we need in order to flourish. Those actions that give us more of the specific "stuff of life" that we need are judged *morally good*. Actions that result in less satisfying material conditions, or that prevent or inhibit flourishing, are labeled in some way *morally wrong*. The most important consequentialist school of thought is called **utilitarianism**.

A second approach holds that the consequences of an action are less important than the nature of *the action itself*. Thinkers with this point of view argue that actions are *intrinsically* right or wrong. If actions respect principles of dignity, honesty, equality, and fairness, they're morally right. Actions that deceive, manipulate, and discriminate are morally wrong.

This approach to ethics is more formally called **deontological** ethics. *Deontos* is the Greek word meaning "duty." So deontological thinkers believe that when faced with an ethical dilemma, we should ask, "What is my duty or obligation in this situation to the people involved? How should I treat them?"

> **deontological** A deontological theory of ethics argues that actions have a moral character apart from their consequences.
>
> **virtue ethics** Virtue ethics focuses on positive character traits like honesty and generosity that should be behind our actions.

A third school of thought focuses on the fundamentally social character of human experience and on the fact that, ultimately, we cannot survive, never mind flourish, without the assistance of others. This ethic of care evaluates actions from the point of view of our moral responsibility to support those in need of assistance and to prevent harm.

Finally, virtue ethics calls attention to what produces our actions—our character.

Consequentialist Ethics: Utilitarianism

A consequentialist approach is both simple and practical. It says, "Something is right or wrong depending on whether it produces tangible good or harm for the people involved and allows or prevents them from flourishing." The school of thought called *utilitarianism* provides us with the clearest explanation of consequentialist ethics. Devised by Jeremy Bentham and elaborated by John Stuart Mill, utilitarianism argues that the ethical character of an action depends on how much pleasure or pain results from it.

Jeremy Bentham

A number of eighteenth-century thinkers advanced the commonsense and practical idea that the best actions are those that promote the greatest happiness of the greatest number of people. The British thinker Jeremy Bentham, however, was the first person to develop the idea into a formal theory, which he called "utilitarianism."

Jeremy Bentham (1748–1832) attended Queen's College, Oxford, and studied law at Lincoln's Inn in London, but he was more a practical reformer than a lawyer or philosopher. A champion of legal and prison reform in the England of his day, Bentham became the leader of a political movement that ultimately did achieve some important reforms. Bentham was also the founding thinker of utilitarianism, and his most famous work is *An Introduction to the Principles of Morals and Legislation*. Friend of James Mill, Bentham was godfather to another powerful utilitarian thinker, John Stuart Mill. Bentham bequeathed his entire estate to the newly founded University College London on the condition that his remains be present at all board meetings. Bentham's embalmed body is still displayed in a movable glass case in the main hall of the college.

Bentham was a practical man who was deeply impressed by **empiricism**, the philosophical outlook that stresses the importance of basing knowledge on objective, observable facts and physical evidence. Thus Bentham thought that actions and policies should be evaluated according to how much tangible good they produce. Bentham called this way of thinking "utilitarianism" because he believed that what is important is how *useful* something is in producing benefits, that is, how much "utility" it has for making people's lives better.[10] Bentham also insisted that actions and their consequences be evaluated in a fair, reasonable, and objective manner. His goal was to make the determination of right and wrong as impartial and objective a process as weighing objects on a public scale.

"Utility" and Pleasure

Given his approach, Bentham needed to articulate a precise and practical idea of what makes something *useful*. He does this with the ordinary concept of *pleasure*. In his

---

10. If you have studied economics, you may already have heard about utilitarianism because in modern economics the "utility" of a good or service lies in the benefit, or satisfaction, it brings to the consumer.

Introduction to the Principles of Morals and Legislation, he writes,

> empiricism Empiricism is the philosophical outlook that stresses the importance of basing knowledge on objective, observable facts and physical evidence.

By utility is meant that property in any object, whereby it tends to produce benefit, advantage, pleasure, good, or happiness (all this in the present case comes to the same thing) or (what comes again to the same thing) to prevent the happening of mischief, pain, evil, or unhappiness to the party whose interest is considered; if that party be the community in general, then the happiness of the community; if a particular individual, then the happiness of that individual.[11]

Linking this explicitly to ethical judgments, Bentham claims, "Nature has placed mankind under the governance of two sovereign masters, *pain* and *pleasure*. It is for them alone to point out what we ought to do. . . . The standard of right and wrong . . . [is] fastened to their throne."[12] As far as utilitarianism is concerned, an act is morally good to the extent that it produces a greater balance of pleasure over pain for the largest number of people involved. Therefore, no action is intrinsically right or wrong. If a lie or some "forbidden" pleasure truly did not hurt anyone, it would make no sense to Bentham to say either act was "wrong."

Measuring Pleasure: Bentham's "Hedonistic Calculus"

But Bentham does not leave things at a general, theoretical level. To ensure that the evaluation of actions should be fair, reasonable, and objective, he devises a method of measuring how much pleasure or pain an action produces. He calls this the **hedonistic calculus**. ("Hedonism" comes from the Greek word meaning "pleasure.")

The hedonistic calculus identifies seven different characteristics of the pleasure or pain that results from a particular action:

> hedonistic calculus The hedonistic calculus is Jeremy Bentham's system for measuring the amount of pleasure and pain that results from an action. It takes into account seven dimensions of a pleasure or pain: intensity, duration, certainty or uncertainty, propinquity or remoteness, fecundity, purity, and extent.

1. The *intensity* of the feeling

2. How long it lasts—its *duration*

3. The odds that the action will actually produce this feeling—its *certainty* or *uncertainty*

4. How soon the feelings will be experienced—its *propinquity* or *remoteness*

5. The likelihood that this experience will produce even more pleasure in the future—its *fecundity*

6. The chance it will produce pain or unhappiness—its *purity*

7. The number of people affected—its *extent*

---

11. Jeremy Bentham, *Introduction to the Principles of Morals and Legislation*, https://www.econlib.org/library/Bentham/bnthPML.html

12. Bentham, *Introduction to the Principles of Morals and Legislation*.

Bentham did not provide explicit directions about how to use the calculus. But if we assign an arbitrary numerical value to each of these seven categories for every option we are considering and factor in everyone involved, we can calculate the totals for each action and get an idea of what Bentham has in mind. Whichever action has the highest total, then, is morally best.

If you apply the hedonistic calculus to specific cases, you'll see there's much to be said for what Bentham argues. (Try your hand at one of the cases in the questions at the end of this chapter, for example.) By requiring scores for seven different categories, the calculus forces us to look at aspects of an action we otherwise might ignore. If we use it correctly, we consider longer-term effects (fecundity and purity) as well as immediate consequences. It is also egalitarian. No one person's pleasure or pain counts for more than any other person's.

Bentham seems to have given us precisely what he wanted to—an objective way to identify which actions produce the greatest balance of pleasure over pain. And that, for Bentham, is all that right and wrong amount to. In reality, however, to resolve an ethical dilemma, we have to do more than grab a calculator and figure out the totals. Bentham's approach is appealing, but it has an important defect.

Go back to the example we started this chapter with—racist Jeff getting Tyson to withdraw his application to the fraternity. Imagine that Jeff tells a bunch of his racist buddies about his success. He also takes lifelong pride in what he did and regularly brags about it to other racists. Meanwhile, Tyson looks at it as just another example of what he's encountered too often. He tries to put it behind him and mentions it to only a couple of friends.

If we were to work through Bentham's hedonistic calculus on this question, Jeff's actions would probably come out a clear winner because more people take pleasure from what he did. And this reveals a fatal flaw in the hedonistic calculus. It measures only the *amount* of pleasure or pain that results from an action. As a result, the pleasure of Jeff and his friends outweighs the pain of Tyson, no matter how intense the unhappiness that one person feels. By the same logic, we could say that slavery is morally justifiable as long as it produces more pleasure in the lives of slave owners and everyone who benefits from an economy based on slave labor than unhappiness in the lives of comparatively fewer slaves.

Bentham excludes the *kind* or *quality* of pleasure and pain involved—deliberately. He actually did consider the issue of kinds of pleasure—but he rejected it. As he put it, "pushpin [a child's game] is as good as poetry."[13] One of his younger contemporaries, however, disagreed. And he developed a revised version of utilitarianism to take the notion of the quality of pleasures into account. This philosopher was Bentham's godson, John Stuart Mill.

---

13. Bentham, *Introduction to the Principles of Morals and Legislation.*

John Stuart Mill

The Quality of Pleasure

John Stuart Mill is, like Bentham, a consequentialist thinker. Mill accepted Bentham's basic idea that the appropriate standard for evaluating the ethical character of actions is the pleasure, or happiness, that results from an action. He writes in *Utilitarianism*:

> The creed which accepts as the foundation of morals "utility" or the "greatest happiness principle" holds that actions are right in proportion as they tend to promote happiness; wrong as they tend to produce the reverse of happiness. By happiness is intended pleasure and the absence of pain; by unhappiness, pain and the privation of pleasure.[14]

Mill, however, rejects Bentham's belief that all pleasures are equal. He insists that there exists a whole range of pleasures—some lower, some higher. He then argues that the better pleasures are so much better that a small amount of high-quality pleasure outweighs a much larger amount of low-quality pleasure.

Mill's revision of Bentham's schema makes sense. Even our ordinary intuition tells us that some pleasures are better than others, and some pains are worse than others. Going back to the case of Tyson and Jeff, the pleasures of feeling safe from threats and discrimination combined with the pleasure Tyson would experience in the fraternity are of a much higher quality than whatever pleasure racist Jeff and his friends would feel in connection with harassing Tyson.

Identifying Higher and Lower Pleasures

However, how do we accurately and fairly differentiate between low-quality and high-quality pleasures? According to Mill, we should rely on the judgment of people who already have experienced the range of pleasures involved. He writes:

John Stuart Mill (1806–1873) was the most important British philosopher during the nineteenth century and remains one of the most persuasive representatives of liberalism. Mill was educated by his father, James Mill, to be a defender of utilitarianism. After a serious bout with depression when he was twenty, Mill rebelled against the narrow, unemotional, and analytical way he had been trained, and he significantly broadened his philosophical outlook. He became an important administrator of the East India Company and served in Parliament toward the end of his life. Mill was one of only a few philosophers to address the subjugation of women, a concern that no doubt was sparked by his long relationship with Harriet Taylor. Mill and Mrs. Taylor met when Mill was twenty-five, and the two remained close platonic friends for nearly twenty years. Three years after the death of Mrs. Taylor's husband, the two married. Harriet died only six years later, however. Mill was convinced that Harriet would have been recognized as one of the time's leading thinkers had she been a man, and he claimed that she was a major influence on his thinking.

---

14. John Stuart Mill, *Utilitarianism* (Indianapolis: Hackett Publishing Co., 2001), 7.

> If I am asked what I mean by difference of quality of pleasures, or what makes one pleasure more valuable than another, . . . there is but one possible answer. Of two pleasures, if there be one to which all or almost all who have experience of both give a decided preference, . . . that is the more desirable pleasure.[15]

This makes sense. Who is best qualified to separate higher- from lower-quality anything? The person who has the greatest amount of experience with both. If you want a good sound system, you don't rely on the opinion of someone whose idea of "great sound" is an AM radio in a 1960 Chevrolet.

Why not approach pleasure and a sense of well-being the same way? The opinion of someone who has always been a lying, manipulative troublemaker is poorly informed and one-sided. So is the opinion of some sheltered innocent who knows nothing of the pleasures associated with greed, lust, and selfishness. We want someone who knows all sides of an issue and can make a truly informed judgment. If such a person, having experienced all the pleasures, claims that some are indeed better than others, shouldn't we listen?

What does Mill say these experienced individuals can tell us? He explains,

> Now it is an unquestionable fact that those who are equally acquainted with and equally capable of appreciating and enjoying both do give a most marked preference to the manner of existence which employs their higher faculties. Few human creatures would consent to be changed into any of the lower animals for a promise of the fullest allowance of a beast's pleasures; no intelligent human being would consent to be a fool, no instructed person would be an ignoramus, no person of feeling and conscience would be selfish and base, even though they should be persuaded that the fool, the dunce, or the rascal is better satisfied with his lot than they are with theirs. . . . Whoever supposes that this preference takes place at a sacrifice of happiness—that the superior being, in anything like equal circumstances, is not happier than the inferior—confounds the two very different ideas of happiness and content. It is indisputable that the being whose capacities of enjoyment are low has the greatest chance of having them fully satisfied; and a highly endowed being will always feel that any happiness which he can look for, as the world is constituted, is imperfect. But he can learn to bear its imperfections, if they are at all bearable; and they will not make him envy the being who is indeed unconscious of the imperfections, but only because he feels not at all the good which those imperfections qualify. It is better to be a human being dissatisfied than a pig satisfied; better to be Socrates dissatisfied than a fool satisfied. And if the fool, or the pig, are of a different opinion, it is because they only know their own side of the question. The other party to the comparison knows both sides.[16]

---

15. Mill, *Utilitarianism*, 8.

16. Mill, *Utilitarianism*, 9–10. Be sure you realize that Mill is not making an illegitimate appeal to authority here—whether it be the authority of experience or the authority of Socrates. Whether it involves determining quality in sound equipment, clothes, sports gear, or pleasure, people with the experience that you lack should be able to show you, on the basis of that experience, how to tell the difference between low and high quality. It is not a matter of taking someone's word. If you let yourself be guided by them, you too could have experiences that would let you develop your judgment.

Mill also suggests a consensus among people who have experienced the full range of pleasures. Such people would say that the "higher" pleasures include intelligence, mental pleasures, education, sensitivity to others, a sense of morality, and health. Among the "lower" pleasures they would place stupidity, ignorance, selfishness, indolence, and physical pleasure—especially sensual indulgence.

You can test Mill's idea for yourself by taking a few minutes to fill out this questionnaire. For each of the following items, indicate how important or serious you think the pleasures and pains are. Use a scale of: LOW, MEDIUM, HIGH. (LOW pleasures still feel good, but, in some way, you feel they aren't quite as good as MEDIUM and HIGH ones.)

Pleasures

1. getting an A in a difficult course

2. getting an A in an easy course in which everyone else gets an A

3. getting an A in a course by cheating

4. getting your ideal job because you were the best candidate

5. getting your ideal job because your parents knew your boss (better-qualified people were passed over)

6. sexual activity with someone with whom you have no special feelings (you're both unattached)

7. sexual activity with someone you're deeply in love with

8. sexual activity with someone you have no special feelings for while you're in love and committed to someone else

Pains/Unhappiness/Feelings That Are in Some Other Way Uncomfortable or Undesirable

(LOW pains are more bearable or less important pains; HIGH pains are more serious or "worse" pains than LOW or MEDIUM ones)

9. the fear you feel at a haunted house at an amusement park

10. the fear you feel as a tire blows out and your car spins out of control on the highway

11. being punished for something that you knew was wrong when you did it

12. being punished for something that you didn't do

13. missing a party so that you can keep your promise to help your best friend study

14. the work and sacrifice involved in taking care of someone close to you who is very sick

15. being physically abused by a significant other

16. discovering that someone stole something out of your car

I have given this questionnaire to hundreds of students in my ethics classes over the years, and their answers have been remarkably consistent. It would be surprising if your answers were very different. Virtually without exception, my students have answered:

Pleasures

1. HIGH
2. MEDIUM
3. LOW
4. HIGH
5. MEDIUM
6. MEDIUM
7. HIGH
8. LOW

Pains

9. LOW
10. HIGH
11. MEDIUM
12. HIGH
13. LOW
14. LOW
15. HIGH
16. HIGH

This questionnaire does two things. First, it provides a simple illustration of Mill's idea that there are qualitative differences among various pleasures and pains—differences that Bentham rejects. Second, it puts to the test Mill's claim that people with roughly the same experience of various pleasures and pains will agree as to which are better and which are worse. The results suggest that there is at least some reason to think he is correct on both counts.

Identifying Long-Term Consequences

The second way that Mill improves on Bentham's utilitarianism lies in his astute treatment of the long-term consequences of actions. Mill uses the act of lying as his example. Most of us probably feel that unless we lie so often that people stop believing us, there really are no long-term disadvantages to lying. To this, Mill would respond that we simply are not identifying all the long-term consequences of a lie. In the *very* long view, Mill says, truth telling is one of the most essential conditions for human well-being, or happiness. Consequently, he claims,

> Any, even unintentional, deviation from truth . . . [weakens] the trustworthiness of human assertion, which is not only the principal support of all present social well-being, but the insufficiency of which does more than any one thing that can be named to keep back civilization, virtue, everything on which human happiness on the largest scale depends.[17]

It may seem to you that Mill exaggerates here. His point, however, is that to identify *all* the consequences that result from an action, we have to see just how far the ripples caused by our actions reach. In this case, Mill says, *any* instance of lying makes all of us a little less likely to believe each other, and you can probably see how this might be so. If you think about how this would play out over the very long term with most of us lying at some point or another, life would definitely end up worse rather than better for everyone.

Problems with Mill's Theory: A Case of Cheating

Despite Mill's improvements of utilitarianism, there is still a fundamental problem with his ideas. Imagine the case of Susan who cheats to get into medical school and takes a place that would otherwise have gone to you. Don't assume, however, Mill's approach would condemn her. After becoming a physician, Susan decides to practice in a rural community chronically short of medical assistance. The pleasures associated with health and helping people rank high in Mill's scheme. Susan will undoubtedly produce substantial high-quality pleasure through-out her career—a career she is sure she can have only by cheating. Taking quality and quantity into account, it looks as if Susan might produce enough pleasure to offset any unhappiness she causes by her dishonesty.

If we say the cheating is ethically acceptable, however, we are actually saying that *the ends justify the means.* And if this is true, given the right conditions, absolutely anything can be ethically justified—murder, child abuse, rape, theft, tyranny, slavery, genocide, and so on—as long as it ultimately produces enough high-quality good.

Deontological Ethics

As you have seen, Bentham's and Mill's approaches can be used to defend some otherwise questionable actions. In response, another group of philosophers, one that rejects consequentialist ethics, says that in order to determine right and wrong we must examine the *actions* people do, not the consequences. This is the *deontological* approach to ethics.

---

17. Mill, *Utilitarianism*, 23.

The "Principle of the Thing"

Deontological ethics is in many ways easier to apply than consequentialist ethics. We can ignore the consequences of an action and simply ask, "Is this an appropriate action for one person to take toward another?"

Deontological ethics appreciates that human beings need to be treated in certain ways in order to flourish. It recognizes that we are constituted in such a way that experiencing unfairness, manipulation, and deceit will significantly diminish our sense of well-being, while being treated with honesty and justice will increase it. A deontological approach to ethics evaluates an action's *intrinsic* strengths and weaknesses.

All of us commonly use a deontological approach to ethics on those occasions where we rustle up our moral courage, ignore the consequences of an act we're considering, and decide instead on a course of action based strictly on "the principle of the thing." At times like this, we believe we simply have a *duty* to act in a particular way, whatever the outcome.

Immanuel Kant

As Bentham and Mill are the classic representatives of consequentialist ethics, so the great German thinker Immanuel Kant created the model for deontological ethics.

Duty and Dignity

Kant's ethics is based on the idea that actions are intrinsically right or wrong. And in our dealings with each other, one way to figure out the difference is to apply Kant's idea that human beings have intrinsic worth by virtue of being unique creatures—free and autonomous beings—who have a *dignity* that must be respected.

Dignity is a special concept for Kant. He separates the world into things with a "price" and things with "dignity." The former are objects that can be bought and sold. But as individuals, we have no price; we have a dignity. We and everyone else like us are entitled to respect for our dignity, freedom, and desire to control our lives.

Immanuel Kant (1724–1804) spent his entire life in the Prussian city of Königsberg. After years as a tutor and lecturer, Kant was appointed a professor at the University of Königsberg. Supposedly, Kant's life was so regular that his neighbors would set their clocks by his daily walk, yet he also had a reputation as a witty and entertaining host at the frequent dinner parties he gave. Kant's initial intellectual reputation came from his writings on physics, astronomy, and metaphysics. But beginning in 1781, when Kant was fifty-seven, the philosopher issued a series of books that transformed the shape of philosophy and established Kant as one of philosophy's greatest thinkers. Kant first wrote *The Critique of Pure Reason*, then during the next nine years he published the *Prolegomena to Any Future Metaphysics, Grounding for the Metaphysic of Morals, Metaphysical Foundations of Natural Science, The Critique of Practical Reason,* and *The Critique of Judgment*.

Kant's Ethical Standard: The Categorical Imperative

On the basis of Kant's ideas about duty, intrinsic worth, and dignity, he formulated a basic moral rule by which everyone could live ethically. He called this the **categorical imperative**. By this he meant a command we must follow (an imperative) that holds in every case without exception (categorically). Actions that followed this command would, he thought, be right actions; those that did not would be wrong. Kant states the categori-

> **categorical imperative** The categorical imperative is Immanuel Kant's conception of a universal moral law. One formulation of this principle is "Act in such a way that you treat humanity, whether in your own person or in the person of any other, always at the same time as an end and never simply as a means."

cal imperative in a few different ways in his classic work *Grounding for the Metaphysics of Morals*. We will look at just one version—the one that's closest to the concept of *dignity*.

Means and Ends

The formulation of the categorical imperative we're going to examine reads: "Act in such a way that you treat humanity, whether in your own person or in the person of another, always at the same time as an end and never simply as a means."[18] What does this mean?

What Kant seems to have in mind is that to treat someone as an "end" is to treat him or her with all the respect due to a human being. We respect people's dignity, their freedom, and their autonomy. When we treat people as "means," on the other hand, we use them for our ends, not theirs. Through lies, coercion, or some other kind of deceit, we use them as a tool to get what we want. We do not respect their freedom and dignity.

A False Promise

Kant illustrates this with the example of a man who needs to borrow money but knows he'll never be able to repay it. If he lies and promises to repay it nonetheless, has he done anything wrong? Kant's answer: yes. "[T]he man who intends to make a false promise will immediately see that he intends to make use of another man merely as a means to an end which the latter does not likewise hold. For the man whom I want to use for my own purposes by such a promise cannot possibly concur with my way of acting toward him . . .".[19] Think about this as it might apply to your own life. Under what circumstances would you make a promise to someone when you have no intention of keeping it? When you know it's the only way to get what you want. Only a lie will persuade the other person to do what you want—something they'd never freely agree to. You use them like a tool, an object for your own purposes—a means to your end. Because such an action fails to respect the freedom, choice, dignity, and autonomy of the person being deceived, Kant says it's wrong.

---

18. Immanuel Kant, *Grounding for the Metaphysics of Morals*, trans. James Ellington (Indianapolis: Hackett Publishing Co., 1981), 36.

19. Kant, *Grounding for the Metaphysics of Morals*, 37.

The Strengths and Weaknesses of Deontological Ethics

Kant's approach to ethics has some important advantages. His "categorical imperative" gives us consistent standards of morality. Actions are right or wrong no matter what the circumstances or consequences. The emphasis on *dignity*—our nature as free, autonomous beings entitled to make our own decisions and be treated with appropriate respect—narrows our focus in evaluating actions.

As much as a deontological approach adds to ethics, it also has limitations. It may appeal to our desire for consistency and stability, but this can slide into a rigid and inflexible standard that virtually all of us would find morally offensive. We all can imagine cases where saying that a particular action is always wrong doesn't seem realistic. If a gun-waving maniac bursts into your philosophy class and demands that your teacher tell him where you are so that he can kill you, surely it would be defensible—even good—for your professor to lie. Stealing food from someone who has plenty in order to save your starving infant may not be the best way to handle a situation, but surely it is ethically superior to letting your child die.

Ethics of Care

The third approach to ethics we're going to look at actually grew out of a debate not among philosophers but between two moral development psychologists: Lawrence Kohlberg and Carol Gilligan.

Kohlberg believed that he had identified the characteristics of a fully developed moral sense in the human personality and that he could chart the stages people go through in developing their ability to reason about ethical issues. The most advanced stage was characterized by an "ethic of justice" that assessed behavior according to universal, abstract moral principles. This is essentially a deontological approach.

Taking her cue from the fact that Kohlberg's initial studies did not include any women or girls and that the application of his ideas consistently placed female subjects in lower stages, Carol Gilligan discovered the weakness in Kohlberg's approach. His "ethic of justice" failed to appreciate an alternative ethical approach based on a moral responsibility to support those in need of assistance and to prevent harm—an "ethic of care."

The central moral command of the ethic of care is to "discern and alleviate the 'real and recognizable trouble' of this world."[20] By contrast, the prime moral imperative of the ethic of justice is "to respect the rights of others and thus to protect from interference the rights to life and self-fulfillment."[21] Gilligan calls the ethic of justice a *morality of rights* and the ethic of care a *morality of responsibility*.

---

20. Carol Gilligan, *In a Different Voice: Psychological Theory and Women's Development* (Cambridge, MA: Harvard University Press, 1982), 100.
21. Gilligan, *In a Different Voice*, 100.

Although it was Gilligan who first recognized the ethic of care, this approach to ethics has been developed and advanced by a group of feminist philosophers that includes Annette Baier, Virginia Held, Alison Jaggar, Eva Feder Kittay, Nel Noddings, Sara Ruddick, and Joan Tronto. We're going to focus on Virginia Held's contributions.[22]

Experience, Emotions, and Equity

The primary features of consequentialist and deontological approaches that thinkers like Held object to relate to their reliance on abstract general principles that are supposed to be applied impartially and objectively after a strictly rational analysis. These thinkers also point to the habit of traditional approaches to conduct ethical inquiry via theoretical and hypothetical cases viewed unemotionally at a distance. Held proposes something very different.

First, instead of claiming that an ethics of care should be seen as the "one, true" theory whose strengths have rendered consequentialist and deontological approaches obsolete, Held sees its value more as a "method of moral inquiry and process of moral improvement."[23] If we recall Janice Moulton's critique of traditional philosophical approaches we saw in Chapter 2, we might say that Held is less concerned with defeating intellectual adversaries than helping people handle real-life ethical challenges.

This real-world orientation puts a premium on what Held calls "moral experience":

> *Moral* experience is the experience of consciously choosing to act, or to refrain from acting, on grounds by which we are trying conscientiously to be guided. *Moral* experience is the experience of accepting or rejecting moral positions for what we take to be good moral reasons or well-founded moral intuitions or on the basis of what we take to be justifiable moral feelings. *Moral* experience is the experience of approving or disapproving of actions or states of affairs of which we are aware and of evaluating the feelings we have and the relationships we are in. And it is experience as subjectively engaged in, not as studied by a scientific observer.[24]

---

22. "Care ethics" has emerged since the 1980s as a philosophically sophisticated alternative approach to ethics. Accordingly, it has led to the exploration of a wide range of questions. What are the relative roles of reason and emotion in giving us morally relevant knowledge? Do care ethics and traditional approaches to ethics rest on different modes of self-definition? Do care ethics express more of our social dimension, while traditional approaches proceed from our autonomous character? Does an ethic of care provide a full account of the ethical dimensions of an issue or is it simply a necessary supplement and corrective to traditional approaches? Given the limits of this chapter, we cannot explore all the important topics or thinkers associated with care ethics, but I encourage you to explore these important issues on your own.

23. Virginia Held, "Feminist Moral Inquiry and the Feminist Future," in *Justice and Care: Essential Readings in Feminist Ethics*, ed. Virginia Held (Boulder, CO: Westview Press, 1995), 166.

24. Held, "Feminist Moral Inquiry and the Feminist Future," 154.

She argues that morality should be seen as the domain of lived, human experience—not imaginative and dramatic hypotheticals we will never encounter. It combines reason and emotion, real persons, and relevant context. An ethic of care worries less about legalistic precedents than determining what is fitting or appropriate to a particular ethical dilemma faced by specific individuals.

Emotions

One of the most important differences between an ethic of care and traditional approaches is the respect given to emotions. Historically, the only role that philosophers see for emotions is helping us do what our *intellect* tells us is the right thing. Held, however, sees emotions as a critical source for understanding the ethical issue at hand. As she explains:

> Many feminists argue, in contrast, that the emotions have an important function in developing moral understanding itself, in helping us decide what the recommendations of morality themselves ought to be. Feelings, they say, should be respected by morality rather than dismissed as lacking impartiality. Yes, there are morally harmful emotions, such as prejudice, hatred, desire for revenge, blind egotism, and so forth. But to rid moral theory of harmful emotions by banishing all emotion is misguided. Such emotions as empathy, concern for others, hopefulness, and indignation in the face of cruelty—all these may be crucial in developing appropriate moral positions. An adequate moral theory should be built on appropriate feelings as well as on appropriate reasoning.[25]

The idea that emotions are an appropriate instrument for moral understanding makes sense. After all, emotions evolved as a mechanism to tell us something about the outside world. Imagine we're out for a walk in the woods, we hear a loud "crack" and see a large tree start falling right toward us. Interaction between our brain's prefrontal cortex and amygdala generates a "flight" response, and we automatically run to safety—no doubt more quickly than if we'd stood there doing a rational calculation.

At the same time, Held's distinction between morally harmful emotions and positive emotions is critical to bear in mind. The heart, like the head, is not always right. If, nervous after our encounter with the falling tree, we come upon what looks like a large, dangerous snake, we'd probably take off again without thinking, in what's called an "amygdala hijack." It would only be after we felt safe and let the parts of our brain that handle memories and judgment go to work that we'd realize it was just a big stick.

Still, when it comes to understanding an ethical issue, emotions like empathy, compassion, and care reveal features of an ethical dilemma that consequentialist and deontological approaches can't.

---

25. Held, "Feminist Moral Inquiry and the Feminist Future," 157.

Equality/Equity?

Another important feature of an ethic of care is its emphasis on the principle of equity. While an ethic of justice stresses the importance of treating everyone *equally*, an ethic of care argues for treating people in a way that's *appropriate to the circumstances and context.* That is, an ethic of care makes a principle of *equity* central.

While equality calls for strict impartiality and blind justice, equity isn't blind at all. It looks very carefully at the particulars of a situation and asks that people be treated differently if they have different needs. Whenever we make exceptions to policies because of extenuating circumstances, we decide according to a principle of equity.

It's important to realize that in order to get the kind of detailed information required for an appropriate response to an ethical problem, a principle of equity values direct, personal *experience* with the issue at hand. How else would we be able to determine what's the right "fit" for this particular situation? As Virginia Held points out, we aren't talking about "the constricted experience of mere empirical observation. It is the lived experience of feeling as well as thinking, of acting as well as receiving impressions, and of connectedness to other persons as well as of self."[26]

A Final Evaluation of an Ethic of Care

An ethic of care originated as a corrective to important weaknesses in an ethic of justice, and we can see ways in which it has succeeded. Its central moral principle is more down to earth than an abstract, deontological concept of justice. It regards the emotions as a significant source of information for understanding and resolving ethical issues. It attempts to work with the complexities of real-life moral dilemmas by stressing the importance of context, equity, and experience.

However, this perspective also suffers from some flaws. As compassionate as it is to recognize the special features of every situation, and to argue that every solution must be tailored to the circumstances, such a perspective poses major practical problems. When every case is "unique" and all circumstances are "extenuating," there is virtually no predictability about what will count as ethically acceptable and unacceptable behavior. Such a narrow focus on the particularities of a situation risks ignoring implications for the bigger picture, that is, losing sight of the forest for the trees. The emphasis on emotions and relationships opens the door for idiosyncratic or self-serving emotional perspectives to be regarded as legitimate.

Virtue Ethics: Aristotle Revisited

The fact that emotions are seen in a largely positive light in an ethic of care might lead you to re-examine the situation from Chapter 4 involving Richard at the baseball game.

---

26. Held, "Feminist Moral Inquiry and the Feminist Future," 154.

Even if his actions aren't totally excusable, do his anger and hair-trigger temper mitigate his culpability? We saw that Aristotle said no because he argued that Richard was responsible for the shape of his character and personality. And this brings us to the final approach to ethics: virtue ethics.

Virtue ethics is in many ways a very traditional and non-philosophical approach to ethics. Instead of analyzing the positive and negative consequences of what we do or brooding about whether our actions follow Kant's categorical imperative, the question is whether our deeds are honest, truthful, and generous, for example. Are our actions expressions of positive personality traits typically thought of as moral *virtues*?

Thinkers debate how many moral virtues there are. Traditional candidates include such traits as: honesty, courage, compassion, generosity, fidelity, integrity, fairness, self-control, civility, compassion, friendliness, kindness, prudence, justice, humanity, temperance, transcendence, and wisdom. Aristotle offers his own list of moral virtues: courage, self-control, generosity, magnificence, high-mindedness, appropriate ambition, gentleness, truthfulness, wittiness, friendliness, modesty, and righteous indignation.[27] The premise underlying any list is that these traits make it more likely that we and the people with whom we interact will be better able to flourish and enjoy a satisfying life.

However, when Aristotle asks if our actions manifest moral virtues, he sets the bar pretty high. He examines not just *what* we do, but *why* and *how* we do it. The question isn't *"Did we do the right thing?"* but *"Are we a good person?"* From Aristotle's perspective, virtue ethics is about *character*, not actions. That is, our actions are morally good only if we do them *in the same way that a truly good person does*. Aristotle explains,

> But for actions expressing virtue to be done temperately or justly and hence well it does not suffice that they are themselves in the right state. Rather, the agent must also be in the right state when he does them. First, he must know that he is doing virtuous actions; second, he must decide on them, and decide on them for themselves; and, third, he must also do them from a firm and unchanging state.[28]

From Aristotle's perspective, we don't get credit for doing the right thing as a way to impress someone, if we do it resentfully, or after lots of inner turmoil about whether we really want to do the right thing. Instead, it's all about character—and whether our personality is thoroughly defined by positive traits. The goal is less about doing good actions and more about acquiring the character of a good person.

Virtue Ethics: Strengths and Weaknesses

There's an obvious appeal to the fact that virtue ethics gives us a less technical way to evaluate our behavior. Everyone has a commonsense understanding of *truthfulness* and

---

27. Aristotle, *Nicomachean Ethics*, 1107a30–1108b10.
28. Aristotle, *Nicomachean Ethics*, 1105a30.

generosity—which can't be said for *categorical imperative*. And many organizations have adopted sets of values they hope will serve as a guide for people working there.

At the same time, becoming something of a moral paragon (which Aristotle seems to call for) is no small challenge. And virtue ethics gives us no obvious help when we face a situation in which virtues clash. Kennedy has a drunken one-nighter and is immediately filled with so much guilt and remorse, it's clear it will never happen again. Jamie is suspicious, however, and asks, "Have you ever cheated on me?" *Honesty* requires the truth. *Kindness* and *compassion*, however, might defend lying, or at least evasion.

Ethics in Summary

The primary object of this chapter has been to introduce you to thinking about ethics from a philosophical point of view. A philosophical approach aims to develop a standard of right and wrong that is rooted in conceptions of human well-being and flourishing—not religion, law, emotions, cultural traditions, or our own idiosyncratic ideas. Philosophical ethics aims at finding objective and universal standards with which to evaluate actions. Such an approach is more useful, practical, and realistic for solving ethical dilemmas than either a detailed, unchangeable code of rules or the general notion that right and wrong are arbitrary and relative to cultures and individuals.

Consequentialist, deontological, care, and virtue perspectives offer us more than one way to make up our minds. Jeremy Bentham and John Stuart Mill direct our attention to the consequences of our actions, specifically to pleasure and pain. They encourage us to produce a complete picture of every result of our acts both in the short and long term—and, with Mill's addition to Bentham, with sensitivity to the quality of the good or harm produced. Immanuel Kant's deontological ethics argues that we should attend simply to the intrinsic ethical character of our actions and treat each other with respect for our dignity. An ethic of care reminds us that ethical issues are grounded in complex real-life situations and calls for us to remember our basic humanity as we live in community with others. Virtue ethics gives us a less technical approach, underscores the importance of why and how we do things, and calls attention to the importance of character.

Facing ethical dilemmas is always difficult. You are torn between two or more desires, and you are awash in conflict and confusion. Even though it's hard to think straight when you feel like this, this is one of those times when a philosophical approach to life's problems is eminently practical. Try to force yourself to take a rational, objective look at the consequences of your different options, at the actions themselves, and at the moral duty we all have to prevent harm in the world. Philosophy often leaves us more confused about problems than when we started, but a philosophical approach is generally helpful in deciding what is the right thing to do.

Of course, *why* you should do what's right is another matter. And that is what we talk about in the next chapter.

Discussion Questions

1. What is your reaction to the idea that notions of right and wrong should ultimately not be based on religious beliefs or laws? What do you say to the idea that if religious and legal judgments about the ethical character of actions cannot be justified philosophically, they should be abandoned as irrational and illegitimate?

2. Do you find the notion of "human well-being" or "happiness" a reasonable and practical standard for determining right and wrong?

3. The Equal Pay Act of 1963 put the notion of "equal pay for equal work" into U.S. law. Does that mean that before 1963 American companies that paid men and women different salaries for the same job were doing something unethical even though it was legal?

4. Consequentialist ethics has a commonsense feel to it. We might say that it is a philosophical version of the maxim in sports, "No harm, no foul." What is your reaction to the fact that such a theory, even with Mill's addition of the concept of "quality," could justify slavery, racism, even terrorism? Should the theory be rejected on this basis?

5. Mill writes, "Few human creatures would consent to be changed into any of the lower animals for a promise of the fullest allowance of a beast's pleasures; no intelligent human being would consent to be a fool, no instructed person would be an ignoramus, no person of feeling and conscience would be selfish and base, even though they should be persuaded that the fool, the dunce, or the rascal is better satisfied with his lot than they are with theirs. . . . It is better to be a human being dissatisfied than a pig satisfied; better to be Socrates dissatisfied than a fool satisfied." Is he right? If someone offered you the chance of being transformed into Mill's "fool" who was actually more content with his or her life than you are with yours, would you do so, even if it meant giving up most of your intellectual abilities?

6. Kant's deontological outlook suggests that certain actions are always either right or wrong. Do you agree?

7. Kant's theory holds that using others as a means to your end in a way that they would not agree with is always morally wrong. What is your reaction to that?

8. One of the most important differences between a traditional philosophical approach to ethics and the alternative one sparked by the ethic of care has to do with the proper role of reason and the emotions. What's your reaction to making emotions more important in an ethical calculation?

9. Both emotion and reason have specific strengths in helping us understand an ethical issue. Both also have clear weaknesses. What recommendation can you make about how to leverage the strengths without being snared by the weaknesses?

10. One criticism of virtue ethics is that traits of Aristotle's admired character type (the good person) could depend on one's culture. What do you think?

11. Reflect on Janice Moulton's criticism of traditional philosophical approaches. Do thinkers like Virginia Held provide an appropriate correction?

12. Does a philosophical approach to ethics offer you any practical help in making decisions about right and wrong in your personal life?

Selected Readings

For a fuller treatment of the themes of this chapter, see: Geoffrey Thomas, *An Introduction to Ethics* (Indianapolis: Hackett Publishing Company, 1993) and Thomas I. White, *Right and Wrong: A Practical Introduction to Ethics*, 2nd ed. (West Sussex, UK: Wiley, 2017). Bentham's ideas can be found in his *Introduction to the Principles of Morals and Legislation*. For Mill, see *Utilitarianism*. Kant's primary ethical work is *Grounding for the Metaphysics of Morals*. For Virginia Held's ideas, see *The Ethics of Care: Personal, Political, Global* (Oxford: Oxford University Press, 2005). Empirical research by psychologists suggests that "character" and "virtue" aren't as important as proponents of virtue ethics argue for determining what people do. This point of view is called "situationism." See, for example, Lee Ross, Richard E. Nisbett, and Malcolm Gladwell, *The Person and the Situation* (Philadelphia: Temple University Press, 1991).

Chapter 6

Why Be Ethical?

You now know something about the nature of philosophical ethics and what it means to examine questions of right and wrong from a rational, secular point of view. But simply knowing what is "right" isn't enough. Lots of times we say to ourselves, "I know I shouldn't do this, but I'm going to anyway."

Take this case. You have a relationship with someone, and the two of you have promised you won't see anyone else. One day, however, you meet someone whom you find very attractive. You'd like to start seeing this person, but you don't want to jeopardize your original relationship in case this new one doesn't work out. The person you've been seeing trusts you, so you could probably get away with a few lies. Would this be justifiable?

There really shouldn't be any question that lying in this situation is wrong. You're breaking your promise, you're being deceptive, and both people you're seeing will be hurt if they discover what's going on. Nonetheless, many of us lie in a case like this, simply because we want the pleasure of dating someone else. Deceiving someone may be wrong, but if it'll make us happier, why not go ahead and do it?

When strong desires tempt us, it's hard to do the right thing. When we do resist the pull of temptation, we usually want to be rewarded. It may not be high-minded, but when confronted with moral dilemmas, most of us ask: If I do what's right, what's in it for me? It doesn't have to be fame and fortune. It may just be a good feeling about who we are. But most of us want a good reason to be good.

Why should we do what's right? The question is simple, but answering it is probably the most difficult task in ethics. Legal systems and religious traditions have an easy time giving us answers, of course. We should do what is right in order to avoid punishment for doing wrong. But philosophy does not approach it this way. It must give a rational, secular account of why living the moral life is valuable in its own right, here and now. And that's not easy.

Think about it for a minute. What reasons would you give someone for why he or she should do what is right? Most of you will be parents; some of you already are. How will you explain to your children, particularly as they get older and can argue with you, why they should act according to the values you hold? Perhaps you will invoke the Golden Rule and tell your children that since they don't want to be hurt, they shouldn't hurt other people. Or perhaps you will say that other people won't like them if they do something wrong. But what if your children say they enjoy hurting others, don't mind being disliked, and are happy to take their chances with the consequences of their misdeeds? What will you say then?

Why Act Ethically? Plato and Socrates

The Case of Gyges's Ring

Few philosophers take up the problem of why we should act ethically. Two who do—the ancient Greek philosopher Socrates and his pupil Plato—address it head on. We begin with Plato because he sets the question up in the toughest form imaginable. He does this in his dialogue called the *Republic*.[1]

The portion of the dialogue that is relevant here concentrates on the question of how we ought to live. A character named Glaucon claims that people are not good willingly and that the only reason any of us does what is right is to get something we want. If we develop a reputation for being honest, telling the truth, and keeping our commitments, then people will do business with us, elect us to office, and be our friends. But Glaucon thinks living ethically is difficult and unpleasant—and worse than living unethically. According to Glaucon, most of us do what is right only because we don't have the power to do what we really want to do and get away with it.

To illustrate his point, he tells the story of a shepherd named Gyges, who finds a ring that can make him invisible. He seduces the queen of the kingdom, kills the king, and takes over. The moral of the story, says Glaucon, is that given the opportunity, everyone would act just the way Gyges did.[2]

Plato raises a very interesting question here. If you knew you could get away with anything you wanted to do, however unethical, how ethical would your behavior be? Plato's character Glaucon thinks that it wouldn't be ethical at all. What would you do if you had a ring like that of Gyges?

Plato uses Glaucon to say what he thinks most people believe, and he is probably right. We don't have to look very far to see that dishonest, unscrupulous, selfish people get most of what they want while the rest of us settle for much less. Many of these people never get caught, and if they do, they aren't punished very severely. If we knew that we could get away with anything we wanted to, most of us would be sorely tempted to cut a few moral corners—or worse.

---

1. The *Republic*, like all of Plato's writings, is a fictional dialogue in which Plato explains his ideas through imaginary conversations that involve several different people. Plato generally uses Socrates as his main character, however, and this produces problems about separating Plato from Socrates. In Plato's early dialogues (like the *Crito* and the *Gorgias*, which we'll encounter later in this chapter), we can take the Socrates of the dialogue to be speaking ideas held by Socrates himself. In later works like the *Republic*, Plato expresses his own philosophical outlook. At that point he simply uses the character of Socrates as a mouthpiece for his own ideas.
2. Plato, *Republic*, Book II.

An Extreme Case

Plato is realistic enough to see the foolishness of arguing that we should do what is right in the hope of being rewarded. Instead, he comes at the question of whether the moral life has any intrinsic value by making the starkest possible comparison. He asks us to compare the life of a *good person with a reputation for vice* with the life of an *unethical person with a reputation for goodness*. Now any reason for being virtuous must depend on the value of moral virtue itself, not anything that reputation brings.

Think about this for a minute. Which would you rather be: an unethical person with a good reputation or an ethical person with a reputation for injustice? Be honest with yourself. Is there any reason to choose the latter?

Moral Virtue, Vice, and the Soul

It should come as no surprise, of course, that Plato and Socrates think that moral virtue is valuable. They believe that virtue is its own reward. The key to their ideas on the subject, however, lies in the interesting notion that moral virtue is "the health of the soul."

People use the term "soul" in many ways. We need not go into a long discussion of what the ancient Greeks mean by "soul." For our purposes, it is enough to know that "soul" means the most important part of who we are—our moral and intellectual essence, our *real* self, our *character*, the source of our consciousness, and the core of our personality. Whether the soul lives on after death in one form or another is irrelevant. Here we are interested in the intrinsic value of moral virtue.

In trying to understand what these philosophers mean by claiming that moral virtue is "the health of the soul," we must explore two critical ideas. First, whatever part of us Socrates and Plato mean when they refer to the *soul*, they believe that, like the body, it can be healthy or unhealthy. And health is something that most of us would agree is intrinsically worthwhile. We all know what healthy and unhealthy bodies are like, but what is the difference between healthy and unhealthy souls?

The other important idea is Socrates's belief that the soul's health is determined by what we do—that is, it is affected by the moral character of our actions. Socrates even describes the soul as "that part of ourselves that is improved by just actions and harmed by unjust actions."[3] In particular, Socrates believes that unethical actions harm the person who does them more than the victim.

Admittedly, these ideas about the value of moral virtue may seem strange to you. How is being good like being healthy? If you lie about denting someone's new car so you don't have to pay the repair bill, how do you hurt yourself more than someone else? These are not the easiest notions to swallow when you first hear them. Yet Plato and Socrates have

---

3. Plato, *Crito* in *The Trial and Death of Socrates*, Third Edition, trans. G. M. A. Grube (Indianapolis: Hackett Publishing Co., 2000), 47d, p. 48.

developed them into a substantial answer to the question, "Why bother about ethics?" Understanding and exploring that answer is our task in this chapter.

Plato: Moral Virtue as the Health of the Soul

Plato thinks that moral virtue is to the soul what health is to the body. What might a "healthy soul" be like? And what is the difference between healthy and unhealthy souls?

Healthy Bodies, Healthy Souls

Everybody understands the difference between healthy and unhealthy bodies, so let's start there.

A healthy body is free of disease and in decent shape. When you are healthy, you may not feel euphoric, but you probably feel calm and contented. When you are healthy, you aren't in pain. Your body has its full range of capabilities, and you can do what you want to. When you are sick, on the other hand, all you can think about is how bad you feel. You are too weak to do things. Your discomfort keeps pushing itself into your awareness. As long as we stay healthy, we can do what we choose. The effects of illness and neglect—clouded minds and weak, damaged bodies—limit our activities. With health comes freedom and control over our lives. Health is intrinsically enjoyable, and it enables us to get more of what we want. Therefore, we are more likely to live happier lives.

What can we say about the healthy soul (or character or personality)? Much the same thing that we said for the healthy body. The absence of disease in your soul means that your mind is clear and that you can see things as they really are. Your view of the world is not distorted by fears, insecurities, irrational anxieties, or overpowering desires. Your judgment is not blinded by greed or self-interest. Thus your assessment of whether something is right or wrong can be objective. We might say that a healthy soul has a fairly clear *moral vision*. Like the healthy body, the healthy soul has its own kind of freedom and control. Once you decide about something, you have the capacity to carry it out. We might call this *strength of will*.

Imagine that a friend asks you to help him cheat in his history course. He'll pay you a few hundred dollars to write a paper for him. "Come on," he says. "You need the money. I've got cash to spare. Nobody gets hurt. There's nothing wrong. Besides, I'd do it for you." You feel uneasy—especially because you'd like the money. He expects you to do it, and you don't want him to get angry. To see this situation for what it is and to do what you know you should do takes clarity of mind and courage—that is, the strength of a healthy soul. If fear of your friend's anger and your own desire for the money control you, you won't have the nerve to stand up to him. With a weak and unhealthy soul, you compromise your own beliefs and allow your fears to take control. With a healthy soul, on the other hand, you have the freedom to live according to your own moral insights. Once you decide what the right thing to do is, you can do it. You have the power to live according to your sense of right and wrong.

Plato's Idea of the Healthy Soul: Balance and Control

In the *Republic*, Plato uses this simple parallel between bodies and souls to distinguish between healthy and unhealthy souls. Each of us, he says, is made up of three parts: the *physical* (physical desires), the *spirited* (emotions), and the *intellectual* (mind). In the healthy soul, these three are perfectly balanced. As we make decisions about how to live, our minds give due regard to our emotional and physical needs, and each of the three parts performs its proper role. According to Plato, the mind should be in control, and our emotions should help us follow the mind's judgment, particularly when it goes against the inclination of our physical desires. In an unhealthy soul, the balance is lost. Our actions flow not from our good judgment but from our emotions or physical appetites.

For example, think of people who are obsessed with their bodies or their physical appearance. You may know people who expend huge amounts of energy playing sports, working out, worrying about their diet, or spending time shopping for the right clothes or getting their hair or makeup just right. Virtually everything in their lives—what they do, what they don't do, whom they hang out with—revolves around the physical side of their beings. They may even be addicted to, say, their daily five-mile run or buying new clothes. Such people are so driven by their bodies that they cut classes, miss work, or neglect relationships because of their obsession. Clearly, the physical part of their nature dominates their lives.

Others are driven by their emotions. They need to be in love, to be popular, to be admired by others, or to be famous. Think of people who will do anything to be liked by someone they are involved with. They may even do things that hurt others—or themselves—to hold on to their latest love. And when that relationship ends, they immediately hunt for someone new. Clearly, their lives are dominated by their emotions.

Plato thinks that the unhealthy soul is out of balance and controlled by the wrong aspect of our being. The mind yields to the body or the emotions.

The healthy soul, however, is balanced. It gives due weight to bodily and emotional needs, but the head remains in control and keeps things from going overboard. In Plato's opinion, the person with a healthy soul has freedom and self-control.

The Soul's Health and Acting Ethically

Plato believes that physical and emotional desires, particularly when they are out of balance, are the primary factors that cloud our judgment about right and wrong. The actions of unethical people serve some physical desire (sex, alcohol, the physical pleasures that money can buy) or some emotion (jealousy, ambition, anger, fear, greed). People with unbalanced, unhealthy souls are so driven by physical or emotional wants that they do not think straight about right and wrong. Their mental power is used to service their wants, not in examining the morality of their actions. Their minds follow their bodies or their feelings. When we allow this to happen, Plato thinks there is a strong chance we will behave unethically

Socrates (469–399 BCE), one of the most famous ancient philosophers, was born, lived, and died in Athens. He came from an honorable but undistinguished middle-class family; his father was a sculptor and his mother a midwife. Socrates never wrote anything, nor did he found a school, but it is impossible to exaggerate his importance to philosophy. While his philosophical predecessors concentrated on issues concerned with the nature of reality, Socrates was the first philosopher to focus on questions of ordinary living. He spent his day in philosophical dialogue challenging his fellow Athenians to scrutinize their lives and to make virtue and caring for their souls their chief concern. Socrates came to believe that he had something like a religious duty to do this after a friend returned from the oracle at Delphi with the message that no one was wiser than Socrates. Because Socrates believed that he was genuinely ignorant, he concluded that the oracle's words must mean that his task was to help others give up their false convictions, among them that money, pleasure, and power were the keys to happiness. If he could help his discussants become as "ignorant" as he was, Socrates believed, then they would see the value of moral virtue. Socrates also shaped the history of philosophy by being the teacher of another philosophical giant, Plato.

Socrates was a devoted son of Athens, fighting in her defense in the army and fulfilling his political obligations as a citizen. He also saw himself as a "gadfly" whose persistent questioning, even if annoying, truly benefited Athens. Not everyone shared this point of view, however, and not long after Athens was defeated by Sparta, Socrates was indicted on the capital charges of impiety and corrupting the young. Socrates's accusers apparently thought that philosophical questioning contributed to Athens's defeat by somehow weakening the city and lessening the respect the young should have for Athens's institutions and its leading citizens. Found guilty by a narrow margin (281 to 220), Socrates was sentenced to death. He died, according to Athenian custom, by drinking a cup of hemlock. His fate remains a sad reminder of the danger that ignorance and fear pose to the honest champion of truth and virtue.

to get what we want. Having a soul that is out of balance—"unhealthy" in Plato's terms—goes hand in hand with wrongdoing.

By contrast, Plato believes the freedom, control, and balanced perspective that come with the soul's health result in ethical behavior. Good decisions come only when we are not dominated by our physical or emotional wants. Thus, acting ethically is an expression of the strong, healthy soul—the soul in which a clear mind is in charge.

Despite Plato's claims, you, like Glaucon, may still be skeptical. If a little larceny helps us get what we want, why is that so bad?

At this point, we must turn from Plato's thought to that of his teacher, Socrates, who had more to say about the unhealthy soul. In particular, it was Socrates who formulated the idea that vice harms the doer more than those who are his or her victims.

Socrates: Vice Harms the Doer

The philosopher who could be said to have "invented" ethics is Socrates. During the two centuries before Socrates, Greek philosophers had speculated about the nature of physical reality. What is the world made of? Is there a basic element out of which everything else is composed? How does the cosmos work? Socrates was the first philosopher to take how we should live as his main concern.

Socrates is an interesting figure for several reasons. For one thing, he represents the rare case of a major philosopher who never wrote down a word. We know about his ideas primarily through the writings of his pupil Plato, who makes Socrates the main figure in most of his dialogues. For another, Socrates was an eccentric character in ancient Athens, having come to believe he had a mission from the god Apollo to encourage people to live a moral life.

Socrates did this by approaching his fellow Athenians individually, engaging them in philosophical dialogues that challenged their deepest beliefs. For example, he would ask someone what the most important thing in life was. If the person answered "money," for example, or "fame," Socrates would ask for an explanation. When the person responded, Socrates would ask for more, pursuing every point of the answer, trying to show the problems with the other person's thinking. Back and forth it went like that until Socrates had convinced his partner about the importance of moral virtue. This "Socratic method" of question/answer, question/answer is still used by many teachers, especially those in law schools.

An Overview of Socrates's Ethical Beliefs

For someone who is universally considered one of philosophy's brightest lights, Socrates advanced some unusual ideas about why we should act ethically. In terms of everyday life and the dominant values of Western culture from Athens to the present day, Socrates's beliefs seem at best peculiar.

- When we treat someone unethically and escape unpunished, we hurt ourselves more than we hurt our victim.
- Our greatest protection is moral virtue. Even though someone may kill us, our virtue makes it impossible for anyone to harm us.
- Using the idea that virtue is the soul's health and vice its disease, Socrates talks about immorality in a way that suggests that moral compromise makes as little sense as deliberately infecting ourselves with a terminal illness.
- If we do something wrong, we should seek out someone to punish us with the same speed and care as when we look for someone to cure us when we are sick.

Religious figures who invoke divine revelation preach ideas every bit as peculiar as those of Socrates. But Socrates does not attribute his beliefs to special wisdom from Apollo. Rather, he takes these ideas to be absolutely certain, observable *facts* of human nature. Most people probably disagree with this claim. But Socrates takes it as an empirical fact that when we do something wrong, we are hurt by it. He thinks that no one can

be strong and fully healthy without moral virtue. Similarly, he claims that unethical people lack critical capacities and strengths. He sees them as genuinely unhealthy, and they
are made that way by their wrongdoing.

How did Socrates try to argue for such an odd idea as that *unethical actions harm those
who perform them*?

How Vice Changes Us: An Ordinary Example

The idea that wrongdoing harms the doer is a prominent Socratic idea, yet it is puzzling.
Socrates says, "Wrongdoing or injustice is in every way harmful and shameful to the
wrongdoer."[4] It is so harmful, counsels Socrates in the Platonic dialogue *Crito*, that even
if somebody else hurts us first, we "should never do wrong in return, nor do any man
harm, no matter what he may have done to you."[5] But precisely how are we hurt if we do
something wrong? How are *we* harmed if we hurt somebody else, especially if they have
already wronged us? At stake here is what Socrates calls "that part of ourselves that is
improved by just actions and destroyed by unjust actions."[6] Today we call this our character, personality, or self. As you saw earlier, the Greeks called it the soul. Whatever we call
it, it is that essence which we feel is most uniquely who we really are, and Socrates takes
it to be far more important than our bodies.

Because Socrates believes that "care of the soul" is our most important task, the only
thing that counts as harm is something that makes us less able to be virtuous. Unethical
actions corrupt us and break down our ability to act virtuously. Thus, each unethical act
makes it more likely that we will act unethically in the future by weakening those capacities and faculties we need to act more morally.

At first, Socrates's belief that doing wrong hurts the wrongdoer may strike you
as odd. Hurting other people seems obvious. But hurting ourselves? That seems
unlikely.

Yet take a simple example. Most people think there is something wrong with telling
lies, even though virtually all of us do it at one time or another. Think back to your first
lie. It was probably after you had disobeyed your parents and knew you'd be in trouble
if they found out. That first lie was probably hard to tell, and you most likely felt guilty
afterward. But if your parents believed you, you discovered that lying can get you out of
some tough spots. Now think of your second lie, your third, and on down the line. Odds
are that lying got easier, and you felt less guilty the more you did it. At this point in your
life, you probably feel that lying is not as wrong as you once thought it was, and you
probably feel less guilty when you do it.

The question here is, "What has happened to you?" Socrates would say that you've
been corrupted. You haven't turned into Jack the Ripper, but you are less likely now

---

4. *Crito*, 49b, p. 49.
5. *Crito*, 49d, p. 50.
6. *Crito*, 47d, p. 48.

to tell the truth than you were before. You've lost some ground. Getting away with lying lowers our resistance to it in the future. This makes it easier and increases the odds that we will do it again in tight spots. It also changes our thinking about how wrong it is. Most people come to feel that there is some good in any act that gets you out of trouble.

How did this happen to you? Did someone force this on you? No, you chose it each time, little by little, by doing what you did. Your allegiance to the truth lessened, even if only to a small degree, with each falsehood. Socrates would argue that you harmed or weakened yourself each time by acting unethically. He would claim that it's now less likely and more difficult for you to do the right thing and tell the truth in a tight spot.

Whether or not you agree that you've been harmed or weakened in this process, you have been changed by it. What you do and what you think about what you do have been changed by actions that were initially at odds with your original values. Socrates's argument, therefore, has a common-sense validity. We haven't seen enough specifics about precisely how you were harmed for you to judge whether you completely accept this notion, but you can probably agree that the process actually exists.

Plato's lineage was as stellar as Socrates's was conventional. His father was descended from the last king of Athens and his mother from a great Athenian lawgiver, and his relatives were prominent citizens in the city. Plato (428–348 BCE) received a privileged upbringing, distinguishing himself in everything from poetry to wrestling, and he was probably being groomed for a political career.

Meeting Socrates changed Plato's life forever, however. He committed himself to philosophy, followed Socrates around, and observed his numerous dialogues. The death of his teacher led Plato to leave Athens and to travel throughout the Mediterranean area for twelve years. When he returned to Athens, he established the first formal school of philosophy, the Academy, where he worked for the rest of his days.

Plato retained an interest in public life, however, and he made a series of unsuccessful attempts to educate the rulers of the city of Syracuse on the island of Sicily along the lines of his ideas of the philosopher–king. He lectured widely at the Academy, and like Socrates, not only was he one of philosophy's greatest lights, but he also was the teacher of another major thinker, Aristotle.

How Vice Harms Us: An Example from the *Gorgias*

The best description for precisely how vice harms us is in the ideas attributed to Socrates in Plato's dialogue titled *Gorgias*. This dialogue begins with a discussion of the value of rhetoric (the art of public speaking). Soon, however, the question of how we should live our lives and the value of moral virtue takes center stage.

Four characters speak in the dialogue. Socrates, of course. Then there is Gorgias, a well-known and highly respected teacher of public speaking, for whom the dialogue is named. Gorgias travels from city to city teaching the skills of rhetoric, and at the beginning of the dialogue, he has just arrived in Athens. Such teachers were common in ancient Greece, and they were particularly popular in Athens where speaking eloquently was essential to success. Athens was a democracy in which any citizen could speak at the city's democratic assembly, and politics was at the heart of the city's life. The key to success in Athens was having a reputation as an intelligent and effective speaker.[7] The third character, Polus, is Gorgias's rambunctious young student and follower. And then there is Callicles.

Callicles is a bright, ambitious young Athenian who is hungry for wealth and power. He is talented, educated, refined—but thoroughly immoral. He believes that people who are bright and cunning should rule because they are superior to everyone else. He also thinks the strong should take whatever they want as long as they can get away with it and indulge themselves in all kinds of pleasures. He rejects fairness, equality, and moderation. Conventional ideas of morality, he claims, come from inferior people making virtues out of their own weaknesses in order to hold superior people in check.

It is in Socrates's discussion with Callicles that we get a clear picture of the harm vice does. After all, considering how unethical—and dangerous—Callicles is, he ought to be a prime example of the damage wrongdoing can do.

Setting Up the Issue

The *Gorgias* starts as a conversation between Socrates and Gorgias about the nature of rhetoric. Gorgias sings the praises of the art he teaches, but Socrates points out its weaknesses—especially that it can be used for unjust ends.

At this point Polus speaks up. Unlike Gorgias, who is a man of great integrity, Polus is not bothered by the abuse of rhetoric. The discussion slides from the nature of rhetoric to how we ought to live, and Polus holds up the example of Archelaus, the king of Macedonia, who acquired his throne through injustice and brutality. To be a tyrant and to have your evil go unpunished, claims Polus, is a life that everyone envies. Disagreeing, Socrates argues that doing wrong, particularly if you go unpunished, is the greatest of evils. It is always better, he argues, to be the victim of injustice rather than the person who does it. Polus laughs at Socrates, but eventually he is shamed into silence. In the presence of his teacher, the virtuous Gorgias, he is too embarrassed to press his point with Socrates.

---

7. Teachers like Gorgias were called sophists. Originally the term "sophist," which means "expert in wisdom," was a title of respect. Gradually, however, a group of sophists arose who were less concerned with teaching how to argue honestly than with teaching rhetorical tricks that would help you in court or in the Assembly even if your case were bad and your reasoning weak. At this point, "sophist" came to mean something akin to "shyster." You can see a residue of this idea in modern English. To engage in "sophistry" or to argue "sophistically" today is to use linguistic trickery. If someone calls you a sophist, you may safely take it as an insult.

Callicles, however, has no such shame. Taking up the dialogue at this point, he too ridicules Socrates's idea that the key to happiness lies in moral virtue. Then he launches into a passionate defense of the unbridled pursuit of pleasure and of the strong dominating the weak. Callicles proclaims:

> the man who'll live correctly ought to allow his own appetites to get as large as possible and not restrain them. And when they are as large as possible, he ought to be competent to devote himself to them by virtue of his bravery and intelligence, and to fill them with whatever he may have an appetite for at the time. But this isn't possible for the many, I believe; hence, they become detractors of people like this because of the shame they feel, while they conceal their own impotence. And they say that lack of discipline is shameful, as I was saying earlier, and so they enslave men who are better by nature, and while they themselves lack the ability to provide for themselves fulfillment for their pleasures, their own lack of courage leads them to praise self-control and justice.[8]

This speech sets the terms of a long debate between Socrates and Callicles that dominates the rest of the dialogue. The philosopher champions virtue and self-control—a life of being "one's own ruler." The aspiring politician endorses the uncontrolled and self-interested pursuit of pleasure by whatever means available.

In the ensuing discussion, Socrates goes on to identify two distinct ways we harm ourselves when we do something wrong. Our ability to control ourselves in the face of desire is weakened, as is our intellect. Although Socrates did not put it in these words, we might interpret him as saying that when we do wrong, we weaken our *strength of will* and our *moral vision*. In other words, Socrates suggests that vice destroys precisely those qualities that, as we saw above, characterize the healthy soul.

The Jar Metaphor: Desires and Strength of Will

Socrates would surely see Callicles as an example of someone who's been badly damaged by vice. And the first thing Socrates would point to is that Callicles's remarks show that he has lost control over his desires. What Callicles takes as a strength, Socrates regards as a weakness.

Trying to show Callicles the error of his ways, Socrates contrasts the uncontrolled life his opponent praises with that of a self-controlled and ethical person. To illustrate his point, he draws an analogy to jars—some intact, others leaky.

> Suppose there are two men, each of whom has many jars. The jars belonging to one of them are sound and full, one with wine, another with honey, a third with milk, and many others with lots of other things. And suppose that the sources of each of these things are scarce and difficult to come by, procurable only with much toil and trouble. Now the one man, having filled up his jars, doesn't pour anything

---

8. Plato, *Gorgias*, trans. Donald J. Zeyl (Indianapolis: Hackett Publishing Co., 1987), 491e–492b, pp. 64–65.

more into them and gives them no further thought. He can relax over them. As for the other one, he too has resources that can be procured, though with difficulty, but his containers are leaky and rotten. He's forced to keep on filling them, day and night, or else he suffers extreme pain.[9]

The healthy, self-controlled individual is like a solid jar, while someone like Callicles, an unethical person who gives in to his desires, is like the rotting jar. If you are like a leaking jar, Socrates suggests, you inevitably feel your yearning growing, no matter what you do. And the longer you wait to "fill up," the more powerful and compelling is the ache. Thus, your desires run your life. You must constantly satisfy them or be aware of the discomfort connected with your yearning. By contrast, if you are like the solid jar, you are content and untroubled. You do not feel the growing craving of unsatisfied desire. You can do with your life what you want, not what your desires compel you to do.

Thus, the unethical person's ability to experience a stable sense of *satisfaction* has been damaged. Someone like Callicles cannot be satisfied because his desires are unchecked, and any satisfaction is only temporary. If an unethical person is like a leaky jar, then he or she is ultimately unsatisfiable. As soon as that person feels a comfortable contentment or fulfillment, the feeling starts slipping away. The unethical person is then unsatisfied again and looking around for the next thrill. And this pattern repeats itself over and over.

Not surprisingly, Callicles is unpersuaded. He rejects Socrates's ideas, saying that the life of someone like the intact jar is dull and boring: "The man who has filled himself up has no pleasure any more, and when he's been filled up and experiences neither joy nor pain, that's living like a stone. . . . Rather, living pleasantly consists in this: having as much as possible flow in."[10]

Most of us would not succeed if we tried to live as Callicles recommends. Constantly finding new sources of pleasure—more money, more power, new jobs, new successes, different lovers, new drugs, exotic places to travel to, novel and exciting experiences—is a tall order. Of course, Callicles believes that a truly superior person—like him—will be able to do this. Surely, he thinks, this refutes the idea that he has been damaged in any way. Socrates, of course, disagrees.

The key to this dispute is who is in control. Callicles himself describes the situation as one in which he ministers to his desires. He does not see, however, that this makes him not simply weaker than his own desires, but their servant.

It is not whether someone can satisfy his or her desires that matters to Socrates, but whether a person is his or her "own ruler." An ethical person like Socrates can decide which of his desires he'll satisfy. Callicles does not have this option—his only decision is *how* to satisfy them. His desires control his life. Furthermore, if Socrates is correct and the desires of someone like Callicles (a rotting jar) are ultimately unsatisfiable, the whole project is doomed to fail.

---

9. Plato, *Gorgias*, 493e–494a, pp. 66–67.
10. Plato, *Gorgias*, 494a–b, p. 67.

In other words, someone like Callicles does not have the *strength of will* to resist his own desires. In Socrates's opinion, when a man goes from virtue to vice, his "jar" goes from being solid to rotting and leaky, and that individual has lost some power over his own life.

Noncognitive Harm: Insatiable Desires and Loss of Control

The first kind of harm that comes from vice, then, is that the person who indulges in it becomes uncontrolled and intemperate. Socrates's jar analogy implies that the intemperate person lives a life that is out of her or his own control. Driven by the need to satisfy the gnawing hunger of unfulfilled want, unethical individuals experience only fleeting satisfactions because such people are essentially unsatisfiable. This literally compels them to seek more and different pleasures.

There are three important points here. First, the fact that a vice-ridden person's desires become insatiable means that at least part of the harm vice does affects the *noncognitive* dimension of the human personality. That is, the first kind of harm that Socrates points out involves not the mind but the will and our feelings of desire and satisfaction. The point at which we are satisfied by food, money, sex, power, or whatever else is to a large extent a psychological matter, not a physical or an intellectual one. For example, people with eating disorders know perfectly well that their behavior is bad for them. Some difficulty beyond their conscious control, however, makes them unable to control themselves. If we become "leaky jars," the psychological mechanism that produces our sense that our wants have been satisfied has been disabled. In this case, instead of feeling a stable sense of contentment with what we have and how we get it, we feel unsatisfied.[11]

Second, it does seem that genuine harm has been done. To go from master to servant in one's own life is a significant reversal. It is much like the dynamic of addiction, in that most of the addict's life is geared to gratifying the desire for whatever he or she craves. Although Socrates did not have the concept of addiction that we have today, he describes it well where he claims that the "leaking jar" person "suffers extreme pain" if he does not satisfy his desires. With desires this compelling, the victim will not spend much time worrying about the ethical character of what has to be done to satisfy them. Such a person is in a downward spiral, becoming even more damaged, out of control, and corrupt the more he tries to satisfy his desires.

Third, Socrates describes a behavior that seems real enough. Think about what happens to people once they give themselves over to self-interest and start acting unethically. Nothing is ever enough. Think about the number of times you've heard about someone rich and powerful—an executive, a politician, a minister—who gets caught doing something crooked. Haven't you said to yourself, "I don't get it. This guy already has it all, and now he risks losing everything"? There is an ongoing stream of such people—many of

---

11. By using modern psychological concepts at this point, our interpretation moves beyond notions available to the ancient Greeks. It does appear, however, that much of the harm that Socrates describes is connected to what we today call "the unconscious." Feelings of contentment are generally not under our conscious control.

them otherwise bright, talented individuals—who are caught taking stupid chances for what amounts to small change. The only explanation that makes sense is that these people somehow lost control. Their *strength of will* all but evaporated. On this evidence, at least, we can say that Socrates has a real point in suggesting that once we cross the line from ethical to unethical behavior to get what we want, our "jar" starts to erode, and we lose some control over what we want and what we do. This loss of control that vice causes is serious. To use an analogy of our own, we might say that vice turns the unethical person into someone trying to navigate a rudderless sailboat, at the mercy of the winds of his or her own desires. If virtue and happiness are analogous to reaching a safe harbor, this person doesn't have a chance of getting there.

Cognitive Harm: Weakened Intellect and Damaged Moral Vision

It may surprise you that this first kind of harm that Socrates sees as coming from vice is not intellectual. Because he is a philosopher, however, you can be sure he also thinks vice harms the mind.

Socrates sometimes points to unscrupulous people who make mistakes in judging what is in their own interest. Vice, he implies, has somehow clouded their view of situations and altered their perception of what advances their own ends.[12] This is nothing new, of course. Take the billionaire who gets caught cheating his way to a little more money. To an outside observer, this man cannot be thinking straight. In terms of what he gets by breaking the law, the risks of losing what he already has are extremely high. A little more money, bending the rules, outwitting a few more people—none of this adds anything significant to his life. Yet the cost is astronomically high—public disgrace, divorce, a ruined career, dreams shattered, prison. It's surprisingly easy to find stories about wrongdoers who end up misreading the odds, misjudging the likelihood of getting away with their deeds, and taking chances so foolish they are almost asking to be caught.

What do people like this think when they take the first step over the line and then get themselves in deeper? They must have thought something—these are usually bright, accomplished, highly rational people. But somehow they just didn't think straight. What they *think* is in their interest is *not* in their interest. Even if they aren't caught, the damage they suffer has to do with their ability to perceive what genuinely advances their own interest. They *didn't* think straight because they *couldn't* think straight. Their earlier unethical behavior had dramatically eroded that ability.

An additional part of that erosion occurs in what we can call someone's *conscience,* or their *moral vision*—their basic sense of right and wrong. Like Callicles, people who have

---

12. For example, Socrates proposes the paradox that the tyrant with the reputation for absolute power in reality has neither great power nor even the power to do what he wants. The tyrant wants what is in his interest, but Socrates believes it is likely that such a person will do only what seems best to him and that his actions will in reality often be to his disadvantage. Since the tyrant never wants what is to his disadvantage, Socrates argues that he often ends up doing what he does not really want to do. If he were as powerful as he seemed, he would not make such mistakes. Hence, the "powerful" tyrant is not powerful.

suffered this damage come to believe that ordinary ideas of right and wrong do not apply to them.

Common sense shows you how Socrates might be right when he implies that vice harms its doer by causing us to lose some control over our desires. Now you can see the validity of the idea that vice also causes the rational faculties to deteriorate.

Callicles as the Embodiment of Vice

Because Callicles embodies so clearly what Socrates regards as vice, we should expect him to display the full range of the harm Socrates alleges that vice does. Callicles enthusiastically endorses the unordered, intemperate, and licentious life as the path to happiness. We might expect, then, that he lives that way himself. We can also expect to see signs of a weakened intellect.

Socrates identifies both of these weaknesses by pointing out how out of control Callicles is. He describes Callicles as someone enslaved by the idea of pleasing the two current loves of his life: the Athenian public (*demos*) and a beautiful young man (Demus).[13] Socrates remarks,

> I notice that in each case you're unable to contradict your beloved, clever though you are, no matter what he says or what he claims is so. You keep shifting back and forth. If you say anything in the Assembly and the Athenian *demos* denies it, you shift your ground and say what it wants to hear. Other things like this happen to you when you're with that good-looking young man, the son of Pyrilampes. You're unable to oppose what your beloveds say or propose, so that if somebody heard you say what you do on their account and was amazed at how absurd that is, you'd probably say—if you were minded to tell him the truth—that unless somebody stops your beloveds from saying what they say, you'll never stop saying those things either.[14]

Socrates claims that in the hope of getting what he wants, Callicles cannot resist agreeing with either of his two loves—the Athenians in the Assembly and Demus. And because each is fickle, he is also constantly changing what he says and does in order to please them. That Callicles's very words are now aligned with his search for pleasure and not with his reasoning and the search for truth is a major sign that his *intellect* has been harmed by the uncontrolled life he is living.

However, the fact that Callicles refuses to change his position during his conversation with Socrates is the most powerful sign that vice has harmed his ability to think rationally. Callicles is Socrates's strongest opponent in the dialogue—far stronger than Gorgias or Polus. Callicles hangs in there against Socrates; he does not allow Socrates

---

13. It may or may not surprise you that homosexuality and bisexuality were quite acceptable among upper-class men in ancient Greece. Socrates is implying no criticism of Callicles on this score at least. Socrates is attempting a clever play on words because of the similarity between "Demos," the Athenian public whose support Callicles craves, and "Demus," the young man he is in love with.

14. Plato, *Gorgias*, 481d–482a, pp. 51–52.

to refute him on trivial grounds, and he even toys with the philosopher a couple of times in the argument to show his mastery of the issue. Socrates gets Gorgias and Polus to back off and change their minds, but he makes no headway with Callicles. Even though Socrates tries to point out a number of contradictions in Callicles's position, Callicles is convinced that he is right and that Socrates hasn't been able to show otherwise.

Callicles no doubt thinks that he is holding his own against Socrates, that his self-ish and relentless pursuit of power and pleasure has in no way diminished his intellectual prowess. Socrates would say, however, that the fact that Callicles does not budge an inch in their discussion is proof of the harm done to him. It is because Callicles's intellect is in such *bad* shape that he thinks he has bested Socrates and can't imagine he's wrong.

The damage to Callicles's intellect shows up in two main ways. First, in the course of the discussion, Socrates tries to show Callicles that as long as he believes what he does about pleasure and power, right and wrong, his thinking will be riddled with confusion and contradictions. Callicles simply cannot see it. His mind has been so clouded that either he doesn't know when he contradicts himself or he doesn't care. And since tolerating contradictions is an obvious sign of weak thinking, to disregard them in such a cavalier fashion is a serious matter.

Second, and more important, is *why* contradictions don't matter to Callicles. It's not that Callicles's unethical behavior has disabled some neurons in his brain. Rather, we can speculate that it's because most of his mental energy is spent on keeping himself convinced that what he thinks is right.

No doubt you have met people who are so intent on being right that they won't listen to anybody with facts to the contrary. Or if they do listen, they're only waiting to shoot back an answer that proves they're right. Such people may even try to convince you they're right about something you don't even care about. You wonder why they're wasting their time with you. You don't care, so whom are they trying to convince? And that question is the key to understanding what's going on here. People like this—like Callicles—are really trying to convince themselves that they're right. It may look like they're trying to convince other people, but other people have nothing to do with it. They're talking mainly to themselves.

When this happens, some part of us other than our conscious mind is controlling our life. As we have already seen, in Callicles's case it's his physical and emotional desires. And when our desires become obsessive, the mind is pulled in to help the cause and keep everything in place. It needs to come up with reasons for why the course we're following is the right way to go. An outside observer, of course, does not see these as good reasons. They're just excuses we give to people so we don't have to consider the possibility that we're wrong.

Psychologists call this process *rationalizing*. When confronted with something negative about ourselves, we often feel internal pressure to make ourselves feel better. We then reinterpret our behavior to make it seem more rational and acceptable. For example, if you cheat on exams because you are too lazy to study, you may convince yourself that it isn't a big deal because "everyone does it." In a genuine case of rationalization, we don't even realize that we're just making excuses. At such times, unconscious forces rule our lives.

If we interpret Callicles's behavior this way, we can say that his arguments are nothing more than a sophisticated set of rationalizations that keep him from seeing his condition. Because Callicles's intellect now serves his desires, he is forced to reinterpret how he lives—justifying it to himself as rational, sensible, and defensible. He has been manipulated by his own greed, lust, and ambition.[15]

A Commonsense Assessment

Socrates sees virtue as necessary for the health of our "souls" and he views vice as unhealthy. Vice, he suggests, harms the doer in two specific ways.

First, when we get caught up in the selfish pursuit of our own ends at others' expense, we damage a basic mechanism within ourselves that gives us emotional stability and a sense of satisfaction, or contentment, with our lives. This means that we lose some control over ourselves. We don't remain content once our desires are satisfied, and we're driven to find and gratify more needs. Ultimately, our desires become insatiable. We're never happy; we just want, want, want.

Second, when we become slaves to our desires, our minds are pulled into their service too. Our intellects become dulled, we may become less sensitive to important contradictions in our thoughts or behavior, and internal pressures cause us to devise rationalizations that keep us on the path we've chosen. We may explain to others—but primarily to ourselves—that such behavior is reasonable, good, and fulfilling. But we're only kidding ourselves, and we don't even know it.

Such a claim about the harm done by vice seems to make sense. Most of us already know that as we do unethical things, they often get easier to do and harder to resist. Ultimately, we may lose our sense that anything is really wrong with them.

This is what corruption is all about. It involves a deterioration of strengths and abilities accompanied by blindness to what is happening. Do you think that corrupt people think they are corrupt? Hardly. They think they've finally gotten smart, or courageous, or realistic. They think they now have the guts to do what ordinary people dare not do. And

---

15. Be sure to realize that all this talk about rationalization and unconscious mechanisms is part of our *speculation about* and *interpretation of* Socrates's ideas. The ancient Greeks, after all, did not have a modern concept of the unconscious, and we certainly cannot say that Socrates did or necessarily would put things this way.

However, the human psyche probably hasn't changed significantly in the last two thousand years, and the unconscious was as much a part of the actions of ancient Athenians as of anyone today. The force of the unconscious is at times painfully apparent, and Socrates must have noticed it, even if he did not have a convenient way of referring to it. In essence, this interpretation of Socrates's ideas suggests that using a contemporary concept may let us better understand this ancient thinker's claims. This kind of interpretation is allowable in philosophy as long as we acknowledge what we are doing and accept the limitations of such speculation.

when they're caught, do they think the punishment is justified? No, they feel that they were trapped unfairly and that they are being held to unreasonable standards while the real crooks get away with murder.

People are not born corrupt. And in most cases no one coerces them into corruption. How, then, does it happen? Unethical behavior starts with a free choice. But once made, we are drawn in until our "souls" have sustained serious harm.

Moral Virtue and Happiness

Ultimately, the reason Socrates's idea that "vice harms the doer" is so important for us to consider is that he thinks we need to live virtuous lives in order to be happy. If acting unethically affects both our ability to be satisfied and our ability to see things clearly, we will never be content. We will constantly want more. And our perception of the world will be so distorted that we will see things incorrectly, make mistakes, and probably get caught. This is not the path to happiness. As Socrates expresses it to Polus, "I say that the admirable and good person, man or woman, is happy, but that the one who's unjust and wicked is miserable."[16]

What About a Moderate Callicles?

Despite the apparent commonsense validity of Socrates's ideas, you may have some doubts about this. "This talk about self-control, rationality, virtue, and happiness seems all well and good," you might say, "but isn't it possible to be a really successful *unethical* individual? The trick is to let your desires grow but not let them get out of hand, to be prudent in your larceny, to assess the odds of success and failure realistically. In short, if you can be a moderate and more restrained Callicles, you'll have the happiest life imaginable. You'll get most of what you want, you'll be satisfied with it, and you won't get caught."

While this sounds good in theory, a "moderate Callicles" may simply be impossible. There are too many examples of highly intelligent, successful, talented people who run foolish risks, make mistakes, and get caught to suggest that everyone who gets mired in scandal is second-rate. It does seem that objective judgment is one of the first casualties of moral corruption. And if the harm done by vice does take place on an unconscious level, it's no surprise that these people couldn't control how corrupt they were becoming.

Why Be Ethical?

Plato and Socrates give straightforward answers to this question. An unethical person is weak, even unhealthy. Such a person lacks the freedom, self-control, and intellectual clarity that are necessary to live happily.

---

16. Plato, *Gorgias*, 470e, p. 34.

Plato describes this in terms of the proper balance between our intellect, on the one hand, and our physical and emotional desires, on the other. In the unbalanced, unhealthy soul, he says, people are so driven by physical or emotional wants that they cannot think straight about right and wrong. When their minds service their wants, they cannot examine the morality of their actions. Only the freedom, control, and balanced perspective that come with the soul's health result in ethical behavior. If you aren't dominated by your physical or emotional wants, you can make good decisions. Thus acting ethically is an expression of the strong, healthy soul, one in which a clear mind is the dominant force in someone's life.

According to Socrates, wrongdoing harms the doer by unleashing our desires, disabling the inner mechanism that makes contentment possible, and diminishing our intellectual power.

So now that you've heard from these two philosophers, ponder this yourself. Examine the effects of virtue and vice in your own life. Look at the lives of people you know and people you read about. Who are the healthier, stronger, and happier people, those who are ethical or those who are unethical? Now look at those people who are clearly unethical. Have they sustained any of the harms Socrates describes? Finally, is there anything in it for you if you live your life trying to do the right thing?

Discussion Questions

1. What would your response be to the issue raised by the story of "Gyges's ring"? If you knew you could get away with absolutely anything you wanted to do, however unethical, how ethical would your behavior be? How would you decide what to do?

2. What about Plato's case of the unethical person with a reputation for virtue? As long as everyone around you believed you were virtuous, would vice really have any negative consequences?

3. Does the idea that virtue is "the health of the soul" make sense to you? How would you describe that notion to someone in contemporary terms?

4. Do you agree with Plato that in the "healthy soul," the proper relationship is for the mind to be making the decisions and for our physical and emotional dimensions to be subservient? Would you agree that giving in to physical or emotional desires against our better judgment is "unhealthy"?

5. What do you make of Socrates's idea that when we do something wrong, we hurt ourselves? In particular, what about the two distinct kinds of harm: (a) that we begin to lose control over our wants, and (b) that even our minds are weakened?

6. Have you found it true in your own life that once you started doing something you believed was wrong, it became easier and you did it more often?

7. What is your reaction to the "wine jar" analogy? Is it accurate or deceptive?

8. To some extent, what Socrates and Plato claim about morality and the healthy soul does not fit with some accepted truths in contemporary society. We are told that competing aggressively and advancing our own interests at all costs is a sign of strength. Many people consider that limiting our wants and being good are not only barriers to success but weaknesses. Many people agree with Callicles, not with Socrates. What is your reaction to this?

9. The discussion of Socrates's ideas in this chapter relied on a good deal of speculation. Was this interpretation plausible to you? Can you think of another way of interpreting the idea that "vice harms the doer"?

Selected Readings

For Plato's ideas about ethics, the importance of moral virtue, and the relationship between the different parts of the "soul," see the *Republic*. Socrates's ideas are set out in Plato's Socratic dialogues, especially the *Apology, Crito,* and *Gorgias*. The *Apology* is an account of Socrates's trial and contains Socrates's own account of his life's work.

Part Three: Fundamental Theoretical Issues

Chapter 7

What Is Real and How Do We Know It?
Rationalism

Imagine you're told that everything you think about what's "real" is wrong. Everything you see, hear, taste, and smell is an illusion. Events you're taking part in and events you're observing around you are actually *not* happening. All your memories are of things that never took place. In effect, you're asleep and living in a dream world. What would you do if someone offered you a way to wake up and learn the truth? What if the offer had a catch—that once you saw the truth, you could never go back to the illusion? You're offered two pills: a red pill and a blue pill. The red one will give you the truth; the blue one will make you forget everything you've just heard and put you back in the dream.

This is the premise of the classic *Matrix* science fiction film series. Thomas Anderson is a computer program writer and a skilled hacker who goes by the name "Neo." Neo is contacted by the legendary hacker Morpheus, who confirms Neo's unsettling fears that things aren't really what they seem to be. As Morpheus puts it when he and Neo first meet, "Let me tell you why you're here. You're here because you know something. What you know you can't explain. But you feel it. You felt it your entire life. Something's wrong with the world. You don't know what, but it's there." Morpheus reveals to Neo that what he thinks is "reality" is actually a computer simulation called "the Matrix." All humans—except the 250,000 living in the hidden rebel city of Zion—are hardwired into a "neural-interactive simulation" that conceals the truth. What Neo thinks is "real" is simply electrical impulses that are part of a computer simulation determining his perceptions. "Reality" is actually "virtual reality."

We thus have the classic philosophical distinction between *appearance* and *reality*. What everyone experiences in the Matrix—ordinary life in 1999—is simply *appearance*. In *reality*, however, it is hundreds of years in the future. Humanity has lost a war against a race of intelligent machines, is now enslaved, and is being used as a source of energy for the machines. The Matrix creates the life that people think they're living—a virtual reality—by sending electrical impulses to the brain. In essence, everyone connected to the Matrix is living in a dream from which they will never wake up. As Morpheus explains to Neo, the Matrix is "the world that has been pulled over your eyes to blind you from the truth . . . that you are a slave, Neo. Like everyone else, you were born into bondage, born into a prison that you cannot smell or taste or touch. A prison for your mind."[1]

---

1. "Screenplay," Lana Wachowski and Lilly Wachowski, in *The Art of the Matrix* (New York: Newmarket Press, 2000), 300.

That's just science fiction, right? But what if you discovered that two important philosophers (Plato and Descartes) said something similar to what Morpheus claimed—that reality is not what it appears to be and that you can't necessarily trust your senses? How curious are you about the answer? Which pill will you take?

Plato: Idealism and Rationalism

Look at a chair. Now close your eyes and imagine a chair—not necessarily *that* chair but *any* chair. Which is more real, the chair or the idea of the chair? You probably said the physical chair, and so would most people. Can you imagine anyone saying that the *idea* of the chair is more real? If you met someone who argued that position, you'd probably think he wasn't playing with a full deck. However, that is precisely the argument the ancient Greek philosopher Plato makes.

Plato's most basic ideas about reality and knowledge are easy to express: *Ideas are more real than the objects that present themselves to our senses. Knowledge we get through our minds is better than what we get from our physical senses.* The world we reach with our minds is more permanent, perfect, real, and true than the world we experience with our eyes, ears, noses, tongues, and hands. Plato represents the school of thought named **idealism**, which maintains that reality is rooted in ideas, not matter. His perspective that knowledge comes from our minds, not our senses, is called **rationalism**, which takes its name from *ratio*, the Latin word for "reason."

Philosophers regularly challenge us to question what we take as self-evident. But this seems extreme. Plato believes that the world of our senses is not fully "real" at all. Physical objects exist; they aren't imaginary. But they are like shadows in comparison to actual objects. What's most "real" exists only in a dimension of reality that we make contact with by means of our minds. This is a superior level of existence populated by perfect, eternal, but invisible objects.

In other words, there is a higher level of reality, invisible to our senses but not to our minds. In this realm, we "see" with our "mind's eye." Plato calls this dimension, which we know by our intellect, the *intelligible world.* He calls the physical world, which we know by our senses, the *visible world.* Both worlds are real, but the intelligible world is as superior to the visible world as a physical object is to a shadow.

> **idealism** In opposition to materialism, idealism maintains that reality is rooted in ideas, not matter. Plato, for example, claims that the **Forms** are more real and better sources of truth and knowledge than the objects that present themselves to our senses.
>
> **materialism** Materialism is a theory about the nature of reality that claims that if something exists, it must be physical and subject to natural laws like cause and effect. Materialism logically implies **determinism**.
>
> **rationalism** Rationalism claims that knowledge comes from or arises in our minds. Rationalist philosophers say that the best examples of knowledge are mathematics and logic.

Plato's Real World: The Line

Plato appreciates the difficulty of explaining his ideas because he represents them in a couple of different ways. First, he illustrates his conception of the nature of reality by another image: a line.

To start, we draw a line.

Next, we divide it in two, taking care not to split it in half. We will make the top part of the line somewhat shorter than the bottom part as a way of representing that the top part is superior to the bottom.

This is the most basic way to represent Plato's conception of the two parts of reality. The bottom portion of the line represents the visible world, the ordinary physical world we live in. The top portion of the line represents the "intelligible" realm, the world that we can reach only with our minds.

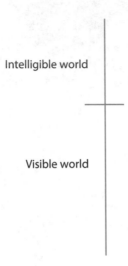

Now we divide each part of the line in two again, using the same proportions. This is Plato's way of saying that in each world there are two types, or grades, of things, each superior to the one below it. The line now represents a hierarchy. As we go up in this hierarchy, we encounter things that are more real, more enduring, and more true.

The Visible World

Let's take a closer look at the section of the line representing the visible world. Label the top portion of the bottom part "physical objects" and the bottom portion "shadows, representations, drawings, reflections." This section now represents the ordinary world we experience with our senses.

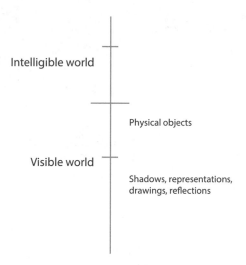

In Plato's scheme, physical objects are superior to images, or representations, of them. There are a couple of reasons for this. First, pictures of a chair are possible only because the chair itself exists. If there were no chair, there could not be a picture of one. Second, if you want to learn about a particular object—say, a car—what will teach you more: the car itself or a drawing of it? The car, of course. A drawing—even a series of drawings or a hologram—can teach you only so much. Each image gives you limited information. If you have the car itself, however, you can climb around inside, look at the engine and trunk, go for a drive, and even take things apart. You cannot do any of this with a drawing or a hologram of the car because it's not really the car. It's just a representation. Thus, Plato ranks physical objects higher than any images of them because they give us more dependable knowledge of their nature.

So far, Plato makes sense. Material objects and images of material objects are both real in some way. But to Plato, some things are more real than others. When we think of what we can do with a real car versus what we can do with an image of one, you can see how the reality of an actual car is a superior kind of reality. Similarly, we get better knowledge about a car by examining the car itself, not images of it.

The Intelligible World

Now let's move to the intelligible world. Label the bottom portion of the upper part of the line "objects of mathematics" and its top portion "the Forms."

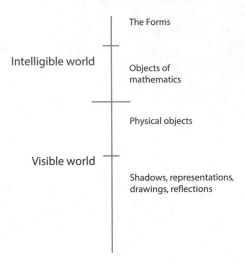

Squares, Circles, Triangles, Points

The lower level of the intelligible world is populated by the "objects of mathematics." These include the lines and points as well as perfect triangles, circles, and the other objects that geometry and trigonometry are built around.

The first thing to see about these objects is that we encounter them only in our minds. We can find physical representations of them in the visible world, of course, but here Plato is talking about the abstract concepts behind the material shapes: perfect circles, squares, rectangles, and triangles; lines and points without dimensions, etc.

The idea that the objects of mathematics actually exist on some immaterial plane may surprise you. But Plato does not stop there. He also says that these objects are superior to anything in the visible world. Indeed, he says, they are perfect and unchangeable.

Look at some object in the room you're in right now. What color is it? How long will it be that color? Only until someone paints it. How long will it exist? Maybe twenty or thirty years at the longest. Consider a triangle. How long will it have three sides? Forever. In five hundred years, will the sum of the interior angles still be the same? Absolutely. How long will it be true that $5 = 5$? Always. Now what about the fact that a particular wooden chair can support the weight of people who sit on it? That will be true only until the chair starts to fall apart—in other words, not forever. No physical object can match the stability and consistency of a mathematical object. That's why Plato thinks they're superior to ordinary chairs and tables.

However, even though mathematical objects are superior to physical things, they occupy only the lower part of the intelligible world.

The Forms

The top of the upper segment of the line is the area that is most important to Plato. Here reside what he calls the **Forms**. By placing the Forms at the top of the hierarchy, Plato assigns them the highest dimension of reality. Knowledge of the Forms is the highest kind of knowledge. But what are the Forms?

The Forms are just what the name implies. They are the forms, or models, for everything that exists. They are perfect, unchanging, and eternal. There are two kinds of Forms. First come the ideal patterns for everyday physical objects—chairs, tables, cats, dogs, trees, grass, and so on. Second come the Forms for concepts and qualities—justice, fairness, equity, perfection. Above all these Forms is the highest Form, one called simply "the Good."

A Form not only captures the essence of an object or an idea, it is that essence. It's a lot like a universal definition, only it's an entity that actually exists.

> **Forms** The Forms are what Plato calls the nonmaterial, perfect models of everything that exists. They are known only by the mind. The chief Form is the Form of the Good.

For example, look at all the chairs around you. Some are wood, some metal; some have four legs, some have none; some are plain, some fancy; some are comfortable, some are not. Now close your eyes, mull over what you've just seen, and then think about what it is for something to be a chair. Think about what qualities all chairs have. In other words, try to define the essence of a chair.

If you have such a description in your mind, you have encountered the Form of a chair; we can also call this "chairness." As you contemplate "chairness," you understand the true, ultimate nature of a chair. Its description fits every chair that has ever been or will ever be. This essence of chair, its Form, will never change. Just as the truths of mathematics will never vary, the Form "chairness," that is, the essence of a chair, will never change. That's the nature of a Form, remember. A Form is perfect, absolute, eternal, and unchanging.

Plato's Forms, then, are abstract, nonmaterial entities. Also realize, however, that Plato believes that they exist—just as independently, just as uniquely, just as surely as you do. Even more so. They are superior to anything in the physical world. They exist in a dimension of reality we reach only with our minds. They are, in Plato's opinion, the most "real" things that exist—perfect, absolute, eternal, immutable. The knowledge we have of the Forms is the best knowledge possible.

Forms and Physical Objects

As hard as it is to grasp what the Forms are, it is more difficult to grasp the relationship between the Forms and physical objects. Plato says that material objects *imitate* or *participate in* the Forms. But that doesn't give you much to hang on to.

One way to capture this is to think of the relationship between an object and its shadow. Just as an actual chair is responsible for the shadow of a chair, Plato thinks that the Form of the chair is responsible for the actual chair. And as the shadow of a chair represents but is vastly inferior to an actual chair, so actual chairs, such as the one you might be sitting in now, represent but are inferior to the Form "chairness" that they somehow represent.

The process by which a Form becomes a model for actual objects needn't concern us here. Plato's intent lies more in explaining the substance of reality than the forces that shape it, anyway. What's important is that you simply understand how to use the analogy, which, again, goes like this:

a Form : a physical object :: an object : its shadow.

The Highest Forms

By now you understand something about the Forms of physical objects. As noted above, however, there are also higher Forms for abstract ideas, concepts, and qualities like Justice, Beauty, Fairness, and Equality. The highest Form of all is simply the Good—the essence of perfect goodness.

These higher Forms are harder to talk about than something more familiar, like "chairness," "tableness," or "treeness." Understanding the essential nature of Beauty or Justice, as opposed to being acquainted with beautiful objects or just actions, is a tall order for most of us. Plato himself expected philosophers to spend their whole lives trying to understand these Forms. And he never said it would be easy. An accomplished, full-time, highly trained philosopher, he thought, would not be able to understand the Good until about the age of fifty.[2]

The Allegory of the Cave

Plato's second explanation about the nature of reality is more figurative than "the Line." It's a story about people imprisoned in a cave. He writes:

> Imagine human beings living in an underground, cavelike dwelling, with an entrance a long way up, which is both open to the light and as wide as the cave itself. They've been there since childhood, fixed in the same place, with their necks and legs fettered, able to see only in front of them, because their bonds prevent them from turning their heads around. Light is provided by a fire burning far above and behind them. Also behind them, but on higher ground, there is a path stretching between them and the fire. Imagine that along this path a low wall has been built, like the screen in front of performers above which they show their puppets. . . .
>
> Then also imagine that there are people along the wall, carrying all kinds of artifacts that project above it—statues of people and other animals, made out of stone, wood, and every material. And, as you'd expect, some of the carriers are talking, and some are silent.

---

2. Given what we've just seen about the Line, it should come as no surprise that Plato sees a close connection between philosophy and mathematics. He supposedly had carved over the entry to his school, the Academy, "Let no one ignorant of geometry enter here." His educational program for philosophers includes a ten-year study of mathematics before they can begin understanding the Forms.

This is a strange image you're describing, and strange prisoners.

They're like us. Do you suppose, first of all, that these prisoners see anything of themselves and one another besides the shadows that the fire casts on the wall in front of them?

How could they, if they have to keep their heads motionless throughout life?

What about the things being carried along the wall? Isn't the same true of them? Of course.

And if they could talk to one another, don't you think they'd suppose that the names they used applied to the things they see passing before them

They'd have to.

And what if their prison also had an echo from the wall facing them? Don't you think they'd believe that the shadows passing in front of them were talking whenever one of the carriers passing along the wall was doing so?

I certainly do.

Then the prisoners would in every way believe that the truth is nothing other than the shadows of those artifacts.

They must surely believe that.[3]

Plato uses this story of the cave to represent his ideas about the nature of reality, or more precisely, the distinction between appearance and reality. The critical fact is that we are the prisoners. The cave and the shadows represent our everyday experience. Here is how the analogy plays out. The shadows of tables and chairs on the cave wall are to the actual objects that produce them what the ordinary tables and chairs we know in our everyday lives are to "real" tables and chairs. Similarly, the dark, shadow-filled cave is to the sun-filled world outside the cave as the natural world we live in is to the "real" world. Or to restate this using analogy symbols:

shadow of a chair : physical chair :: physical chair : Form of the chair

cave : outside world :: physical world : world of the Forms

The Practical Implication of Plato's Ideas About Reality and Knowledge: Plato's Contribution

If you see yourself as a practical, commonsense person, you might be inclined to dismiss Plato's wondering whether chairs and tables are actually "real" as the sort of odd thing philosophers are notorious for, such as asking how you know the furniture in your room doesn't disappear when you aren't there. If you're feeling generous, you might think that **metaphysics** and **epistemology** are interesting. But you more likely think they're irrelevant to life in the real world. Plato, however, thinks his conclusions about reality and knowledge are anything but impractical. And there's a good chance you'll find the implications of his ideas concerning.

---

3. Plato: *Republic*, translated by G. M. A. Grube (Indianapolis: Hackett Publishing Company, 1992), 514a–515c, p. 186.

Plato thinks it's a long and difficult process to get to ultimate knowledge of the Forms. This includes studying mathematics for ten years before even beginning to study the Forms. As a result, a true understanding of the nature of reality is limited to a minority of the population, and a very small minority at that. At first, you might be tempted to say, "If a small group of people want to spend their lives hidden in some ivory tower doing math, metaphysics, and epistemology, why should I care?" Before we answer that, however, take a few minutes to do this questionnaire.

Using a scale of −5 to +5, rate how much you enjoy the following activities or how important they are to you:

1. buying and having things

2. trying to solve the crime in mysteries

3. dancing and/or partying

4. knowing that someone loves or cares about you a great deal

5. thinking about the meaning of life

6. having sexual pleasure

7. being impulsive and spontaneous

8. making decisions in a calm, logical manner

9. having deep friendships

10. being in good shape physically

11. analyzing why people do things

12. doing something adventurous

13. having a "signature scent" or wearing various colognes or perfumes

14. discussing serious, intellectual topics

15. eating your favorite foods

16. doing something romantic

17. being logical

18. understanding yourself

19. looking good

20. making new friends

21. attending an interesting lecture

22. being popular

23. making or having money

24. watching a movie that evokes strong feelings (love story, scary film, tragedy, etc.)

Now add up your scores in the following three groups.

Group A: questions 1, 3, 6, 10, 13, 15, 19, 23

Group B: questions 4, 7, 9, 12, 16, 20, 22, 24

Group C: questions 2, 5, 8, 11, 14, 17, 18, 21

You should now have three scores: an A score, a B score, and a C score. Hold on to them for the time being while we return to Plato's argument.

Remember that Plato's Forms include Justice, Goodness, Fairness, and the like. The reason this is so important is that Plato thinks that only people who have this kind of knowledge should be in charge in a society. As he says in a very famous passage from the *Republic*, where he describes his ideal city:

> Until philosophers rule as kings in cities or those who are now called kings and leading men genuinely and adequately philosophize, that is, until political power and philosophy entirely coincide, . . . cities will have no rest from evils, Glaucon, nor, I think, will the human race.[4]

Philosophers in charge? Is Plato kidding? Just imagine what it would be like if the people in your school's philosophy department ran the country. Most of you would think that a prescription for disaster! Philosophers often live so much in the world of ideas that they don't know—or care—what day it is. You probably think that running things is the last thing philosophers should be doing, and you'd probably recommend leaving them in the classroom where they can't hurt themselves.

Yet Plato sees things differently because he thinks that ultimately being able to understand the Forms requires not only superior intelligence but also a certain kind of personality.

Plato thinks that all people fall into one of three types, depending on which of three basic parts of their being dominates their nature. These elements are *physical desires*, the *emotions*, and the *intellect*. Each of us has all three, but Plato claims that one part usually predominates.

In "physical people," the body and physical pleasures dominate. This includes people whose lives revolve around food, alcohol, or sex; those whose first concern is to be rich; people strongly motivated by luxuries; and people who get more pleasure from working out than from participating in a good discussion. This physical focus can be expressed positively or negatively. Being concerned with staying in shape is positive; aspiring to the "good life" is fine, as long as it's kept within limits; being addicted to drugs or alcohol is negative. In any case, "physical people" make physical and material things the most import-ant parts of their lives. They have emotional and intellectual interests as well, but these are less compelling and less satisfying.

---

4. Plato, *Republic*, 473c–d, p. 148.

In another type of person, emotions hold sway. "Feeling people" get their greatest satisfaction from emotional things. They may make romantic relationships the most important part of their lives. They may devote themselves to caring for others, getting emotional nourishment in the process. Such people may be artists, social workers, or nurses, for example. As with a "physical" orientation, an "emotional" orientation can be positive or negative. One person may be attracted to doomed love affairs, another to healthy relationships. One may get the Nobel Peace Prize; another may die as a terrorist seeking vengeance.

The "intellectual person" may enjoy physical and emotional pleasures perfectly well but is drawn most strongly to intellectual interests. Such people are driven to learn new things, understand the world around them, or solve problems. They may be scholars or scientists, but they may also be writers, detectives, psychiatrists, management consultants, architects, or anyone else motivated by an intellectual challenge. Most at home in the world of ideas, and they are highly motivated to understand things. They hunger for intellectual stimulation. Again, this quality can show itself positively, as with scientists like Albert Einstein and Stephen Hawking, or negatively, as in the case of some brilliant criminal who executes the "perfect crime."

It is from this last group that Plato draws his "philosopher-rulers" because their personalities are dominated by *reason* more than anything else. The force of reason in their personalities should be so strong that they can resist any emotional pull in their decisions or be similarly influenced by physical desires or greed. Plato wants his philosopher-rulers to be intelligent, controlled, and idealistic—which are admittedly good qualities for political leaders.

Now take out the results of the questionnaire you answered earlier. This is not a scientific instrument with guaranteed accuracy, but your scores should tell you roughly which of the three types you are. If your A score is highest, you are probably a "physical" person. "Feeling" people will have a high B score. And if C is highest, you are most likely an "intellectual" person. Two or even all three of your scores may be close, but most people have one that is highest. See if your category is right. Ask other people in your class if they think it's accurate. Odds are you'll find that one of Plato's categories describes you pretty well.

In a representative group, the C people will make up the smallest group. Plato would draw his philosopher-rulers from Group C. What's your opinion about their qualifications to be powerful government officials?

Strictly speaking, the kind of government Plato suggests here is the rule of an *aristocracy*. But this isn't what you think it is. Most of us use "aristocracy" to refer to a hereditary nobility. But the word literally means "rule by the best," or "rule by the most capable," and that is how Plato uses it. His ideal government is made up of those who are most qualified because of their knowledge of the Forms of Justice, Fairness, and the like and their being more "intellectual" than "physical" or "emotional."

And here's the most troubling part of Plato's ideas. His philosopher-rulers are not chosen by popular vote. Why should they be? What expert is elected? Are medical licenses given out by a vote of the general public? No, aspiring physicians have to go through medical school and an internship; then they take state examinations and go through a residency. Lawyers, architects, veterinarians, teachers, clergy, psychologists, electricians, beauticians, and most other experts also must go through some certification process. Even people who drive cars must get licenses.

The idea behind certification is that people are not automatically competent to do jobs that require advanced knowledge and training just because a majority of people say they are. The stakes are too high. Who determines whether people actually possess the competencies in question? Others who already practice the profession—*not* the general public, or even a small group of nonpractitioners.

In a democracy, of course, political officeholders are one of the few groups of people performing important tasks who are chosen by nonexperts, that is, by "the people." And too often in democracies, personality plays a large part in the people's choice. Given Plato's metaphysical and epistemological conclusions, he thinks this is a ridiculous way to identify the most competent people for the job. He believes that citizens are too easily misled by ignorance or emotion to make wise choices about who should be in charge. Just as we leave decisions about our next generation of lawyers, nurses, teachers, and physicians to experts, so Plato leaves the decision about who qualifies as a philosopher-ruler to experts in that arena. There's nothing democratic about it.

Whether you agree with Plato or not, his challenge to democracy based on his ideas about "reality" and "knowledge" are a good reminder that even the most abstract issues can have very important practical implications.

The Rationalism of René Descartes

Plato may get the rationalist ball rolling, but he is actually not the most important rationalist thinker in the history of philosophy. That honor should probably go to the seventeenth-century French philosopher René Descartes. Perhaps the most important reason is that Descartes concentrates much more on the concept of knowledge. In so doing, he breathes new life into the claim that the mind comes to more certain conclusions than the senses. At the same time, he places more limits on what the mind can know than Plato does. His Greek predecessor believed that the mind lets us have knowledge of intelligible objects like the Forms. Descartes, however, maintains that all we can really know is what's in our own consciousness, thus giving us a more constrained theory of idealism.[5]

Descartes had a major impact on every thinker that followed him. He came to think that instead of starting with the question "What is the nature of reality?" we should start with "What is the nature of knowledge?" After Descartes, epistemology moves to the center of philosophy. In fact, Descartes's approach ultimately prompts a number of

---

5. Because Plato believes that the Forms exist independently of our knowing them, his approach is called *objective idealism*. Descartes's theory is called *epistemological idealism*.

important thinkers in the history of philosophy to explore deeply how the human mind works as an instrument that produces knowledge. The fact that Descartes changed how all philosophers after him think counts as a genuine revolution in philosophy.

The first thing to note about Descartes is how systematic and rigorous his methodology is. In his *Discourse on Method* (1637), he sets down four rules:

> The first was never to accept anything as true if I did not have evident knowledge of its truth: that is, carefully to avoid precipitate conclusions and preconceptions, and to include nothing more in my judgments than what presented itself to my mind so clearly and so distinctly that I had no occasion to doubt it.
>
> The second, to divide each of the difficulties I examined into as many parts as possible and as may be required in order to resolve them better.
>
> The third, to direct my thoughts in an orderly manner, by beginning with the simplest and most easily known objects in order to ascend little by little, step by step, to knowledge of the most complex, and by supposing some order even among objects that have no natural order of precedence.
>
> And the last, throughout to make enumerations so complete, and reviews so comprehensive, that I could be sure of leaving nothing out.[6]

What's most important for our purposes is to see how Descartes claims that he must be *absolutely certain* of something before he can say he *knows* it. He takes absolute certainty as the most important characteristic of genuine knowledge. Like Plato, he finds it by using his mind, not his physical senses.

Descartes's Radical Doubt

Descartes describes the application and purpose of his method very clearly. He confesses that he had earlier accepted some beliefs he now knows are false. In order to make sure that his mind is on the strongest footing going forward, he will question everything and accept only what he is absolutely certain is true.

René Descartes (1596–1650) was born in France and educated at the Jesuit college of La Fleche. After a period of travel, including a short stint as a soldier, Descartes began writing about the proper method of intellectual investigation (*Rules for the Direction of the Mind*), a method that would give philosophical knowledge the same certainty as the conclusions of mathematics. He completed scientific and mathematical writings, but he suppressed his own defense of the idea that the earth revolves about the sun when he heard of Galileo's fate for taking the same position. In 1641, Descartes published the book he is best known for, *Meditations on First Philosophy*. In 1649, he agreed to teach philosophy to Queen Christina of Sweden, but he died of pneumonia the following year.

---

6. Tarek R. Dika, "Descartes' Method," *The Stanford Encyclopedia of Philosophy* (Summer 2020 Edition), ed. Edward N. Zalta, https://plato.stanford.edu/archives/sum2020/entries/descartes-method/.

In his intense, skeptical examination of what he thinks he knows, Descartes takes the simple act of questioning, or doubting, to an unprecedented extreme. In fact, he is best known for what is called his *radical doubt*. The term "radical" means both "fundamental" and "extreme," and both meanings are intended here. Simply put, he decides to doubt everything he thinks he knows and perceives.

Descartes will accept only things that are "certain and indubitable." There can be not one trace of doubt in his mind. If he can make up any scenario, no matter how unlikely or bizarre, in which what he claims to know might be false, then he must say he does not know it. As long as it is theoretically or logically possible that something is false, he cannot claim to know it. The only way to find genuine knowledge is to doubt everything that suggests itself as true. Whatever survives the heat of such intense skepticism must be certain. Will anything survive such a blistering assault and qualify as something he genuinely knows?

Doubting the Obvious: Dreaming

Here is how Descartes describes his first steps in his *Meditations on First Philosophy*:

> There is no novelty to me in the reflection that, from my earliest years, I have accepted many false opinions as true, and that what I have concluded from such badly assured premises could not but be highly doubtful and uncertain. From the time that I first recognized this fact, I have realized that if I wished to have any firm and constant knowledge in the sciences, I would have to undertake, once and for all, to set aside all the opinions which I had previously accepted among my beliefs and start again from the very beginning. But this enterprise appeared to me to be of very great magnitude, and so I waited until I had attained an age so mature that I could not hope for a later time when I would be more fitted to execute the project. Now, however, I have delayed so long that henceforward I should be afraid that I was committing a fault if, in continuing to deliberate, I expended time which should be devoted to action.
>
> The present is opportune for my design; I have freed my mind of all kinds of cares; I feel myself, fortunately, disturbed by no passions; and I have found a serene retreat in peaceful solitude. I will therefore make a serious and unimpeded effort to destroy generally all my former opinions. In order to do this, however, it will not be necessary to show that they are all false, a task which I might never be able to complete; because, since reason already convinces me that I should abstain from the belief in things which are not entirely certain and indubitable no less carefully than from the belief in those which appear to me to be manifestly false, it will be enough to make me reject them all if I can find in each some ground for doubt. And for that it will not be necessary for me to examine each one in particular, which would be an infinite labor; but since the destruction of the foundation necessarily involves the collapse of all the rest of the edifice. I shall first attack the principles upon which all my former opinions were founded.
>
> Everything which I have thus far accepted as entirely true and assured has been acquired from the senses or by means of the senses. But I have learned by experience

that these senses sometimes mislead me, and it is prudent never to trust wholly those things which have once deceived us.

But it is possible that, even though the senses occasionally deceive us about things which are barely perceptible and very far away, there are many other things which we cannot reasonably doubt, even though we know them through the senses—as, for example, that I am here, seated by the fire, wearing a winter dressing gown, holding this paper in my hands, and other things of this nature. . . .

Nevertheless, I must remember that I am a man, and that consequently I am accustomed to sleep and in my dreams to imagine the same things that lunatics imagine when awake, or sometimes things which are even less plausible.[7]

Descartes begins with ordinary perceptions that seem too obvious to doubt: "I am here, seated by the fire, wearing a winter dressing gown, holding this paper in my hands." But remember, he's committed to consider *any* possible reason he could be wrong. He wonders, then, whether or not he might be dreaming. Taking that possibility seriously, he even concludes that he is almost able to convince himself that he is not awake—but sleeping and dreaming:

How many times has it occurred that the quiet of the night made me dream of my usual habits: that I was here, clothed in a dressing gown, and sitting by the fire, although I was in fact lying undressed in bed! It seems apparent to me now, that I am not looking at this paper with my eyes closed, that this head that I shake is not drugged with sleep, that it is with design and deliberate intent that I stretch out this hand and perceive it. What happens in sleep seems not at all as clear and distinct as all this. But I am speaking as though I never recall having been misled, while asleep, by similar illusions! When I consider these matters carefully, I realize so clearly that there are no conclusive indications by which waking life can be distinguished from sleep that I am quite astonished, and my bewilderment is such that it is almost able to convince me that I am sleeping.[8]

At first glance, you may think Descartes is going off the deep end here. Few of us have trouble figuring out whether we've dreamt something or actually lived it. There is, however, an incredibly vivid kind of dreaming called "lucid dreaming," in which the experience is in many ways indistinguishable from ordinary waking experience. So it's possible that if we were having a lucid dream, we might at first mistake it for being awake. Hallucinations—whether the result of drugs or brain pathology—seem real to the people having them. Or what about something even more exotic? Consider where the technology involved in virtual reality may ultimately go. A variety of science fiction films,

---

7. René Descartes, *Meditations on First Philosophy*, trans. Laurence J. Lafleur (Indianapolis: Bobbs-Merrill, 1960), 17–18.

8. Descartes, *Meditations*, 18.

like *The Matrix* discussed earlier, use the idea that complex computer simulations can be as convincing as "reality." In theory, Descartes's doubts about ordinary perception aren't totally off base. Remember, if it's even remotely possible to question the authenticity of what we're perceiving, we can't say we *know* it to be true. Descartes quickly concludes that our physical senses aren't totally dependable.

Having dismissed the senses as a source of certain knowledge, Descartes moves to the conclusions of our minds—the pure truths of mathematics. Perhaps we can find a way to doubt the reports of our eyes, but how can we question "2 + 3 = 5" or "a square will never have more than four sides"? Wouldn't we be crazy to doubt such things?

Doubting the Obvious: Deception

Yes, we would be crazy or *deceived*. Remember that the radical doubt allows for *any* scenario, no matter how bizarre. Descartes definitely goes for the bizarre here, writing:

> I have long held the belief that there is a God who can do anything. . . . But how can I be sure but that he has brought it to pass that there is no earth, no sky, no extended bodies, . . . and that nevertheless I have simply the impressions of all these things . . . ? . . . How can I be sure but that God has brought it about that I am always mistaken when I add two and three?[9]

Or, if God is not doing this, Descartes says that there is no reason why we cannot imagine that this massive deception is being masterminded by "a certain evil spirit, not less clever and deceitful than powerful." But whether God or some Master Deceiver is behind this deceit, the bottom line is the same. We still have no way to say that we are absolutely certain of anything—from physical perception ("snow is white") to intellectual calculation ("2 + 3 = 5").

The One Certainty: Existing

So far, we're coming up dry. If some Master Deceiver really is at work, everything may be an illusion—the room you're in, your friends, the events you think you have experienced, even your hands, your feet, and all the rest of you.

At this point, however, Descartes finally hits on something he cannot doubt. Because even if he is being deceived about absolutely everything around him, the one thing he cannot be deceived about is that *he exists. He must exist in order to be deceived.* And no matter how hard he tries, although he can doubt absolutely everything that goes on outside him and even everything that goes on within his mind, he cannot doubt his own existence. Descartes concludes:

> Even though there may be a deceiver of some sort, very powerful and very tricky, . . . there can be no slightest doubt that I exist, since he deceives me; and let

---

9. Descartes, *Meditations*, 20.

him deceive me as much as he will, he can never make me be nothing as long as I think that I am something. Thus, . . . *I am, I exist,* is necessarily true every time . . . I conceive it in my mind.[10]

You have probably heard Descartes's famous line: *Cogito ergo sum,* "I think, therefore I am." This is what it means. Doubting is a kind of thinking—even being deceived requires thinking on our part—and as long as you're aware of yourself thinking or doubting, it must necessarily follow that you exist.

The Standard of Truth: Clarity and Distinctness

Having discovered what he considers to be one example of certain knowledge—his own existence—Descartes looks to see what philosophical conclusions he can draw from it. He studies this piece of knowledge and claims that it has a *clarity* and *distinctness* that set it apart from ideas that can be doubted. These criteria, then, become his general standard for truth: "And therefore it seems to me that I can already establish as a general principle that everything which we conceive very clearly and very distinctly is wholly true."[11]

Self-knowledge is not the only thing Descartes perceives so clearly and distinctly, however, and this leads him to draw some important conclusions. First, he claims that the existence of God is clear and distinct. However, if God exists, there is no Master Deceiver—a good God would not allow such deception. And if there is no Master Deceiver, mathematics must be sound. (The integrity of mathematics is, not surprisingly, very important to a rationalist.) Descartes also argues that two other basic concepts, Substance and Identity, are legitimate. Taken together, this forms the foundation for his general interpretation of reality.

These "very clear and very distinct" perceptions—Self, God, Substance, and Identity—are *innate ideas,* Descartes says. Describing them as "certain germs of truth which exist naturally in our souls," he believes that God puts them there. This theory of innate ideas, we might say, envisions the human mind like a computer that already comes with a few basic programs installed. Because these concepts are innate, they are also self-evident, and their truth is absolutely certain.

Whether Descartes's innate ideas are as self-evident as he claims and whether they are put there by God are beyond the scope of our investigation. But appreciate that even the logical operations of our minds give us conclusions that are not only "clear and distinct" but significantly more stable, dependable, and permanent than any physical truth. Recall the riddle from J. K. Rowling's *Harry Potter and the Philosopher's Stone* that we examined in Chapter 2. Hermione solved it using logic. Her conclusion was solid. Like the rules of mathematics, the rules of logic give us absolutely certain conclusions.

---

10. Descartes, *Meditations,* 24.
11. Descartes, *Meditations,* 34.

- No sentence of the form "A and not-A" can be true because it's a *contradiction*. ("Today is Tuesday and today is not Tuesday.")
- Any argument of the form "if A, then B; A; therefore, B" will be valid. This is called *affirming the antecedent*. ("If Eliud was born in Nandi County, Eliud was born in Kenya; Eliud was born in Nandi County; therefore, Eliud was born in Kenya.")
- Any argument of the form "If A, then B; not-B; therefore, not-A" will be valid. This is called *denying the consequent*. ("If Jones was born in Atlanta, Jones was born in Georgia; Jones was not born in Georgia; therefore, Jones was not born in Atlanta.")
- Any argument of the form "If A, then B; not-A; therefore, not-B" will not be valid. This is a fallacy called *denying the antecedent*. ("If Murdoch was born in Toronto, Murdoch was born in Canada; Murdoch was not born in Toronto; therefore, Murdoch was not born in Canada." Murdoch could easily have been born in a different town or city in Canada.)

Self-consciousness, the conclusions of mathematics, and logic. Not a bad set of "clear and distinct" perceptions that qualify as significantly more stable, dependable, and permanent than anything we can conclude from our senses.

A Contemporary Radical Doubt

Even though you understand Descartes's conclusions, you may not be as impressed with his "radical doubt" as he would wish. Most people don't seriously question whether they are awake or dreaming. They also don't normally wonder whether some malevolent spirit is trying to deceive them by manipulating their thoughts. You know that you dream, and you know about optical illusions. But most of us know when we are awake, alert, and thinking straight.

If Descartes's ideas about dreaming and a Master Deceiver did not shake your confidence in what you "know," perhaps we can discover a more contemporary "radical doubt" that does. Our goal is to find out if we can know anything with absolute certainty. If we can imagine the slightest theoretical doubt about something, using Descartes's rules, we will give up any claim to "know" it.

An Alternative to the Senses: "Inner" Data

Like Descartes, we can quickly reject the senses as dependable sources of knowledge. This brings us to an examination of our inner selves, our minds. Here is where Descartes conjures up his clever, deceitful, and powerful Master Deceiver whose capacity for deception forces us to question even the most apparently evident conclusions of the mind.

You probably think that Descartes's idea of a Master Deceiver is unconvincing. It is theoretically possible, of course, but it doesn't persuade the average person that the conclusions of our minds are doubtful. Nonetheless, there *are* good reasons why we cannot trust our minds any more than we can trust our senses, and those are what we should consider here.

Let's take a familiar mental operation: memory. Do you remember the most important events of your life—major birthdays, graduation, romances, accomplishments? Not the first thing you said as a baby or what you wore in the spring pageant in the fourth grade. Just major events that took place after you're old enough to remember things. Did these events actually happen? No doubt you're absolutely certain that they did.

Now is it possible that there were any major events that you do *not* remember? Again, not small stuff—genuinely important things. You probably think this is a stupid question. How could you *not* remember a crucial event in your life? You're no doubt certain you remember all the big events, but can you really be sure? Can't the mind be deceived as the senses can?

In fact, the mind is often unreliable, and many people do not remember major events in their lives, or do not remember them accurately. For example, it is well known that when we experience certain terrible events, our minds often cope with the trauma by selectively changing our memories. One psychological mechanism is called a *screen memory,* in which we reconfigure reality and remember an event very differently. Someone who was sexually abused as a child, for instance, might remember the event as an attack by a fierce dog.

Another strategy is to remove an event from our conscious minds altogether. Some people will recount their past totally omitting certain experiences. As far as they are concerned, these events never happened. For example, someone who grew up with an alcoholic parent might have no memory of any alcohol abuse. When a sibling recalls the details, the person without the memory thinks that this other person is exaggerating, making things up, or crazy. No one could forget something that important, we think—but we can.

However, if the mind can simply "forget" a major event that happened or reconstruct an incident in a more acceptable way, then the mind is not a completely accurate and reliable instrument for representing reality. And of course, following Descartes's lead, if there is the slightest room for doubt, we cannot claim that something, in this case the mind, is a source of certain knowledge.

Or consider this. Take a moment and freely choose to do something. Pick up a pencil. Move your head to the left. Stand up. Do you have any doubt that you caused that action? Presumably, you clearly and distinctly perceived that you made a decision about something. It absolutely, positively feels like free choice, doesn't it? However, as discussed in the chapter on determinism, neuroscientist Benjamin Libet discovered that there's clear, scientific evidence that measurable activity in your brain took place *before* your "free, conscious" decision. That is, there's reason to doubt that what you experienced was an instance of free choice.

Accordingly, we have various reasons to cast genuine doubt on the workings of the mind. In other words, we do not have to imagine a Master Deceiver to say that knowledge stemming from our minds may be less than perfect.

Descartes's Insight

Seen through contemporary eyes, Descartes's conclusion that the only thing we can know for sure is that we exist still seems legitimate. Whether or not there are contemporary ways to talk sensibly about his "innate ideas" remains a question for you to ponder. Descartes appeals to the concept of God to prove the truth of the outside world, but those arguments and the issue of God's existence exceed the scope of this chapter.

If nothing else, however, Descartes gives us powerful reasons for being more than a little skeptical about what we are sure is true, and that insight alone assures the indispensability of Descartes's thought in any examination of our own lives and of the world around us if we want to be certain that what we claim to know is, in fact, true.

There are also decidedly practical implications to Descartes's skeptical method and his insistence on clarity and distinctness. Think about the various beliefs you have that you are *positive* are true. How many of them do you have direct evidence for? Probably not many. You likely hold a number of them because you trust the people who told you they were true. What would Descartes say? Remember, if we discover any possibility that we might be wrong, we can't claim to know something for certain. The people who told us something could be mistaken. Perhaps they're relying on their trust in someone else. They might even be lying to you. According to Descartes's strict standards, we aren't entitled to as much certainty as we think. And if that's the case, we may need to leaven our certainty about these beliefs with no small amount of intellectual humility.

The Strength of Plato's and Descartes's Rationalism

Plato and Descartes make a strong case for the idea that only the truths we arrive at through our minds alone can count as knowledge. Only purely intellectual disciplines like mathematics and logic enable us to reach conclusions that are permanent and certain. By contrast, the facts we derive from observing the physical world are temporary and changing. Our senses give us inferior information. It may not be fiction or illusory. But, according to Plato and Descartes, it is too insubstantial to qualify as knowledge.

Even if you don't find Plato and Descartes entirely convincing, at least recognize the fact that they provide important support to the idea that "things aren't what they appear to be."

Discussion Questions

1. To Plato, philosophers are people who have left the cave, gone outside, and seen the brightness of the sun. Plato points out that when such people return to the cave, however, they have trouble adjusting to the darkness and identifying the shadows on the wall. Furthermore, if they try to convince the other prisoners that the shadows are paltry images of what is "real," the philosophers are scoffed at and thought strange. Doesn't this fit with the way most people think about

philosophers? Might this mean that philosophers have "seen the light" while most other people are still preoccupied by shadows?

2. What do you make of the fact that the truths of mathematics are eternal and perfect? Does this mean that a "mathematical reality" is superior to "physical reality"? In trying to determine the nature of reality, is the mind or the physical senses the better tool?

3. If Plato's theory of the Forms is correct, would you agree with Plato that only people who understand Forms like Justice, Fairness, Equity, and so on should be in positions of responsibility in our society? Should such knowledge be a requirement of public office? How would you test for it?

4. In *The Matrix*, one of the characters decides that he'd prefer the illusion of good food and a comfortable life over the reality of utilitarian food and a life of struggle. So he makes a deal with Agent Smith to turn over Morpheus. If the technology made it possible, would you choose a "virtual" luxurious, pleasure-filled life over a "real" life that invariably would include times of challenge, failure, and unhappiness? Which pill would you take?

5. Descartes concedes the possibility that he may be dreaming at a time when he believes that he is awake. Have you ever had dreams that were so vivid that they felt real? How do you know that you are awake now? Wouldn't you say or do the same things in a dream to prove that you were "awake"? Don't our perceptions while we are dreaming seem to match Descartes's notions of clarity and distinctness? Is there any way to prove for sure that you are not dreaming at this instant?

6. Descartes thinks that we have a "very clear and very distinct" perception of God. Do you agree? If not, do you think this undermines anything else Descartes claims?

7. How dependable is the mind as an instrument of knowledge? Reflect on the content and structure of your mind. Do you find any innate or self-evident ideas at all? How do you know they are innate?

Selected Readings

Plato's allegory of the cave can be found in his *Republic*, Book VII, and the discussion of the Line in Book VI. For Descartes, see his *Meditations on First Philosophy*, particularly the first two meditations.

Chapter 8

What Is Real and How Do We Know It?
Empiricism

We saw at the start of the previous chapter that *The Matrix* gave us an excellent place to begin an inquiry into a fundamental theoretical issue: what's *real*, and how do we *know* it? It's also the case that the basic idea of the film—that the experience most people have in Neo's world is an illusion produced by electrical impulses sent to their brains—perfectly reflects, in its own way, a challenge that the **rationalism** of Plato and Descartes faces. After all, these two thinkers claim that the mind is the only sure source of knowledge. But isn't the situation described in *The Matrix* theoretically possible? Can't the brain be influenced by electrodes or chemicals to create experiences—hallucinations, altered states, and the like—that aren't *real*? Even Descartes proposed that a Master Deceiver could fool us about everything except that we exist. Maybe the mind isn't as dependable a source of knowledge as Plato and Descartes claim.

Even in Descartes's time, the development of modern science was challenging rationalism. Galileo was contemporaneous with Descartes, even though he was censured by church authorities. Isaac Newton's *Principia* was published fewer than forty years after Descartes died. It shouldn't be surprising, then, to find major philosophers after Descartes rejecting his ideas and claiming that genuine knowledge comes only through the senses. This philosophical tradition is called **empiricism**, from the Greek word *empeiria*, meaning "experience." Empiricism holds that physical objects are indeed "real," and that knowledge and truth are the products of sensory experiences and not purely mental operations, as Plato and Descartes would claim. In this chapter, we'll begin by examining the work of two early modern thinkers, John Locke and David Hume, and see whether their views on reality and knowledge are convincing. We'll proceed to the findings of a contemporary scientist that seem to support some of Hume's most radical claims, and we'll conclude with Immanuel Kant's attempt to bridge rationalism and empiricism.

> **empiricism** Empiricism holds that knowledge and truth are the products of sensory experiences and not of purely mental operations. Modern science employs a thoroughly empirical approach.

Empiricism's Objections to Rationalism

There's no question that empiricism has great commonsense appeal—especially if you live in a scientific century like ours. For the most part, we proceed through life quite comfortably if we assume that the physical objects we encounter in our daily lives are real and if we think that the knowledge we get from our sense perceptions is dependable.

Nonetheless, there's no denying that rationalism has to be taken seriously. After all, the truths of mathematics and logic—which are, after all, the rationalist's model of knowledge—have a permanence, stability, and duration that empirical truths lack.

Why, then, did the empiricists reject rationalism? Despite the impressive qualities of rationalist truths, the fact is that empirical philosophers find nonempirical claims, even the claims of mathematics and logic, *trivial*. When it comes right down to it, the empiricists say that a rationalistic piece of knowledge does not tell us anything new. Empirical knowledge, by contrast, reveals something we did not know before.

Another way to describe this difference between the rationalist's and the empiricist's idea of knowledge is to talk about two different kinds of statements: *analytic statements* and *synthetic statements*. (Some of this language is fairly technical, but if you take your time with it, everything will be clear.)

Analytic Statements

Analytic statements are what we find in definitions, logic, and mathematics. They get their name from the fact that they simply analyze a concept and identify its parts. For example: "Smith is a *bachelor;* therefore, Smith is *unmarried.*" Is it true?

Yes. But does the conclusion "Smith is unmarried" tell us anything new? Not if we already understand what "bachelor" means. The idea "unmarried" is already part of the concept "bachelor." We might represent it like this:

BACHELOR
Unmarried
Man

The box stands for what we mean by the word "bachelor." That concept contains two parts: the characteristic of being unmarried and the characteristic of being male. So if you say that anyone who is a bachelor is unmarried, you are merely identifying one of the characteristics contained in the idea. You are specifying one piece of what goes into the definition of "bachelor." The same thing goes for saying "Smith is a *bachelor;* therefore, Smith is a *man.*" In either case, we have not moved outside of the box, and we have not learned anything beyond the concept "bachelor."

> **analytic statement** An analytic statement attributes a property to something, and that property is already implicit in the definition of that object or concept. For example, "A square has four sides" and "A bachelor is unmarried" are analytic statements.

We also find analytic statements in mathematics. Let's take: "That building is built in the shape of a *cube;* therefore, it has *equal sides.*" We can represent that statement this way:

CUBE
All angles 90 degrees
Six surfaces
All sides equal

As you can see, our statement "That building is built in the shape of a cube; therefore, it has equal sides" is just like our "bachelor" statement. It is true. But all we are doing is specifying its essential properties. We are not speaking about anything outside the box, that is, outside the concept "cube."

Here is one more example: "2 + 2 = 4."

4
iiii   IV

3 + 1   2 + 2
1.5 + 2.5
. . .
. . .
2^2 10 − 6

The box stands for every conceivable aspect of what "four" means. (Ours is incomplete, and we have used ellipses to represent the rest.) But "2 + 2" is just one of the many ways that "four" can be represented. If I ask, "What is two plus two?" and you say, "Four," you still are not moving outside the box and beyond what is already intrinsic to the concept we are talking about.

Another way of expressing this is that the claims, or **conclusions**, involved in analytic statements automatically follow from the **premises**.

- Smith is a *bachelor* [premise]; therefore, he is *unmarried* [conclusion].
- This object is a *triangle* [premise]; therefore, it has *three sides* [conclusion].

Can you imagine any scenario in which you can find a "married bachelor" or a "four-sided triangle"? No, it's theoretically impossible. The idea "unmarried" automatically follows from "bachelor," in the same way that "three sides" follows from "triangle."

All analytic statements are like this: "Triangles have three sides," "All grandfathers are the parents of parents," "8 × 2 = 16." They are all absolutely and necessarily true, which is why rationalists like them so much. But all they do is describe parts of a concept. They do not add anything to it. By staying "in the box," we are looking only at the specific features of the concept.

Synthetic Statements

Synthetic statements, on the other hand, do precisely what analytic statements do not. They *add* something to the concept at issue. They "move out of the box." They are called "synthetic" because they synthesize, or put together, ideas or facts that do not necessarily go together. Unlike analytic statements, synthetic statements make claims that do not automatically follow from the premises.

> **synthetic statement** A synthetic statement attributes a property to something, but that property goes beyond what is contained within the definition of the object or concept involved. For example, "The page is white" is a synthetic statement.

Here is a synthetic statement that applies to many books: "The page is white." It is synthetic because if you were to examine a definition of the concept "page," you would not find the idea "white." Nothing about the concept "page" automatically implies the color "white." "Page" suggests "material that can take writing or printing," "flat surface," "part of a book or letter," and so on. That a page is "material" does imply the notion "color," but that does not mean the page has to be white. "White" is not contained in the concept "page," and that is what makes the statement synthetic. Using our box image, we can represent it like this:

> **PAGE**
> Material for writing
> Flat surface
> Has color and weight
> Part of a document

Obviously, this picture differs dramatically from our pictures of analytic statements. It shows that a synthetic statement claims that there is a relationship between two things that do not have a necessary connection. And that is what synthetic statements are all about—asserting relationships between intrinsically unrelated concepts. "The tree outside my window is 30 feet high," "the oceans are inhabited by different life forms," "the fourth planet in this solar system has two moons." These are all synthetic statements.

Synthetic statements also differ from analytic ones in needing a different kind of proof to show that they are true. Strictly speaking, analytic statements are self-evident and logically necessary. "Proving" them amounts only to making that more obvious. If you understand the meaning of the words and concepts in analytic statements, you should be able to tell whether or not they're true without having to "check the world" to confirm or disconfirm them. But with synthetic statements, we need empirical proof, actual data that backs up our claim. If we want to say "the capital of Oregon is Salem," we have to be ready to prove that by citing the appropriate, verifiable facts that support our statement.

The Empirical Advantage

It should be clear by now why empiricists reject rationalism. They see the rationalist idea of truth and knowledge as little more than an intellectual game. Such statements lead to no new facts about the world, no insights, no expanded understanding of reality—in particular, nothing new that will help us navigate the physical world in which we live. The point of the process is to arrive at conclusions by purely mental gymnastics. Rationalism stays within its intellectual "box" and never moves outside into the "real world." And that is what empiricists mean when they say analytic statements are trivial.

There is a trade-off, of course. The empiricist loses the absolute certainty of knowledge that rationalism provides. However, the knowledge produced by empirical methods may be more interesting and useful. You must decide for yourself whether that trade is worth it when you have finished examining the issues.

The Empiricism of John Locke

Descartes's rationalism was defended by a group of European thinkers called the "Continental Rationalists." However, across the English Channel, there developed a rival, empirical school of thought. These philosophers are called, not surprisingly, the "British empiricists."

John Locke, a British empiricist, was a pioneer in empirical thinking who thoroughly disagreed with the way Plato and Descartes thought about knowledge. He rejects the notions that the mind can encounter non-substantial, universal essences and that it comes equipped with innate ideas that are self-evidently true. As a classic empiricist, Locke believes that everything we know must come through the senses. He lays out the arguments for this position in *An Essay Concerning Human Understanding* (1690).

John Locke (1632–1704) studied philosophy and medicine at Oxford, but he became deeply involved in the political turbulence of his day. His association with the leader of Parliament's opposition to the Crown caused him to flee England for the Netherlands in 1683 where, in addition to his intellectual work, Locke remained active in the movement to make William of Orange the King of England. Returning to England when this was accomplished, Locke published his two most important works, *An Essay Concerning Human Understanding* and *The Two Treatises of Government*. The rest of his years were spent in both intellectual inquiry and government service.

The Mind as a Blank Piece of Paper

Locke uses a famous image to make his point. The mind, he says, is initially like a blank slate or a blank piece of paper. When we're born, our minds are a *tabula rasa*—empty. Any knowledge that we acquire comes from the world outside of us. He writes,

> Let us then suppose the mind to be, as we say, white paper, void of all characters, without any *ideas*; how comes it to be furnished? Whence comes it by that vast store, which the busy and boundless fancy of man has painted on it, with an almost endless variety? Whence has it all the materials of reason and knowledge? To this I answer, in one word, from *experience*: in that, all our knowledge is founded; and from that it ultimately derives itself.[1]

Locke claims that our minds contain nothing which did not come first through our senses. Anything in our heads, then, is the result of either "sensation" (our sense perceptions) or "reflection" (our thinking about these perceptions). Everything we think and know originally comes from outside us.

The "Copy Theory": Primary and Secondary Qualities

The next job for the empiricist is to explain how it is that what we *think* we know about the outside world can be genuine *knowledge*. As the image of the "white paper, void of all characters" implies, Locke assumes that the mind passively takes in impressions. In so doing, it does not distort reality. What it mainly does is to copy it.

However, Locke is sensitive to the fact that we sometimes contribute something to our perceptions of the world. To account for this, he distinguishes between *primary qualities* and *secondary qualities* of the objects we experience.

Primary qualities are the most fundamental and essential properties of an object, which Locke identifies as "solidity, extension, figure, motion or rest, and number." They are *primary* because they are fundamental properties of physical objects, and, no matter what we do to an object, it will still have those properties. He uses the example of wheat:

> Take a grain of wheat, divide it into two parts, each part has still *solidity*, *extension*, *figure*, and *mobility*; divide it again, and it retains still the same qualities; and so divide it on, till the parts become insensible, they must retain still each of them all those qualities. For division (which is all that a mill, or pestle, or any other body, does upon another, in reducing it to insensible parts) can never take away either solidity, extension, figure, or mobility from any body, but only makes two or more distinct separate masses of matter.[2]

---

1. John Locke, *Essay Concerning Human Understanding* (Indianapolis: Hackett Publishing Co., 1996), Book II, 1, p. 33.
2. Locke, *Essay Concerning Human Understanding*, Book II, 8, p. 49.

Anything in our minds about an object comes from the impact of these qualities on our minds. Locke thinks that invisible particles must come from the objects themselves to our eyes and then into our brains to create our mental ideas of them. Locke explains, "the *ideas of primary qualities* of bodies *are resemblances* of them, and their patterns do really exist in the bodies themselves."[3] Consider a pencil. Our mental *idea* that the pencil is so many inches long by so many inches wide, with a specific circumference, weighing so many ounces, and so on, is the result of the *impression* the pencil makes on us. That idea "resembles" the actual primary features of the pencil itself.

However, our interaction with physical objects isn't entirely passive. Locke claims that qualities like color, sound, smell, and taste are not actually *in* the object itself. Instead, they're the result of *our body's response* to an object's primary qualities. We add them. Locke calls these an object's *secondary qualities*. He explains,

> a violet, by the impulse of such insensible particles of matter of peculiar figures, and bulks, and in different degrees and modifications of their motions, causes the *ideas* of the blue color, and sweet scent of that flower to be produced in our minds. . . . There is nothing like our *ideas,* existing in the bodies themselves. They arc . . . only a power to produce those sensations in us: and what is sweet, blue, or warm in *idea*, is but the certain bulk, figure, and motion of the insensible parts in the bodies themselves, which we call so.[4]

Or consider the case where a bucket of water can feel cold to one hand (if you've warmed up that hand) but hot to the other (if you've cooled it down). Our mental impressions—"cold" and "hot"—come from our body's reaction to the water, not from the object itself. Locke writes, "it is impossible that the same water, if those *ideas* were really in it, should at the same time be both hot and cold."[5]

Locke's position is clear. Sense experience is the sole source of every detail of everything we know. If the mind does anything, it simply responds to primary qualities already in an object and translates impulses transmitted by objects into secondary sensations. The mind discovers nothing on its own. You can't get a more categorical rejection of rationalism than that.

The Radical Empiricism of David Hume

One of the appeals to empiricism is that it fits with our commonsense view of the world. However, the Scottish philosopher David Hume, another of the British empiricists, is going to challenge that. Hume agrees with Locke, and against Descartes, that knowledge must come through the senses. But more than any other empiricist, Hume questions just how much of what we *think* we know is genuine *knowledge*. As you will shortly

---

3. Locke, *Essay Concerning Human Understanding*, Book II, 8, p. 51.
4. Locke, *Essay Concerning Human Understanding*, Book II, 8, pp. 50–51.
5. Locke, *Essay Concerning Human Understanding*, Book II, 8, p. 53.

see, Hume's special contribution is his challenge to some "obvious" truths. For David Hume, some important aspects of reality aren't at all what they appear to be. A renegade in his personal life as well as his philosophical career, Hume takes empiricism so far that we can legitimately call him a radical thinker. His epistemological ideas are set out in two definitive works: *A Treatise on Human Nature* and *An Enquiry Concerning Human Understanding*.

Impressions and Ideas

Like Locke, Hume thinks that everything in the mind originates in our sense experience. With no innate ideas or Platonic Forms to discover, with nothing in there at all to start with, our minds are in no position to create or uncover immaterial, intuitive, spiritual, or mystical truth. All they can do is receive sense impressions.

> David Hume (1711–1776) was a Scottish philosopher who was educated at Edinburgh University. At the age of twenty-eight, he published one of his most famous works, *A Treatise of Human Nature*. The work got so little notice at the time that Hume remarked that it "fell still-born from the press." Hume published different revisions of material from the *Treatise* in *An Enquiry Concerning the Principles of Morals* and *An Enquiry Concerning Human Understanding*, but he preferred to cultivate a reputation as a man of letters. During his life he was best known for his work in history, moral and political thought, and economics. He also held a series of government posts. Hume was an unorthodox thinker, and his *Dialogues on Natural Religion* was published only after his death.

Hume divides the contents of our minds into *impressions* and *ideas*. *Impressions* encompass "all our more lively perceptions, when we hear, or see, or feel, or love, or hate, or desire, or will." We are aware of our impressions *during* an experience—they are strong, forceful, and vivid. *Ideas* include "the less lively perceptions, of which we are conscious, when we reflect on any [impressions]."[6] *Ideas* are what our *impressions* are like when we think about them or remember them *after* the experience. For example, if you look around the room you are in right now, you will take in various vivid sights, sounds, and smells. These are Hume's *impressions*. But if tomorrow you think back on this moment, those perceptions will be less intense. Those less vivid recollections are Hume's *ideas*.

For Hume, genuine knowledge comes through the senses. Objects in the outside world produce impressions in our minds, which we retain, in less vivid form, as ideas. Yet these ideas accurately represent what we have encountered in the world outside us. We truly know something certain about the world through this process. Furthermore, this knowledge lets us make *synthetic* statements. (If you say "my desk is brown wood," you are confidently claiming something about color and material that is not already part of the concept "desk.") And finally, the validity of this knowledge can be tested. We can

---

6. David Hume, *An Enquiry Concerning Human Understanding* (Indianapolis: Hackett Publishing Co., 1993), Sect. II, p. 10.

verify the accuracy of our *ideas* by reexperiencing certain *impressions*. Or we can check our experience against other people's. A primary virtue of empirical knowledge is that it can be objectively confirmed.

So far, both Locke and Hume seem to endorse common sense. Unlike Plato, they think that physical objects are completely real. Unlike Descartes, they place their trust in the senses. We can trace the ideas in our minds to their sources in the outside world and say we know something. These philosophers seem to give us back what rationalism took away, the ability to say we genuinely know something on the basis of our everyday sense perceptions—and to say we know something beyond the mere meaning of any concepts involved.

Not All Ideas Are Genuine

Don't think all our problems are over, however. Just because Locke and Hume say that all our ideas are based on sense impressions, this doesn't mean that our every idea refers to some object that physically exists. Locke's "secondary qualities," like color and taste, are the product of the interaction between us and the objects we encounter. And Hume thinks that our minds sometimes imaginatively join ideas that in reality do not go together. Because our minds are so creative, we easily produce ideas of objects that do not and cannot exist. Hume offers the following two examples:

> When we think of a golden mountain, we only join two consistent ideas, *gold* and *mountain,* with which we were formerly acquainted. A virtuous horse we can conceive; because, from our own feeling, we can conceive virtue; and this we may unite to the figure and shape of a horse, which is an animal familiar to us.[7]

You can think of many examples—unicorns and centaurs, gods and goddesses, all sorts of imaginary objects and creatures. Given our tendency to create such ideas, Hume thinks we should look for the sense impressions that underlie them. If we cannot find anything in the real world that we can physically correlate with an idea, we must say that the idea is just a fiction, like the "golden mountain." As Hume puts it,

> When we entertain any suspicion that a philosophical term is employed without any meaning or idea (as is but too frequent), we need but enquire, *from what impression is that supposed idea derived?* And if it be impossible to assign any, this will serve to confirm our suspicion.[8]

Hume seems to be making sense here. We're so creative that we can imagine all sorts of things that don't actually exist. But he argues that this is a bigger danger than we realize. You probably agreed with Descartes that the one thing we absolutely, positively

---

7. Hume, *An Enquiry Concerning Human Understanding*, Sect. II, p. 11.
8. Hume, *An Enquiry Concerning Human Understanding*, Sect. II, p. 13.

can be certain of is that we exist. *Cogito ergo sum.* After all, we have "a self" that possesses self-awareness and persists through time. According to Hume, we shouldn't be so sure.

Testing for Meaning: The Self

Descartes regards the "self" as an innate idea of such vividness and clarity that its existence is absolutely certain. However, Hume considered Descartes's notion of the self completely meaningless. For an idea to be other than a fiction concocted in our minds, Hume said, we must first identify the *impressions* that produce the *idea* and then identify the actual *objects* that produce the impressions. To talk accurately about a "self," then, we must isolate the impressions that produce our idea of a "self" and trace them to the object that is their cause.

Before we look at Hume's reasoning, try to think this problem through yourself. Do you have a "self"? Surely everyone would say yes. You are the same person who has lived through all your varied experiences in life. Even though all the cells in your body change every seven to ten years, the same you persists. Different cells, yet the same "self." But exactly what is it that you're referring to when you say "I"? Take a moment and see if you can come up with an answer.

Now hold on to your hat. We ask Hume, "What is the 'self'?" and he answers, "Nothing. The concept is meaningless, empty, the product of imagination." How radical can you get? The *self*, claims Hume—Descartes's rock-solid, ultimately undoubtable truth, the "I" at the very core of our existence—is meaningless. Is Hume serious?

Yes. He is deadly serious. Taking aim at Descartes, Hume makes his case in his *Treatise of Human Nature*:

> There are some philosophers, who imagine we are every moment intimately conscious of what we call our Self; that we feel its existence and its continuance in existence; and are certain, beyond the evidence of a demonstration, both of its perfect identity and simplicity. . . . To attempt a farther proof of this were to weaken its evidence; since no proof can be deriv'd from any fact, of which we are so intimately conscious; nor is there any thing, of which we can be certain, if we doubt of this.
>
> Unluckily all these positive assertions are contrary to that very experience, which is pleaded for them, nor have we any idea of self, after the manner it is here explain'd. For from what impression cou'd this idea be deriv'd? . . . If any impression gives rise to the idea of self, that impression must continue invariably the same, thro' the whole course of our lives; since self is suppos'd to exist after that manner. But there is no impression constant and invariable. Pain and pleasure, grief and joy; passions and sensations succeed each other, and never all exist at the same time. It cannot, therefore, be from any of these impressions, or from any other, that the idea of self is deriv'd; and consequently there is no such idea. . . . For my part, when I enter most intimately into what I call myself, I always stumble on some particular perception or other, of heat or cold, light or shade, love or hatred, pain or pleasure. I never can

catch myself at any time without a perception, and never can observe anything but the perception.[9]

To David Hume, the "self" is an idea like the "golden mountain." We have impressions that come from our experience of actual objects, but our imagination combines these impressions to create a new, fictitious idea—"I." However, we do not admit that it is a fiction. Instead, we just assert that there is some "self," even if it is "something unknown and mysterious."

You're probably thinking that Hume is crazy. You *know* that the same "you" has persisted throughout your life, right? *You* aren't some fiction! But Hume isn't buying it. By Hume's strict rules, if you cannot identify a single, specific source of an impression, any idea based on that impression is something you have just made up in your mind. When we apply Hume's rules, we do not find anything we can point to as the "self" which is the source of whatever impressions lead us to say "I."

Hume does not say that because he cannot find a "self," we don't really exist. His point is that Descartes's claim to *know* that he exists is wrong. Hume's strict empirical view means that Descartes (and the rest of us) may *believe* or *think* that he exists. But he cannot *know* it because he cannot prove it according to strict empirical criteria.

Hume's insistence on grounding all knowledge in the evidence of the senses at first seems appealing. It makes sense in our scientific age. But once he shows how easily the mind creates illusions of knowledge, we are back in the same quicksand we stood in when Descartes asked, "How can I be absolutely certain that I can trust what my senses tell me?" Furthermore, Descartes's claim to knowledge of the self now gives way to Hume's assertion that we cannot find a "self" to know. If this makes you jittery, brace yourself. The other shoe is about to drop.

The Attack on Causality

Hume is relentless. It is disturbing enough that he claims that the "self" is a fiction. And it is hard to imagine that he could find something else to question that would leave us similarly troubled. But the hallmark of a great philosopher is that he can surprise you. And Hume does that.

When you look around at the world, what do you see? Things happening. Cars move, planes fly, trees fall, people do things. The world is dynamic, ever-changing. One event takes place, which causes something else to happen, and so on. When we observe what goes on around us, we see an ongoing chain of events. Everything has a cause. If you're thinking like an empiricist, you'd probably say, "The physical world is built on the idea of cause and effect. You can always find a cause of an object or event." That's what a scientific view of reality tells us, after all. To understand something, we study what caused it and what effect it has on other things. We know that some events cause others to happen.

---

9. David Hume, *A Treatise of Human Nature* (Oxford: Oxford University Press, 1968), IV, 6, p. 251.

Take plants, for example. If you water them correctly, give them food, and move them so that they get the right kind of light, they grow. If you ignore them, don't water them, or let them get too much or too little sun, they wilt. It's obvious that how you treat them *causes* them to be healthy or unhealthy. It's as obvious as the fact that their leaves are green.

We have so much empirical proof that some events cause others to happen that it seems ridiculous to doubt it. But couldn't we also say that it's just as obvious that we have a "self"? And if Hume claims that the "self" is a fiction, might he not also claim the same thing for cause and effect? That is precisely what he does. In fact, Hume's claim that we can never really *know* that one thing *causes* another to happen is probably the most important part of his philosophy.

If you have understood Hume so far, you can probably anticipate his line of reasoning about "causality." Remember, Hume thinks that for something to count as "knowledge," we must be able to identify the outside, empirical source of the "impressions" that underlie our "ideas." If we cannot do that, we must assume that the mind is somehow taking a variety of different impressions and combining them into new ideas that do not correspond to observable reality. As you have probably guessed, Hume doesn't think we can find observable, empirical evidence for "causality." Therefore, it is just such an idea. We manufacture it in our minds—like the golden mountain, the virtuous horse, and the self.

But causality seems so obvious, you say. How can Hume suggest that it is a fiction?

Let's start this way. Pick up a pen or pencil. Examine it to determine what it's made of. Now put it out of sight. Is it wood, metal, or plastic? Are you sure that your "idea" is right? Of course you are. Do you have to go back and check to be sure? Hardly. You just put it down. One look was enough. One set of "impressions" from the object was plenty.

Now take one of your books and drop it on the floor. You hear a sound, don't you? But can you say with absolute certainty that you will hear exactly the same sound if you drop it again? Isn't it possible that just as the book hit, a car backfired or someone made another noise down the hall? That's possible, as are other explanations that we have not imagined. When will you know for sure? After you have dropped the book a few times. Unlike the case of knowing what the pen or pencil you looked at was made of, you need to examine the situation a few times. You need *a series of impressions* of the event to make you comfortable thinking that "dropping the book on the floor causes this particular sound."

Why do you need to look at the pen or pencil only once, but you need to drop the book at least a few times? If we are going to claim to know some fact, we must be certain of it. Looking at the pencil once is enough to determine what it is made of. But we need more than one test to be sure that one thing causes another. Science uses this approach all the time. A single experiment may suggest a causal relationship between one event and another, but other scientists must repeat that experiment over and over to see if they get the same results. No reputable researcher will say she "knows" something without a substantial body of supporting evidence. In short, one instance cannot demonstrate with a reasonable degree of certainty that one thing *causes* another.

Constant Conjunction

The need to do experiments more than once before we claim cause and effect makes perfect sense. But the very fact that we need to repeat an experience at all makes Hume suspicious. It shows that "cause" is not immediately present in the initial impression. (Contrast this with the idea of the material a pencil is made of.) Consequently, Hume says, the idea of causality "arises entirely from experience, when we find that any particular objects are constantly conjoined with each other."

Hume discusses causality using his now-famous example of two billiard balls. We see one ball, ball A, hit another, ball B; then we see ball B move away. When we see these two events take place over and over again, these events are "constantly conjoined with each other," to put it in Hume's terms. But we don't say to ourselves simply, "Every time I saw ball A hit ball B, ball B then moved"—which is actually all that we have seen. After we have seen these events together for a while, we say to ourselves, instead, "Ball A hit ball B and *caused* it to move; *and the same thing will happen in the future.*" However, Hume writes in the *Enquiry*, "These two propositions are far from being the same, *I have found that such an object has always been attended with such an effect,* and *I foresee, that other objects which are, in appearance similar, will be attended with similar effects.*"[10]

Predicting the Future from the Past

The bridge we use to get from one statement to the other is the assumption that the future will be like the past. And that's where we get into trouble. According to Hume, there is simply no way to know this.

Think about the book-dropping example. Can you be 100 percent certain that the next time you drop this book on the floor, it will make the same noise it made the last time you dropped it? Maybe you can be 99 percent certain. But can you honestly rule out all possibility that for whatever reason, the noise will not be different? Of course you can't. There are too many variables, including whether the book hits the floor at precisely the same angle, the speed of the earth's rotation, the strength of gravitational fields, etc. The slightest change in any of them as the book falls to the floor may cause the sound to change.

Probability, Not Knowledge

Even if you are 99 percent sure, you cannot say you *know* what sound the book will make. From a practical standpoint, however, you may say this is close enough. No one can ever know anything for sure about the future. To be realistic about it, a 99 percent certainty is so close to a 100 percent certainty that what difference can it make?

From a practical standpoint, you have a point. But "practical" is not Hume's standard. The Scottish philosopher's conclusion is that when we make statements about what will happen in the future, we are talking only about probability, not knowledge: "If we be, therefore, engaged by arguments to put trust in past experience, and make it the standard of our future judgement, these arguments must be *probable* only" (emphasis added). Our

---

10. Hume, *An Enquiry Concerning Human Understanding*, sect. IV, p. 22.

minds, however, having gotten into the habit of seeing things "constantly conjoined" in the past, create the fiction that the future will repeat the past. Thus we think that one event causes the other, always did, and always will. In Hume's view, however, we have no empirical grounds for such claims. We simply cannot find enough evidence in physical reality to justify the idea of "causality." Like the "self," cause and effect has to be written off as a product of our imaginations.

How Convincing Is Hume?

First the "self," then "causality." By calling into question the most obvious truths (we have a "self," and we can identify "causality"), Hume's skepticism leaves us with very little to hang on to. His empirical ideas may allow for *synthetic* propositions in a way that rationalism doesn't. But it seems that all he'll concede is very limited. From this perspective, what Hume is willing to grant as knowledge is almost as limited in its own way as the analytical propositions of rationalism.

Is Hume convincing? You're probably about as convinced by Hume's doubts as you were by Descartes's Master Deceiver. You still think your senses are reliable, don't you? If they aren't 100 percent trustworthy, they're close enough. You're probably willing to say that you *know* the world is the way your senses tell you it is. If you remember our examination of **pragmatism** from Chapter 4, you might say that assuming that your senses are reliable simply "works better." If that's what you think, Hume hasn't made much of an impact on you.

Testing the Senses

In the same way that we considered a contemporary "radical doubt" to test Descartes's ideas, let's set up a test to determine what counts as genuine knowledge using an empirical standard. The question we will explore is very basic: how certain can we be of the evidence of our senses? We want to discover two things: (1) how accurate our sense impressions are and (2) whether they refer to something that actually exists.

An Experiment with the Senses

Consider this experiment. Imagine that you take a red light and a white light and shine them on some object. You will get two shadows. What colors will they be? One, predictably, will be red. But the second, not so predictably, is *green*!

Ordinarily when we see a color, we can confidently say that we know that something of that color (an object, a colored stream of light, etc.) is there. Thus the green shadow in this experiment should lead us to say something like, "I know a patch of green light exists." But it doesn't. If we measure the wavelengths of the light in that experiment, we find only various shades of red, white, and pink. This is not a trick; red and white light do not somehow mix to produce green. There is no light here with wavelengths matching those that scientists tell us we see as "green." Everyone who sees this phenomenon will see green, but if you take a photograph of it, no green will appear in the picture. In reality, no matter what we see, *there is no green* there.

How is it possible for there to be a green shadow where there isn't green? The answer lies in the fact that our eyes are not just passive receptors of external sensations. They are part of a very active nervous system that responds to stimuli in particular ways. Researchers think that in this experiment the red and white light stimulates certain cells in the eye in the same way green light does. The signals they send to the brain are there translated as "green" when reality is presenting you with "red," "white," or "pink."

Perceiving Reality: There Is More Going on Than You Think

The fact that we can see green when no green is there is not an isolated case. Indeed, the neurobiologist Humberto Maturana, who has done extensive work on vision in humans and other animals, has concluded that we are wrong if we think that we passively perceive exactly what goes on in the world around us. Maturana explains that when he and another scientist began doing research on frog vision,

> we did it with the implicit assumption that we were handling a clearly defined cognitive situation: there was an objective (absolute) reality, external to the animal, and independent of it (not determined by it), which it could perceive (cognize), and the animal could use the information obtained in its perception to compute a behavior adequate to the perceived situation. This assumption of ours appeared clearly in our language. We described the various kinds of retinal ganglion cells as feature detectors, and we spoke about the detection of prey and enemy.[11]

The Influence of the "Knower"

Most of us trust our senses as sources of knowledge because we ordinarily assume that perception is basically a passive process. The "green" shadow and Maturana's work with frog vision, however, to take only two examples, suggest that the "knowing mechanism" itself affects the way we identify what we perceive. This further undermines any unquestioned belief in the objectivity and certainty of our sense impressions.

---

11. Humberto Maturana, "Biology of Cognition" (1970), in Terry Winograd and Fernando Flores, *Understanding Computers and Cognition* (New York: Addison-Wesley, 1986), 42–43.

For a simple example of how the mind can shape what we perceive, look at this picture.

What do you see? The picture should present you with two distinctly different images—a vase and two faces.

How is this possible? The sense data that your eyes take in—the arrangement of lines and shading—remain the same. But you can "shift" the picture you see. What you "see," then, is the meaning your mind imposes on the sensory data, and your mind can reprocess that data so that they represent something different.

This is yet another example of the influence of the knower. What we would say we see in the picture based on our perceptions is heavily influenced by internal mental processes. This is essentially the same idea suggested by Maturana's work and by the "green" shadow that isn't there. It is also, of course, what Hume intimates when he discusses the "self" and "causality."

Isn't it possible that this sort of thing goes on more than we realize, that our minds more or less create the meaning of the sensory data we take in? And if this is so, how can we be sure that we perceive reality as it actually is?

Apparently, there is good reason to doubt what is right in front of our eyes. The green in our experiment is produced by our nervous system and not by green light. Which of two images we perceive in the picture above depends on how our own minds direct our thinking. If our senses cannot pass these simple tests, we are entitled to question whatever we experience through them. Maybe Hume is right after all when he suggests that even though genuine knowledge comes only from the senses, some bits of "knowledge" that seem too evident to doubt are really fictions created by our minds.

Does Hume Go Too Far?

As we see, Hume's skepticism can be devastating—leaving us uncertain about the trust-worthiness of our own senses. However, it's worth pausing to ask whether we've gone too far. In fact, even Hume ultimately pulls back.

Hume is keenly aware that his radical empiricism takes him far from how most people see the world and leads him into a gloomy isolation. His conclusions leave him so con-fused about virtually everything that he ends up feeling depressed and powerless. In his *Treatise of Human Nature*, he comments:

> The intense view of these manifold contradictions and imperfections in human reason has so wrought upon me, and heated my brain, that I am ready to reject all belief and reasoning, and can look upon no opinion even as more probable or likely than another. Where am I, or what? From what causes do I derive my existence, and to what condition shall I return? Whose favour shall I court, and whose anger must I dread? What beings surround me? And on whom have I any influence, or who have any influence on me? I am confounded with all of these questions, and begin to fancy myself in the most deplorable condition imaginable, inviron'd with the deepest darkness, and utterly depriv'd of the use of every mem-ber and faculty.[12]

However, when discouraged, not even a famous philosopher is immune to the pull of everyday life. Hume writes,

> Most fortunately it happens, that since reason is incapable of dispelling these clouds, nature herself suffices to that purpose, and cures me of this philosophical melancholy and delirium, either by relaxing this bent of mind, or by some avo-cation, and lively impression of my senses, which obliterate all these chimeras. I dine, I play a game of back-gammon, I converse, and am merry with my friends; and when after three or four hours' amusement, I wou'd return to these specula-tions, they appear so cold, and strain'd, and ridiculous, that I cannot find in my heart to enter into them any farther.[13]

Hume doesn't reject his philosophical positions, but he's reminded that trusting his senses actually does work in everyday life most of the time. So perhaps we need to ask whether a dose of common sense will temper his radical empiricism.

The Self Reconsidered

Recall that Hume claimed that when he looked inside, he could never encounter "the self." He concluded that it must be a creation of our imaginations like the "golden mountain."

---

12. Hume, *A Treatise of Human Nature*, I, 4, pp. 268–69.
13. Hume, *A Treatise of Human Nature*, I, 4, p. 269.

But consider the following story that the twentieth-century British philosopher Gilbert Ryle (1900–1976) tells as part of his criticism of Descartes's concept of the mind.

> A foreigner visiting Oxford or Cambridge for the first time is shown a number of colleges, libraries, playing fields, museums, scientific departments, and administrative offices. He then asks, "But where is the University? I have seen where the members of the Colleges live, where the Registrar works, where the scientists experiment and the rest. But I have not yet seen the University in which reside and work the members of your University."[14]

To anyone familiar with "universities," the visitor's mistake is obvious. He doesn't understand that "classroom building," "playing field," and "library" (on the one hand) and "university" (on the other) refer to very different kinds of logical categories. Ryle coined the phrase "category mistake" to describe this error—although you're probably more familiar with the phrase "comparing apples to oranges." Hume's comment that whenever he looks for his "self," all he comes upon are perceptions (cold, hot, love, anger, pleasure, pain, etc.) sounds suspiciously like the visitor saying that he's seen buildings and facilities but no "university." Is Hume guilty of a "category mistake" in wanting the "self" to refer to something other than the perceptions that we're conscious of? Is it a more solid concept than some fiction like a unicorn?

Causality Reconsidered and the Value of Induction

Recall, too, that Hume also dismisses the idea of cause and effect as something that is just a product of our imagination. If we want to make claims about what will happen in the future on the basis of what we've observed in the past, Hume says that "these arguments must be probable only."

But again, we can ask if Hume isn't making a kind of category mistake when he suggests that probability is a failing in this context. Remember that one of the major differences between rationalism and empiricism is that the latter aims to make synthetic statements that take us beyond the contents of the concepts we start with. Another way to talk about this is that a standard empirical inquiry is based on *inductive reasoning* of the sort we see in scientific investigations, not the *deductive reasoning* that we use in geometry and symbolic logic. Deductive logic ("all triangles have three sides; this object is a triangle; therefore, this object has three sides") gives us absolute certainty, whereas induction usually gives us only degrees of probability. But this doesn't mean that induction is epistemologically inferior to deduction. Imagine that a chemist makes an important discovery. At first, any predictions she makes about it are little more than guesses. That is, they have a low probability of being right because they're based on a small amount of evidence. However, the more that she experiments with the materials involved, the

---

14. Gilbert Ryle, *The Concept of Mind*, introduction by Daniel C. Dennett (Chicago: University of Chicago Press, 2000), 16.

greater the probability that her predictions will be true. The inductive, scientific method that she uses is to formulate hypotheses, test them, refine them in terms of what she's learned, test some more, and continue to gather evidence. Other scientists will engage in the same process, and a substantial body of data about this discovery will accumulate. An inductive process may never give any of these scientists certainty, but it will strengthen the basis of any claims so that they become more and more probable.

Given the nature of empirical reality, the goal of inductive inquiry is greater and greater probability—not certainty. But be sure to realize that this doesn't make it a weak intellectual tool. On the contrary, a solid inductive approach lets us assess the likelihood that one theory or another is true or false. If we have competing theories about, for example, how the universe came into existence, an inductive process lets us see what the universe itself tells us about which one is more likely. The physical evidence that is uncovered combined with the objective judgment of trained scientists will reveal which theory has the greater probability of being true. If such an approach reveals that one theory has a significantly smaller probability of being right than the other, we can see how valuable an inductive process is.

Perhaps, then, it is simply inappropriate to ask for certainty when talking about empiricism. Maybe doing so shows a fundamental misunderstanding of both the value and limits of induction. Could asking for certainty from an inductive process be so off target that it amounts to a kind of category mistake?[15]

Knowledge Is Limited to Appearance: Immanuel Kant

Rationalism and empiricism leave us with something of a standoff. Fortunately, one of Western philosophy's greatest thinkers, Immanuel Kant, whom you met in Chapter 5, came along and offered a theory that tries to harmonize the two extremes of his predecessors. In the *Critique of Pure Reason*, Kant proposes a fascinating theory that tries to bridge the gap between rationalism and empiricism—but he does so at a very high price.

Kant accepts the claim of rationalism that only the mind provides absolute certainty. He also accepts the claim of empiricism that knowledge depends on having sense data. Unlike Hume, however, he accepts the legitimacy of causality. The key here is Kant's rejection of the idea that the mind is a *tabula rasa* passively receiving information from our senses. Instead, he argues that the mind takes all our sense impressions and actively orders, arranges, and gives shape and meaning to them. The mind acts as an active agent through which all sense impressions pass; the mind actually imposes a certain structure on those sense data.

---

15. Hume is not silent on this question, and he's famous for one more epistemological conundrum: the "problem of induction." At issue is whether we can make claims about what will happen in the future based on what has happened in the past. Hume wrestles with the problem but is unable to find a solution that lets us make legitimate claims about the future. Because some thinkers believe that the problem is unsolvable, it's a more advanced issue than is appropriate for our inquiry. If you're interested in looking into this, you'll find Hume's discussion in Book 1, part iii, section 6 of *A Treatise of Human Nature*.

Into what shape does the mind mold things? First, it gives sense data a spatial and temporal dimension. For Kant, space and time are not properties of reality as such but characteristics the mind imposes on it. Second, our sense data are also fashioned in terms of such basic concepts as substance, causality, unity, plurality, necessity, possibility, and reality. Kant calls these concepts "categories."

Knowledge, for Kant, is what our minds produce as they actively arrange the data supplied by our senses. All human minds have the same structure, so we all experience the world the same. We impose space, time, and the "categories" on what we perceive. For example, we create a causally ordered world, and we impose these relationships on the sensations that we encounter. We do not imagine causality as a fiction, as Hume suggests. Thus, in Kant's view, it is possible to claim with certainty that we know that billiard ball A *causes* billiard ball B to move when the former strikes the latter. Our knowledge claims are objectively true because the basic rules for how all humans experience are, as it were, hardwired into our minds.

Kant's idea that the mind orders sense data with the categories to give us our everyday experience of reality can be difficult to grasp, so think of it this way. If you look at the screen on a computer, what do you see? Depending on the website you're viewing or the app you're running, you see images and words, and you might also hear sounds. But what if I said that what you're *really* watching and hearing is electricity that has simply been configured to produce what you're experiencing? The electricity powers the laptop; it initiates a variety of functions—the screen, the keyboard, the sound card, etc.; it runs through electronic pathways, programs, and apps that you can manipulate to find what you're looking for or to make the computer do what you want it to do. What you ultimately see and hear is the result of how the computer transforms the electricity by means of its various elements (hardware and software).

This is not unlike what Kant has in mind when he suggests that the data we take in through our senses (something equivalent to the electricity that your computer draws in) are then organized by the categories (something equivalent to the software) to give us what we "know" (the image on the monitor).

Kant is also suggesting something similar to—but much more aggressive than—what Maturana described above as the way that our nervous system "participates in" determining how we experience reality.

Kant's achievement is not without its cost. To make knowledge possible, Kant must distinguish between an *object-in-itself* and an *object-as-it-appears*. (To guarantee the objectivity and dependability of knowledge, Kant may not allow for the possibility of a perception that is not filtered and molded by the mind.) Objects-in-themselves inhabit what Kant calls the "noumenal world," whereas things-as-they-appear constitute the "phenomenal world." The catch is that when we encounter an object—"a thing-in-itself"—the filtering and ordering that our minds do change that object into a "thing-as-it-appears." Thus all human experience and all human knowledge is limited to the phenomenal realm, that is, to things-as-they-appear, and not to things-as-they-are-in-themselves.

This has two serious consequences. First, we once again find major restrictions placed on the concept of knowledge. This time, we can never know the nature of reality *as it truly is* (noumenal reality), only as it *appears* to us (phenomenal reality). Knowledge is possible but limited. Second, because knowledge is the result of the mind's operations on empirical data, Kant argues that it is impossible to have any knowledge of such ultimate, intangible things like the soul, immortality, and God. Kant does not reject these notions outright. He says only that knowledge of them is impossible, and he thinks that the demands of morality are good reasons for people to believe in them. However, in one move, Kant proclaimed that the traditional attempts of metaphysics to understand such concepts were doomed to failure.

However, even if we decided we could make our peace with Kant's views, there is no way around the fatal problem of anthropocentrism—species bias in favor of humans. It may be understandable that, writing in the eighteenth century, Kant claims that "animals are not self-conscious and are there merely as a means to an end. The end is man."[16] There was no scientific evidence at the time for self-consciousness in such nonhuman animals as dolphins, elephants, and nonhuman primates. Now, however, there is.[17]

If Kant's idea that the mind takes sense data and imposes an order on it is correct, however, there is no way to know whether the "dolphin mind," "elephant mind," or "chimp mind," for example, have the same features as the "human mind" in the way they process sense data. Accordingly, the most that Kant can argue is that the kind of knowledge we have is "species-specific." We experience "phenomenal reality as humans"—and that's a significant limitation for a philosopher hoping to establish a firm basis for knowledge.

The Search for Reality and Knowledge—Where Are We?

We have considered a variety of views in this chapter—Locke's more or less commonsense view that the senses are a good source of knowledge about what exists, Hume's radical empiricism that challenges such "obvious" notions as "the self" and "causality," and Kant's attempt to bridge rationalism and empiricism. In giving us answers to the questions we've been considering in the last two chapters ("What's real and how do we know it?" and "Are things the ways they appear to be?"), how do these thinkers' ideas fare against Plato's and Descartes's?

Plato gives us the most aggressive rationalist version by saying that things aren't at all the way they seem. He argues that we live our life in an inferior reality—essentially a world of shadows. The information our senses give us doesn't come close to "knowledge." Only years of study of mathematics and philosophy will let us achieve true knowledge of the Forms.

Descartes's rationalistic universe isn't as expansive as Plato's. The French thinker asserts that, at the very least, our sense that we absolutely, positively exist is real. He also thinks that the mind gives us knowledge of the innate ideas of Self, God, Substance,

16. Immanuel Kant, "Duties toward Animals and Spirits," in *Lectures on Ethics*, trans. Louis Infield (1780; New York: Harper & Row, 1963), 239.
17. See the discussion of this about dolphins, in particular, in Chapter 10.

and Identity. But other than the truths of mathematics and logic, nothing qualifies as knowledge.

Locke and Hume's empirical approach initially seems more agreeable to a modern world that has been shaped by science. But when Hume puts the self, causality, and predicting future events in the "sorry, you can't know any of these" category, we're almost back to Plato's view of the physical world.

Kant at least gives us greater overall certainty in what we can know. The problem, however, is that because our minds are processing and imposing a certain order on the sense data we experience, we can never know what things *really are*, only how they *appear to be*. Even the work of neurobiologist Humberto Maturana suggests something similar. However, because of the limitations of the time in which he wrote, Kant is oblivious to the fact that he falls victim to anthropocentrism.

Our search in these last two chapters may have seemed hopelessly confusing at times. But Plato, Descartes, Locke, Hume, and Kant have shown us how difficult it is to discover "knowledge" when we set absolute certainty as our standard. Would it be so bad if the only absolute certainties we can discover are the limited truths of mathematics and logic and the empirical truths that we can trace back to observable events and objects? Would it be so bad if we had to evaluate everything else in terms of degrees of probability?

A Final Thought: Recognizing the Limitations and Benefits of Philosophy

Before concluding the inquiry we've been engaged in over the last couple of chapters, it's worth taking a moment to recognize both the limitations and the achievement of what Plato, Descartes, Locke, Hume, and Kant were able to do.

Especially if you have a strong background in science, there's a good chance you felt frustration with some of the theories advanced. After all, physicists can explain Hume's billiard ball problem by referring to the measurable, predictable transfer of kinetic energy from one ball to the other. As far as predictability goes, the number of times humans have ventured to the moon and back—which some have likened to hitting a moving target in a hurricane—speaks for itself. Advances in neuroscience give us a growing picture about how the brain influences both our intellectual and emotional perception of our experiences and our reaction to them. In one way, modern science seems to make a good bit of traditional metaphysics and epistemology obsolete.

However, while there's some truth in that, it is worth appreciating that these thinkers offered distinctive, serious, sophisticated explanations of the nature of reality and what we're able to know about it using *just their minds*. They unquestionably advanced the idea that *things are not as they seem*—which, if you're familiar with twentieth- and twenty-first-century physics—is even recognized as the case by physicists. Moreover, given the frequency with which humans overestimate what they know and/or are deceived by critical issues, there's much to be said for looking at the world with a certain amount of skepticism and intellectual humility. And what does that say to you about what *The Matrix* suggests?

Discussion Questions

1. Empiricism claims that nothing is in the mind that did not come through the senses. Reflect on the contents of your mind again. Are the empiricists right? Or can you find an idea that could have come through the mind alone?

2. Consider Hume's argument about causality. In light of how easily and frequently we create an enormous range of fanciful ideas, is there any way to reject Hume's claim that causality and our idea of "self" are simple fictions? Is there any way to refute him? Could any scientific experiments prove that one billiard ball causes the second to move?

3. Kant makes the human mind an active participant in how we experience the world around us. Isn't this precisely what the experiment with the red and white lights shows? Is it possible, as Kant's theory intimates, that everything we experience is like that—an experience that our mind has a major hand in shaping?

4. How dependable do you believe your senses are? Have you ever had an experience when your senses completely deceived you?

5. Have you ever had your cards or palm read or gone to some other kind of psychic? What was the experience like? Did you leave thinking that the person genuinely knew things about you that he or she could not possibly know? If so, how do you explain this?

Selected Readings

Locke's ideas are elaborated in *An Essay Concerning Human Understanding*. See Hume's *A Treatise of Human Nature* and *An Enquiry Concerning Human Understanding*. For Hume's discussion of the self, see Book I, Section VI, and comments to this section in the Appendix of the *Treatise*. The billiard ball example appears in Section IV, Part I of the *Enquiry*. For Gilbert Ryle's ideas, see Gilbert Ryle, *The Concept of Mind*, introduction by Daniel C. Dennett (Chicago: University of Chicago Press, 2000).

Chapter 9

Does God Exist?

Philosophy covers a wide territory. Some of its topics are abstract: the nature of reality and the nature of knowledge. Others are closer to our daily lives. What is the difference between right and wrong? Why should we do what is right? Do we freely choose our actions or are they determined? As practical or impractical as these investigations may be, however, the question of whether God exists touches all of us most personally. After all, the way we answer this question may make a difference in how we live.

If you believe in an all-powerful, all-knowing, supreme being, this is probably the cornerstone of your life. If God sets a standard for behavior and judges you in those terms after death, it makes good sense to keep that in mind as you go through your days. God's existence can be a great comfort or a source of fear. If, on the other hand, you believe that God does not exist, this also has a major impact on your life. You may have more flexibility in how you behave and the consequences of your deeds do not stretch into eternity. But you must now decide for yourself how to conduct your life and how to make sense of the universe. You must reconcile yourself to the fact that there is no "great divine plan" for everything around you. You, then, determine what will give your life meaning and purpose.

Is there some Great Being out there on whom we can depend, or are such ideas merely projections of our deep longing to avoid taking charge of our own lives or our fear that this life is all there is? Such a fundamental question has attracted the attention of philosophers and spawned a host of arguments. When someone claims that God does or does not exist, however, that person is claiming that statements about God's existence are *true* or not *true*. As you saw in Chapters 7 and 8, there are two main schools of thought in Western philosophy as to the better source of truth and knowledge. **Empiricism** trusts the senses while **rationalism** holds with the mind. Not surprisingly, in Western thought, arguments about God's existence break down the same way. In this chapter we start with empirical "proofs" that claim that nature reveals to us the existence of God. Later we examine a very different rationalistic argument that arrives at the same conclusion.

What Do We Mean by "God"?

Any discussion of the existence of God should begin with a definition of "God." Since we are limiting ourselves here to the ideas of Western philosophers, we shall also limit ourselves to the monotheistic conception of God found in Judaism, Islam, and Christianity.

In this religious tradition, only one God exists: a divine being who created and rules the world. Everything that happens is an expression of God's divine providence, that is, God's care and direction of the universe. God knows everything and is all-powerful.

God has specific standards of right and wrong, and God rewards virtue and punishes vice. (Christians believe that God rewards and punishes each of us after we die. Orthodox Jews do not believe in an afterlife, but they still maintain that God is righteous and responds to vice and virtue appropriately in this world, particularly in God's dealings with "God's people.") The God of the Jews and Christians is the epitome of all virtues. God is: the essence of goodness, love, justice, compassion, and mercy; the protector of the innocent and the faithful; the enemy of the wicked and the infidel.

God is pure spirit with no material substance and neither beginning nor end. We cannot experience God directly with our senses. The only people who claim to have had direct contact with God are mystics, who all agree that this experience is totally spiritual and private. Arguments for God's existence are, therefore, *indirect*. Believers do, however, point to certain facts that, they claim, imply God's existence. Are these empirical facts and implications sufficient to make a reasonable person conclude that a Supreme Being actually exists?

Proofs of God: Arguments from the Character of the World

When archaeologists sift through the many-layered sites of ancient civilizations, what do they look for? Something "artificial." The evidence they want is handmade, produced by people—pottery shards, tools, amphorae, statuettes, coins—things that do not occur naturally. How do they assess the accomplishments of the people they are literally unearthing? By the complexity of what these civilizations have produced. Well-designed cities, houses with mosaic floors, and the extensive use of metals all suggest more sophisticated skills than mud huts and wooden bowls.

Can we use the archaeologist's approach in our search for God? Are there "divine pottery shards"? Can we find something so complex that it could have been produced only by a divine being? Many people think so. If you ask a friend to explain why she believes in God, she may tell you that the world seems so well planned that it could not be as it is by accident. God must have conceived of it and created it. Another friend might come up with sunsets, beaches, and love as God's proof. So much beauty and goodness assure him that some Supreme Being caused it.

Some philosophers also think this way. What do they point to? The world; the basic characteristics of the universe; its order and design; the way that everything from the cells of a leaf to the gravitational forces between planets somehow "make sense" and blend together to form a wondrously coherent whole. These thinkers argue that nothing so complicated could be the result of accidental, natural processes. Therefore, it must have been designed by some supremely wise and powerful being: God.

The Argument from Design: William Paley

The most simple and straightforward strategy for proving God's existence from the character of the material world is called the **argument from design**. The universe is so intelligently crafted, the argument goes, that it must have a creator. The thinker most famous for this argument is eighteenth-century British churchman William Paley.

Paley's argument rests on the now well-known analogy in which he compares the world to a watch. Just as the existence of a watch implies a watch-maker, so the existence of our world implies a world-maker (or world-architect). Paley writes,

William Paley (1743–1805) was educated at Christ's College of Cambridge University, ordained a priest, taught at the university for nine years, and held a variety of positions in the church. He wrote three widely read books: *The Principles of Moral and Political Philosophy* (1785), A *View of the Evidences of Christianity* (1794), and *Natural Theology; or Evidences of the Existence and Attributes of the Deity, Collected from the Appearances of Nature* (1802). The first work discusses civic duties and obligations in a way that anticipates Bentham's utilitarianism; the second argues for the authenticity of Biblical miracles; and the third claims to prove the existence of God from various natural phenomena.

In crossing a heath, suppose I pitched my foot against a stone, and were asked how the stone came to be there, I might possibly answer, that, for any thing I knew to the contrary, it had lain there forever; nor would it perhaps be very easy to show the absurdity of this answer. But suppose I had found a watch upon the ground, and it should be inquired how the watch happened to be in that place; I should hardly think of the answer which I had before given, that, for any thing I knew, the watch might have always been there. Yet why should not this answer serve for the watch as well as for the stone? Why is it not as admissible in the second case as in the first? For this reason, and for no other, namely, that when we come to inspect the watch, we perceive (what we could not discover in the stone) that its several parts are framed and put together for a purpose, e.g., that they are so formed and adjusted as to produce motion, and that motion so regulated as to point out the hour of the day; that, if the different parts had been differently shaped from what they are, of a different size from what they are, or placed after any other manner, or in any other order, than that in which they are placed, either no motion at all would have been carried on in the machine, or none which would have answered the use that is now served by it. . . . This mechanism being observed . . . and understood, the inference, we think, is inevitable, that the watch must have had a maker: that there must have existed, at some time, and at some place or other, an artificer or artificers who formed it for the purpose which we find it actually to answer; who comprehended its construction and designed its use. . . .

[E]very indication of contrivance, every manifestation of design, which existed in the watch, exists in the works of nature; with the difference, on the side of nature, of being greater and more, and that in a degree which exceeds all computation. I mean that the contrivances of nature surpass the contrivances of art, in the complexity, subtlety, and curiosity, of the mechanism; and still more, if possible, do they go beyond them in number and variety; yet, in a multitude of cases, are not less evidently mechanical, not less evidently contrivances, not less evidently accommodated to their end, or suited to their office, than are the most perfect productions of human ingenuity. . . .

Every observation which was made in our first chapter, concerning the watch, may be repeated with strict propriety concerning the eye; concerning animals; concerning plants; concerning, indeed, all the organized parts of the works of nature. . . .

Were there no example in the world, of contrivance, except that of the eye, it would be alone sufficient to support the conclusion which we draw from it, as to the necessity of an intelligent Creator. It could never be got rid of; because it could not be accounted for by any other supposition, which did not contradict all the principles we possess of knowledge; the principles, according to which, things do, as often they can be brought to the test of experience, turn out to be true or false.[1]

This lengthy passage contains a simple argument. Watches are not natural objects. They do not grow on trees but are made by skillful craftspeople. Therefore, watches imply watchmakers. The world is infinitely more complex than a watch. How did it get made? There must be a supreme, infinitely skilled creator—God.

> **argument from design** The argument from design is an argument for the existence of God that claims that the universe is so intelligently crafted that it must have a creator.

Does the Argument Work?

This analogy has an obvious appeal. Paley claims that the world's design shows such a high degree of sophistication that only God could conceive of and execute it. The comparison with a watch is particularly apt. A watch is both complicated and precise. So is the world, with its cycles of the sun, the moon, the seasons, and the birth, growth, and death of plants and animals. Everything moves in a way that contributes to order and balance. The wonderful patterns and intricacies of the universe really do seem extraordinary. It is natural, then, to think of it as the handiwork of a divine craftsman.

This argument from design also seems to have the virtue of being strictly empirical. Paley does not base his "proof" on religious beliefs—he reflects on the observable, physical workings of nature. Then he draws what seems like a reasonable conclusion, which he illustrates by the "watch : watchmaker :: world : God" analogy. Many religious people are fond of this argument. As the workings of nature are a sign of God's great design, so the world is a signpost to God.

But does the argument by design prove what it claims to?

---

1. William Paley, *Natural Theology*, http://darwin-online.org.uk/content/frameset?itemID=A142 &pageseq=1&viewtype=text.

False Analogy?

The argument from design has a series of problems. Let's begin with the most serious.

Paley says that after appreciating the design of the world, we cannot account for it in any other way than by assuming that God did the designing and therefore exists. Paley even makes it sound as though any other cause is logically impossible. But don't the theories of contemporary science contradict this claim? What about the evidence of the "big bang" and natural evolution? Surely, natural processes could produce the kind of world we have. Why must the order and purpose in nature come from a supernatural source?

The problem with Paley's argument crops up when we take his watch analogy too literally. Paley's reasoning works for a mechanical device like a watch. Machines are not alive; they have no inner force that gives them shape and drives their behavior. Plants and animals are quite different. They grow and adapt to their environment on their own. They become ill and heal. They respond and change. They reproduce according to their own unique genetic code in a way that a watch does not. That's what being alive is all about. Some biologists even speculate that the whole planet can be understood as a single organism. If that were the case, the entire material universe would have properties that would distinguish it from any artifact ever made. This is essentially the criticism offered by the British philosopher David Hume, whose thoughts about knowledge you encountered in Chapter 8. As you saw there, Hume is so rigorous and skeptical that he doubts such seemingly self-evident ideas as the "self" and "causality." You can just imagine how he attacks the question of God's existence. In his *Dialogues Concerning Natural Religion*, Hume specifically rejects the argument from design:

> If we see a house, . . . we conclude, with the greatest certainty, that it had an architect or builder; because this is precisely that species of effect which we have experienced to proceed from that species of cause. But surely you will not affirm, that the universe bears such a resemblance to a house, that we can with the same certainty infer a similar cause, or that the analogy is here entire and perfect. The dissimilitude is so striking, that the utmost you can here pretend to is a guess, a conjecture, a presumption concerning a similar cause.[2]

If Paley's argument is indeed based on a false analogy, it proves nothing. What do you think? Can you defend the argument from design, or must we discount it as an interesting but ultimately unpersuasive approach?

What Kind of "Watchmaker"? What Kind of "Watch"?

Even if we go along with Paley and concede that the design of the world does imply an architect of some sort, does that prove that the Judeo-Christian God is that architect? Maybe some great being did in fact design and create the world. But what makes us think

2. David Hume, *Dialogues Concerning Natural Religion*, https://www.gutenberg.org/files/4583/4583-h/4583-h.htm.

that this being was more than simply "one terrific world-architect"? The Judeo-Christian God has a vast array of attributes. Does the ability to design a world necessarily mean that someone is perfect and omnipotent in all respects? Don't you do some things well and some badly? Maybe you're a great auto mechanic who cannot cook, or a great cook who cannot play the piano. It is certainly not necessary that the creator of the world should also be just, fair, loving, merciful, and so on.

Next, think of the following different watches: a watch that must be wound every day; a self-winding watch whose spring is wound by the movement of your wrist; a battery-powered watch that runs for two years before the battery needs changing; a watch powered by light; a watch with a special computer chip that lets it repair itself; a self-repairing watch whose battery runs for billions of years. Which of these is best? The last one, of course. And wouldn't it take a better watchmaker to make it than one who makes only spring-run watches that must be wound, cleaned, oiled, and repaired? One would think so.

Applying the same logic to worlds, we should expect the greatest possible world-architect to create a self-regulating world that does not need any tending. Yet Paley's God continues to exist and tinker with the workings of the universe—presumably on a daily basis. If you were a perfect being designing a universe, surely you would make a self-contained, self-powered, and self-regulating universe. Doesn't it insult God's power to say that God created a world that needs a divine being's constant attention? On the other hand, if the universe does not need God's oversight, it is possible that the world was designed and made by some world-architect who subsequently went away or died. This would mean that all we could conclude is that there once was a world-architect.

Saint Thomas Aquinas was born in 1225 to a family of the Italian nobility. Destined for the monastery from an early age, Thomas was sent to the abbey of Monte Cassino when he was only five. Monte Cassino was the main monastery of the Benedictines, a famous and highly influential order of monks, and Thomas's family probably had political intentions in placing the boy there. At fourteen, Thomas began studying at the University of Naples, where he became interested in and joined a new religious order—the Dominicans—that took both learning and poverty quite seriously. Thomas's family was so upset that they kidnapped him for a year in an attempt to change his mind. After his release, he studied at the University of Paris with Saint Albert the Great, a teacher who introduced Aquinas to the thought of Aristotle. Thomas taught theology at Paris, was assigned to the Papal Court, and, most unusually, was allowed a second term in Paris teaching theology.

Aquinas was a controversial thinker and prolific writer who constructed a vast and intricate theological system that attempted to explain Christian belief in terms of Aristotelian philosophy. On December 6, 1273, however, he stopped writing, claiming that such things had been revealed to him that everything he had written now seemed like straw. He died in 1274 on his way to a church council and was canonized in 1323, a remarkably short time after his death to receive such recognition. In 1879, his system of thought was made the official doctrine of the Roman Catholic Church.

The Argument from "Governance of the World": Saint Thomas Aquinas

In fairness, it's reasonable to ask if we're focusing too much on Paley's watch analogy. If we take a step back and take a wider view of how the universe works, do we see empirical evidence of God? Saint Thomas Aquinas, one of the greatest philosophers of the Middle Ages, thought so.

Canonized as a saint by the Roman Catholic Church shortly after his death, Thomas Aquinas built a philosophical system that is often likened in structure and in feeling to a Gothic cathedral. His system is not only intricate but also inspired by religious faith. Out of the synthesis of philosophy and theology, Aquinas built a towering intellectual edifice.

> **argument from the governance of the world** The argument from the governance of the world claims that the order and intelligence of the activities of nature imply the existence of a being directing them.

Aquinas is a Christian thinker, of course, so it is not surprising that he sets out to prove the existence of God. Actually, he offers five different arguments. One of them is based on a concept Aquinas calls the **governance of the world**. It is similar to Paley's argument from design in the sense that Aquinas claims that the workings of nature reveal God's existence. However, it makes an even stronger claim. Aquinas writes,

> We see that things which lack knowledge, such as natural bodies, act for an end, and this is evident from their acting always, or nearly always, in the same way, so as to obtain the best result. Hence it is plain that they achieve their end not fortuitously, but designedly. Now whatever lacks knowledge cannot move towards an end, unless it be directed by some being endowed with knowledge and intelligence; as the arrow is directed by the archer. Therefore some intelligent being exists by whom all natural things are directed to their end; and this being we call God.[3]

When Aquinas surveys the workings of nature, he sees signs of intelligence, an intelligence absent in the objects of nature themselves. This, he thinks, suggests the existence of God, just as a flying arrow implies the existence of an archer. Arrows do not just shoot themselves at their targets. Similarly, God directs nature's activities. To Aquinas, the workings of nature are akin to the movements of a glove worn on the hand of God. The purposefulness we observe in nature is the result of the intelligence of God. To Aquinas, then, God didn't just create the world and walk away. God governs the world through bringing intelligence into the operations of nature.

Aquinas's argument may seem for the moment stronger than Paley's.

Unfortunately, both thinkers still have a big problem to overcome.

---

3. Saint Thomas Aquinas, *Summa Theologica*, Question II, Article 3, in *Basic Writings of Saint Thomas Aquinas*, ed. Anton C. Pegis (New York: Random House, 1945; reprinted Indianapolis: Hackett Publishing Co., 1997), Volume 1, p. 23.

How Good Is the "Watch"?

Think about it this way. The basic assumption on which the arguments from design and governance are built is that something about the nature of the creator can be inferred from the nature of the world that has been created. This assumption by its very nature, however, produces major problems for the arguments that rest upon it. Consider, for example, the reaction to the argument from design from one of the most important philosophers of the twentieth century, British thinker Bertrand Russell (1872–1970):

> It is a most astonishing thing that people can believe that this world, . . . with all its defects, should be the best that omnipotence and omniscience have been able to produce in millions of years. I really cannot believe it. Do you think that, if you were granted omnipotence and omniscience and millions of years in which to perfect your world, you could produce nothing better than the Ku Klux Klan or the Fascists?[4]

Look very carefully at the world around you. Paley and Aquinas say that this world is so wondrous that clearly its existence proves the existence not only of a God but also of a *good* God. But is this world of ours really so wonderful? The order and design of nature are sometimes breathtaking. At other times, however, things do not work out so well. There are earthquakes, droughts, floods, hurricanes, tornadoes, tsunamis, all of which are uncontrollable and devastating expressions of nature's destructive power. Is this the best way to design a world?

Then consider *Homo sapiens,* the creature supposedly fashioned in the creator's "image and likeness." We regard everything on this planet as ours to use or abuse as we see fit. We hunt species to extinction, strip-mine, pollute the oceans, and destroy ecological systems with our toxic wastes. Our behavior has heated the planet to catastrophic levels. Is this really the best a wise creator could do?

Look at how we treat each other. We have war—tribal, religious, political. We have discrimination—racial, sexual, religious. We have poverty, slavery, greed, murder, rape, child abuse. It seems incomprehensible that a creature that is even vaguely fashioned after a God of goodness could so regularly savage our brothers and sisters. On top of this, we have used our intellect to invent devices with which we can destroy all life on this planet, and we have put them under the control of military and political organizations that consider it rational to use them. As a species, we do not even follow what one would assume is the most basic instinct: survival for ourselves and our children. It's almost as though our genes command us to somehow destroy ourselves. How can this be a sign of a competent world-architect?

Even an ordinary electrician designs systems that work better. An overheated electrical line will cause a fire. To guard against that, the electrician installs mechanisms that

---

4. Bertrand Russell, "Why I Am Not a Christian," in *Why I Am Not a Christian and Other Essays on Religions and Related Subjects* (New York: Simon & Schuster, 1957), 10.

prevent disaster, either circuit breakers or fuses. Why are there no similar mechanisms in human beings? The absence of "circuit breakers" that at least limit the harm we can do should give us pause. It might also make us question whether the apparent natural order of things is as good as we sometimes think. For all the glory of creation, an objective assessment shows that the world, and especially *Homo sapiens*, leaves much to be desired.

What does this imply about the being who designed a world that includes so many natural disasters and so much calculated evil? At least that he or she was not very capable, and possibly sadistic. When we push the fundamental premise of Paley's and Aquinas's arguments to their logical conclusion, about the best we can do is to say that our "world architect" still needs more practice—or, as Bertrand Russell concludes, that God does not exist.

The Problem of Evil

Any argument for the existence of God from the character of the world must overcome the presence of evil in the world. That is, it must answer the question of how you reconcile evil with a good God. This **problem of evil** is particularly critical for the arguments from design and governance of the world. After all, the properties and features of the world are precisely those things that reveal the nature of its creator or overseer. When we observe massive flaws, can we escape the conclusion that their creator is inept or evil—or that there never was a creator in the first place?

> **problem of evil** The problem of evil refers to the conflict between the notion of a good God and the existence of evil in the world. This idea is generally used to argue against the existence of God.

The Free-Will Argument

At this point, you might rise to God's defense. The argument from design is based on the idea that we can conclude something about the creator from the creation. An important part of that creation, you might argue, is people who are created with **free will**. Evil is a human product, not a divine one. God made us free, but people abuse that freedom. Isn't it better for God to make us free than incapable of doing wrong?

If you are thinking this way, you are in the company of the great early Christian thinker Saint Augustine. Augustine believes that "a wicked will is the cause of all evil."[5] For Augustine, evil is not some dark force with its own life whirling throughout the world. It is simply the result of our not choosing properly. According to this position, our world-architect gave us the power of choice. Because we are responsible for what we choose, the creator's competence and benevolence are neither at issue nor at risk.

---

5. Saint Augustine, *On Free Choice of the Will* (Indianapolis: Hackett Publishing Co., 1993), 104; translation adapted.

But there are more problems with this "free-will" argument. First, any appeal to free will ignores natural disasters and diseases. The "watch" still explodes every now and then, apparently on its own. Second, isn't genuine freedom an ability to choose what we think best without pressure of any sort that takes our decision away from us? Yet as we saw in our discussion of **determinism**, an argument can be made that freedom is an illusion.

Freedom to choose our actions would be fine if we were designed in a way that we could always make intelligent, objective assessments of our options. But we are not designed this way. Instead, irrational forces—greed, anxiety, fear, and hatred—can lead to terrible events: the slaughter of six million Jews, the White people's aggression against Native Americans and Blacks, centuries of male domination of women. When our dark emotions are aroused, there's a way that our actions are not what any decent person would want them to be. A better-designed human being would be more powerful, that is, freer, and have the capacity to ward off the influence of prejudice and fear. Wouldn't such control and such freedom be the only handiwork of which a perfect world-architect would be capable?

Thus, we are still confronting the same conclusion. Any world-architect who designed us as we are either lacks the power or resources to carry out an otherwise good plan, or just isn't very skilled.

The Suffering of the Innocent: The Book of Job

You may never have seriously questioned God's existence. You may even be thinking that these problems with the argument from design are simply petty academic complaints. You may see faith as the issue here, and proofs are irrelevant to faith.

Or instead of acknowledging the problem of evil, you may be tempted to say that only an evil person would question God. If so, you should realize that there is a long *religious* tradition of facing the problem of evil. In fact, the most powerful and eloquent expression of this problem appears in the Bible, in the Book of Job. This classic statement of a universal human phenomenon, the terrible suffering endured by innocent people, was written about 2,500 years ago, but its theme is as true today as it was then. Job may get more than his share of bad luck, but we don't have to look very far in our own world to find good people facing terrible hardships.

Most of you are familiar with the story of Job. He is a good and prosperous man whom God allows to suffer mightily in order to prove a point to Satan—that Job is not righteous just because of the rewards it brings. On a single day, Job's oxen and camels are stolen, his flocks are destroyed, and his children and servants are killed. Then Job himself is afflicted with a particularly painful form of leprosy. His wife urges him to "Curse God, and die." His friends turn against him because they think Job must have done something terrible to be the victim of such suffering. They believe in a world designed by a good God and in a covenant between the Jews and Yahweh that calls for goodness to be rewarded and evil punished. Insisting on his innocence, Job demands an audience with God. God eventually replies to Job along the lines of "Who are you to criticize me?" God also rebukes Job's friends for accusing him of wrongdoing. Job "repents," and God gives him a new family and fortune.[6]

What does this story tell us about the argument from design? Only that even the Bible, the basic text of the Judeo-Christian tradition, testifies to flaws in the design of the world. In the real world, the innocent are *not* rewarded for their suffering. But even if we grant God's effort to make it up to Job, what kind of a God does the Book of Job give us? In trying to win an argument with Satan, God allows great suffering to an innocent person—even the death of Job's children. Does God apologize to Job? No. Does he claim Job's fate was deserved or just? On the contrary. What are we left with? A world-architect who is incredibly powerful but apparently insensitive to the pain of those whom He is supposed to protect. In other words, not even the Bible gives us a satisfactory answer to the problem of evil.

Does the Material World Prove God's Existence?

When we survey proofs for God's existence based on the nature of the physical world, the results are mixed. These arguments certainly do not establish any necessity for a Supreme Being of goodness, love, mercy, and justice who designed and created a good and orderly universe. Attributing the problems in the universe to human free will does not account for all the imperfections in the design of the world.

The best these proofs do, then, is suggest that there once may have been (and there may still be) a world-architect. However, logically, it is just as possible that the world simply exists as a product of natural forces.

Arguments from Reason Alone

We have not yet settled the question of whether God exists. But remember that the question we are investigating is somewhat different. Here we are examining claims about whether we can *know* that God exists.

We have just looked at *empirical* arguments—those that would be offered by someone who thinks knowledge comes from the evidence we gather using our senses. In the rival *rationalist* tradition, knowledge derives from the purely mental operations like those used in mathematics or logic. And not surprisingly, there are rationalist proofs of God's existence as well.

---

6. Many Biblical scholars think that Job's "repentance" and new fortune were not in the original version of the Book of Job. After all, Job has nothing to "repent" for. And how realistic is it that innocent people ultimately are rewarded for their suffering? It is not realistic at all.

The Ontological Argument: Saint Anselm

The most famous argument of this sort, the **ontological argument**, is offered by the early medieval thinker Anselm of Canterbury. Anselm himself did not use the word "ontological" when he made his argument. But ever since Immanuel Kant referred to it this way, the label has stuck. He chose "ontological" because the argument is based on the concept of the most perfect *being*. (*Ontos* is Greek for "being.")

Saint Anselm (1033–1109) was born in Italy, entered the monastery against the objections of his father, and became a monk, abbot, and teacher in the monastery of Bec. In 1093, he was made Archbishop of Canterbury and took an active role in a dispute concerning the relationship between the authority of the King and that of the Pope. His most famous works on the existence of God are the *Monologion* and *Proslogion*.

Anselm's argument has had a long and controversial history. During its first seven hundred years, the argument had as many defenders as attackers. About two hundred years ago, most philosophers decided it was wrong, but debate over it has started again in our own day. Some people hail it as a genuine proof of God's existence. Others dismiss it as philosophical flimflam.

For all of that, Anselm's argument is unquestionably one of the most important proofs offered for the existence of God. The argument is found in Anselm's *Proslogion*.

That God Truly Exists

Therefore, Lord, you who grant understanding to faith, grant that, insofar as you know it is useful for me, I may understand that you exist as we believe you exist, and that you are what we believe you to be. Now we believe that you are something than which nothing greater can be thought. So can it be that no such nature exists, since "The fool has said in his heart, 'There is no God'"? [Ps. 14:1; 53:1] But when this same fool hears me say "something than which nothing greater can be thought," he surely understands what he hears; and what he understands exists in his understanding, even if he does not understand that it exists [in reality]. For it is one thing for an object to exist in the understanding and quite another to understand that the object exists [in reality]. When a painter, for example, thinks out in advance what he is going to paint, he has it in his understanding, but he does not yet understand that it exists, since he has not yet painted it. But once he has painted it, he both has it in his understanding and understands that it exists because he has now painted it. So even the fool must admit that something than which nothing greater can be thought exists at least in his understanding, since he understands this when he hears it, and whatever is understood exists in the understanding. And surely that than which a greater cannot be thought cannot exist only in the understanding. For if it exists only in the understanding, it can be thought to exist in reality as well, which is greater. So if that than which a greater cannot be thought exists only in the understanding, then the very thing than which a greater *cannot* be thought is something than which a greater *can* be thought. But that is clearly impossible. Therefore, there is no doubt that something than which a greater cannot be thought exists both in the understanding and in reality.

That [God] Cannot Be Thought Not to Exist

This [being] exists so truly that it cannot even be thought not to exist. For it is possible to think that something exists that cannot be thought not to exist, and such a being is greater than one that can be thought not to exist. Therefore, if that than which a greater cannot be thought can be thought not to exist, then that than which a greater cannot be thought is not that than which a greater cannot be thought; and this is a contradiction. So that than which a greater cannot be thought exists so truly that it cannot even be thought not to exist.

And this is you, O Lord our God. You exist so truly, O Lord my God, that you cannot even be thought not to exist. And rightly so, for if some mind could think something better than you, a creature would rise above the Creator and sit in judgment upon him, which is completely absurd. Indeed, everything that exists, except for you alone, can be thought not to exist. So you alone among all things have existence most truly, and therefore most greatly; for whatever else exists has existence less truly, and therefore less greatly. So then why did "the fool say in his heart, 'There is no God,'" [Ps. xiii. I, lii. I] when it is so evident to the rational mind that you among all beings exist most greatly? Why indeed, except because he is stupid and a fool?[7]

What Anselm Has in Mind

Anselm's argument is fairly simple. Push your imagination as hard as you can and think of the most perfect, most supreme being. That is Anselm's "that-than-which-a-greater-cannot-be-thought." In particular, imagine that this being is so great, so perfect, that it cannot even be thought not to exist. Do you have that in mind? If so, you realize that it is logically impossible for such a being not to exist. Anselm would say that this most perfect being that you have envisioned is God. So, he thinks, anyone who truly understands the idea of the greatest possible being should realize that God must actually exist.

Moreover, by realizing that God is a being whose nonexistence we cannot even imagine, Anselm would say that we are aware of God's "necessary existence." That is, if God's existence is "necessary," to say that God does not exist is as self-contradictory as saying "Fire is cold." To claim that something that must exist cannot exist is so illogical that it is ridiculous.

In other words, Anselm thinks that as our minds explore the idea of the greatest possible being imaginable, we will realize that in addition to being all-powerful, all-knowing,

> **ontological argument** The ontological argument is Saint Anselm's argument for the existence of God. It claims that by merely contemplating the notion of God as "something-than-which-nothing-greater-can-be-thought," we become aware that God must exist.

---

7. *Anselm's Proslogion; with the Replies of Gaunilo and Anselm,* translated and introduced by Thomas Williams (Indianapolis: Hackett Publishing Co., 2001), II.2, pp. 7, 8.

all-just, all-merciful, and all-loving, its level of existence is so great and so necessary that it must have existed from eternity, will go on forever, and cannot even be thought of as not existing. Anselm is convinced that if we have a clear understanding of the idea of the "greatest possible being," then we should have no doubt about God's existence. Only a fool would think otherwise.

Reason Alone

Notice that this argument relies on nothing but reason alone. Unlike Paley and Thomas Aquinas, Anselm does not draw his reasons for God's existence from the world of nature. Rather, he takes an idea, the concept that God is the most perfect being imaginable— "that-than-which-a-greater-cannot-be-thought"—and claims that a purely intellectual examination of that concept shows that such a being must exist in *reality* as well as *in our minds* as an idea. Furthermore, Anselm thinks that if we understand the concept properly, we should see that the statement "God does not exist" is a logical contradiction. Anselm makes his point about God's existence purely by logic, not by reference to the physical world.

Anselm's Platonism

The material world offers us no evidence of a necessarily existing, most perfect being. Where does such an idea come from, then? Anselm would say it results from the fact that such a being actually exists and that our minds discern that fact. This style of thinking makes Anselm in essence a Platonist.

Like Plato, Anselm assumes that the ideas in our minds are not simply arbitrary creations of our imagination. Instead, he believes they are connected to some higher reality that is superior to the senses. Plato thinks that our conceptions of justice, fairness, beauty, and the like come from actual existing, nonmaterial entities that we discover with our "mind's eye," as it were.[8] If there were no such thing as the metaphysical entity "Justice itself," for example, Plato would say that we would have no idea of justice in our minds. Anselm is from the same school of thought. We are able to fashion a mental image of a "most perfect" being only because one actually exists. And if we do have such an idea, we can conclude that such a being must exist.

Anselm's argument has a certain appeal. We can all think of a being "that-than-which-a-greater-cannot-be-thought." But does this mean that Anselm has proven that God exists?

---

8. See Chapter 7 to review Plato's understanding of the nature of reality.

Anselm's Critics

Gaunilo

As persuasive as Anselm's argument may seem, it has no shortage of critics. Its first critic was a French monk named Gaunilo of Marmoutiers, who lived at the same time as Anselm. Speaking "on behalf of the Fool," Gaunilo rejects Anselm's contention that simply imagining the idea of a most perfect being proves that it exists. If that were the case, he says, imagining something like a "most perfect" island would "prove" that it exists. He explains,

> For example, there are those who say that somewhere in the ocean is an island, which, because of the difficulty—or rather, impossibility—of finding what does not exist, some call 'the Lost Island.' This island (so the story goes) is more plentifully endowed than even the Isles of the Blessed with an indescribable abundance of all sorts of riches and delights. And because it has neither owner nor inhabitant, it is everywhere superior in its abundant riches to all the other lands that human beings inhabit. Suppose someone tells me all this. The story is easily told and involves no difficulty, and so I understand it. But if this person went on to draw a conclusion, and say, 'You cannot any longer doubt that this island, more excellent than all others on earth, truly exists somewhere in reality. For you do not doubt that this island exists in your understanding, and since it is more excellent to exist not merely in the understanding, but also in reality, this island must also exist in reality. For if it did not, any land that exists in reality would be greater than it. And so this more excellent thing that you have understood would not in fact be more excellent.'—If, I say, he should try to convince me by this argument that I should no longer doubt whether the island truly exists, either I would think he was joking, or I would not know whom I ought to think more foolish: myself, if I grant him his conclusion, or him, if he thinks he has established the existence of that island with any degree of certainty, without first showing that its excellence exists in my understanding as a thing that truly and undoubtedly exists and not in any way like something false or uncertain.[9]

Gaunilo sees no contradiction in conceiving of a most perfect being and at the same time doubting its existence. He continues,

> When did I ever say that any such thing as that "greater than everything else" exists in actual fact, so that on that basis I am supposed to accept the claim that it exists to such a degree that it cannot even be thought not to exist? Therefore you must first prove by some absolutely incontestable argument that there exists some superior nature, that is, one that is greater and better than all others that exist, so

---

9. Gaunilo, "A Reply to the Foregoing by a Certain Writer on Behalf of the Fool," in *Anselm's Proslogion*, 32.

that from this we can also prove all of the qualities that that which is greater and better than all other things must necessarily possess.[10]

Thomas Aquinas

About a century later, Thomas Aquinas joined Gaunilo in criticizing Anselm. As you saw earlier in this chapter, Aquinas tries to derive God's existence by pointing to the material world rather than proving it by reasoning alone. Like Gaunilo, Aquinas thinks that the idea of a most perfect being can certainly exist only as an idea with no counterpart in reality, and he explicitly rejects Anselm's argument on grounds similar to Gaunilo's. Aquinas writes,

> Perhaps not everyone who hears this name *God* understands it to signify something than which nothing greater can be thought. . . . Yet, [even] granted that everyone understands that by this name *God* is signified something than which nothing greater can be thought, nevertheless, it does not therefore follow that he understands that what the name signifies exists actually, but only that it exists mentally. Nor can it be argued that it actually exists, unless it be admitted that there actually exists something than which nothing greater can be thought; and this precisely is not admitted by those who hold that God does not exist.[11]

David Hume

About five hundred years after Aquinas, we find David Hume also challenging Anselm. Like Aquinas, Hume thinks it is impossible to argue for God's existence from reason alone. Nor does he see any logical contradiction in imagining God's nonexistence. As Hume puts this:

> I shall begin with observing that there is an evident absurdity in pretending to demonstrate a matter of fact, or to prove it by any arguments *a priori* [by reason alone]. Nothing is demonstrable unless the contrary implies a contradiction. Nothing, that is distinctly conceivable implies a contradiction. Whatever we conceive as existent, we can also conceive as non-existent. There is no being, therefore, whose non-existence implies a contradiction. Consequently there is no being whose existence is demonstrable. I propose this argument as entirely decisive, and am willing to rest the whole controversy upon it.
>
> It is pretended that the Deity is a necessarily existent being; and this necessity of his existence is attempted to be explained by asserting that, if we knew his whole essence or nature, we should perceive it to be as impossible for him not to exist, as for twice two not to be four. But it is evident, that this can never happen, while our faculties remain the same as at present. It will still be possible for us, at any time, to conceive the non-existence of what we formerly conceived to exist; nor can the mind

10. Gaunilo, "A Reply to the Foregoing," 32.
11. Saint Thomas Aquinas, *Summa Theologica*, Question II, Article 1, p. 20.

ever lie under a necessity of supposing any object to remain always in being; in the same manner as we lie under a necessity of always conceiving twice two to be four.[12]

Stop and think about the statement "2 + 2 = 4." Now try to think logically that "2 + 2" equals something else. It is hard to do. In fact, as long as you are thinking in line with the rules of reason, it is impossible. Now call to mind your image of a "most perfect being" and imagine that it really exists. Now try to imagine that it does not exist. It is much easier to do that than it is to imagine that "2 + 2" equals something other than 4, isn't it?

This is just Hume's point. As long as we can even conceive of God's nonexistence, it is not contradictory to say, "God does not exist." In short, Hume not only thinks that Anselm's argument doesn't win the day; he thinks it doesn't even leave the starting gate.

Anselm's Critics Reviewed

Anselm's case is simple and straightforward; Gaunilo, Aquinas, and Hume reject it in an equally simple and straightforward way. Anselm says it is contradictory to think that "that-than-which-a-greater-cannot-be-thought" does not exist in reality as well as in the mind. The other three thinkers flatly disagree. Understanding a concept does not prove that the entity represented by the idea exists. A phoenix is a beautiful bird that lives for five hundred years, then is consumed by fire in order to be reborn out of the ashes. We can all understand what a phoenix is, but that doesn't prove that such a bird exists.

Lest you think that these philosophers are merely biased against the idea of God, remember that at least two of them, Gaunilo and Aquinas, believe devoutly in God. They agree with Anselm's conclusion. They just don't think that Anselm's argument proves it.

Anselm's Reply: A One-Concept-Only Argument

Good philosophers always have intelligent responses to their critics. Since Gaunilo lived at the same time as Anselm, we have the good fortune of knowing exactly how Anselm replied to the criticism.

The essence of Anselm's defense is that his argument works for one concept, and one concept only—the concept of "that-than-which-a-greater-cannot-be-thought." Gaunilo's claim that we can imagine a fantastic "Lost Island" is beside the point. As Anselm explains,

> The only thing that cannot be thought not to exist is that which has neither beginning nor end, and is not made up of parts, and which no thought discerns except as wholly present always and everywhere.[13]

---

12. David Hume, *Dialogues Concerning Natural Religion*, Second Edition, ed. Richard H. Popkin (Indianapolis: Hackett Publishing Co., 1998), 55.

13. Saint Anselm, "A Reply to the Foregoing by the Author of the Book in Question," in *Anselm's Proslogion*, 40.

Any other concept we can imagine is irrelevant. His argument, Anselm says, applies to only one concept. And if we come up with a being that we can imagine not existing, then we have the wrong concept in mind:

> Therefore, if, while he is thinking that than which a greater cannot be thought, he thinks that it can fail to exist, he is not thinking that than which a greater cannot be thought. But it is not possible for the same thing at the same time both to be thought and not to be thought. Therefore, someone who thinks that than which a greater cannot be thought does not think that it can, but rather that it cannot, fail to exist. For this reason the thing that he is thinking exists necessarily, since whatever can fail to exist is not what he is thinking.[14]

This answer is either very clever or very good. Anselm claims that his two "proofs"— (1) conceiving an idea of the "greatest possible being" automatically implies the existence of that being and (2) imagining the nonexistence of this being is self-contradictory— hold for one and only one concept, "that-than-which-a-greater-cannot-be-thought." If his proofs are true for only this concept, Anselm can dismiss any counterexample as comparing apples and oranges.

How does Anselm's reply hold up? Is Anselm cheating, or is he right? Ordinarily, we would not take a "one-concept argument" seriously. Intellectual custom usually does not let us defend a conclusion by saying that the idea on which it is based is so unique that special rules apply. Still, there is something about this concept that is hard to ignore. Might not things indeed be different when it comes to the greatest imaginable being? Is it absolutely impossible to conceive of an argument that applies only to one case? In this one instance only, might it not be that the nonexistence of such an entity is in fact self-contradictory?

The simple fact that this argument has been debated as a viable proof for God's existence for almost a thousand years is worth noting. Anselm's argument may not be conclusive, and it may not be universally accepted. But its enduring appeal and its tenacity suggest that it has something important to say.

Defining the Greatest Possible Being by Reason or Faith?

When we looked at the arguments of Paley, Aquinas, and Hume, the most we ended up with was not the God of the Bible but a world-architect. Now we have to see if the same thing happens with Anselm's argument. Anselm begins his argument by referring to the line from the Book of Psalms, "The Fool has said in his heart, there is no God." This lets us know right away that he aims to prove the existence of the Judeo-Christian God of the Bible. Does he accomplish this?

---

14. Saint Anselm, "A Reply," 45.

The key here is Anselm's concept "that-than-which-a-greater-cannot-be-thought." To Anselm, of course, this phrase refers to nothing but the God of the Old and New Testaments. But couldn't it mean something else? When we examine the thought of the ancient philosophers, we find candidates for "greatest possible being" that differ significantly from Anselm's God—Aristotle's "Unmoved Mover," for example, and "the One" of Plotinus (205–270). Both philosophers put a "supreme being" at the top of their systems, but these beings differ from the Biblical God in many ways.

Both men describe a supreme being so perfect it needs nothing and no one else. The Unmoved Mover and the One exist in a state of pure self-contemplation, meditating on the most perfect thing in the universe—itself. They have no awareness of anything else, least of all the petty events of human life. Why would the greatest possible being have any interest in anything less than perfect? Neither of these beings watches over the world the way the Judeo-Christian God does, keeping a tally of right and wrong and handing out rewards and punishments. In addition, these two supreme beings do not have the identifiable personality that the God of the Bible does. They are simply pure intellect. Furthermore, the Unmoved Mover and the One are so overwhelmingly powerful in their very essence that the universe is merely a by-product of their existence. Plotinus says the universe "emanates" from the One the way heat and light emanate from a flame. In other words, the One does not create the world by an act of will the way God creates the world in Genesis. The world is simply a product of its nature.

These two supreme entities, then, are examples of the "greatest possible being," yet they are very different from Anselm's conception of God. Other examples might have still other qualities. And there is no reason why there should be only one such being. Why couldn't there be two, three, or a countless number of perfect beings? It should be clear, therefore, that "that-than-which-a-greater-cannot-be-thought" can easily mean something other than what Anselm has in mind when he says "God."

Thus *reason* does not support Anselm's claims. In order to prove the existence of the Judeo-Christian God, Anselm has to draw on the conception of God given to him by his religious faith. Without that, the most he can claim is that his proof shows the existence of some "that-than-which-a-greater-cannot-be-thought." After that, we have to figure out exactly what this means.

Anselm finds nothing wrong with this. Remember how he starts his proof:

> Therefore, Lord, you who grant understanding to faith, grant that, insofar as you know it is useful for me, I may understand that you exist as we believe you exist, and that you are what we believe you to be.[15]

Clearly, he puts faith above reason when it comes to discerning God's nature. This being the case, we have to see his proof, like Paley's and Aquinas's, as operating under those limitations.

---

15. *Anselm's Proslogion,* 7.

For the strictly philosophical reader, then, Anselm's argument is not as strong as Anselm hopes it is. Yet this is the most famous argument for the existence of God that seeks to prove its point by appealing to reason alone. Whether it is brilliant thinking or philosophical sleight of hand, it still gives you much to think about.

Reason or Faith?

God's Existence: A Question of Reason

We have looked at Paley's and Aquinas's attempts to infer God's existence from the nature of the material world. We have considered Anselm's purely intellectual proof based on the concept of the greatest possible being. On balance, do these arguments prove that God exists?

These proofs certainly require us to consider seriously the possibility that some superior being created, designed, and governs the world. But none of them proves beyond the shadow of a doubt that such a being exists. Even if they do work, they fail to demonstrate the existence of the Judeo-Christian God. But the conclusion that there is no such being is not established either. Perhaps the issue simply can never be settled.

God's Existence: A Question of Faith

Is exploring possibly unanswerable questions a waste of time, then? Not at all. Even if the arguments we have looked at here do not "prove" whether God exists, they may be useful expressions of faith for people who already believe in God. It should be clear by now that although a number of interesting arguments can be made in favor of God's existence, ultimately it may be a matter of personal, unconfirmable, and unprovable belief.

Religion and Emotion

The fact that the issue of God's existence may ultimately be a matter of personal belief opens the door for one other challenge from Bertrand Russell. You noticed previously that Russell can bring an unusual perspective to philosophical discussions—as when he suggests that believing in God might come from a poverty of the human imagination. Russell poses another important question to us in suggesting that *fear* also plays a large role. He writes:

> Religion is based, I think, primarily and mainly upon fear. . . . Fear is the basis of the whole thing—fear of the mysterious, fear of defeat, fear of death. Fear is the parent of cruelty, and therefore it is no wonder if cruelty and religion have gone hand in hand. . . . In this world we can now begin a little to understand things, and a little to master them by help of science, which has forced its way step by step against the Christian religion, against the churches, and against the opposition of

all the old precepts. Science can help us to get over this craven fear in which mankind has lived for so many generations. Science can teach us, and I think our own hearts can teach us, no longer to look around for imaginary supports, no longer to invent allies in the sky, but rather to look to our own efforts here below to make this world a fit place to live in.[16]

Weak imaginations and fear certainly characterized humans in the earliest days of the species. Can we really be sure that we've outgrown them as far as we think we have? Is there a relationship between faith and fear?

Belief and Harm

The epistemological limits of faith are also important to keep in mind when we decide to take action on the basis of our religious beliefs. Although religious beliefs have produced much good in the world, they have also led otherwise good people to hurt one another very badly. In the course of history, much harm has come when people argued over which is the "true religion" and whose beliefs are "correct." The Romans persecuted the Christians because they refused to worship the gods of the state. For centuries the Jews have been persecuted as practitioners of a false faith. Islam spread via "holy wars," and Christian nations responded against the "infidel" during the Middle Ages with the Crusades. During the Reformation, opposing Christian sects executed people as a way of combating what the religious authorities judged to be "false beliefs." And in reaction to the development of science, the Catholic Church punished thinkers like Galileo for holding a different view of the universe than that found in the Bible.

Throughout all this, the issue is not so much how "heretics" and "infidels" *act*, not how they treat others, but what they *believe*. For example, Catholics and Protestants killed one another in sixteenth-century Europe because they believed different things about "grace," the "authority of Scripture," and "papal authority." Heretics were not executed because they were cruel, vicious people, although they were often falsely accused of that to make their deaths seem more defensible. They were burned at the stake for the beliefs they voiced or simply for what they held in their hearts. That most of them were good, decent, loving, and spiritual people was irrelevant.

Unfortunately, the tragic consequences of this focus on belief rather than behavior extend even to today. "Heretics" may not be burned at the stake any longer, but we do not have to look very far for examples of otherwise decent people experiencing everything from intimidation to death threats because their religious beliefs, or lack thereof, do not blend with someone else's idea of the truth. If "heretics," "blasphemers," and "infidels" went around actively harming other people, getting rid of them forcibly might be defensible. But whom do they hurt by their beliefs? God? Jesus? Muhammad? Buddha? Of course not. They may cause some distress among the "faithful," and we can sympathize

---

16. Russell, "Why I Am Not a Christian," 22.

with the feelings of these people when they hear "blasphemy." But offended sensibilities are surely not the sort of harm that merits imprisonment or death.

The only argument against "false belief" must refer to an afterlife. If people need to believe certain things in order to be "saved" by God, heresy or blasphemy can endanger the salvation of the true believer—and everyone is potentially a true believer or should be. But if we cannot prove God's existence, the most basic component of religious belief, we certainly cannot prove the existence of an afterlife or the conditions we have to meet to get there. This leads us right back to where we started. We are facing matters of belief, not knowledge.

In other words, when we take action against people because of their "false beliefs," their "blasphemy," or their "heresy," we do so based on premises that may be true or false. This, of course, is the nature of belief. We subscribe to an idea knowing that we do not have enough reasons to label it "knowledge." If we did have those reasons, questions about who is right and who is wrong would be settled easily.

Hurting anyone because they have offended your religious beliefs is a case of perpetuating a known harm in order to achieve an uncertain good. Do we have any right to hurt other people for such reasons? Perhaps most importantly, would a God of love want us to?

Discussion Questions

1. When you look at the physical world, do you see anything that makes you think it was designed, constructed, and continues to be governed by someone or something? What might that be?

2. If you agree with the argument from design, how do you account for the existence of so much evil—both natural disasters and human evil—in the world?

3. What is your reaction to the idea that at best the design of the world implies the existence of a somewhat incompetent world-architect? How would someone argue against this claim?

4. Even if we were to concede Aquinas's point that some "first cause" is necessary, would that prove the existence of the Judeo-Christian God?

5. If you think that the character of the natural world implies that it was created, is there any reason to think that such a being is still alive?

6. Do you find Anselm's rationalistic proof more or less convincing than Paley's and Aquinas's empirical arguments? What is your reaction to the Platonic notion that we could not have ideas of perfection, goodness, the greatest possible being, and so on, unless such intangible entities actually existed in some way?

7. Is there a way of proving God's existence that you find convincing but that we have not discussed in this chapter? What is it?

Selected Readings

William Paley's argument from design can be found in his *Natural Theology*. Hume's critique is elaborated in *Dialogues on Natural Religion*. For Bertrand Russell, see his "Why I Am Not a Christian." Immanuel Kant discusses various proofs for the existence of God in chapter 3 of the Transcendental Dialectic in the *Critique of Pure Reason*. The five proofs of Thomas Aquinas are defended in Question 2, Article 3 of the *Summa Theologica*. Anselm discusses the existence of God in both the *Monologion* and *Proslogion*; the latter contains the "ontological argument." On Aquinas, see also: Matt Fradd and Robert Delfino, *Does God Exist? A Socratic Dialogue on the Five Ways of Thomas Aquinas* (St. Louis: En Route Books & Media, 2018), and Taylor Marshall, *Thomas Aquinas in 50 Pages: A Layman's Quick Guide to Thomism* (Colleyville, TX: Saint John Press, 2013).

Part Four: Perhaps Things Aren't Really the Way They Appear

Chapter 10

Dolphins—Personhood, Rights, and Flourishing

One claim you've probably heard your entire life is that humans are the *only* intelligent being on the planet. And even if we grudgingly concede that other animals might have some sort of intelligence, we're confident it doesn't compare with ours. After all, we're hands down the *most* intelligent being on the planet. Right?

But what if this is a case of things not being what they seem? In particular, what if the scientific research on dolphins suggests these cetaceans possess not only a very impressive intelligence but a specific trait we humans have always claimed was unique to us—self-awareness? Are we prepared for the philosophical—and especially ethical—implications of this? Is it possible that we at least have to share the top rung of "intelligent beings on earth" with someone else? Should dolphins be considered nonhuman **persons**? Which *rights* are they entitled to? From a practical standpoint, what does this mean about how humans are required to treat them?[1]

Basic Facts About Dolphins

We cannot "do philosophy" on an issue like this, however, until we know the relevant facts. We should begin, then, with what scientists have learned about dolphins.

Dolphins are members of the biological group of marine animals called *Cetacea*, the same family that includes the large whales. Dolphins are not fish. They evolved from a land mammal about fifty million years ago. Like all mammals, they are warm-blooded, breathe air, reproduce via sexual intercourse, bear their young alive, and suckle them from female mammary glands. Even though dolphins live in the water while we live on land, they must still breathe just as humans do. However, while we breathe automatically, even when we are unconscious, dolphins do not. For them, every breath is a voluntary act.

There are more than thirty different kinds of dolphins, including *Orca orcinus* (killer whale), the largest member of the family. But you are probably most familiar with *Tursiops truncatus*, the Atlantic bottlenose dolphin. These are the dolphins you see in shows at marine parks and in movies and television programs.

An adult bottlenose dolphin is seven to twelve feet long and weighs about six hundred pounds. Its body is marvelously streamlined, allowing it to move through the water at

---

1. While this chapter is limited to discussing dolphins, be aware that other nonhuman animals—elephants and chimpanzees, for example—have also demonstrated self-awareness and appear to have a variety of sophisticated intellectual and emotional abilities. See the Selected Readings at the end of this chapter.

about fifteen to twenty miles per hour. It powers itself with its tail, using its dorsal fin on top and two side flippers for stability.

Female dolphins carry their young for about twelve months. After the mother delivers her baby, she nurses it for about a year. By the time it is nine months old, the baby makes many of the sounds dolphins use to operate in the world.

Bottlenose dolphins can live into their thirties or forties.

The Sonic World of the Dolphin

While dolphins have good eyesight, vision isn't very useful in the ocean. Dolphins rely more on sound and have within them the equivalent of a sonar system called "echolocation." They send out sonic signals—"clicks"—and interpret the echoes that bounce back from objects.

These internal sonar abilities are very sophisticated—more so than any machine we have been able to build. Researchers in one experiment put two discs 1/16-inch thick behind something that would block the dolphin's sight but not its sonar. The only difference in the discs was that one was aluminum and the other copper, but the dolphin could tell the difference. Echolocation also gives them three-dimensional images about the shape, size, and density of objects. Furthermore, because of the high frequencies they use, dolphins can actually "see through" things that we cannot. For instance, dolphins can probably see into each other's bodies—and ours too, if they chose to.

Some Facts About Dolphin Social Behavior

Dolphins live in groups, or schools, sometimes large, sometimes small. They are highly social and cooperative, and indeed, their survival at sea depends on it.

Dolphin societies are different from ours. The core consists of groups of mothers and their calves, aunts, and grandmothers. Females will sometimes "babysit" for a mother. And a group of mothers will even form protective circles, like playpens, so that babies can play with each other in the middle. After about three to six years, a young dolphin joins a group of other young adults, both male and female. When females begin giving birth, they return to their mothers' groups. Adult males tend to swim together.

Dolphins form strong social bonds. Researchers know of dolphins who have sustained close relationships for ten to twenty years. Interaction with one another is probably the central fact of their lives. Dolphins are so social that they can spend up to a third of each day making physical contact with all the other members of their school. Apparently, they do this to affirm their relationships with each other. Tending to these relationships may be what makes possible the cooperative behavior that is essential to their survival.

Dolphins express concern for their group's welfare in helpful behavior toward individual members of the group. Most notably, they attend to sick members of their group. When one dolphin is in danger of losing consciousness, for example, other dolphins have been seen to swim under it, buoy it up to the surface, and waken it so that it will breathe. They will continue to help one another like this for long periods of time.

Dolphin interaction is very physical and sexual. They are naturally bisexual and are one of the only animals other than humans who appear to engage in sex strictly for pleasure. Because of the importance of knowing and relating to other members of their group, much of dolphins' apparently sexual behavior may be more social than sexual. Rather than sexual gratification, its aim may actually be forming, renewing, or strengthening social bonds.

Some dolphins show a strong interest in humans, and there's nothing recent about this. The ancient Greek writer Plutarch observed, "To the dolphin alone, beyond all others, nature has granted what the best philosophers seek: friendship for no advantage. Though it has no need at all of any man, yet it is a genial friend to all and has helped many."[2]

Beyond their curiosity about humans, one of the most surprising things about dolphins is that they do not harm us. A dolphin could easily kill a human. Yet despite the fact that we kill, injure, and capture them, reports of dolphins hurting humans are rare. In fact, there are many stories, from preclassical times to the present, of dolphins assisting humans. These range from helping sailors navigate through dangerous waters to supporting people who have fallen overboard to helping swimmers being threatened by sharks.

Dolphins do have an aggressive side, however. They can be physically aggressive with each other, but their disputes typically don't escalate to the point where they kill each other. They express their displeasure in many ways: chasing each other, slapping their tails against the water, clapping their jaws at each other, even striking each other. Even so, they are much less aggressive with their own species than humans are with theirs. "Because they live in schools," observed the late Kenneth Norris, one of the world's most famous dolphin researchers, "they are by nature extremely cooperative. A cooperative element pervades their whole psychology. They have a sweetness of disposition that makes them sweeter than we are."[3]

Dolphin Emotions

Norris's reference to their "disposition" brings up the topic of whether dolphins experience emotions. The presence of the limbic portion of the cetacean brain means that they experience emotion. Scientist Carol Howard even suggests they have "dolphinalities," the equivalent of our "personalities."[4] Dolphin trainers see differences in curiosity, timidity, playfulness, aggression, speed of learning, and patience. Some captive dolphins enjoy swimming with humans more than others. Some like learning new behaviors more than others. Even mothers differ. Some refuse to cut the apron strings, whereas others

---

2. Plutarch, "Whether Land or Sea Animals Are Cleverer," in *Moralia*, trans. Frank Cole Babbit (Cambridge, MA: Harvard University Press, 1931), 473.
3. Private communication.
4. See Carol J. Howard, *Dolphin Chronicles* (New York: Bantam, 1995), chapter 5, "Dolphinalities."

encourage their young to become independent. Dolphins also seem to have what we call moods. Captive dolphins can be eager to work some days, lackadaisical on others, and stubbornly uncooperative on still others.

On the question of dolphin emotions, scientist Denise Herzing provides a particularly moving account of a dolphin who suffered a miscarriage or lost her calf to predators or natural causes. "Swimming slowly and despondently on the edge of the group, she stayed in line but left a space beneath her, as though she had a phantom calf in tow. She showed no interest in her friends or in mating again. Month after month, [she] left her train of grief, as clear as a luminescent streak in the dark water."[5]

Some Facts About the Dolphin Brain

A dolphin's brain resembles a human brain more closely than that of any other animal. It clearly contains, as Lori Marino, the leading researcher on cetacean brains, puts it, "the neurobiological underpinnings of complex intelligence."[6] Bottlenose dolphins' brains are larger than ours: human brains weigh about three pounds, dolphins' about three and one half. If we look at the "encephalization quotient" (the ratio of the brain volume to the surface area of the body), we find humans at 7.4, bottlenose dolphins at 5.6, and chimpanzees at 2.5. In almost all other mammals this ratio is under 2.0.[7] A similar picture emerges from examining another potential indicator of comparative intelligence: ratios of brain weight to spinal cord weight. In humans, the ratio is 50 to 1; in bottlenose dolphins, 40 to 1; in apes, 8 to 1; in cats, 5 to 1; in horses, 2.5 to 1; and in fishes, the brain weighs less than the cord. All the relevant scientific measures suggest that the dolphin brain is very sophisticated. It's also interesting to note that dolphin brain structure is older than ours. Our species has had the brain that we do for only about one hundred thousand years. Dolphins have had brains the same size or larger than ours for about fifteen million years. It's reasonable to imagine, then, that their brain might have some features or efficiencies that ours lacks.

A particularly interesting comparison between human and dolphin brains lies in what is called the cerebral cortex, or "gray matter." The cerebral cortex is the brain's outer layer of cells and is generally acknowledged to be where our higher mental functions take place. We form associations, remember things, make judgments, use language, and think abstractly and creatively because our cerebral cortex enables us to do these things.

---

5. Denise Herzing, "A Trail of Grief," in *The Smile of a Dolphin*, ed. Marc Bekoff (New York: Discovery Books, 2000), 138.

6. Lori Marino, "The Marine Mammal Captivity Issue: Time for a Paradigm Shift," in *The Palgrave Handbook of Practical Animal Ethics*, ed. Andrew Linzey and Clair Linzey (London: Palgrave Macmillan, 2018), 210.

7. Lori Marino, "A Comparison of Encephalization Between Odontocete Cetaceans and Anthropoid Primates," in *Brain, Behavior, and Evolution*, 51 (1998): 230–38, and "Brain Size Evolution," in *Encyclopedia of Marine Mammals* (second edition), edited by William F. Perrin, Bernd Wursig, and J.G.M. Thewissen (San Diego, Academic Press, 2009), 149–52.

The dolphin brain looks much like ours. It is more spherical, but its cortex and ours are much more highly convoluted than the brains of other mammals. Actually, in comparison to the human brain, there are even more sulci and gyri (the grooves and convolutions found in the brain's outer layer) in the dolphin brain, so it has more surface area. If we compare the brains of a typical bottlenose dolphin and a normal human being, the dolphin's brain is 40 percent larger. And all that difference is in the cerebral cortex. As Marino summarizes,

> Cetaceans possess . . . prodigious cognitive capacities both individually and socially. . . . First, their brains are large relative to their body size. Second, they possess a highly expanded neocortex, the evolutionarily newest part of the brain. Third, the cellular architecture of their neocortex is well differentiated, which forms the foundation for complex information processing. . . . [This includes] spindle cells or Von Economo neurons considered to be involved in facilitating neural networks subserving aspects of social cognition and thought to play a role in adaptive intelligent behavior.[8]

Are Dolphins "Intelligent"?

Even this cursory description of the dolphin brain leads to the question of how "intelligent" dolphins are. "Intelligence," however, is a tricky concept to work with. Determining levels of intelligence among humans has been difficult at best. Standardized "intelligence tests" have been accused of having underlying racial and cultural biases that distort the results. If we have so much trouble defining human intelligence, much less measuring it, you can imagine how difficult it is to discuss intelligence in a dolphin.

Even so, it would help if we had at least a rough, commonsense understanding of intelligence to work with. Keeping in mind the limitations of any definition of this concept, then, let's say that "intelligence" refers to a being's ability to engage in advanced mental processes like abstract thinking, reasoning, and understanding. Furthermore, this ability must be apparent in an "intelligent" being's behavior—particularly in how it handles problems and novel situations. Thus, "intelligence" also refers to the quality that allows a being to *decide* how it will act—to *choose* its actions, rather than automatically respond to instinct, physical desires, or some physical stimulus. We also usually assume that an "intelligent" being can communicate in some fashion. Ultimately, then, "intelligence" refers to those fundamental features that make us think of a being as some*one* rather than some*thing*.

Keeping in mind all the complexities implicit in this concept, does dolphin behavior suggest a significant degree of awareness of the world around them? Do their impressive brains let them behave "intelligently"?

---

8. Marino, "The Marine Mammal Captivity Issue," 210, 212.

Tool Use

Humans consider our ability to invent and use tools to be a sign of our intelligence. At least some dolphins use natural objects as tools.

In both Sarasota Bay, Florida, and Shark Bay, Australia, scientists have observed bottlenose dolphins using bubbles to help them capture fish. A dolphin lifts the back part of its body out of the water and then brings it down sharply into the water. This causes a loud splash and creates a trail of bubbles that may keep the fish from getting away. Scientists call the practice "kerplunking" after the sound made by the dolphin's tail. It looks like the dolphins make something like a "bubble net" and use it as a tool in their fishing.

In Shark Bay, some of the dolphins appear to use sponges as a tool. Rachel Smolker has observed several female dolphins carrying around sponges on their beaks, and she believes they use them for protection as they forage for food. The floor of Shark Bay is inhabited by scorpionfish, stingrays, stonefish, and other creatures that could produce a painful, even potentially lethal injury to a dolphin. As Smolker explains, "The dolphins are most likely using their sponges to shield themselves from the spines, stingers and barbs of creatures they encounter."[9] Interestingly, she also discovered that this behavior is apparently taught by one generation to the next.

Problem Solving

Another sign of intelligence that humans are particularly proud of is our ability to solve problems. Many nonhuman animals are able to solve problems by either repeatedly using trial and error until they hit upon the right solution or by accidentally stumbling on it. But *thinking* one's way to a solution has traditionally been considered to be an exclusively human ability.

Some of the most important research about the ability of dolphins to solve problems was done by Stan A. Kuczaj and John Gory. These two scientists studied the cognitive abilities of two bottlenose dolphins named Bob and Toby.[10] Their experiments suggest that these two cetaceans could invent a strategy for solving a problem by *thinking*.

In one experiment, three clear plastic containers were placed in the pool close to each other. In all three of them, when the dolphin dropped a weight into the top, the food compartment opened. In two of the containers, the weight would then fall to the tank floor—where it could be used again to open the food compartment of one of the other boxes. But the third had a closed bottom. Dropped into that container, the weight was unavailable.

---

9. Rachel Smolker, *To Touch a Wild Dolphin* (New York: Doubleday, 2001), 112–13.
10. Stan A. Kuczaj II and Rachel S. Thames, "How Do Dolphins Solve Problems?" in *Comparative Cognition: Experimental Explorations of Animal Intelligence*, ed. Thomas Zentall and Edward Wasserman (Oxford: Oxford University Press, 2006); John D. Gory and Stan A. Kuczaj II, "Can Bottlenose Dolphins Plan Their Behavior?," paper presented at the Biennial Conference on the Biology of Marine Mammals, Wailea, Maui, Hawaii, November–December 1999.

Kuczaj and Gory wanted to see if the dolphins could understand the implication of having both open-bottomed and closed-bottomed containers—that is, to get the maximum amount of fish, use the open-bottomed container first. The scientists theorized that if the dolphins understood this, they would plan their behavior accordingly. The dolphins did.

The second experiment involved a container that required the dolphins to use two tools in a particular order to get the food inside. They were also relatively successful at that.

Kuczaj and Gory concluded that their experiments strongly suggest that Bob and Toby were able to "create a novel and appropriate solution in advance of executing the solution."[11] This seems like a reasonable sign of "intelligence."

Equally impressive are examples of dolphins in their natural habitat solving problems by asking for human help. Scuba diver Wayne Grover, for example, tells the story of an encounter he had with three bottlenose dolphins in which the dolphins solicited his help.[12] Grover was about sixty feet deep in the waters off of Palm Beach, Florida, when he was approached by two adults and one baby bottlenose. The baby had a large fishing hook stuck into its tail about a foot ahead of its tail fluke. Also, monofilament fishing line attached to the hook was wrapped around the dolphin and was cutting into the tail fluke area. "Whether it was my imagination or a logical deduction," Grover writes, "I suddenly felt that I was being asked for help. . . . The large [dolphins] closed in on the baby from either side until they were touching it with their pectoral flippers. They settled the baby to the sea floor right in front of me, still holding it from each side." After discovering that the hook was in too deep to be removed by simply unwinding the fishing line and pulling it out, Grover steadied the baby on the ocean floor and used his diving knife to remove the hook. The two adults observed the entire procedure. After the hook came out, Grover reports,

> The largest dolphin came to me, stopped at eye level, and looked into my eyes behind the mask. For a brief moment, we looked deeply into each other's eyes, and then the dolphin nudged me with its snout, pushing me slightly back.
>
> I had the distinct impression that we were communicating but, even as I thought it, my logical mind tried to dissuade me, saying it was imagined.
>
> Then the three dolphins were gone. Without a sound, they rapidly climbed upward toward the surface, leaving me alone again.

Grover's story is a remarkable tale of ingenious problem-solving on the part of the dolphins. Even more remarkable is that it's not the only such example. Rachel Smolker writes, for example,

---

11. Gory and Kuczaj, "Can Bottlenose Dolphins Plan Their Behavior?"
12. Wayne Grover, "Dolphins: One Diver's Touching Experience," *Sea Frontiers*, January–February 1989, 28–30.

Wilf Mason had described an incident where a strange adult dolphin who was clearly in trouble came into the shallows at Monkey Mia and approached him. She had a large fishing hook lodged in her mouth. This dolphin, unaccustomed to human contact, had permitted Wilf to remove the hook with a pair of pliers. This is all the more remarkable because it must have hurt like hell to have the hook dislodged, yet she somehow understood that Wilf was helping her, that the pain was ultimately necessary, and that she would be better off in the long run if she tolerated it. I'd heard other similar and equally remarkable stories of dolphins seeking help from humans.[13]

Communication

Another trait of intelligence humans point to is our ability to communicate with each other. Where do dolphins stand on this?

Like most animals, dolphins communicate with other members of their species. Dolphins do not have vocal cords, so they cannot "speak." Instead, the sounds they make are high-frequency "clicks" and "whistles" that extend over a wide range of frequencies from 1,000 to 80,000 Hz. (Human sounds, by comparison, span a lower and more limited set of frequencies from 300 to 3,000 Hz.) The dolphin's sound system is so efficient that they can communicate with each other even when they are as far as six miles apart. Dolphins probably use a combination of whistles, clicks, and gestures, although scientists admit that they currently know little about both the content and the process of that communication. However, each dolphin has a unique signature whistle that identifies him or her as the speaker.

Do dolphins have the equivalent of a language? No one knows. However, at least one fascinating research study suggests that they have the capacity to understand the basics of human language. In research that spanned thirty years, the late University of Hawaii psychologist Louis Herman used hand signals and computer-generated whistles to teach a vocabulary of fifty words to two dolphins, Phoenix and Akeakamai. Herman combined these words into sentences with as many as five words that instructed the dolphins to perform certain tasks. Herman discovered that the dolphins had little difficulty understanding more than a thousand commands the first time they were given. In addition, the dolphins were sensitive to syntax or word order. They knew that "hoop pipe fetch" (which told the dolphin to take a hoop to a nearby pipe) meant something different from "pipe hoop fetch." The significance of this, according to Herman, is that "this is the first convincing evidence that animals can process both semantic and syntactic features of sentences."[14]

Dolphins, then, unquestionably possess some linguistic abilities of the sort usually associated with "intelligence" in humans.

---

13. Smolker, *To Touch a Wild Dolphin*, 250.
14. Louis M. Herman, Douglas G. Richards, and James P. Wolz, "Comprehension of Sentences by Bottlenosed Dolphins," *Cognition* 16 (1984): 130.

The Unexplained

Even the most cursory description of cetaceans needs to respect the fact that stories about dolphins that have no easy explanation are not uncommon. One of the most intriguing comes from Denise Herzing. On one of her research trips, someone on the boat went below to nap. When Herzing shortly encountered the dolphins she was studying, "they acted very unusual, coming within fifty feet of the boat but not closer." The crew then discovered the man had died.

> Could the dolphins have sensed something strange on board? . . . As we turned to head back south, the dolphins came to the side of our boat, not riding the bow as usual but instead flanking us fifty feet away in an aquatic escort. . . . After matters were attended to on land, we once again headed up to the dolphin grounds to finish our trip. The dolphins greeted us normally, rode the bow, and frolicked like they normally did, and we finished the trip without incident. Twenty-five years later I have never again observed the dolphins escort our boat in the same manner.[15]

One possible explanation is that the dolphins realized that the man had died and were showing their respects by their "aquatic escort." But how could they have known? Dolphin sonar doesn't work in air. Their clicks couldn't have penetrated the boat's hull and told them the passenger was dead, not asleep. When the dolphins were acting differently at the outset and not approaching the boat, the crew didn't know the man had died. What they were saying or doing, then, couldn't have informed the dolphins of the tragedy. So how did they know and what was the meaning of their escort? Or was this just a very strange coincidence?

The Significance of the Science: Dolphins, Personhood, Rights, Harm, and Flourishing

An impressive body of scientific research, then, shows that dolphins are beings who are intellectually, emotionally, and socially advanced. In that way, they have a great deal in common with us. But this isn't just an interesting scientific fact. What we've learned suggests that dolphins' advanced traits might mean that they are *persons*. Are they?

Are Dolphins *Persons?*

You might be surprised at the question of whether dolphins are *persons*. After all, you may use "human" and "person" as synonyms. The terms actually differ, however. "Human" is a biological concept, simply denoting membership in a particular species—in our case,

---

15. Denise L. Herzing, *Dolphin Diaries: My 25 Years with Spotted Dolphins in the Bahamas* (New York: St. Martin's Press, 2011), 31.

Homo sapiens. "Person" is a philosophical concept, indicating a being with capacities of a particular sort—no matter what their species. Although philosophers debate the appropriate criteria for personhood, there is a consensus that a person is a being with a variety of advanced capabilities. The following is a set of criteria that sets the bar especially high.

- A person is alive.
- A person is aware.
- A person feels pleasure and pain.
- A person has emotions.
- A person has a sense of self.
- A person controls its own behavior.
- A person recognizes other persons and treats them appropriately.
- A person has a variety of sophisticated cognitive abilities. It is capable of analytical, conceptual thought. A person can learn, retain, and recall information. It can solve complex problems with analytical thought. And a person can communicate in a way that suggests thought.

Let's go down our list and see how dolphins fare.

A person is alive, aware, and feels pleasure and pain.

Dolphins are animals, and they are quite alive. All animals are aware of their environment, at least to some degree, and experience pain and pleasure.

A person has emotions.

There's no small amount of evidence suggesting that dolphins have emotions. The dolphin brain has a limbic system—the part of the brain that generates emotions. Recall, too, Denise Herzing's report about an apparently grieving dolphin. Among scientists and dolphin trainers, there is also little doubt that dolphins have emotions, that is, that dolphins behave in ways that suggest that they have such feelings. For example, Susan Shane writes, "Captive dolphins have been known to refuse food and starve themselves to death when a tank companion dies. Mother dolphins have carried the decomposing bodies of their stillborn calves for two weeks and longer. Such behavior indicates that social bonds between individual dolphins are very strong and emotional attachments are deep."[16]

A person has a sense of self.

It's one thing to experience physical pleasure, pain, and a variety of emotions. It's quite another to be aware that one is having these experiences and to be able to reflect on them. And so, we come to one of the most important requirements for personhood: self-awareness. Can a dolphin look inside and say, "I"?

---

16. Susan Shane, *The Bottlenose Dolphin in the Wild* (San Carlos, CA: Hatcher Trade Press, 1988), 28.

There are a number of grounds for believing that dolphins have some concept of self.

- Dolphins have a unique whistle called a "signature whistle." Each dolphin has the equivalent of a "name," a concept that seems to require some sense of self. They can use these whistles to initiate interaction, to stay in contact with each other when separated from a distance, and to communicate information about themselves.
- Dolphins can recognize reflections of themselves in mirrors as just that, reflections.[17] For dolphins to do this, they clearly need the capacity to say the equivalent of "The image in this surface is a representation of me. It is not some other dolphin."
- Dolphin self-awareness is also suggested by this intriguing remark from a trainer: "When you look into their eyes, you know there's someone looking back."[18] Although obviously subjective, this comment captures the experience of those of us who have spent any time in the water with dolphins.

A person controls its own behavior.

The capacity for self-awareness is particularly important because it appears to give a person the ability to generate their actions from within. That is, a person's actions are not the result of irresistible internal or external forces such as instinct, biological drives, or conditioning. We might say, then, that we are talking about what philosophers traditionally refer to as "free choice" or "free will." These terms refer to our ability to do things because we choose to do them, not because we are driven by some other force.

Do dolphins control their actions sufficiently that we can say they *choose* them? There is evidence on several fronts suggesting that they do.

Again, Kuczaj and Gory's work suggests this. There seems little question that the behavior of the two dolphins involved in this research resulted from thinking and choice.

Rachel Smolker, cofounder of the Monkey Mia Dolphin Project at Shark Bay on the west coast of Australia, describes a fascinating event involving a bottlenose dolphin she named Holly. In May 1988, a terrible storm rolled over the study site. Smolker was fortunate. The only thing of value that she lost was a tool kit that had been in her small boat. The dinghy had been tossed about and sunk by powerful winds, and the tool kit had obviously been thrown out. An interesting incident took place about a week later. The scientist writes,

---

17. Kenneth Martin and Suchi Psarakos, "Evidence of Self-Awareness in the Bottlenose Dolphin (*Tursiops truncatus*)," in *Self-Awareness in Animals and Humans: Developmental Perspectives,* ed. Sue Taylor Parker, Robert W. Mitchell, and Maria L. Boccia (New York: Cambridge University Press, 1995), chapter 24, pp. 361–79; Lori Marino, Diana Reiss, and Gordon Gallup, "Mirror Self-Recognition in Bottlenose Dolphins: Implications for Comparative Study of Highly Dissimilar Species," in Parker et al., *Self-Awareness in Animals and Humans,* 380–91.
18. Laura Engleby, private communication.

A week or so after things have settled back down again, I wake up early and go down to see the dolphins. Holly is in at the beach and in a languid mood. I have the urge to jump into the water with her this morning, so I don my snorkel and mask. She stays just offshore, watching me get dressed, and I can tell by her patient, attentive waiting that she too is in the mood for a swimming partner. . . . Holly is whistling as I slide into the water alongside her. . . . Side by side we progress slowly out into deeper water. . . . Then she gently moves out from under my arm and heads down toward the bottom. . . . Below me, she is poking at something on the bottom, but the water is too murky for me to see. A moment later she comes back up toward me, dragging something large, white, and apparently heavy, which she is holding in her jaws. She comes directly to me and delivers a plastic bag into my hands. . . . I tread water for a moment and untie the plastic bag. It looks vaguely familiar somehow. Inside are a ratchet wrench set, pliers, screwdrivers, some spark plugs, and flares. It is the tool kit from my boat.[19]

It is difficult to imagine a more likely explanation for this unusual event than deliberation and choice on the part of Holly.

A person recognizes other persons and treats them appropriately.

Do dolphins act in ways that suggest not only that they have a sophisticated inner world but also that they can recognize it when they encounter this trait in others? That is, do they recognize other persons? Do they behave in ways that suggest that this recognition matters to them? Specifically, do dolphins act toward humans in ways that suggest that they recognize us as the type of beings we are?

The most basic sign that we recognize someone else as a person is that we treat that individual as "some *one*," not "some *thing*." We regard people's lives as special. We respect their rights and vital interests. We appreciate their intrinsic worth, and we act accordingly. Surely, one sign that we recognize other persons and treat them appropriately is that we go out of our way to help them.

What we would call "altruistic" behavior is one of the most intriguing characteristics of dolphins. Dolphins have a long-standing and well-documented concern for other beings. They try to save other dolphins from drowning, and there are many stories of dolphins assisting humans. During one ocean race, for example, a sailor fell into the ocean while moving forward on his boat to drop a sail. Because the seas were so rough, the rest of the crew lost sight of him. As boats in the race searched for a couple of hours, the swimmer found himself surrounded by a group of dolphins. At the same time, one of the boats saw two dolphins swim toward it, swim away, and then repeat the pattern. Even though the boat had searched the area that the dolphins were swimming toward, the crew felt that the dolphins were trying to tell them something. They followed the dolphins and were led to the swimmer.[20] If dolphins recognize that we and they are both aware and intelligent, it wouldn't be unreasonable that they might value our lives and well-being as they do their own.

---

19. Smolker, *To Touch a Wild Dolphin*, 221–22.
20. "Dolphins Find Missing Sailor," *Cruising World*, March 1998, 10–12.

A person has a variety of sophisticated cognitive abilities. It is capable of analytical, conceptual thought. A person can learn, retain, and recall information. It can solve complex problems with analytical thought. And a person can communicate in a way that suggests thought.

To most humans, the most important criteria for personhood are intellectual. Persons must be able to think analytically and conceptually. Their behavior must demonstrate cognitive capacities. They must be "intelligent." What do we see on this front in dolphins?

- The findings about the dolphin brain noted above show that it is very impressive.
- The mirror self-recognition research shows that dolphins appear to have not only consciousness but also self-consciousness.
- Lou Herman's research into whether dolphins can understand artificial human languages is particularly striking. He showed that the two dolphins he studied can understand and work with the basic elements of human language (vocabulary, grammar, syntax, complex sentences, etc.).
- The fact that some dolphins apparently use natural objects as tools is also impressive. Consider the following episode that took place a number of years ago at Florida's Dolphin Research Center when it was asked to take in a sick dolphin from an aquarium. In order to ease her transition to her new home, this dolphin was put in with two dolphins who had lived at the center for a number of years, Mr. Gipper and Little Bit. You need to know that this particular research center is situated in a natural habitat on the Gulf side of Grassy Key. The dolphins live in a series of pools separated from the ocean only by low fences, which the dolphins can jump over—or make holes in. They come and go as they please, some of the dolphins often visiting the nearby waters. Mr. Gipper, in particular, enjoyed coming and going, and he had made a hole in the fence to make his travels easier. Before putting the new dolphin in with Mr. Gipper and Little Bit, the staff patched the hole so that the sick dolphin would stay put.

Unknown to the staff, however, Mr. Gipper had reopened the hole. The new dolphin quickly found the hole and headed for the open seas. This presented a serious problem. As sick as she was, had she gotten lost, she probably would have died. But what happened is that, apparently sensing the danger, Mr. Gipper and Little Bit went after her, turned her around, and brought her back. Remember, dolphins have a history of helping each other in times of need.

That in itself is impressive, but the story continues. When the dolphins returned, the new animal wouldn't go back through the fence. Despite the fact that she'd gone through the hole once, it is not surprising that she'd balk about coming back through again. Dolphins instinctively shy away from going through openings like that ("gating," as it is called, is ordinarily difficult to teach), so what was surprising was that she went through it the first time. Faced with the sick dolphin's refusal, Mr. Gipper stayed with her while Little Bit went back and forth through the hole to show her that it was safe. Reassured, she went through the fence, and once all three were back inside, the other two kept her away from the hole until it could be reclosed.

Here we have two dolphins facing a potentially dangerous situation and a complicated problem with several parts. Again, we cannot know for certain what went on in the heads of these dolphins. But it looks like one or both of them assessed the situation well enough to know that the third was in jeopardy, decided on an appropriate course of action, enlisted the other's aid, reassured the runaway and showed her how to get back through the fence, and then kept her from leaving again until the hole was patched. If that's what happened, the reasoning is impressive.

• As far as communication goes, research with dolphins and language indicates that dolphins can learn to understand some aspects of human language. Within the limits of their "vocabulary," they can carry out commands they have never heard before, and they are sensitive to word order or syntax. Ken Norris believed that, between whistles and body movements, wild dolphins can communicate a good deal of vital information to each other. Some of the information is probably about specific facts, for example, the boundaries of the school and the presence or absence of predators or food. But much of the information is probably about the physical condition or emotional state of individual dolphins. From these different pieces of information communicated throughout the group, each dolphin apparently constructs a mental image of a critical but abstract concept: the state of the school.[21] It is difficult to believe that such a system of communication does not require a fair degree of cognitive ability and "thought."

Summing Up

With respect to the criteria for personhood, dolphins do well. Obviously, we do not know as much as we'd like about these marine mammals. And we must remember that dolphins' evolutionary history and present reality are so different from ours that we would be wrong in insisting that they be "just like us" to be regarded as "persons." However, according to a rigorous set of criteria for the various traits of a person, the scientific research suggests a strong case for recognizing them as "nonhuman persons." Dolphins seem to be self-aware beings with complex cognitive and affective capabilities. A dolphin appears to be a "who," not a "what"—a being, not an object—with a sophisticated individual awareness of the world.

---

21. Norris claims that the spinners' "sensory integration system" allows each dolphin "to sense the spatial disposition of its comrades and thus to define the school's protective envelope for its members. This implies the capabilities that underlie the emergence of animal culture. That is, each dolphin must construct in its own mind a gestalt of the shape of the school at any instant from just a few data points. It must mentally fill in the spaces in three dimensions. At the same time, it must also make predictions about the immediate future. Receiving information that some members are indicating the imminence of a turn tells the dolphin what it must do. The dolphin is not following a leader *seriatim* but is instead behaving in terms of a more abstract conception—the state of the school." Kenneth Norris, "Comparative View," in *Hawaiian Spinner Dolphin* (Berkeley: University of California Press, 1994), 334.

The Ethical Implications of Personhood

Strictly speaking, personhood is a topic discussed in the part of philosophy called metaphysics. This area deals with the most fundamental theoretical issues like the nature of reality and the debate between free will and determinism. However, the conclusions of certain metaphysical investigations have profound practical impact and connect with other parts of philosophy. In our case, claiming that dolphins are nonhuman persons raises important *ethical* issues.

Persons are traditionally seen as deserving special treatment. What does this mean for dolphins?

Persons are also recognized as having moral standing as *individuals*. That is, the life and well-being of each *individual* dolphin must be respected, not just the welfare of a cetacean species or community.

Recall that one of the most basic features of personhood is that every person is a "who," not a "what." One of the most important implications of dolphin personhood, then, is that they have a right not to be treated like property or used as an object. That is, owning dolphins, keeping them captive, and using them as a means to some end—whether it be for entertainment, research, therapeutic, or military purposes—are ethically unacceptable. Recall that when we studied Immanuel Kant's deontological approach to ethics earlier in this text, we found him saying, "Everything has either a price or a dignity. Whatever has a price can be replaced by something else as its equivalent; on the other hand, whatever is above all price, and therefore admits of no equivalent, has a dignity."[22] From Kant's perspective, persons are inherently valuable. We are "above all price." Therefore, it is inconsistent with respecting the dignity of persons to treat them as a piece of property or to use them as means to an end. No matter how much pleasure humans may get from watching or studying dolphins in captivity, from this perspective, it is wrong.

As is regularly the case with ethics, however, the situation quickly gets complicated. Recall that Jeremy Bentham and John Stuart Mill gave us an approach to ethics based on consequences, not actions. It's easy to imagine someone arguing that as long as captive dolphins are treated well, the benefits that come to humans (profit, enjoyment, satisfying curiosity, etc.) outweigh any harm. At the same time, we must keep in mind that Mill claimed that a smaller amount of a high-quality pain counts more than a larger amount of low-quality pleasure. How do we assess quality in this case? In addition, the vast majority of dolphins live in the planet's oceans, not in captivity. They are affected by humans in many ways on a daily basis, for example, through human fishing, shipping, and various sorts of pollution. What do we say about how they deserve to be treated?

---

22. Immanuel Kant, *Grounding for the Metaphysics of Morals*, trans. James W. Ellington (Indianapolis: Hackett Publishing Co., 1993), 40.

Harm and Flourishing

In order not to get lost in the complexities connected with human/dolphin interaction, the simplest way to begin an effort to describe how dolphins are entitled to be treated, especially in light of their status as nonhuman persons, is to say that they should not experience high-quality *harm*. Virtually all of us would agree that any person—no matter what their species—has a right not to be seriously *harmed*. However, since we're talking about a species very different from us that lives in conditions foreign to our own, determining what constitutes high-quality *harm* is challenging. Conveniently, earlier in this book in Chapter 5, we met an approach that can help: Martha Nussbaum's idea about *flourishing*.

The most basic way to define *flourishing* is that it is the full, healthy growth and development of an individual's capacities. Flourishing refers not simply to how *physically healthy* someone is or how *long* they live. It also refers to how *well* that individual can live. To say that individuals can *flourish*, then, is to say that they can grow in a full and healthy fashion, and are able to develop the traits, skills, and dispositions that give a member of that species a reasonable opportunity to have a satisfying and successful life. Interfering with someone's attempt to flourish surely constitutes serious *harm*. Also, because we are talking about flourishing *as a member of a particular species*, this gives us *species-specific* criteria for defining *harm*—which allows us to determine what counts as high-quality harm for dolphins.

The key to recognizing flourishing as a multi-species ethical standard is to appreciate that it is an essentially biological concept that underscores the importance of evolution and adaptation. Any animals now alive possess the traits and capacities they do because of how their ancestors adapted to the conditions they faced in the past. The well-being of the members of any species is, therefore, made possible by the development and use of these capacities—capacities that turned out to be the key for successfully dealing with their environment. To say that animals can *flourish*, then, is to say that they can grow in a full and healthy fashion, and can develop the traits, skills, and dispositions that evolution and adaptation have determined give a member of that species a reasonable opportunity to have a satisfying and successful life. Modern humans, for example, possess our defining traits and capacities because of their role in human evolution. Developing and using these traits—that is, human *flourishing*—is responsible for our success as members of our species and for our experience of individual satisfaction with our lives.

For each species, then, it is possible to identify the conditions necessary to flourish—that is, for members of a species not simply to remain alive and healthy but to grow and develop in a way that gives them the possibility for success in their environment and a sense of well-being. Flourishing gives us an excellent standard for identifying the conditions or treatment at the hands of others that would constitute serious *harm*.

Human Flourishing and Harm

Before seeing how we would use flourishing to determine what constitutes serious harm to dolphins, let's illustrate the idea with the species we're most familiar with: us. In order for *Homo sapiens* to flourish, we require: physical and emotional health and safety; years of care and education as we mature; a variety of skills (cognitive, emotional, physical, and social) and the opportunity to apply them; various relationships; certain social and economic conditions; and so on. When these conditions are met, we have the opportunity to flourish, that is, to realize our potential, and to experience a basic sense of satisfaction or well-being. When these conditions are *not* met, we are unable to develop skills critical to our success, and we face serious, practical disadvantages in making our way in the world. It is fair to say that to the extent that being unable to flourish compromises our ability to have a reasonable opportunity for a satisfying and successful life, we have been *harmed*. Keeping Mill's ideas about quality in mind, it's fair to say this would count as *high-quality harm*.

It's also important to note that the conditions required for human flourishing can be broken down into two different categories. The first set is conditions that are largely tangible: physical and emotional health and safety; social relationships; education; the ability and opportunity to meet any physical and emotional needs; and the like. The second set—which proceeds essentially from the fact that humans have such highly developed cognitive and emotional capacities—includes conditions that are more or less "intangible": freedom to choose our actions and beliefs; privacy; having trustworthy relationships; being able to make decisions about our actions, our beliefs, and our purpose in life; freedom; fairness; justice; equality; being treated with appropriate respect; and the like. The importance of these intangible needs is obvious if we imagine a group of humans who are physically safe and healthy but lack freedom and fairness. They would surely *not* experience a sense of well-being and feel that their life was satisfying.

This discussion, then, leads to a series of claims. First, the concept of flourishing is an appropriate, species-based standard for identifying serious, high-quality harm. Second, in addition to the clearly *tangible harm* humans experience if we're prevented from developing critical skills and traits, our highly developed mental and emotional capacities make us vulnerable to *intangible harm*. That is, what humans feel as painful extends beyond physical harm to include the frustrations of being blocked from satisfying a variety of intangible needs. Precisely because of our highly developed mental and emotional capacities, pains associated with the frustration of such intangible needs can be greater than the pains associated with tangible needs.

Cetaceans, Flourishing, and Rights

Having seen the connection between flourishing and harm in our own species, we can now return to dolphins.

If we apply this same approach to these cetaceans, it is clear why *flourishing* is an appropriate standard for evaluating dolphin well-being and human behavior toward them. Like humans, dolphins are highly developed cognitively, emotionally, and socially. As is the case with every animal, the conditions that allow for cetacean flourishing have been determined by their evolutionary history. The last few decades of marine mammal science make clear that these conditions include: a large, natural habitat; membership in cultural communities; relationships with other members of their species; the opportunity to develop and apply such characteristic skills as echolocation, navigation, diving, and hunting; the opportunity to make choices (e.g., forming relationships, mating, engaging in or avoiding conflict, seeking stimulation, exploring objects, etc.).

As is the case with humans, cetaceans who are prevented from flourishing very likely experience high-quality *harm*. Similarly, as is the case with humans, cetaceans are probably also vulnerable to what we referred to above as "intangible" harm. While we can never be certain about the inner, subjective experience of cetaceans firsthand, it is reasonable to think that when key conditions for flourishing are frustrated, they experience emotional pain. Precisely because of their highly developed abilities and capacity for a rich inner life, the pain associated with the frustration of such intangible needs as control over key decisions, whom they'll form significant relationships with, whom they'll bear children with, and so on can be even greater than the pain associated with tangible needs.

Personhood, Flourishing, and Human Treatment of Cetaceans

Where, then, does all of this take us in terms of the ethical issues related to human treatment of dolphins?

The combination of our analysis of personhood and our application of Martha Nussbaum's concept of flourishing now puts us in a position to make informed judgments about the ethical character of human treatment of dolphins.

- More than three thousand whales and dolphins live in entertainment facilities in a variety of countries, and it can be argued that they endure a grim existence.[23] Their lives are far more barren, boring, and lonely than those of wild dolphins. They live in small, artificial tanks. They have relationships with only a very small number of other dolphins. Their lives are much less complex and challenging. Their breeding is controlled. Not even the largest tanks allow them the conditions necessary for them to flourish.
- Thousands of dolphins die each year in hunts in which these cetaceans are driven into coves to be slaughtered and in the nets that humans use to fish. (In the last thirty years, more than six million dolphins have perished in this fashion.) If this were happening to humans—for example, if the population of an area were wiped

---

23. https://us.whales.org/our-4-goals/end-captivity/.

out in connection with forestry or mining—we would call it an indefensible massacre.

- Military testing and use of sonar by, for example, the US Navy can do irreparable damage to cetacean hearing, leaving those affected, for all practical purposes, "acoustically blind."
- Environmental pollution of various sorts can harm the health of cetaceans in the ocean. Chemical toxins from water runoff can end up stored in a dolphin's body fat. Plastic litter, in particular, can lead to dolphin deaths. Noise pollution from commercial shipping makes communication more difficult.

Even a cursory examination of these practices reveals that virtually all human treatment of dolphins is ethically problematic. We treat these nonhuman persons as property and use them as means for various ends. We make flourishing impossible in captivity and unnecessarily difficult in the oceans. The high-quality harm dolphins experience at our hands includes: death, injury, shortened life spans, degraded environments, and disruption of their societies.

Final Thoughts and a Startling Suggestion

The conclusions we can draw from the scientific research on dolphins are clear. These cetaceans are intelligent, self-aware beings with highly developed intellectual and emotional abilities. They are nonhuman persons who, from an ethical perspective, deserve to be treated far better by humans than is currently the case.

But as difficult as it may be to concede that we were wrong ever to regard dolphins as property, that is, as objects we could treat however we wanted, there is one other—more troubling—assumption we might need to consider. Is it possible there are ways in which dolphins are *more* intelligent than humans?

Douglas Adams, in his fantasy novel *The Hitchhiker's Guide to the Galaxy*, makes an amusing observation in this vein. He writes,

> It is an important and popular fact that things are not always what they seem. For instance, on the planet earth, man had always assumed that he was more intelligent than dolphins because he had achieved so much—the wheel, New York, wars and so on—whilst all the dolphins had ever done was muck about in the water having a good time. But conversely, the dolphins had always believed that they were far more intelligent than man—for precisely the same reasons.[24]

It's easy to dismiss this as a clever quip. But what if there's merit to what he's suggesting?

Certainly, one of the first markers of "intelligence" is the ability to evaluate threats and to take appropriate action to mitigate them. The minimum that our big brains should give us is the ability to make it more likely that we—as individuals and as a species—can stay

---

24. Douglas Adams, *A Hitchhiker's Guide to the Galaxy* (New York: Pocket Books, 1979), 156.

alive. In many ways, of course, humans do that. Medical scientists identify risks to our health and discover cures for diseases. Agricultural researchers find ways to produce more and better food. We try to organize societies so that more people get the opportunity to survive. But it's a mixed picture with humans. We also regularly engage in war, spending vast amounts of time, energy, and money killing each other. We tolerate extraordinary levels of ignorance and poor education. This not only condemns millions of people to dying from threats they didn't recognize or respond to appropriately, it deprives the species of discoveries that could have been made by these individuals if they'd been educated. We ignored the threat of global warming and population growth for decades. We created weapons that could end all life on earth, and some among us would happily use them.

At the same time, it could be argued that dolphins have done better. They do not go to war. They manage aggression without killing each other. They do not overpopulate or deplete the fish they need to survive. Because the modern versions of dolphins have lived successfully on earth for millions of years, they appear to have solved the problem of the long-term survivability of their species.

It's clear that humans are imaginative, inventive, and clever. Is it possible that one of the ways that "perhaps things aren't the way they appear" is that we aren't "intelligent," or at least not the *most* intelligent being on the planet?

Discussion Questions

1. Considering what marine mammal scientists have discovered about the intellectual and emotional abilities of dolphins, do you think that these cetaceans should be considered "persons"? Why or why not?

2. If you think that dolphins are persons, does that mean that they have certain rights? Which ones? What about life, liberty, and the pursuit of happiness? If dolphins are persons, is it wrong to keep them in captivity? Is it wrong to train them and use them in shows?

3. If you are undecided about whether a dolphin is a person, what criteria are most troublesome? In which areas would you want more evidence?

4. What do you think about using Martha Nussbaum's concept of "flourishing" as a way to avoid species bias in determining "harm"?

5. In this kind of philosophical investigation, we have to infer certain conclusions from the available facts. Did the discussion in this chapter ever make unreasonable inferences, that is, conclusions that the data did not warrant?

6. Can you think of any other animals that could be persons? Some chimpanzees, gorillas, and orangutans have been taught some human sign language. Elephants apparently have complex cultures. Does this make them possible candidates for personhood?

7. What is your reaction to the idea that humans aren't the *only* intelligent being on earth—or that we aren't the *most* intelligent?

Selected Readings

For discussions of the concept of personhood, see D. C. Dennett, "Conditions of Personhood," in *Brainstorms: Philosophical Essays on Mind and Psychology* (Cambridge, MA: Bradford Books, 1976–78), 267–85. On the possibility of cognitive states in other animals, read: Donald R. Griffin, *The Question of Animal Awareness: Evolutionary Continuity of Mental Experience* (New York: Rockefeller University Press, 1976) and *Animal Thinking* (Cambridge, MA: Harvard University Press, 1984). On the possibility of nonhuman persons, see: David DeGrazia, *Taking Animals Seriously* (Cambridge: Cambridge University Press, 1996); Gary Varner, *Personhood, Ethics and Animal Cognition* (Oxford: Oxford University Press, 2012); and the essays in *What Is a Person?* edited by Michael F. Goodman (Clifton, NJ: Humana Press, 1988).

For a more detailed discussion of the philosophical implications of the scientific research on dolphins and the ethical questions related to how humans treat dolphins, see my various writings on these topics, especially: Thomas I. White, *In Defense of Dolphins: The New Moral Frontier* (Oxford: Blackwell, 2007); "Whales, Dolphins and Humans: Challenges in Interspecies Ethics," *Palgrave Handbook of Practical Animal Ethics*, ed. Andrew Linzey and Clair Linzey (London: Palgrave Macmillan, 2018), 233–45.

Regarding ethical issues related to other likely nonhuman persons, see: the essays in *The Great Ape Project: Equality Beyond Humanity,* edited by Paola Cavalieri and Peter Singer (New York: St. Martin's Press, 1993); *Etica & Animali: Special Issue Devoted to Nonhuman Personhood* (September 1998), edited by Paola Cavalieri; *An Elephant in the Room: The Science and Well-Being of Elephants in Captivity*, edited by Debra L. Forthman, Lisa F. Kane, David Hancocks, and Paul F. Waldau (North Grafton, MA: Tufts Center for Animals and Public Policy, 2009); and *Elephants and Ethics: Toward a Morality of Coexistence*, edited by Christen Wemmer and Catherine A. Christen (Baltimore: Johns Hopkins University Press, 2008).

Chapter 11

Alternative Perspectives—Marx and Einstein

One of the most important things to realize about our discussion about dolphins is just how much it undercuts some central claims you've heard your entire life. Humans are the *only* intelligent beings on the planet. Humans are the *most* intelligent beings on the planet. But as you saw, it's not outrageous to question ideas we've taken for granted and assume there are good reasons to believe. Socrates's observation that "the unexamined life is not worth living" is apparently true on so many fronts, it's important to subject even the most obvious ideas to critical analysis.

This chapter continues this impulse by looking at the ideas of two thinkers who pose powerful challenges to ideas that most of us probably take for granted. We begin with a thinker who claims that some of our most deeply held beliefs about what's important in life aren't the result of our *choosing* them. Instead, Karl Marx argues that our values are a product of the economic arrangement of our society. But as troubling as that is, even more so are the ideas of Albert Einstein, who makes some pretty strange claims. The everyday perception of space and time that's so obvious to us is actually an illusion. Certain subatomic particles exist for 2.2 millionths of a second while traveling 700 meters before they decay, and *at the same time* they exist for 15.4 millionths of a second while traveling thousands of meters. When you drop a book on a moving train, it falls in *both* a *straight* line and a curved line. Two lightning bolts strike both at the *same* instant and at *different* times. Einstein may sound like one of the rationalist philosophers from Chapter 8 who argued that the senses weren't a good source of knowledge. But Albert Einstein is a physicist who used an empirical methodology to conclude that the physical world is not what our senses tell us it is. These men may be studying very different phenomena using different methodologies, but both agree that things are not what they appear to be.

Karl Marx and Marxism

Karl Marx and his theories are widely misunderstood. Most Americans, for example, think that Marx was Russian (he was German), or that he lived in Russia (he spent most of his life in England), or at least that after spending his life as a bomb-throwing revolutionary (he was a journalist and philosopher), Marx was buried in Moscow's Red Square (Marx's tomb is in London). Karl Marx was indeed a revolutionary thinker, but he did not live his life on the ramparts urging the violent overthrow of European capitalism. He certainly wanted to have a powerful effect on people and to stimulate change. But most of his writings are difficult to read and about as incendiary as a dictionary.

Karl Marx was born in 1818 in Trier, Prussia, in what is now Germany. Marx's father was a successful lawyer, and Karl was supposed to enter the same profession. He began studying law at the University of Bonn but transferred to the University of Berlin, where he studied law, philosophy, history, English, and Italian. He wrote his dissertation on Greek philosophy and received his PhD. Unable to get a teaching position, Marx began a career as a political journalist, first in Prussia and then in France. This brought him into contact with Frederick Engels, the son of a textile manufacturer, who would become Marx's main collaborator. Marx was expelled first from France and then from Belgium and Germany for his radical ideas. In 1849, he moved to London, where he and his family spent the rest of his life in poverty, often supported by Engels. Marx wrote numerous revolutionary books and articles, and he was active in workers' movements and in the founding of the Communist League. He worked on his masterpiece, *Das Kapital*, for the last twenty-five years of his life and died in 1883 with it unfinished.

Marx's ideas did eventually have a major impact on political revolutionaries like Vladimir Lenin and Mao Zedong. Because the former Soviet Union and China regarded Marx as a kind of patron saint, and since these countries were cast as enemies of the democratic societies, it is not surprising that many people have faulty notions about what Marx wrote and did.

What does Marx actually say, then? Two of his ideas are particularly important for us to consider.

First, he argues that our ideas about what is valuable in life come not from our own personal choices, as we think they do, but from the economic system that dominates our lives. He believes that our ideas about what makes us happy are just as much the product of capitalism as the cars that come off the end of an assembly line. Marx thus claims that capitalism imbues people with a particular view of the purpose of life. Second, Marx believes that living according to this vision of happiness in fact puts a satisfying life out of reach for everyone, rich and poor alike. In particular, Marx thinks that the way capitalism has us spend our workdays goes against the grain of the human spirit. Obviously, if either of Marx's claims is true, that would have an important effect on how we live our lives and how we choose our life's goals.

Capitalism as the Source of Our Ideas: "Dialectical Materialism"

One of the most interesting aspects of Marx's ideas is his insistence that economic factors are the single most important force in any society. Not only do economic factors shape individual values, they also determine the overall political goals of a society, and even its view of history. Behind these views is a theory of history that has subsequently been called **dialectical materialism**. To understand Marx's thinking, however, we have to look briefly at the work of the philosopher who pointed Marx in this direction, Georg Hegel.

Hegel's Dialectic and Its Influence on Marx

Georg Wilhelm Friedrich Hegel is the most important representative of nineteenth-century German **idealism**. Idealism is a school of thought that claims that reality is ultimately intangible and nonmaterial, as opposed to **materialism**, which sees reality as physical and concrete.

Hegel took an extreme idealist position, claiming that all reality was ultimately "Mind," "God," or, as he put it, "Spirit." Through time, Spirit fashions the world as we know it, following an evolutionary pattern. As Hegel sees it, however, this process is full of conflict, and all history is thus the story of the clash of opposites. One force or idea gives rise to its opposite and collides with it. The two then unite and produce a new third state of affairs that combines elements of both. Hegel labels the three elements involved in this process *thesis, antithesis,* and *synthesis.*

Human history may look chaotic, with nations making war and factions within societies vying for predominance. But Hegel believes this is all part of a grand, positive process. The clash of conflicting forces produces progress because the best of the opposites is preserved in their joining. The clash gives rise to growth, development, and advancement. History is thus ordered and organic. The process is positive, and Hegelian thinking is understandably optimistic.

> Georg Wilhelm Friedrich Hegel (1770–1831) studied at the theological seminary at the University of Tübingen. He began as a tutor to aristocratic families, and he taught at the University of Jena. After the Prussians were defeated by Napoleon, Hegel was forced to give up his position. He edited a daily paper in Bavaria and then served as headmaster of a school for eight years before being appointed professor of philosophy at the University of Heidelberg in 1816 and then at the University of Berlin in 1818. He died in 1831 in a cholera epidemic. His main works include *Phenomenology of Spirit* and *Science of Logic.*

Hegel's ideas had a powerful effect on Marx, although Marx argued that Hegel's idealism was wrong. Hegel, Marx said, is standing on his head. "Mind" or "Spirit" is not the creative force; it is *matter.* In other words, nothing intellectual or abstract creates matter; it is the other way around. Matter is so strong that even our ideas are produced by different aspects of empirical reality. Marx's materialism thus stands in direct opposition to Hegel's idealism.

Marx docs accept Hegel's dialectical method, however, and he agrees that the clash of opposing forces in human history is ultimately ordered and purposeful. Everywhere he looks he sees the pattern of "thesis, antithesis, and synthesis" playing itself out in human events. Taken together, these two ideas, materialism and the process of thesis, antithesis, and synthesis, provide the substance of Marx's philosophical outlook.

Historical Materialism and Economic Forces

When Marx looked at history, then, he saw it as the dynamic interplay of opposing material forces, not Platonic Forms, Divine Providence, or anything else abstract and intangible. Of the various material forces at play in any society, he thought that the most important were *economic*—the material production of what we need to live. For Marx, material production is so fundamental that it must be regarded as the basic fact of human history. As he expresses this,

> But life involves before everything else eating and drinking, a habitation, clothing and many other things. The first historical act is thus the production of the means to satisfy these needs, the production of material life itself. . . . Therefore in any interpretation of history one has first of all to observe this fundamental fact in all its significance and all its implications and to accord it its due importance.[1]

> **dialectic** Dialectic is Hegel's label for the dynamic and conflict-filled process whereby one force (thesis) collides with its opposite (antithesis) to produce a new state of affairs that combines elements of both (synthesis). Given the primacy of Spirit in Hegel's thinking, Hegel's outlook can be described as "dialectical idealism."
>
> **dialectical materialism** Dialectical materialism is Marx's revision of Hegel's dialectical idealism in terms of Marx's belief in the primacy of material, specifically economic, forces. Marx thus sees human history as the clash of opposing economic forces, creating new stages.

For Marx, history is ultimately the chronicle of economic forces at work. Marx calls this the "materialist conception of history."

But remember that these economic forces do not work together peacefully in some smooth progression. Instead, they clash with each other. Thus, history progresses only by means of opposition and conflict, and the main conflict that Marx saw in human society was that between different economic classes. As Marx writes in the *Communist Manifesto*, "The history of all hitherto existing society is the history of class struggles." The clash between the "proletariat" (the propertyless workers) and the "bourgeoisie" (the people with money, those who own property and hire others) that Marx witnessed in his own time, he believed, would inevitably lead to a synthesis that Marx called "communism." Once achieved, this synthesis would end the class struggle forever.

To appreciate how revolutionary Marx's thinking is, it is helpful to contrast it with interpretations of human history that we are more accustomed to. Religious thinkers, for example, see history as the inevitable working out of God's plan, perhaps as the account of the struggle between good and evil. Astrologers explain what happens with reference to cosmic influences. Proponents of free will see events as determined by individual choices. Scientists describe our history in terms of evolution and adaptation. "Humanists" believe that events reveal a gradual maturation on the part of humanity with enlightenment and respect for freedom and dignity slowly gaining around the world.

Each theory of history claims to account for what "really" happened. For example, was the expansion of the United States from the Atlantic coast to the Pacific coast the achievement of a divinely ordained "Manifest Destiny"? Was it the aggressive domination

---

1. Karl Marx, *The German Ideology: Part I*, in *The Marx-Engels Reader*, ed. Robert O. Tucker (New York: W. W. Norton, 1972), 120.

by the Whites of the indigenous Native American nations? Different views of history provide different explanations.

Marx would say that all these interpretations of human history are wrong. In the case of American expansion across the continent, he would argue that it resulted from capitalist exploitation of the land, its resources, and its peoples. Historical materialism argues that what was "really" going on can be explained only in economic terms.

How the Material World Shapes Us: A Simple Example

Marx's sweeping claim that the material conditions of our lives, and especially economic conditions, are the most important force in shaping human history has profound implications. According to Marx, the material features of our lives determine a dizzying array of things that most of us assume have nothing to do with economics. In Marx's eyes, the material conditions of our lives determine not only what kind of work we do and how we do it, but where and how we live and work, the structure and expectations of our private relationships, our personal values, and even the forms of our society's laws, politics, art, and religion. Some simple examples will show you what this means.

First, think of different professors' offices, and specifically about how their furniture is arranged. Some have it placed so they remain behind their desks while you sit in a smaller chair facing them. Others put their desks against the wall and swing their chairs around when you come in and sit down.

Now try to identify your feelings in each situation. With whom do you feel most comfortable? Whom are you most intimidated by? Odds are you feel least comfortable with someone who has you sit on the other side of a big desk, and you feel best with someone who sits with you in a similar chair. A Marxist would explain that these feelings come from your reaction to what the physical arrangement of the office communicates about power. When people put desks between themselves and anyone who comes in, they are saying, "I'm in charge here." Part of you picks this up, whether you're consciously aware of it or not. Placing the desk so that it is not a barrier or sitting in similar chairs conveys openness, equality, and trust.

Physical conditions do influence our thoughts and feelings in fundamental and powerful ways—even when we're not aware of it.

How the Conditions of Life Determine Consciousness

Marx has something bigger in mind, however. He believes that the way an economy is arranged, that is, the physical facts of production and distribution of material goods, determines everything about a society (and how people react within it), including its politics, laws, art, ethics, religion, and so forth. Most of us believe just the opposite. We assume we come up with ideas and then we apply them to the world. We think we use our views and values as a kind of blueprint according to which we then fashion a society that has certain institutions and economic arrangements.

Marx claims, however, that the "foundation" of a society is its economic structure. On top of that is a "superstructure" consisting of laws and politics. On top of that are the society's ideas about art, philosophy, religion, science, and the like. The nature of everything in the "superstructure" is determined by the economic "foundation." As Marx puts it, "Life is not determined by consciousness, but consciousness by life."[2] He writes,

> The production of ideas, of conceptions, of consciousness, is at first directly interwoven with the material activity and the material intercourse of men, the language of real life. Conceiving, thinking, the mental intercourse of men, appear at this stage as the direct efflux [outcome] of their material behavior. The same applies to mental production as expressed in the language of politics, laws, morality, religion, metaphysics, etc., of a people. . . .
>
> [W]e do not set out from what men say, imagine, conceive, nor from men as narrated, thought of, imagined, conceived, in order to arrive at men in the flesh. We set out from real, active men, and on the basis of their real life-process we demonstrate the development of the ideological reflexes and echoes of this life-process. The phantoms formed in the human brain are also, necessarily, sublimates of their material life-process, which is empirically verifiable and bound to material premises. Morality, religion, metaphysics, all the rest of ideology and their corresponding forms of consciousness, thus no longer retain the semblance of independence. They have no history, no development; but men, developing their material production and their material intercourse, alter, along with this their real existence, their thinking and the products of their thinking. Life is not determined by consciousness, but consciousness by life.[3]

One way we might illustrate Marx's ideas is to say that the economic structure of a society is analogous to the trunk of a tree; a society's laws and politics to its branches; and philosophy, art, and religion are analogous to the leaves. The branches and leaves depend on the trunk for their existence, and they organically express the tree's nature. In the same way, the laws, politics, art, and philosophy of a society are the direct outgrowth and expression of the material relationships that define that society's economy.

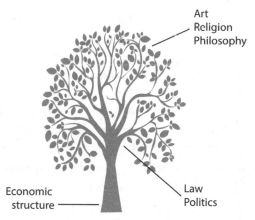

Social/Political Values

According to Marx, the political organization of a society and its major political ideas result from the practical arrangement of things—the distribution of wealth and the consequent power of those who hold it. As he puts it,

---

2. Marx, *The German Ideology: Part I*, 119.
3. Marx, *The German Ideology: Part I*, 118–19.

> The ruling ideas are nothing more than the ideal expression of the dominant material relationships. . . . For instance, in an age and in a country where royal power, aristocracy and bourgeoisie are contending for mastery and where, therefore, mastery is shared, the doctrine of the separation of powers proves to be the dominant idea and is expressed as an "eternal law."[4]

Marx would contend, for example, that the guiding principles expressed in the Declaration of Independence and the American Constitution grew directly out of economic conditions in the late eighteenth century. The Founding Fathers, he'd claim, came up with their political ideals as a result of the fact that thirteen competing economic units, the original colonies, were moving toward free-market, competitive capitalism. Thus, they united into a "confederation of states" rather than subsuming their identities completely in a single entity. "States' rights" and the "separation of powers" became important political principles, expressing in the political arena the diffusion of power needed to make a market economy work.

Whatever examples we take, then, the Marxist thinks that all social institutions owe their form to the prevailing material conditions at the time. If Marx is right, we should even see a direct connection between our economic system, capitalism, and the ideas and values we hold. Can we discover such a link?

Capitalism and Capitalist Values

Let's first make sure we have a clear understanding of capitalism. It is an economy in which the means of production—factories, farms, shops, and so on—are owned by private individuals, not the government. These individuals are entrepreneurs, or capitalists. They take their own money ("capital") and invest it in a business, in hopes of getting a return ("profit") on the investment. The goods produced are distributed through a "free market." Producers offer what they make to potential customers. Prices are neither set in advance nor decreed by some central agency. They are what buyers and sellers agree on and result from what are called laws of "supply and demand." When consumer demand for a product outstrips the available supply, people are willing to pay more for it and prices go up. When producers make more of a product than people will buy, prices fall. Under capitalism, competition among producers is essential to make sure that prices are fair. Producers are thus encouraged to become more efficient and deliver honest value to consumers, or they will lose the consumers to other producers. Capitalism also assumes that buyers and sellers, employers and employees will simply advance their own individual interests. The different interests among opposing parties and the existence of a free competitive market for goods and labor is supposed to keep the game honest.

In essence, then, capitalism is an economic system based on private ownership, capital, self-interest, and a free, competitive market. We shall see shortly that Marx finds capitalism inhumane, an economic system that makes genuine freedom and happiness

---

4. Marx, *The German Ideology: Part I*, 136–37.

impossible. For now, however, let's take capitalism at face value and see what effect such an arrangement of "material conditions" has on the values we live by every day.

Competition. For openers, Marx would say that living under capitalism makes us think that *competition* is a good thing. Instead of cooperating with other people, we feel it is more valuable to pit ourselves against them. Everyone is an adversary. Learning how to advance our own interests against the interests of others becomes an important survival skill.

As a result, we promote competition throughout our society. We especially push athletic competition and team sports. We say that such contention, with its emphasis on winning, is good for us. It keeps us in shape, rewards us for hard work, and builds character. The Marxist would say, however, that we are enamored of athletic competition simply because it mirrors the economic competition that is at the heart of contemporary capitalism.

Our society could have evolved differently, of course. We could have enshrined *cooperation*, which produces equally good results if not better ones, instead of competition. In a cooperative society, competition, winning, being a "star," and excelling as an individual would all be seen as "bad taste" and being insensitive to others. How well we help people who do something less well than we do would be more important than how badly we beat them at it. Competition is not a law of nature, and other societies think quite differently about it. Yet, Marx claims, it is no accident that people in capitalist societies think and behave as they do. Indeed, we think this way *because* we live in a capitalistic economy.

Inequality. A second effect of capitalism on our values is that we accept and even approve of *inequality*, particularly financial inequality. Most of us think it is perfectly all right that some people are extraordinarily rich, while others are too poor to afford food and shelter. We see nothing wrong with the fact that the higher someone goes in an organization, the more advantages he or she receives simply by virtue of that person's position. We even develop a logical rationale for inequality by believing that, ultimately, each of us is the author of our own happiness or unhappiness. We say that everybody has the same opportunities, and that we deserve the fate we end up with. A Marxist would say that this way of thinking is inevitable in our culture because it mirrors the profit motive that is basic to capitalism, because it promotes the wealthy class that capitalism needs to provide money for investment, and because, by rationalizing inequality, it advances the interests of those who dominate the economy.

The fact that so many people accept the idea that everyone has the same chance for success is especially intriguing. In reality, we do not all have the same opportunities. Some people are born with many natural abilities. Some are born into rich families, or at least very supportive ones. Others are born to poverty and illness. The odds that someone born into a lower socioeconomic class will become successful are dramatically lower than those for someone born into the middle or upper classes. With these odds being so different because of circumstances none of us has any control over, you would expect most people to think that something is wrong with the system. Yet most of us apparently accept the idea that everyone has the same chance and that there is nothing wrong with the inequality.

Think how people react when they hear of someone beating the odds. When they hear some rags-to-riches story, they usually say something like, "See, the system works. Everyone has a chance." Or maybe just, "Well, that's life." What most of us do *not* say is that something is wrong with a system in which so few people ever really move up. Yet one as good a chance to move from poverty to extreme wealth as one has to break the bank playing roulette. The only way for a casino to survive is for most people to lose, and our society distributes wealth in the same fashion. A Marxist would hardly admire such an economic structure. But the fact that most of us accept the unequal way our economy distributes wealth shows how fully we have internalized the idea of institutionalized inequality.

"Bettering" Ourselves. A Marxist can even point to phrases in our language that reveal the impact of capitalism. Consider what we mean when we say we want to "better" ourselves. What does that phrase mean to you? The average person will say that to "better yourself" means "to make more money" or "to move into a higher social and economic class." But this does not make sense. Making more money is one thing; becoming a better person is another. Yet in a culture that judges everything by economic measures, we have come to equate one with the other.

If a highly paid executive decided to leave the company to work with the homeless, would most people say that she had "bettered" herself? Most of us would probably praise her selflessness, but we would not say she had "bettered" herself. Yet she would face new challenges, develop her existing skills, make the welfare of other people her first priority, and make the world a better place. By every measure but one—financial—she would grow and develop as a human being. Yet no one would describe her as "bettering" herself.

Materialistic Values. It should come as no surprise by now that Marx sees capitalism as the cause of the *materialistic values* of Western industrial society. Numbers, money, and profit are what capitalism is all about. Tangible, material wealth is all that counts. When confronted with something like the harm done by pollution, instead of treating this as a "quality of life" issue, hard-line capitalists insist on putting a price tag on it via something called "cost-benefit analysis." As far as they are concerned, if it cannot be measured financially, it does not exist.

In a culture that exalts material things this way, it is no wonder that so many of us are driven to buy things in order to feel good. We define "the good life" in terms of cars, high-tech gadgets, expensive clothes, jewelry, big houses, boats, a large salary, financial security, and golden parachutes. We even elevate the material aspects of ourselves—our bodies— above our minds and our souls. How good looking are we? Are we in good shape? And how long can we stay that way?

The Structure of Our Days. Marx would argue that even the *shape of our days* reflects the character of industrial capitalism. Most of us traditionally travel to offices, stores, or factories away from our homes for our jobs because that is the most efficient way to produce. We assume that rush-hour traffic is the way it has to be. And our work life is separated from our home life.

In very important ways, this situation splits our lives into separate fragments. How much do you know about the jobs your parents and relatives hold? How often do you go to where they work? Would the people working there welcome you and take the opportunity to teach you something? Or would your presence interfere with their getting their work done? Most likely, you know little about what people in your family do or where they work, and that is probably all right with you. You may even think that work is more important than family life.

Education. A Marxist would even argue that the way education is structured is a product of the type of economy we have. What are some of the qualities we need in employees in order to make contemporary capitalism work efficiently? We value the ability to adapt to a production schedule, for example, and the willingness to meet deadlines. We value the ability to concentrate on tasks while surrounded by other people without being distracted. We value the willingness to do what we are told, and the wish to compete against the performance both of fellow workers and of other companies.

Do schools teach these qualities? All the time. They are encouraged just by the way education is conducted, particularly in elementary, middle, and high schools. We must come to school on time and have an ironclad excuse for being absent. Homework must be done on time. We sit and take tests in a classroom full of people whom we are told to ignore. We follow directions and learn through a largely passive process. And we are constantly measured against each other. A Marxist would argue that education is conducted this way because our capitalist system requires workers who are trained this way. Thus economic imperatives determine even educational goals.

Do We Choose Our Values? This is what Marx means, then, when he claims that the "material conditions" of our life—that is, the nature of the economy we live in—determine who we are and what we think. Marx maintains that the core values most of us have result from our living under capitalism. And he can certainly make an intelligent case for his claim that whatever the worth of our ideas, we have not chosen them independently—they have simply seeped into our hearts. If Marx is right, our most cherished beliefs are not freely chosen. Instead, they are determined by forces we never even think about.

As disturbing as Marx's insight might seem at first, ultimately it holds some hope. By realizing the influence of these forces on our minds, we can free ourselves from them. Once we become free, we really can choose what we think and do.

Happiness and Unhappiness

We have looked at Marx's claim that the economy we live in determines almost everything about our lives, including how we understand what our aim in life should be. His second claim is just as far-reaching. Capitalism, Marx believes, has so flawed a vision of human happiness that people living under its sway cannot possibly achieve genuine happiness.

Homo Faber: *"Man the Maker"*

Marx's dim appraisal of capitalism stems from his conception of human nature. For Karl Marx, humans are essentially producers. He sees us not so much as *Homo sapiens* ("the thinking human") but as *Homo faber* ("the tool-making human").

Marx believes that in the deepest part of our beings, humans are makers. Our essence is to create, to build, to make things. Productive work is the fullest and highest expression of who we are. Indeed, in Marx's mind, it *makes* us who we are. He writes,

> Production must not be considered simply as being the reproduction of the physical existence of the individuals. Rather it is a definite form of activity of these individuals, a definite form of expressing their life, a definite *mode of life* on their part. As individuals express their life, so they are. What they are, therefore, coincides with their production, both with what they produce and with how they produce. The nature of individuals thus depends on the material conditions determining their production.[5]

Given what we have seen of Marx's materialism and the power he grants to the material conditions of our lives, it is no surprise that Marx claims that we *become* what we *do*. Who we are deep down depends heavily on what kind of work we do. If our jobs consist of interesting, challenging activities, we become interesting, well-developed people. But if we spend our days doing boring, repetitive, mindless work, then we become dull, boring individuals.

"Alienated Labor"

If our productive life is positive, then, we are happy and satisfied with life. If our work life does not allow us to express our true selves, to develop our talents, and to fulfill our productive nature, these most basic needs go unmet, and we are unhappy. Marx's criticism of capitalism hinges on this very point. The kind of work capitalism has us do, according to Marx, is fundamentally unsatisfying. Rather than making us fulfilled, complete, and at one with ourselves, it leaves us deeply unsettled and "alienated" from our true selves. Marx calls this **alienated labor**.

Marx wrote in the middle of the nineteenth century during the development of industrial capitalism, and his main image of labor is factory work. However, his thinking also covers white-collar work. What he is talking about is what most of us would agree is the normal way

> **alienated labor** According to Marx, alienated labor is the type of labor that characterizes capitalism. It has four dimensions. The worker is alienated from the product produced, from the activity of production, from his or her own productive nature, and from other people.

---

5. Marx, *The German Ideology: Part I*, 114.

that work is designed under capitalism—large operations, run by professional managers, using division of labor, with an emphasis on technology and machinery. This may be an efficient way to produce goods, but Marx thinks that it goes against the grain of the human spirit. It may be good for us as *consumers*, but it is terrible for us as *producers*. Consequently, we can only end up unhappy.

Marx sees four distinct ways in which work under industrial capitalism is unsatisfying, that is, four different ways in which we become *alienated* from things that are rightfully ours and that we need in order to be satisfied.

Alienation from the Product. Under capitalism, Marx says, we lose the products of our labor. If we work in a factory, we make things. But at the end of our shift we own nothing that we produced. Who owns it? The person or the company that hired us. "The capitalist," as Marx always puts it, keeps what we make and sells it for a profit. Whether we work in an office, a store, a restaurant, a hospital, or a factory, it's all the same. We perform certain tasks or services, but the owner of the company retains control over what we do and sells it for a profit. We may be paid for our time and effort, but unless we're involved in "profit sharing," we do not get "a piece of the action."

"But that's the way it is," you might say. "Everybody knows those are the rules." Those may be "the rules," but Marx thinks they are the wrong rules. He believes that we are entitled to own and control what we produce. And he is particularly unhappy that the whole process increases the power of "the capitalist" over the workers. The owner earns much more money than the workers and keeps the profits from the sale of the product as well.

Worse yet, because money is power under capitalism, what workers produce actually increases the capitalist's power over them. Not only do the workers lose control over the products of their labor, Marx sees the fruits of these products, money, ultimately being turned against the very people who produced them. Under such circumstances, how can the workers be happy?

Alienation of the Process. Alienation also results from what happens on the job. Workers usually have little say in how their skills are used or in how their jobs are designed. Managers make the big decisions, set the company's goals, plan the process, and decide who does what.

This may be an efficient way of doing things, but Marx finds it unsatisfying. Who wants to spend their work lives doing nothing but what other people tell them to do? Under those circumstances, work is not at all like what Marx thinks it should be. The worker is forced to be passive, unthinking, and compliant when she or he would be happier being active, engaged, and creative.

Capitalism also makes work unsatisfying because it relies so heavily on the "division of labor." Instead of hiring a staff of high-priced but skilled chairmakers for a furniture factory, for example, factory owners break down the process of building a chair into a series of simple steps. Each small step is then taught to a low-paid, unskilled worker. (This is the assembly-line principle that Henry Ford pioneered in the automobile industry.) The division of labor works out very well for the capitalist. Instead of paying an expensive hourly rate for master chairmakers, he can pay minimum wage. Then he can sell more chairs because he can sell them more cheaply than the competition. For the workers, however, it's another story. What once was a highly skilled, well-paid, challenging, and satisfying job immediately changes. Marx gives us a grim account of what happens:

> As the division of labor increases, labor is simplified. The special skill of the worker becomes worthless. He becomes transformed into a simple, monotonous productive force that does not have to use intense bodily or intellectual faculties. His labor becomes a labor that anyone can perform. Hence, competitors crowd upon him on all sides, and . . . the more simple and easily learned the labor is, the lower the cost of production needed to master it, the lower do wages sink, for, like the price of every other commodity, they are determined by the cost of production.[6]

Work becomes dramatically less satisfying under these circumstances. Marx writes that work ultimately loses all its intrinsic appeal, and the worker becomes "an appendage of the machine."[7]

Alienation from Our Nature. A third kind of alienation occurs as a consequence of the first two. Because we give up what we produce to someone else and because the activity of work is itself unsatisfying, we become alienated from our basic nature as producers, from what Marx calls our "species being."

Marx thinks that work should be an end in itself for humans. We should find it intrinsically satisfying and nourishing, the primary vehicle by which we express and develop ourselves. But the way things go in capitalism, work becomes only a means to an end, not an end in itself. Because we must earn money to live, our labor becomes a commodity we are forced to sell. Even if we are paid well, our labor is still a commodity that we sell. As a result of all of this, we become separated from our true nature.

To Marx, being forced to sell our labor as a commodity is literally unnatural and shameful, something like being forced into prostitution. Sex is an intimate and special part of ourselves, and we feel that it should be completely under our control. To be forced into sexual acts, even for money, surely offends all of us. It violates the person coerced and denies his or her basic rights. Marx sees our work life as being just as personal and precious—the core of who we are. If what we do as workers determines who we become as people, then the kind of work we do, its design, the working conditions, and the like are all important. To be forced to sell our labor and perform "alienating" labor damages and debases us, just as rape harms and debases its victims. Both flatly deny our nature and destroy our dignity.

Alienation from Other People: Competition. Finally, alienation also occurs because capitalism pits us against each another as competitors. People looking for work compete with each other to get a job. Once hired, workers vie for raises and promotions. Workers

---

6. Karl Marx, *Wage Labour and Capital*, in Tucker, *Marx-Engels Reader*, 188.
7. Karl Marx, *Manifesto of the Communist Party*, in Tucker, *Marx-Engels Reader*, 341.

in rival companies compete for customers. Ultimately, even the owners fight against each other in their unending quest for more money.

Such thoroughgoing competition, Marx thinks, guarantees unhappiness. He sees humans as essentially social creatures who are meant to live in harmony with our neighbors. He thinks that cooperation, not competition, is the more natural and satisfying condition. Yet rather than fostering common interests and solidarity among people, capitalism breeds self-interest, distrust, and dishonesty. Capitalism clearly fosters self-interest. Our "job," as it were, is to look after ourselves, not anybody else. The spirit of capitalism is "everyone for himself." Under these conditions, we can trust others to only a limited degree. If we are all self-interested competitors (adversaries, really), it makes more sense to distrust the people we do business with than to trust them. Thus we are inclined to be a shade untruthful in our dealings with one another. Who believes the salesperson who says, "This price is the best I can do. At that price I'm losing money on the deal. I'll get in trouble with my boss, but I'll sell it to you anyway because you remind me of myself when I was your age"? Aren't you likely to lie yourself and say, "Look, if I go any higher, I'll have to drop out of school"?

Marx's point is that the nature of capitalism forces us to act this way. But how satisfying is a world in which the people around us are adversaries?

Capitalist Alienation Versus Marxist Happiness

Marx's case is worth thinking about. He sees the values of capitalism as diametrically opposed to human nature. Under capitalism, workers typically have no control over their work. Alienated from their true nature, they are set in competition with the people around them. Under such circumstances, Marx argues, capitalism cannot make people happy.

But, you say, capitalist economies produce an abundance of luxury goods. If you make plenty of money doing work that Marx labels "alienating," doesn't that make you happy in spite of everything?

Not in Marx's opinion. No matter how much money you make, you still become what you do. You may make a pile of money at some dull, boring job, but the job is making you a dull, boring person. You may have lots of nice things, but without developing some inner resources, you cannot enjoy them. Even rich capitalists are adversely affected. Their own workers are adversaries and everyone else is a competitor. Distrust and aggression must be their operating style. Money simply cannot buy mutual trust and peace of mind.

At this point, you may be bursting with objections. What if, for example, your idea of happiness is different from Marx's idea? Aren't many people perfectly happy with a dull job as long as they're paid well enough?

To counteract the common argument, Marx would simply say that it is based on an erroneous idea of human nature. If it is our nature to be producers who flourish in an economic setting marked by cooperation with other people, any other arrangement will rub us the wrong way. We cannot change this any more than we can change the conditions our bodies require to be healthy. Capitalism may make us feel good in lots of ways, but in the last analysis it leaves us frustrated, or "alienated." Marx contends that under capitalism we can never feel as content or happy as if we lived in agreement with our nature.

Capitalism: The "Bottom Line"

Marx's theory presents us with a serious criticism of capitalism. His theory of historical materialism leads him to claim that the economic forces around us are powerful enough to shape our attitudes about what is valuable in life. This means that the largely individualistic and materialistic outlook that pervades our society has not been freely chosen by anyone. It has, instead, been produced by our economic system. It is imposed on us as we are born into and socialized to fit into the economy.

Marx also argues that living according to the requirements of capitalism means we can never be happy. Primarily because of the shape of our work life, we have become alienated from our true nature and have been set in opposition and conflict with the people around us. According to Marx, happiness does not come from what we have—money, clothes, gadgets, cars, or houses. Rather, it comes from what we do in our lives, who we become, and whether we have positive, cooperative relationships with other people.

Accordingly, Karl Marx presents you with a real challenge. What is the path to happiness? Can we really be happy if we accept the values of contemporary capitalism?

Einstein: A Scientific Explanation for How Things Aren't the Way They Appear to Be

Even though Marx saw himself as an empiricist, you might be tempted to dismiss him as just another philosopher whose explanation about how "things aren't the way they appear to be" is simply a product of his imagination. But what if a physicist like Albert Einstein argued that our commonsense understanding of reality is all wrong?

Einstein Replacing Newton

To properly understand Einstein, however, we have to appreciate the picture of reality he overthrew. Before Einstein, the ideas of Sir Isaac Newton were universally accepted as the description of how the universe operated. Newton discovered that the gravitational force that causes objects to fall to the ground is the same gravitational force that keeps the moon in place orbiting around the earth and operates everywhere in the universe. He also proposed his three famous laws of motion. But the one achievement of Newton

Isaac Newton (1642–1727) was educated and taught at Cambridge University. His most famous work is *Mathematical Principles of Natural Philosophy*, a work that revolutionized the understanding of the universe. Newton discovered the laws of motion that are now named after him, developed the theory of gravitation and orbits, studied optics and acoustics, and made many contributions to mathematics. Newton also served in a variety of public posts: member of Parliament, master of the mint, and president of the Royal Society. He was unusually sensitive to criticism, and he engaged in a number of vindictive disputes, most notably over whether he or Leibniz invented calculus.

that has probably had the greatest impact on your thinking, whether you realize it or not, is his account of space and time.

Absolute Space and Time

Newton's most basic assumption is that the two most fundamental properties of reality—space and time—are "absolute." In their deepest essence, they are steady, unchangeable, uniform, and constant. In Newton's view, space and time are independent of anything that happens. It's as if there is a huge empty stage with a great cosmic clock over it where all the events of the universe take place. No matter what else happens—the Big Bang, the birth and death of stars, cosmic explosions, wars, pestilence, famine—the stage remains the same and the clock keeps ticking. Space and time are absolute, unchanged by any object that comes "onstage" or goes "offstage" or by any action that takes place there.

Newton's description of the universe provides us with a clear and unshakable account of the nature of reality. Reality is describable, measurable, mechanical, understandable, bound by natural laws of cause and effect, and fixed in the bedrock of space and time. Truth can be empirically discovered, and puzzles solved. Newton gives us a stable and dependable universe.

It turns out, however, that Newton is wrong.

One of the most brilliant minds of the twentieth century, Albert Einstein (1879–1955) was born in Germany to Jewish parents. After an undistinguished career as a student, Einstein was able to obtain a position in the Swiss Patent Office in 1902. His writings on theoretical physics attracted much attention, but he was not able to obtain a university post until 1909. After starting at the University of Zurich, he moved to the German University of Prague, the Federal Polytechnic in Zurich, and the University of Berlin. Einstein established or made foundational contributions to many fields of physics, including special relativity, general relativity, astrophysics, quantum physics, and statistical physics. He received the Nobel Prize in 1922. Teaching occasionally at the California Institute of Technology, he accepted a permanent position at the Institute for Advanced Studies in Princeton after Hitler came to power.

Einstein's Relativity Theory

The rejection of Newton's ideas culminates in the theories of Albert Einstein. The story of scientific thinking from Newton to Einstein revolves around the problem of getting Newton's principles to square with new discoveries. Newton's laws of nature explained the behavior of gases well, but electric and magnetic forces posed a new challenge. A little over one hundred years after Newton's death, the equations of a scientist named James Maxwell suggested that light is electromagnetic. By concentrating on the behavior of light, then, Einstein focused on a phenomenon that had major implications about the accuracy of Newton's system. Einstein's genius was to see that what he learned about light presented a picture of the universe that differed completely from that of Newton, particularly with regard to the nature of space and time.

The Speed of Light

In Newton's universe, space and time are constant and absolute. For Einstein, however, it's the *speed of light* that is absolute. By "absolute," Einstein means not only that light always moves at the same speed in a vacuum (186,279 miles per second) but also that light will be perceived as moving at the same speed by every observer, whether that observer is standing still, moving away from the light, or moving toward the light. Despite physical conditions that affect the speed of everything else, the speed of light always remains the same. This is the one great constant in Einstein's thinking, and it is the constant on which he builds his explanation of reality.

Once Einstein elevates the speed of light to the premier spot in his thinking, the ideas that follow from it defy Newtonian "common sense." Thus Einstein's explanation of the nature of reality differs not only from Newton's description but from anything we would ordinarily imagine. It takes some doing to accept this.

Measuring Speed

Before we see how Einstein's ideas defy common sense, we need to note some of the odd things that happen when we measure the speed of light. Measuring is a basic activity of science, and measurements are a big part of an empiricist's description of reality. If simple measurements do not work out right, then, it is a very big problem from a scientific viewpoint. And that's exactly what happens when we try to measure the speed of light. But before we talk about that, let's look at what happens when we measure the speed of something more common, like cars.

Measuring the Speed of Cars. You're driving along the highway at 70 mph. Your speedometer says 70 mph, and we can clock you at that speed with a radar gun. Suddenly a black Porsche roars by you at 100 mph. Now when we say the Porsche is doing 100, we mean that its speed is 100 miles per hour *in relation to someone standing still*—someone like the state trooper down the road waiting to give both of you speeding tickets.

But what is the speed of the Porsche *in relation to your moving car*? You see it move past you and continue down the road. How fast is it going? That's easy. Relative to your moving car, the Porsche is going 30 mph. If the two of you keep cruising at the same speed for 1 minute from the time he passes you, the distance between the two of you will be 1/2 mile (30 mph × 1/60 hour = 0.5 mile).

Now imagine that a few miles down the road, the driver of the Porsche suddenly remembers that he left the stove on at home after he finished cooking his breakfast this morning. He turns around and now races back toward you—still at 100 mph. If you're still going 70, what is the Porsche's speed relative to your speed now? Again, the answer is easy. As anyone who watches auto safety ads on television knows, the correct answer is the sum of the two speeds: 170 mph. If the two of you were to collide, the impact of the crash would be the same as if you had run into a stationary wall at approximately 170.

Or you can think of it this way. If we measure the decrease in the distance between the two of you in a minute's worth of driving toward one another, what do we get? Let's say you start five miles apart. At 70, your car will travel 1.17 miles. Doing 100, the Porsche will cover 1.67 miles. The distance between the two of you, then, has shrunk by 2.84 miles in one minute. To cover 2.84 miles in one minute, you would have to be driving 170 mph.

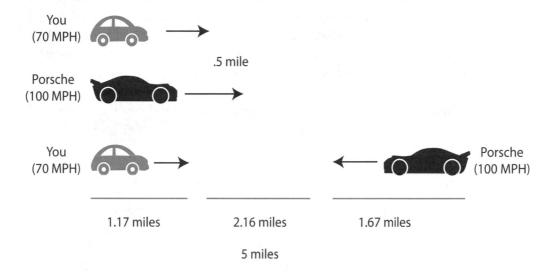

All this sounds perfectly sensible. It also fits Newton's ideas about motion. But look at what happens when we take the speed of light into consideration.

A Galactic Highway. It is now 2348 CE, and you are studying physics. Your instructor assigns you to do some experiments on the speed of light for homework. You get into your spaceship, which is equipped with the space-age equivalent of a radar gun. You can lock onto a single particle of light and track its speed.

First, you're supposed to clock the speed of light when you're stationary. You stop your ship, point your instrument at the nearest star, and lock onto a light particle. You already know what to expect—186,279 miles per second. (To make things easier, we'll use 186,000 mps as a round number.) Next, you're supposed to travel at 100,000 mps, let a particle of light pass you (as the Porsche did), and then measure its speed relative to you. You expect that speed to be 86,000 mps. (You are going 100,000 mps; the light is going 186,000; the difference must be 86,000.) But that's not what your speed gun shows. It says that the light went past you at 186,000 mps. At first you think your equipment has a glitch. Then you remember that your instructor told you not to be surprised by anything you observe. So you crosscheck your speed gun by asking your ship's computer to calculate how much farther the light particle traveled than your ship did in 1 minute. You assume that the light went only 5.16 million miles more than you did (86,000 mps × 60). Your computer tells you it went 11,160,000 miles—the distance something travels in 1 minute going at 186,000 mps.

This doesn't make sense. But you want to get home early, so you go on to the third part of your assignment. You're supposed to get your ship going 100,000 mps again, and this time head into the light. Again, you are to determine the speed of the light particle coming right at you relative to your own speed. This time it should be 286,000 mps, you think—your speed (100,000) plus the speed of light (186,000). But again you're surprised when your speed gun registers only 186,000. Cross-checking with the computer verifies this. You assumed that during 1 minute of travel, the distance between your ship and the light particle would have decreased by 17,160,000, but your computer tells you it went down by only 11,160,000. The speed of the light particle relative to your speed, even when you are moving toward it, is 186,000 mps. There's no disputing it. The speed of light relative to you is always the same—186,000 miles per second. It doesn't matter whether you are stationary, moving away from the light, or moving toward it. Yet this cannot be true if the laws of nature hold universally.

Does this mean we have to give up logic and natural laws as we know them in order to understand the phenomenon? In a way it does. Or rather, we have to give up one kind of logic and natural laws for another.

Einstein's Constant

Einstein theorized that light will always be measured as traveling at the same speed, whether the measurer is standing still or moving at some tremendous velocity, and experiments have borne out this theory time and again. The idea that the speed of light is constant under all conditions throughout the universe dealt a major blow to Newtonian physics. Absolute space and time had been a kind of baseline in Newton's account of the universe. Einstein's theory holds that everything but the speed of light is up for grabs, and that includes space and time. And that has some profound consequences.

The Speed of Light and the Relativity of Time

The connection that Einstein develops between the speed of light and the passage of time has some astonishing implications. Einstein claims that as a moving object speeds up and gets closer to the speed of light, time slows down. Or to be more precise, *from the point of view of someone standing still*, time changes for the moving object. If this sounds strange, what Einstein has in mind is even stranger. Note once again the phrase "from the point of view of someone standing still." *From the point of view of the object itself,* however, time is constant—it neither speeds up nor slows down, despite what the observer perceives. But here is the most incredible part of Einstein's theory. Which point of view is the "right" one? What is "really" happening? Is one time speeding up or is the other slowing down? Which time is the "real" or "official" time? According to Einstein, as strange as it may seem, the answer is that both are.

Einstein claims there is no such thing as absolute time (or absolute space, for that matter). Time (or space) *is relative to a frame of reference.* That's why the theory is called the "relativity" theory.

You're probably thinking that two contradictory reckonings of time, or anything else, cannot both be accurate. It simply isn't logical, at least not in the terms of a Newtonian world. But such a proposition is perfectly logical in an Einsteinian world. Whether or not space and time are changing is all relative to a frame of reference. Experiments have shown conclusively that this is so.

The Relativity of Time: The Twin Paradox

Let's talk about time and see where we can go with it. In modern physics there is a famous paradox called the "twin paradox." Imagine you have an identical twin. You get into a spaceship and blast out into the galaxy traveling close to the speed of light. Your twin remains behind on earth. You hurtle through the galaxy for what you count as a few months. Upon your return to earth, you find that your twin is now many years older than you. Your ship's clock ticked off what seemed to you to be normal seconds, minutes, and hours. It tells you that a relatively short amount of time elapsed since you left. But you cannot doubt your senses. Your twin is now old enough to be your parent. In fact, depending on how close you got to the speed of light and how many months you were in space, you may return hundreds of years (from earth's perspective) after you left.

The point is that in relativity theory the character of any variation in time depends on the frame of reference from which we make the assessment. From your viewpoint, earth time speeded up. From your twin's viewpoint, your time slowed down. If you and your twin could communicate with each other during your trip via video, you would both see some very strange things. Your twin would observe you moving and speaking in slow motion. If your spaceship had a wall clock, it would be going so slowly that your twin would think it had stopped. You would see the exact opposite. Your twin would seem to be racing around and speaking incredibly quickly. The clock on your twin's wall would spin around wildly.

Proofs of the Relativity of Time

Experiments have shown that time is indeed variable. One of the most well-known demonstrations of this fact took place in 1972 when scientists took an atomic clock onto a plane, flew it around the world, and then compared it to another atomic clock on the ground with which it had been synchronized. The clock that went on the plane now registered a slightly earlier time. Even though the plane went nothing close to the speed of light, in comparison to the clock on the ground, the clock on the plane had slowed down—even if minutely—while it was moving. Of course, to be precise and to respect the fact that neither one was "wrong," we must also say that in comparison to the clock on the plane, the one on the ground sped up.

Another stunning confirmation of the relativity of time involves a subatomic particle called a muon. Muons are created at high altitudes in our atmosphere when subatomic particles from space enter the atmosphere and strike air molecules. Muons decay very quickly, so quickly that their lifetime is only 2.2 millionths of a second. Strictly speaking, they should be able to travel only about 700 meters before they decay, and it should be physically impossible for a muon to travel all the way down to the earth in 2.2 millionths of a second. To go that distance in that time it would have to travel faster than the speed of light. Yet muons strike the earth all the time. How is it possible?

What happens is this. The force of the collision at the edge of the atmosphere that creates the muons sends them speeding toward the earth at 99 percent of the speed of light. As you know by now, from the observer's point of view, the closer to the speed of light an object travels, the more time slows down. Since a muon moves almost at the speed of light, time slows down a great deal, which—in its frame of reference—gives it plenty of time to reach the earth. To be more precise, the muon still exists only 2.2 millionths of a second in its time frame. Yet it can cover the distance because as measured by our time frame it exists for 15.4 millionths of a second.

In other words, the natural laws that determine that a muon exists for only 2.2 millionths of a second are valid no matter what is happening in the universe. According to Einstein, however, time is not an absolute, fixed property. Instead, time is a property that is determined by the motion of an object in relation to the speed of light. Perhaps we could say that time is the product of an object's relationship to the speed of light. You can see from this that it does not make any sense to ask whether a muon "really" exists for 2.2 or 15.4 millionths of a second. Both statements are true. The measurement that is used simply depends on your frame of reference.

Philosophical Implications: Alternate Realities

The philosophical implications of Einstein's relativity theory should be occurring to you by now. Most of us have always assumed that time is as Newton described it. But Einstein's work alters our most fundamental understanding of the nature of reality. Specifically, Einstein's theory that time is relative to motion means that more than one reality can exist. (Muons exist only 2.2 millionths of a second *and* muons exist 15.4 millionths of a second.) This idea of the *simultaneous existence of different realities* is very powerful in its philosophical implications.

To explore this startling notion, we'll consider two examples. Let's start with one of Einstein's simpler ones. You're on a railroad car that is moving along. You stand up, take an object, and let it fall to the floor of the car. As you watch its path, you see that it falls straight down. If you were asked to trace the trajectory the object took, you would draw a straight line.

Now imagine a friend of yours sitting on the embankment beside the train tracks can see you do this. (Pretend the car has a glass side.) She can also study the trajectory of the object as it falls. Is she going to say that it fell straight down? No, because it does not just fall down, it also moves forward with the train. If she were asked to trace the trajectory of the object's fall, she would draw a curved line, or a parabola.

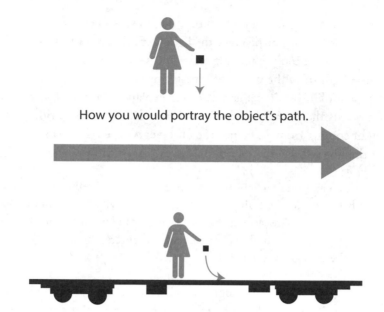

How you would portray the object's path.

How someone on the embankment would portray the object's path.

How does the object "really" move, in a straight line or in a parabola? You are probably inclined to think that a curved path is the better answer. When you're on the train it appears to fall straight down because you don't take the forward motion of the train into account. The stable embankment seems like a better point of view from which to measure the "real" motion. But remember that the earth itself is moving. From yet another vantage point—the moon, a planet, a spaceship—the trajectory of the falling book looks different again.

Thus you can see that we have no basis for saying that one path of the object is "real" and the others "illusion." We have different realities, all existing at the same time.

The Relativity of Simultaneity. Now let's move on to an example that Einstein says demonstrates the "relativity of simultaneity." Imagine that two bolts of lightning strike the train track at two points far from each other, points A and B. These bolts of lightning, Einstein says, hit "simultaneously." You know what he means, right? But you may not know what *Einstein* means, because as he sees it, these two lightning bolts actually hit both at the *same* instant and at *different* times. How is this possible?

Suppose you're standing on the embankment by the train track at a point we call M. We see the bolts hit points A and B simultaneously. No doubt about it, they hit at the same instant. "Simultaneous," then, means that the light, which is traveling at a particular speed, reaches us at M at the same moment.

But here's the complication. Is someone on a train moving past us going to see the same event you see from the embankment? Einstein says no. The observer on the train is moving toward one of the lightning bolts, shortening the distance the light from that bolt has to travel and lengthening the distance the light from the other has to travel. The light from the bolt that hits behind the moving train thus will take a little longer to reach the observer than the light from the bolt that hits in front of it. To someone on the moving train, the bolts do not hit simultaneously. Einstein explains that the observer on the train "is hastening towards the beam of light coming from B, whilst he is riding on ahead of the beam of light coming from A. Hence the observer will see the beam of light emitted from B earlier than he will see that emitted from A." Accordingly, he concludes,

> Events which are simultaneous with reference to the embankment are not simultaneous with respect to the train, and vice versa (relativity of simultaneity). Every reference-body (coordinate system) has its own particular time; unless we are told the reference-body to which the statement of time refers, there is no meaning in a statement of the time of an event.[8]

Why is this so? Because the speed of light remains the same, no matter what the point of view. It moves at 186,000 miles per second in relation to the person watching the lightning from the embankment. It travels at the same speed relative to the person on the train. As a result, two different events occur. The bolts strike simultaneously; the bolts strike at different times. The only way both observers could see "the same thing" is for light to travel at different speeds for each of them. And there is no scientific reason to think that this is possible. Thus Einstein's ideas imply that simultaneous but *different* realities are possible. Remember, there is no "official" description of the event that negates either one. Each is scientifically valid.

Another Example of Simultaneous Different Realities. If you're telling yourself that there are not "really" different realities, that the problem is one of things *appearing* in two different ways, how do you handle this example? Keep the moving railroad car in mind. This car, however, has a bright light installed in the middle and two light-sensing devices installed on the doors at the front and back of the car. When the light hits the sensor, the door flies open. Now think again of two points of observation, or reference points, one inside the moving car and the other outside as it goes by.

Here is what happens. The observer inside the car sees the light go on and the doors open at the same instant. The observer outside, however, sees the light go on and the back door open just a little before the front door opens. Why? Remember the principle at work in the example of the lightning bolts. The path of the light to the back of the car is shortened by the forward motion of the train, while the path to the front of the car is lengthened. Thus it takes less time for the light to reach the sensor on the back door, and that door opens first.

Once again, both events "really" happen: The doors open simultaneously, and they do not open simultaneously. It just depends on the frame of reference of the observer,

---

8. Albert Einstein, *Relativity: The Special and General Theory*, trans. Robert W. Lawson (London: Routledge, 2001), 28.

whether that person is moving with the train or remaining stationary outside the train. This gives us two different events, as it did in the lightning example. The doors open simultaneously *and* the back one opens first.

By now you should understand just how changeable space and time are in Einstein's account of reality. Both are relative properties, directly connected to the speed of an object's motion and the frame of reference from which that object is viewed. Therefore, the spatial and temporal dimensions of an object are, in a sense, manufactured. They are the product of conditions external to the object—its speed relative to the speed of light and the observer's point of view. Different observers experience different conditions, so space and time differ relative to those conditions. In short, Einstein gives us an account of the nature of reality that is very different from anything we experience in our everyday lives.

Marx and Einstein: Things Aren't What They Seem

Marx and Einstein study extremely different phenomena. Marx focuses on the economy; Einstein, space and time. However, they come to disturbingly similar conclusions—things aren't at all what they appear to be to our everyday perception of reality.

Our culture tells us that "the one who dies with the most toys wins" and that money and "stuff" will make us happy. Marx says these ideas lead us to being used as tools.

Our senses tell us that the two most fundamental properties of reality—space and time—are constant and unshakable. Einstein says we're wrong. It's not that what we see is an illusion. It's that it's only one of a variety of possible realities, e.g., two lightning bolts strike at the same time and at different times. (And that's not even getting into the implications of quantum physics.)

What are we to make of this?

Discussion Questions

1. How much do you agree with the conventional wisdom of our society that success and happiness come through material success? How important are things like love, family, community service, and religion, and are they at odds with material success? Are the most successful people in our society also the happiest? What leads you to your answer?

2. Competition is so much at the heart of contemporary Western society that the Marxist critique of competition is virtual heresy in our culture. What is your reaction to the Marxist preference for cooperation? Is competition as good as we think it is? What are its virtues?

3. Is satisfying labor as important as Marx claims for human happiness? What is your idea of a "good job"? If you had to choose between a highly paid but boring job versus a low or moderately paid but very interesting one, which would you choose? Why?

4. Is there any connection between the structure or content of your college education and the demands of capitalism, as Marx would suggest? How "alienating" is the work you do in school? Does this argue for a change in the way higher education should be conducted?

5. How does Newton's description of the universe fit with your commonsense ideas of reality? Would it be safe to say that most people today are Newtonians in the conceptions of space and time they use in their everyday lives?

6. Have you ever had an experience in your everyday life that even remotely suggests the conclusions about space and time that relativity theory draws? Hardly anyone has. What is your reaction to the idea that the ultimate nature of reality is something completely different than our senses suggest, and what might this mean in concrete terms for your life?

7. Think some more about the "relativity of simultaneity" and the example of the two lightning bolts. How do you handle the idea that the lightning bolts strike both at the same time and not at the same time? This seems logically impossible, so how can it be true? What is your reaction to the idea that reality can be this flexible?

8. Do the conclusions of relativity theory mean that knowledge of reality is impossible? Or must knowledge claims always be qualified by some reference to a "frame of reference"? Is truth, then, always conditional?

Selected Readings

Marx's materialist conception of history is outlined in *The German Ideology: Part I*; his theory of alienated labor can be found in the *Economic and Philosophical Manuscripts of 1844*; and his criticism of the division of labor appears in *Wage Labour and Capital*. Marx's master work is *Capital (Das Kapital)*. *The Marx-Engels Reader*, edited by Robert C. Tucker (New York: Norton, 1972), is a convenient edition of Marx's writings.

Isaac Newton's main ideas can be found in his *Philosophiae Naturalis Principia Mathematica (Mathematical Principles of Natural Philosophy)*. Albert Einstein gives an account of his ideas for a general audience in *Relativity* (New York: Crown, 1961). For a popular account of modern physics, see Stephen W. Hawking, *A Brief History of Time* (New York: Bantam Books, 1988).

Chapter 12

Alternative Perspectives—Buddhism and Native American Thought

In the last two chapters, we've seen important challenges to some ideas that many people would think are too obvious to be questioned. Chapter 10 argues that humans aren't the unique beings we claim to be. Scientific research has clearly established that dolphins have the kind of advanced intellectual and emotional capacities that support the idea that they are nonhuman "persons" and that they have moral rights—and these cetaceans aren't the only nonhuman animals on the planet with these capacities. Marx claims that, in many important ways, we're products of the economic systems in which we live. He argues that our values may not be the result of our free, considered choice. And Einstein defies "common sense" even further by implying, for example, that reality is *relative* to the observer; the train doors open both at the same time *and* at different times. We end this book with one final challenge to what's "obvious" by looking at two perspectives very different from how most people in the West see things: Buddhism and Native American thought.

Some Differences Between Eastern and Western Thought

We have barely looked at the contributions of Eastern thinkers so far in this text because philosophy never established itself as a separate and distinct area of inquiry in Eastern cultures. Religion and philosophy separated in the West into two different ways of thinking, but they thoroughly intermix in the East. This makes it difficult to talk about any distinctly philosophical positions held by Eastern thinkers. Indeed, the great thinkers of the East, like Buddha and Confucius, are primarily religious teachers. They are not philosophers as Aristotle and Kant were. Yet this mixture of the philosophical and religious gives Eastern thinking a unity and richness lacking in Western philosophy. In particular, it offers us a way of incorporating spirituality into our philosophical inquiries.

As you might expect, then, Eastern religions are very different from Western religions. The Judeo-Christian tradition is built around the idea of a personal God who created the world and rules over it. Our one and only life on earth is a test to see whether or not we will be saved or damned after we die. Which way we go depends on some combination of what we believe and how we behave.

Eastern religions, by contrast, have a more amorphous concept of God. They recognize a great force in the universe, but that force transcends the limits of a personal God with a specific personality. Particular religious beliefs are far less important than individual spiritual development. From the perspective of Buddhism, for example, we live through many lives in a quest for an advanced spiritual state of enlightenment, and once we achieve it, we reach a new level of being that transcends our former state and we no longer have to return for additional lives. How far along we are in our spiritual journey, however, and how many more lives it will take us to become enlightened, are completely our own work. No deity saves us or punishes us. We do that ourselves.

Beliefs such as these are not completely alien in the West. They are frequently advocated by various "New Age" writers and thinkers, and an increasing number of Westerners are at least sympathetically considering the value of this Eastern outlook.

The Teaching of Buddha: Spiritual Enlightenment as the Aim of Life

One of the world's most important ancient religions, *Buddhism,* began in India in the sixth century BCE. and was founded by Siddhartha Gautama, the man known as "the Buddha." "The Buddha" is thus not a personal name but a title of honor meaning simply "the Awakened One" or "the Enlightened One." Gautama reached Enlightenment when he came to understand the true nature of reality and the way to achieve release from the ongoing cycle of life after life. Gautama is not unique in becoming a Buddha. Tradition maintains that he is the fourth Buddha during the current period of human history. He is, however, considered "Supreme Buddha."

The most obvious difference between Buddhism and the outlook held in Western, capitalistic countries lies in its vision of what life is all about. Westerners are preoccupied with material success. The Buddha thought that spiritual enlightenment should be our goal. "Success" to the Buddhist is measured in terms of the progress we make toward getting off the "Wheel of Life." That is, our aim should be to advance spiritually to the point where we no longer have to return to this plane of existence to live another life.[1]

Siddhartha Gautama (563–483 BCE) was born in Nepal to a family of great wealth. As a boy, he led the protected and sheltered life of someone from a privileged family. He won his wife in a contest of arms at age sixteen and had a son with her. He became deeply troubled by disease and death, and at age twenty-nine, he renounced his former life and began a search for the cause of and solution for human suffering. For six years he wandered, studied with various sages in India, meditated, and lived ascetically, yet he still remained unsatisfied. Shortly after giving up asceticism, however, he achieved enlightenment and became "the Buddha" (the enlightened one). He established a religious order and spent the rest of his life guiding his followers, preaching, and meditating.

---

1. It is important to note that as Buddhism spread, its teaching became more diverse. Theravada, Mahayana, and Tibetan Buddhism, for example, emerged as different branches of Buddhism. The ideas described in this chapter, then, are best considered to be something like "essential Buddhist teachings."

Rebirth

One of the most fundamental truths of Buddhism, then, is that we live many lives. To the Buddhist, "rebirth" or "reincarnation" is an accepted fact. The great task of spiritual development is simply too difficult and too complicated to accomplish in one lifetime.

While reincarnation is more frequently an Eastern than Western idea, its advocates claim that important Western figures—among them possibly Plato, Benjamin Franklin, Ralph Waldo Emerson, and Walt Whitman—have held such a belief or at least have seriously considered it. Some point to passages in the New Testament which imply that reincarnation was generally accepted in the ancient West.[2] However, the Christian church ultimately rejected the idea.

Everyone admits there is no way to prove the truth of reincarnation, but its proponents claim that all of us have experiences that imply its truth. For example, you have probably visited some place for the first time and felt certain that you had been there before. (This feeling is commonly called *déjà vu*.) Or perhaps you meet someone for the first time with whom you are instantly comfortable. The two of you feel as though you have known each other all your lives. Or perhaps you have an uncanny gift or special ability. Those who believe in reincarnation say that these recognitions of places and people are in fact recollections of former lives, and any special talents you have were developed in earlier lives and carried forward with you into this one.

Karma

If rebirth is the first fact of life in Buddhism, the second is the principle that determines what happens from life to life, **karma**. *Karma* is the Sanskrit word for "action" or "deed," and as a concept it equates with the most fundamental law of the universe. As is often the case with Eastern ideas, we have no Western word for this concept.

The law of karma holds that all deeds produce positive or negative effects for the one who does them, and these effects extend from one life to the next. Thus by our actions, we determine what lies ahead for us in our next life—we determine our own destiny. As the Buddha explains it,

> **karma** Karma is a fundamental Buddhist law of the universe. The law of karma holds that all deeds produce positive or negative effects for the one who does them, and these effects extend from one life to the next. Karma is the Eastern equivalent to the Western law of cause and effect, or principle of action and reaction, or balance. It is also described as a law of sowing and reaping.

---

2. Matthew 16:13–16; Mark 6:14–16.

> If a man speaks or acts with an evil thought, pain follows him, as the wheel fol-
> lows the foot of him who draws the carriage. But if a man speaks or acts with a
> pure thought, happiness follows him, like a shadow that never leaves him.[3]

Karma is the Eastern equivalent to the Western law of cause and effect, or principle of
action and reaction, or balance. It is also described as a law of sowing and reaping. It's as
though our actions are seeds that inevitably produce good or bad fruit at some point in
our lives. We might even see it as a spiritual version of what we mean when we say "what
goes around comes around." If we do something negative, if we hurt someone, we set in
motion a process that will eventually bring negativity back on us. Thus karma supposedly
determines both the good and bad circumstances in any of our lives. If we were arrogant
and insensitive in a former life, we will experience the same hostility at others' hands now.
But if we were unusually helpful to others in need, we will now receive help as we need it.

What Karma Is and Is Not

We need to set a few things straight here so that the nature of karma is more or less clear.

First, karma is not a simple force that is easily interpreted. We cannot assume that if
people are poor, ill, or falling on hard times in this life, such misfortune is a direct result
of their wickedness in a former life. It may be the case, but it may not be. Their karma
may call for them to be helped by others in this life. In such a case, their problems may be
more related to the karma of other people, perhaps people who need to learn compassion
and generosity.

Misfortunes may even be the result of *good* karma. Handling difficult experiences is an
important way for us to develop spiritually. Hard times challenge and push us far more
than good times do. "Resistance training" is as necessary for spiritual development as it
is for training the body. Accordingly, people with difficult lives may not be experiencing
the consequences of an evil former life, but rather taking advantage of opportunities for
spiritual growth.

Second, karma is not a system of rewards and punishments administered by some
divine judge. What happens to us is the natural consequence of what we do. As one
writer puts it, "a Christian is punished *for* his sins; a Buddhist is punished *by* his sins.[4]
This is like Newton's third law of motion: "For every action there is an equal and opposite reaction." These are simply laws of nature. Newton describes the behavior of physical
energy. Karma describes the behavior of moral or spiritual energy.

Indeed, as a law of the universe, karma is just as unavoidable as the laws of physics. As
one of the Buddhist scriptures explains, "Not in the sky, not in the midst of the sea, nor
anywhere else on earth is there a spot where a man can be freed from (the consequences
of) an evil deed."[5] It doesn't matter if we regret what we did or if we apologize for it.

---

3. *The Dhammapada*, translated by P. Lal (New York: Farrar, Straus & Giroux, 1967), v. 1.
4. James Basquet, "The Five Precepts and the Reduction of Suffering," https://templetales.substack.
com/p/ep-016-the-five-precepts-and-the?s=r.
5. *Dhammapada*, v. 127.

When we do something negative, there is no way to avoid the consequences in this or in some future life. It is precisely as if we pushed a piano off the top of a building. Nothing can stop it from hitting the ground.

Deterministic Yet Optimistic

Certainly one of the most important philosophical implications of karma is that it predetermines much of our lives. The challenges and circumstances we face in this life result directly from what we did in our past incarnations—they are the inevitable consequence of our actions. This is just the way the universe works. If you plant an apple seed, a tree will grow. If you aren't careful about what you plant, you might get something you don't want.

Paradoxically, however, this determinism is built on the idea of free choice. There is nothing we are fated or forced to do. We choose our actions, but we must live with the consequences of our decisions. If we approach life with the proper attitude, however, and make better choices in the future, we work off bad karma and advance toward enlightenment. Even the determinism of karma is essentially optimistic.

There is also no guarantee that we will take advantage of the opportunities for spiritual growth when we are presented with them in this life. Our karma from past lives may require us to be more compassionate and tolerant. But we still have to choose to be that way when confronted with certain situations. We can respond properly and advance spiritually. Or we can fall back on old habits and waste a chance to move along. In this respect, we are completely free.

No One Else to Blame

One of the least forgiving aspects of Buddhism is that, according to the principle of karma, each of us must take all the credit or all the blame for our happiness. No one else is in any way responsible. As one of the Buddhist scriptures explains, "By oneself evil is done; by oneself one suffers. By oneself evil is left undone; by oneself one is purified."[6] If there is something about our lives we do not like, we should not handle this by blaming God, the Fates, our parents, or anybody else. The law of karma says that we are the author of all our unhappiness. We may not be able to control the actions of people who hurt us, but we can choose to hold on to the hurt and, in effect, let our enemies continue to torture us. Or we can try to accept our troubles and achieve some kind of equanimity and peace of soul.

This unremitting individual responsibility is a very tough idea to accept.[7] If you haven't thought about it before, the idea of being responsible for everything about your life can feel like a terrible burden. The good parts of life are no problem. We enjoy taking credit for things that go right for us. (We worked hard. We deserved it.) But we are always

---

6. *Dhammapada*, v. 165.
7. Buddhism's emphasis on individual responsibility is similar to Existentialism's. This is simply to note the parallel, not to suggest any causal relationship.

tempted to blame someone or something else for what goes wrong. (The teacher is unfair. The boss plays favorites. The circumstances are beyond our control. We had bad luck.) Feeling just as responsible for our reaction to bad outcomes as to good ones is not at all easy to accept.

But keep in mind that the workings of karma are not simple to sort out. Troubles are not punishment. Rather, they are opportunities for spiritual development, part of our "spiritual workout." Furthermore, if we are responsible for our reaction to everything we face, we ultimately have complete control over our destinies. One major lesson we learn from adversity is that we are much stronger and more powerful than we thought we were. Since our troubles are ours alone, we are the only ones to fix them—and we do have the power to do that.

The Teaching of Buddha: How to Get Off the Wheel of Life

As powerful as karma is, it does not trap us eternally. In fact, the aim of life is to achieve a level of spiritual development that lets us end the cycle of rebirth. The glory of the Buddha's teaching, then, is that it tells us how to do this. The key is contained in what Buddhists call the Four Noble Truths and the Noble Eightfold Path.

The Four Noble Truths are the Buddha's account of the challenge we face in life. Each truth tackles the same problem—*dukkha,* or suffering. (Actually, the Sanskrit word *dukkha* means anything from "pain," "disease," and "evil" to "imperfection" and "frustration.") The Buddha considers this the basic state of life. He said, "One thing I teach, *dukkha* and the ending of *dukkha.*" The Noble Eightfold Path tells how we can end it.

The Four Noble Truths

The Buddha's First Noble Truth makes clear that every part of life involves suffering. He explains,

> Birth is suffering, decay is suffering, disease is suffering, death is suffering, association with the unpleasing is suffering, separation from the pleasing is suffering, not to get what one wants is suffering.[8]

This is the suffering that confronts us over and over again in life, and this is the suffering we have to master.

The Second Noble Truth identifies the cause of suffering: desire. Desire is also the force that keeps us coming back for more lives. Like the word for "suffering," the Sanskrit word *trishna,* which is translated "desire," has many meanings. It includes: our appetite for sensual gratification, money, and power; craving for excitement; our clinging to or

---

8. *Dhammapada,* v. 190.

grasping after the things we enjoy, even life itself. But the Buddha sees all this as a trap. Our desires inevitably lead to suffering because our satisfaction grows cold or we lose the object of our desire. We grow bored with what we have and demand something new. We want more money. The objects of our desire are not what we thought they were. Those we love—and we ourselves—grow old and die.

Strictly speaking, however, the problem is not desire but wanting the wrong things. The Buddha believes that most of us are ignorant of what really makes us happy. We assume that once we get things like money, or a great job, or the perfect lover, everything will be set, and we can coast happily for the rest of our days. But it doesn't work that way. Life constantly changes, and nothing makes us immune to "suffering." What we should want are things more permanent and more useful to our spiritual growth—wisdom, altruism, and reducing our desires. As long as we desire the ordinary satisfactions of life, however, we will continue being reborn. After all, that is the only way our desires for the transient and material things of human life can be fulfilled.

The Third Truth, then, teaches that stopping desire is the only way to stop suffering. When we accomplish this, we reach a state of consciousness called *Nirvana*.[9] By extinguishing greed, hatred, and ignorance in ourselves, we achieve perfection. We grow beyond a limited sense of our own selves and feel a sense of union with the universe.

How do we do this? That is what the Fourth Noble Truth tells us. We follow the path that the Buddha himself followed and pointed out to the rest of us. This is the Noble Eightfold Path—right views, right intentions, right speech, right action, right livelihood, right effort, right concentration, and right meditation. By living this way, we lose our false desires, develop compassion and selfless love for others, and achieve a high level of spirituality. This combination lets us break out of the cycle of birth and rebirth.

The Noble Eightfold Path

The Eightfold Path is also called the "Middle Way" of Buddhism. It is a middle path between the two extremes of sensual indulgence and rigid asceticism.

Right views refer to understanding the Buddha's teaching—the Noble Truths, karma, rebirth, and the like.

Right intentions are the proper motives of our actions—helping others. If extinguishing desire is critical, the intentions we put in its place are of paramount importance.

Right speech obviously means truthfulness. But it also includes speaking to other people with kindness, respect, and courtesy, avoiding frivolous speech and hurting other people through gossip.

Right action is conduct that conforms to five basic moral precepts: "refrain from injury to living things; refrain from taking what is not given; refrain from sexual immorality;

---

9. Be sure you realize that Nirvana is not a place, as the Christian heaven is. It is a state of mind. As a state that transcends all of our ordinary human, and therefore limited, experience, it cannot be adequately described.

refrain from falsehood; refrain from liquors which cloud the mind." The Buddha, like the Christ, sees morality as primarily a matter of the heart, and these precepts apply to our minds as well as to our bodies. They refer to our inner desires, motives, and thoughts as much as to the actions we perform.

The right-thinking Buddhist understands the precepts governing right action in an expansive, all-inclusive way. For example, not hurting living things extends to our attitudes toward animals. What does this say about hunting or eating meat? Taking only what is given means that we should be less hungry to acquire material things. Wealth is not bad in itself, but we should not lust after it in our hearts. The Buddha said, "It is not life and wealth and power that enslave a man, but the cleaving to them. He who possesses wealth and uses it rightly will be a blessing unto his fellow beings." Sexual immorality is best understood as referring to any kind of sexual activity that could hurt others, sensual indulgence, or negligence about our health.

Refraining from falsehood refers as much to public rhetoric, like that found in advertising and political campaigns, as it does to exchanges between two individuals. We must strive to be completely honest, never exaggerating or shading the truth even a little. Avoiding liquors that cloud the mind obviously refers to alcohol or any other drug that affects how we think. But it also includes emotional states that "intoxicate" us: anger, greed, jealousy, envy, revenge, excitement, love of power. Such feelings may be an inevitable part of being human, but the Buddha cautions against indulging in them, and especially against making decisions under their influence.

The next step on the Eightfold Path is *right livelihood*. This means that we should conduct ourselves in whatever profession we choose according to the Noble Truths and the five precepts.

Right effort refers to the steps we must take to purify and strengthen our minds. We do this by developing our positive qualities, working on our current weaknesses, and avoiding new ones. This means, for example, mastering feelings of jealousy, anger, fear, and anything else that would distract and weaken us internally.

Right concentration also concerns the mind. Here the Buddha means we should develop the skills of mental concentration fostered by meditation. This ability to control our minds in a highly disciplined fashion is absolutely necessary if we are to reach the final stage.

Right meditation is the highest state of mental control and development. It is an inner stillness and focus that transcends ordinary consciousness. It includes the development of morally good attitudes, but the perfection of this state cannot be described by words.

Ideally, following the Eightfold Path produces a combination of wisdom, compassion, and an advanced state of consciousness. Our intuitive abilities (in Sanskrit, *Buddhi*) develop and increase our tolerance and serenity. At that point, Nirvana is possible and we ourselves become "an Enlightened One"—a Buddha.

The Essence of Buddhism

Although its pursuit is difficult, the essence of Buddhism is quite simple. It was set out in its entirety in the very first sermon that the Buddha gave to a handful of monks. The sermon speaks eloquently for itself:

> Avoid these two extremes, monks. Which two? On the one hand, low, vulgar, ignoble, and useless indulgence in passion and luxury; on the other, painful, ignoble, and useless practice of self-torture and mortification. Take the Middle Path. . . .
>
> What, you will ask me, is the Middle Path? It is the Eightfold Way. Right views, right intentions, right speech, right action, right livelihood, right effort, right concentration, and right meditation. This is the Middle Path, which leads to insight, peace, wisdom, enlightenment, and Nirvana.
>
> For there is suffering, and this is the noble truth of suffering—birth is painful, old age is painful, sickness is painful, death is painful; lamentation, dejection, and despair are painful. Contact with the unpleasant is painful, not getting what you want is painful.
>
> Suffering has an origin, and this is the noble truth of the origin of suffering—desire creates sorrow, desire mixed with pleasure and lust, quick pleasure, desire for life, and desire even for nonlife.
>
> Suffering has an end, and this is the noble truth of the end of suffering—nothing remains of desire. Nirvana is attained, all is given up, renounced, detached, and abandoned.
>
> And this is the noble truth that leads to Nirvana—it is the Eightfold way or right views, right intentions, right speech, right action, right livelihood, right effort, right concentration, and right meditation.
>
> This is the noble truth of suffering. This must be understood.[10]

Buddhism Compared to Western Thought

Buddhism and Western Religions

Buddhism is more self-consciously spiritual than philosophical in its nature, but it is very different from Western religions. The most important difference, perhaps, is that Buddhism does not focus on God. Buddhists do not believe in a God that will punish them now or in the future if they do not behave. The only religious beliefs important to them are those that explain the nature of life, and failure to accept them does not mean punishment, only more lives. Buddhism is primarily a guide to living.

Buddhism is also an especially tolerant and accepting religion. It does not claim to be the "one true Faith" as Roman Catholicism and Islam do. You always get another chance. There is no ultimate "mortal sin" that irrevocably damns us to eternal fire. No matter

---

10. *Dhammapada,* trans. Lal, 22–23. [Translation altered.]

how many mistakes we make, we always have another opportunity to set them right. Buddhism also differs from many other religions in stressing the importance of kindness to animals.

Buddhism puts a heavier burden on the individual than the Judeo-Christian religions do, however. It isn't just that we have as many chances as we need to set our mistakes right—we *must* set them right. And we must do it alone, with no grace, or forgiveness, or salvation handed out in due course by an all-powerful deity. In the same way that Buddhists do not believe in a God who hovers over us waiting for us to do something wrong, they do not believe in a deity who will pull us out of trouble. Everything is in our own hands. The Buddha's last words underscored this. "Work out your own salvation with diligence," he said.[11] Such responsibility is surely a heavy load to carry.

In addition, the process takes a long time and requires a tremendous amount of patience. You cannot do something wrong, feel remorse, apologize to the person you hurt, or confess it to God or His representative, and then feel that the slate is clean. Regret and remorse are good because they show you have learned something. But karma is not forgiving. You may even have to wait until another life to make things right.

In comparison to Western religions, then, Buddhism is both softer and harder on people.

Buddhism and Western Philosophy

How does Buddhism compare to Western philosophy? Setting aside the spiritual and religious focus of Buddhism, which it shares with other Eastern modes of thought, an intriguing similarity with philosophy in the West is its emphasis on developing the mind. Most Western religions emphasize faith, feeling, and belief over intellectual development. In contrast, Buddhism teaches that if we want to advance spiritually, our minds and spirit must grow.

Buddhism and philosophy may agree on the primacy of the mind, but they differ on the best way to cultivate its powers. Philosophy stresses logic, analytical thought, and argument. Buddhism recommends meditation. This emphasis on meditation suggests that the traditional way we teach philosophy does not train the entire mind. In fact, if the Buddha is right, we should probably reconsider the way we generally conduct education in the West.

And still another, more technical difference exists between Buddhism and Western philosophy with regard to the nature of the self. Most philosophers argue for something inherent and unchanging in us that constitutes what they call a "self." We grow, develop, and change—indeed, the cells in our bodies change every seven to ten years—but there is some "self" that endures. Some thinkers even posit an immortal soul that inhabits the body.

---

11. Christmas Humphreys, *Buddhism: An Introduction and Guide* (New York: Penguin Books, 1951), 41.

The Buddha denies all this. He sees everything, even our very selves, as being in constant change. Buddhists believe that we are composed of five elements: the body, the emotions, the perceptions, the mental processes involved in choice, and consciousness. What passes from life to life, then, is not a specific entity, but what one interpreter of Buddhism refers to as "an ever-evolving, karma-created bundle of characteristics."[12] The metaphor the Buddha uses to illustrate his idea of the essence that survives from life to life is the flame of a candle. When we light one candle from another, what do we say of the second flame? It is completely different; yet it is also the same.

Buddhism and Western Social Values

The Buddhist view of life in general also differs greatly from that held in the West. Western cultures espouse a materialistic, individualistic, and secular outlook. Happiness is found in wealth, the exercise of power, celebrity, and personal achievement.

By contrast, Buddhism is spiritual and altruistic. The aim of life is spiritual development, and an important part of this is learning compassion, empathy, tolerance, and love for other people, and indeed for all other creatures. "Happiness" in the sense we use the term, that is, what we feel when all our desires are met, is not even a goal in Buddhism—quite the contrary. The Buddha sees desire as the source of our troubles, and he recommends that we reduce our wants and needs, not indulge and increase them. If we really want to be content with life, the Buddha recommends that we meditate, develop our minds, think of others, pursue wisdom, and learn to control our desires. Our goals in life should be spiritual and ethical, not material.

Keep in mind, however, that Buddhism recommends the "Middle Way." The Buddha does not say we all should retreat to monasteries in the Himalayas. The Middle Way is a practical path that lets us live in the world. And that is the real challenge—how to live according to Buddhist principles in the "real world."

Take ambition. We can aspire to success, but we must be careful lest it become an end in itself. Success lets us do much good for others, but when it tempts us to be self-absorbed, it retards our spiritual development and leads us to do things that will produce bad karma. Or consider running a business. Buddhism does not say that every business must become a charitable operation. It does suggest that businesses should examine whether they are helping or hurting the spiritual growth of their employees, customers, and owners. Do they encourage "right speech" and "right action"? Do they encourage something beyond an aggressive, competitive pursuit of profit? Do companies do violence to living things?

Buddhism's main ideas may differ from the ideas we are used to, but their strengths can be incorporated into our lives in practical ways.

---

12. Christmas Humphreys, *Buddhism: An Introduction and Guide*, 21.

The Challenge of Buddhism

Buddhism's outlook on life differs dramatically from that of our own society. The Buddha locates unhappiness in our desires and recommends a path of spirituality, meditation, and limited wants. Buddhism argues that the conventional wisdom of our society is all wrong. The Buddha thinks that pursuing money, power, and fame—the main things that our society values—leads us away from happiness, not toward it. Furthermore, there is not one major philosopher over the last two thousand years who would disagree with him on this point. This should unquestionably give us pause.

Native American Thought

One of the most shameful aspects of the European exploration and colonization of the Americas is the treatment of indigenous populations. Powered by greed, political ideologies, religious intolerance, and a sense of cultural and racial superiority, a wave of explorers, soldiers, missionaries, and colonizers swept through the two continents taking whatever they wanted, conquering any who resisted, spreading diseases from which indigenous peoples had no immunity, and forcing tribes onto reservations.

Particularly egregious was the destruction of native cultures, many of which, because they were transmitted orally, have been lost forever. In North America—from one coast to the other—the story was the same. Native Americans were driven from their homelands, their treaties were repeatedly violated, and they were forced to give up their traditional way of life. They were disparaged as "savages" and "pagans" who needed to be either civilized and saved or destroyed. Their culture was systematically eradicated by means of everything from laws forbidding religious practices to the notorious "Indian Residential Schools"—boarding schools that followed the principle of "kill the Indian, save the man." Removed from their families, indigenous youth were given new names, new appearances (short hair and school uniforms), prevented from speaking their own languages, taught English, and forced to convert to Christianity.

Contemporary society ultimately recognized the cruelty in how Native Americans were treated, but hundreds of years of cultural warfare have made it extremely difficult to study and appreciate the worldview and values of the indigenous peoples. Despite that difficulty, Native American thought provides us with an alternative perspective on some important philosophical issues worth examining—in particular, what kind of "knowledge" we should value and how we come to understand everything around us.

However, there are some serious challenges to studying Native American thought. There are fewer "primary sources" available than we would like. As a result, we must rely primarily on the research of contemporary philosophers who study Native American thought, although we will occasionally cite two Lakota holy men of the late nineteenth and early twentieth centuries, Black Elk and Lame Deer.

In addition, in a way that is similar to Eastern perspectives, Native American thought doesn't make a sharp distinction between religious and philosophical issues. As Brian

Yazzie Burkhart (Cherokee) explains, "Literature and philosophy, science and religion are all very different branches of knowledge in Western thought. . . . However, in American Indian thought this is not the case. None of these four can really be separated from the others."[13] Trying to isolate philosophical issues, as we will do in this chapter, then, admittedly gives us a limited picture of a complex and sophisticated perspective.

It's also important to recognize that there are many differences in the ideas of various tribes and nations. Therefore, we will focus only on the some of the broadest features that seem to be common across these different groups as we consider only three aspects of Native American thought: worldview, knowledge, and values. Also, for the sake of consistency, we will rely primarily on Lakota sources.

Native American Cosmology and Metaphysics

To the extent that there is a common view among Native peoples about the nature of the universe, it begins with a recognition that everything is alive—spirits, humans, non-human animals, the land, rocks, minerals, even forces of nature. Also, as Lame Deer explains, everything is not only connected, it is connected to the Great Spirit. He writes,

> Nothing is so small and unimportant, but it has a spirit given to it by Wakan Tanka [the Great Spirit]. Tunkan is what you might call a stone god, but he is also part of the Great Spirit. The gods are separate beings, but they are all united in Wakan Tanka. . . . The spirit split[s] itself up into stones, trees, tiny insects even, making them all *wakan* by his ever-presence. And in turn all these myriad of things which makes up the universe flowing back to their source, united in the one Grandfather Spirit.[14]

Consequently, everything in nature has a unique power, and we're able to connect with that power. Lame Deer writes,

> All animals have power because the Great Spirit dwells in all of them, even a tiny ant, a butterfly, a tree, a flower, a rock. . . . You have to listen to all these creatures, listen with your mind. They have secrets to tell. . . . You ask stones for aid, to find things which are lost or missing. Stones can give warning of an enemy, of approaching misfortune. . . . Butterflies talk to the women. A spirit will get inside a beautiful butterfly, fly over to a young squaw, sit on her shoulder. The spirit will talk through that butterfly to the young squaw and tell her to become a medicine woman.[15]

---

13. Brian Yazzie Burkhart, "What Coyote and Thales Can Teach Us," in *American Indian Thought*, ed. Anne Waters (Oxford: Blackwell, 2004), 22.
14. "The Circle and the Square" and "Talking to the Owls and Butterflies," in *Lame Deer, Seeker of Visions*, by John (Fire) Lame Deer and Richard Erdoes (New York: Simon & Schuster, 1994), 113, 127.
15. Lame Deer, "Talking to the Owls and Butterflies," 112, 136, 139.

As Gregory Cajete (Tewa) explains, "every act, element, plant, animal, and natural process is considered to have a moving spirit with which we continually communicate." Even physical places can have spiritual properties and be *sacred*. "Particular places," Cajete writes, "are endowed with special energy that may be used, but must be protected. This sentiment extends from the notion of sacred space and the understanding that the earth itself is sacred."[16] In contrast, a Western philosophical approach to reality regards time and space as, for lack of a better way to put it, "spiritually neutral."

Native American cosmology, then, describes a universe that is alive and infused with a variety of spiritual energies, unlike what we find in a Western philosophical approach. The universe is an essentially organic, multifaceted entity.

Understanding the World: A Polycentric Approach to Knowledge

Native American epistemology also stands in important contrast to Western epistemology. As we saw in Chapters 7 and 8, even when philosophers advance diametrically opposed theories about how we acquire knowledge (reason versus the data from our senses), they nonetheless assume *there is a single truth to be discovered*.

Native American thought takes a different view. Dennis McPherson (Ojibwa) and J. Douglas Rabb describe it as "a **polycentric** perspective." "[P]olycentrism," they explain, "recognizes that we finite human beings can never obtain a God's-eye view, a non-perspectival view, of reality, of philosophical truth. Every view is a view from somewhere. . . . [N]o one perspective can contain the whole truth."[17]

Vine Deloria (Lakota) recounts an episode that illustrates this point of view—and the stark contrast with a Western perspective (in this case in the context of religious ideas). He writes,

> A missionary, Reverend Cram, once came to the Senecas to convert them and recited the story of Adam and Eve. When he was finished the Senecas insisted on relating one of their creation stories. Cram was livid, arguing that he had told the Senecas the truth while they had recited a mere fable to him. The Senecas chastised him for his bad manners, saying that they had been polite in listening to his story without complaining and he should have been willing to hear their tales.[18]

The Seneca rebuke wasn't simply about courtesy, however. They were objecting to the arrogance of thinking that that any one perspective can capture the truth.

It is important to note that the benefits of a polycentric approach come only through a willingness to listen, to suspend judgment, and to ruminate on what one has heard.

16. Gregory Cajete, "Philosophy of Native Science," in Waters, *American Indian Thought*, 53.
17. Dennis H. McPherson and J. Douglas Rabb, *Indian from the Inside: Native American Philosophy and Cultural Renewal* (Jefferson, NC: McFarland, 2011), 20.
18. Vine Deloria, "Philosophy and the Tribal Peoples," in Waters, *American Indian Thought*, 9.

polycentric A polycentric approach to knowledge, characteristic of Native American thought, claims that no one perspective can capture the truth.

Accordingly, there is an important methodological component associated with this outlook. This is illustrated in the description by Michael Hart (Cree) of the sacred tradition of the "sharing circle": "Everyone expresses their views so that a full picture of the topic is developed. Individual views are blended until consensus on the topic is reached. A community view is developed and knowledge is shared for the benefit of all members."[19]

There are three especially important points to be appreciated about polycentrism. First, while this is somewhat of an oversimplification, we might say that a traditional Western view of truth is binary. A knowledge-claim is either true or false. Through our inquiries, we *discover* which it is. A polycentric approach, however, offers more possibilities because it is perhaps best represented by looking at an object through a series of lenses or a multifaceted crystal. We get different perceptions and must think about their significance in determining what we're ultimately experiencing. On the basis of the various perspectives we experience, we ultimately *construct* the truth.

Second, we need to be open to new evidence or perspectives. As McPherson and Rabb explain, "We never know what we will discover next and we can never be certain that we have finally put together a complete picture. It is therefore very helpful, we could even say essential, to compare what we have learned with the wisdom of others."[20]

Third, a polycentric approach echoes Janice Moulton's criticism of the way philosophical inquiry is traditionally done, which we saw in Chapter 2. She points out that "it is assumed that the only, or at any rate, the best, way of evaluating work in philosophy is to subject it to the strongest or most extreme opposition," and she calls this the "Adversary Method." The attitude of participants in a "sharing circle," for example, is anything but adversarial.

One of Moulton's ideas about an alternate philosophical approach is especially intriguing because it is similar to another aspect of Native American thought. Pointing to the role of *experience* in philosophical inquiry, she notes that in the Adversary Method,

> It is believed that philosophical discussions ought to proceed as if experience plays no essential role in the philosophical positions one holds. . . . It is thought that all genuine philosophical differences can be resolved through language. This belief supports the Adversary Paradigm, for adversarial arguments could be pointless if it was experience rather than argument that determined philosophical belief.

She discusses the possibility that "experience may be a necessary element in certain reasoning processes." The Native American perspective goes even further, however. Experience is an *essential* element in acquiring knowledge. As Gregory Cajete explains, "Direct subjective experience, predicated on a personal and collective closeness to nature, will

---

19. Cited in McPherson and Rabb, *Indian from the Inside*, 121.
20. McPherson and Rabb, *Indian from the Inside*, 21.

lead to an understanding of the subtle qualities of nature."[21] Indeed, the Native American perspective takes experience so seriously as a source of understanding that some experiences are even formalized into ceremonies. Referring to one especially important ceremony, Arthur Amiotte (Lakota) writes that "the Sun Dance is probably the most formal of all learning and teaching experiences. Inherent in the Sun Dance itself is the total epistemology of a people. It tells us of their values, their ideals, their hardships, their sacrifice, their strong and unerring belief in something ancient."[22]

Knowledge-That Versus Knowledge-How

The importance of experience as a source of knowledge in the Native American tradition leads us to another significant contrast with a traditional philosophical approach—which type of *knowledge* is most valuable.

Western philosophers focus on "propositional knowledge," which, Burkhart writes,

> is knowledge of the form "that something is so." It is the kind of knowledge that can be written down, that can be directly conveyed through statements or propositions. This kind of knowledge is thought to have permanence. If we make true and justified claims that something is so, those claims will continue to be true for eternity. In Western thought, this kind of knowledge is generally thought to be the pinnacle of philosophy.[23]

For shorthand, we can call this kind of knowledge *knowledge-that*. We *know that* "water freezes at zero degrees Celsius" and "2 + 2 = 4." Descartes would say we *know that* "we exist." *Knowledge-that* involves propositions we can establish as either true or false through some process of *justifying* our claims. We can observe and measure the process by which water freezes. Descartes would point to our "clear and distinct" awareness of ourselves thinking.

However, there is also what we can call *knowledge-how*. This is *experiential* knowledge related more to *skills* than *statements of fact*: *knowledge-how* to ride a bicycle, *knowledge-how* to make an omelet. We acquire this knowledge primarily through practice and experience.

Given Cajete's point about the important of experience, it's no surprise that a Native American perspective places more value on knowledge-how. "For American Indians," Burkhart explains, "knowledge is knowledge in experience . . . the kind of knowledge we carry with us. This is the kind of knowledge that allows us to function in the world,

---

21. McPherson and Rabb, *Indian from the Inside*, 53.
22. Cited in John DuFour, "Ethics and Understanding," in Waters, *American Indian Thought*, 35. The epistemological importance of powerful, subjective experiences culminates in the "vision quest." See below.
23. Burkhart, "What Coyote and Thales Can Teach Us," 19.

to carry on our daily tasks, to live our lives. This knowledge is embodied knowledge. We might do best to call this knowledge 'lived knowledge.'"[24]

It's fair to say that what Burkhart describes is *knowledge-how to live successfully*. This means that there is a strong *pragmatic* dimension to the Native American understanding of knowledge, a perspective that we already met when we considered William James's defense of freedom in Chapter 4. Recall that James claimed that Pragmatism was interested in "what works best in the way of leading us, what fits every part of life best and combines with the collectivity of experience's demands, nothing being omitted."

When the Native American approach to knowledge is seen in this light, the "polycentrism" that McPherson and Rabb refer to above makes sense. *Knowledge-that* claims are largely settled once and for all. After we determine the temperature at which water freezes, we don't need to go back and re-examine the issue. However, if we're talking about experience-based or skills-based knowledge, there's benefit in keeping an open mind to find out if there's *a better way* to do something than what we're doing now. For Native peoples, then, the central epistemological question isn't "What is true?" but "What *works?*"

Burkhart illustrates the kind of knowledge he is talking about by recounting the famous American Indian "Three Sisters" story:

> Centuries ago, the Senecas acquired a piece of knowledge. Three sisters, corn, beans, and squash, came to them, . . . gave the people certain ceremonies and told them that if they carried out these ceremonies (that supported the continued existence of the three sisters) the sisters would become plants and feed the people. Part of this requirement was that the sisters be planted and harvested together.[25]

If you understand even the basics of agriculture, you know that what this story conveys is the knowledge necessary for replenishing nitrogen in the soil so that crops can flourish year after year.[26]

The Role of Stories

The tale of the three sisters also points out another feature of the Native American approach to knowledge. It is often conveyed in narrative form, and the stories regularly convey important lessons. Consider the following four Lakota stories.[27]

---

24. Burkhart, "What Coyote and Thales Can Teach Us," 20.
25. Burkhart, "What Coyote and Thales Can Teach Us," 21–22.
26. It's worth noting that while this approach to planting was practiced in North America in the fourteenth century, if not much earlier, European farming traditionally favored planting single crops, with its consequent soil depletion. The value of "intercropping" has been rediscovered, however, and recommended as a way to increase yield especially on small farms.
27. Marie McLaughlin, "Myths and Legends of the Lakota," https://www.gutenberg.org/files/341/341-h/341-h.htm.

"The Forgotten Ear of Corn"

An Arikara woman was once gathering corn from the field to store away for winter use. . . . When all was gathered she started to go, when she heard a faint voice, like a child's, weeping and calling. . . . The woman was astonished. "What child can that be?" she asked herself. "What babe can be lost in the cornfield?" . . . She searched for a long time. At last in one corner of the field, hidden under the leaves of the stalks, she found one little ear of corn. This it was that had been crying, and this is why all Indian women have since garnered their corn crop very carefully, so that the succulent food product should not even to the last small nubbin be neglected or wasted, and thus displease the Great Mystery.

"The Little Mice"

Once upon a time a prairie mouse busied herself all fall storing away a cache of beans. . . . The little mouse had a cousin who was fond of dancing and talk, but who did not like to work. . . . The season was already well gone before she thought to bestir herself. . . . So she went to her hardworking cousin and said:

"Cousin, I have no beans stored for winter and the season is nearly gone. But I have no snake skin to gather the beans in. Will you lend me one?"

"But why have you no packing bag? Where were you in the moon when the snakes cast off their skins?"

"I was here."

"What were you doing?"

"I was busy talking and dancing."

"And now you are punished," said the other. "It is always so with lazy, careless people. But I will let you have the snake skin. And now go, and by hard work and industry, try to recover your wasted time."

"The Pet Donkey"

There was a chief's daughter once who had . . . twin sons. . . . As the babes grew older, their grandmother made for them two saddle bags and brought out a donkey.

"My two grandchildren," said the old lady, "shall ride as is becoming to children having so many relations. Here is this donkey. He is patient and surefooted. He shall carry the babes in the saddle bags, one on either side of his back."

It happened one day that the chief's daughter and her husband were making ready to go on a camping journey. The father, who was quite proud of his children, brought out his finest pony, and put the saddle bags on the pony's back.

"There," he said, "my sons shall ride on the pony, not on a donkey; let the donkey carry the pots and kettles."

So his wife loaded the donkey with the household things. . . . But no sooner done than the donkey began to rear and bray and kick. . . . The more he was beaten the more he kicked.

At last they told the grandmother. She laughed. "Did I not tell you the donkey was for the children," she cried. "He knows the babies are the chief's children." . . . She fetched the children and slung them over the donkey's back, when he became at once quiet again.

The camping party left the village and went on their journey. But the next day . . . a band of enemies rushed out. . . . After a long battle the enemy fled. But when the camping party came together again—where were the donkey and the two babes? No one knew. For a long time they searched, but in vain. At last they turned to go back to the village, the father mournful, the mother wailing. When they came to the grandmother's tepee, there stood the good donkey with the two babes in the saddle bags.

"The Simpleton's Wisdom"

There was a man and his wife who had one daughter. Mother and daughter were deeply attached to one another, and when the latter died the mother was disconsolate. She cut off her hair, cut gashes in her cheeks and sat before the corpse with her robe drawn over her head, mourning for her dead. Nor would she let them touch the body to take it to a burying scaffold. She had a knife in her hand, and if anyone offered to come near the body the mother would wail: "I am weary of life. I do not care to live. I will stab myself with this knife and join my daughter in the land of spirits."

Her husband and relatives tried to get the knife from her, but could not. They feared to use force lest she kill herself. . . . At last they called a boy, a kind of simpleton, yet with a good deal of natural shrewdness. He was an orphan and very poor. His moccasins were out at the sole and he was dressed in wei-zi (coarse buffalo skin, smoked).

"Go to the tepee of the mourning mother," they told the simpleton, "and in some way contrive to make her laugh and forget her grief. Then try to get the knife away from her."

The boy went to the tent. . . . As the mother sat on the ground with her head covered she did not at first see the boy, who sat silent. But when his reserve had worn away a little he began at first lightly, then more heavily, to drum on the floor with his hands. After a while he began to sing a comic song. Louder and louder he sang until carried away with his own singing he sprang up and began to dance, at the same time gesturing and making all manner of contortions with his body, still singing the comic song. As he approached the corpse he waved his hands over it in blessing. The mother put her head out of the blanket and when she saw the poor simpleton with his strange grimaces trying to do honor to the corpse by his solemn waving, and at the same time keeping up his comic song, she burst out laughing. Then she reached over and handed her knife to the simpleton.

"Take this knife," she said. "You have taught me to forget my grief. If while I mourn for the dead I can still be mirthful, there is no reason for me to despair. I no longer care to die. I will live for my husband."

The simpleton left the tepee and brought the knife to the astonished husband and relatives. . . . When the old men of the village heard the orphan's story they were very silent. It was a strange thing for a lad to dance in a tepee where there was mourning. It was stranger that a mother should laugh in a tepee before the corpse of her dead daughter. The old men gathered at last in a council. They sat a long time without saying anything, for they did not want to decide hastily. The pipe was filled and passed many times. At last an old man spoke.

"We have a hard question. A mother has laughed before the corpse of her daughter, and many think she has done foolishly, but I think the woman did wisely. The lad was simple and of no training, and we cannot expect him to know how to do as well as one with good home and parents to teach him. Besides, he did the best that he knew. He danced to make the mother forget her grief, and he tried to honor the corpse by waving over it his hands."

"The mother did right to laugh, for when one does try to do us good, even if what he does causes us discomfort, we should always remember rather the motive than the deed. And besides, the simpleton's dancing saved the woman's life, for she gave up her knife. In this, too, she did well, for it is always better to live for the living than to die for the dead."

The lessons of the first two stories are obvious, practical, and straightforward. The point of "The Forgotten Ear of Corn" is explicit: gather every bit of the corn crop. "The Little Mice," like Aesop's "The Grasshopper and the Ant," stresses the importance of planning for the future.

Note, however, how many different topics "The Pet Donkey" and "The Simpleton's Wisdom" present to a listener for consideration. It is the plain, plodding donkey, not the flashy, fast pony, who saves the lives of the babies. The donkey understands his responsibilities and, even though he is beaten, he insists on performing them. Similarly, "The Simpleton's Wisdom" reminds us that we are often wrong when we base our assumptions on thoughtless, biased judgments (a simpleton can't possibly be intelligent enough to help a suicidal woman) or on traditional wisdom (dancing and laughing over a corpse is disrespectful and wrong).

There are several points to appreciate about these stories.

First, stories should not be dismissed out of hand as a primitive and unsophisticated way to operate in the world. Psychologist Robin Dunbar argues that language appeared among humans primarily as a way to increase social cohesion by exchanging information about other members of the group—to gossip, that is, to tell *stories* about each other.[28] Neuroscientist Steven Pinker also points to stories' usefulness in navigating life: "Fictional

---

28. Robin Dunbar, *Grooming, Gossip, and the Evolution of Language* (Cambridge, MA: Harvard University Press, 1996).

narratives supply us with a mental catalogue of the fatal conundrums we might face someday and the outcomes of strategies we could deploy in them. . . . The cliché that life imitates art is true because the function of some kinds of art is for life to imitate it."[29] In cultures that rely on oral traditions for shaping and passing along their culture, stories are an excellent tool. They're easy to remember and enjoyable.

Second, these four stories represent many Native American tales that reflect a bias for *knowledge-how*, specifically, knowledge-how to live successfully in a particular set of physical and social conditions.

Third, in many American Indian stories, the main characters aren't human. They're mice, coyotes, bears, rabbits, bison, turtles, etc. This expresses the Native American belief that everything is alive, has power, and deserves respect.

Fourth, McPherson and Rabb argue that stories are also used for the explicit purpose of developing "self-reliance and independent thinking." They write,

> Native elders . . . are not known for offering advice, at least not directly. In actual fact they have a reputation of never giving a straight answer. You will often be told a story which seems to have nothing whatsoever to do with whatever question you asked or problem you raised. You are given the autonomy, the complete freedom, to discover the relevance of the reply, and hence to work out the problem for yourself. This is a sign of respect.[30]

In the Native American tradition, then, stories are important tools for everything from passing along practical information to reinforcing a tribe's values to developing intellectual abilities and independence.

Moral and Social Values

While Native American perspectives clash sharply with Western philosophy's ideas about knowledge, the contrast with philosophical ethics is not as dramatic.

Given the idea that everything is alive, powerful, and has a connection with the Great Spirit, it should be no surprise that Native American thought has respect for anything alive—beings, objects, places, the earth itself. In particular, this applies to nonhuman animals. In a Western perspective, nonhuman animals are typically regarded as economic commodities, having few rights of their own. To Native Americans, however, these animals are beings who deserve respect and appreciation. "When we killed a buffalo," Lame Deer explains, "we knew what we were doing. We apologized to his spirit, tried to make him understand why we did it, honoring with a prayer the bones of those who gave their flesh to keep us alive, praying for their return, praying for the life of our

29. Steven Pinker, *The Way the Mind Works* (New York: W. W. Norton, 1997), 543. See also Lisa Cron, *Wired for Story* (Berkeley, CA: Ten Speed Press, 2012).
30. McPherson and Rabb, *Indian from the Inside*, 105.

brothers, the buffalo nation, as well as our own people."[31] McPherson and Rabb argue the Native American perspective contains "a moral obligation to protect the habitat of the moose, the beaver, the muskrat, and the lynx; the habitat of geese, ducks, grouse and hare, not just because members of the Band wish to continue hunting and trapping, but because these other-than-human persons are also extended members of Ojibwa society."[32] Indeed, they go so far as to endorse the claim of philosopher J. Baird Callicott that the Native American perspective is very close to the ideas of environmentalist Aldo Leopold, who considers the touchstone of environmental ethics to be "the integrity, stability, and beauty of the biotic community," not the rights of individuals.[33]

Note that if the Native American perspective is that we're all part of one large, living community, it makes the concept of *responsibility to others* central. Vine Deloria elaborates, "In contrast to the West, where 'rights' reign supreme, the tribal peoples through family, clan, and societies created a climate in which 'responsibility' would be the chief virtue."[34] Interestingly, this parallels one of the central differences we saw in Chapter 5 between an "ethic of justice" and an "ethic of care." Once again, as in the case of Janice Moulton, we see Western *female* philosophers articulating insights that parallel the Native American tradition. Recall that while an ethic of justice focuses on *rights,* the ethic of care evaluates actions from the point of view of our *responsibilities* to support those in need of assistance and to prevent harm.

Other Native American values emphasize the importance of fostering the conditions that allow groups to work well together. As we saw, the sharing circle encourages respect for different perspectives. The practice of passing an object (a pipe, for example) from speaker to speaker enforces courtesy and a non-adversarial atmosphere. Speakers must be listened to without interruption or judgment.

The practice by elders of telling a story when a young person asks for advice, noted above, not only encourages self-reliance and independent thinking, it also expresses the importance of noninterference. The value is so important that, as McPherson and Rabb report, "in the Western Apache tradition one would never directly criticize another person, regardless of age. That would be considered rude." This stance toward others should not be understood as an attitude of "everyone for themselves," however. If it becomes necessary to interfere in someone else's life—as we saw in "The Simpleton's Wisdom"—it should be done in a way that doesn't offend them.[35]

However, there is one aspect of the Native American attitude toward others that is explicitly intrusive—but in a positive way, through generosity. Standing Bear, a Lakota Chief and friend of Black Elk, reports that before a particular bison hunt, the person in charge "would go around and find the best men in the bunch with good horses and bring

31. Lame Deer, "Talking to the Owls and Butterflies," 122–23.

32. McPherson and Rabb, *Indian from the Inside*, 91.

33. McPherson and Rabb, *Indian from the Inside*, 92; Aldo Leopold, *A Sand County Almanac, with Essays on Conservation from Round River* (New York: Ballantine Books, 1970), 262.

34. Deloria, "Philosophy and the Tribal Peoples," 10.

35. McPherson and Rabb, *Indian from the Inside*, 105–6.

them forward and [he] said to them: 'Good young warriors, . . . today you shall feed the helpless and feed the old and feeble and perhaps there is a widow who has no support. You shall help them. Whatever you get you shall donate to the poor."[36] Giving to others without looking for anything in return—whether the gifts are material objects, someone's time, kindness, sympathy, and so on—continues to be a part of Native American societies.

Dreams and Visions

The final topic we're going to touch on in this chapter is in many ways its most controversial and difficult to study. Accordingly, this section should be seen as doing nothing more than acknowledging the critical role of dreams and visions in Native American thought and encouraging you to take the time to explore this topic in more detail—especially via the visions of the Lakota holy man and healer Black Elk (1863–1950).

As we saw in Chapters 7 and 8, Western philosophers think that knowledge comes either from reason or the senses. Dreams and visions are generally regarded as the brain doing some therapeutic housekeeping, a window into our unconscious, or hallucinations. For Native Americans, however, dreams and visions are valuable sources of knowledge, offering a glimpse into the spirit world.[37]

Visions are particularly powerful sources of understanding. Traditionally, a "vision quest" is an initiation into adulthood and begins with a period of fasting and solitude at a sacred site in the hope of receiving a vision that will illuminate one's purpose and role in life. Probably the most venerated and studied vision, however, that of Black Elk, came without warning when he was nine years old and, to outward appearances, was sick for twelve days.[38] He received this and two subsequent visions when there were open hostilities between the Native Americans and the Whites. This was the period in which the massacre at Wounded Knee took place. Whites were pushing across the continent, displacing Native Americans from their homeland, reneging on treaties, and limiting them to reservations.

In Black Elk's highly symbolic vision, two men (whom he had seen in an earlier vision) call to him and lead him on a cloud that takes him into the sky, where a group of horses leads him to the six Grandfathers (the Powers of the world). They give him a series of objects (including a cup, an herb, a peace pipe, and a red stick) and tell him about powers he will have (the power to heal, do good, and defend his people from their enemies). He is shown a red road ("the road of good") and a black road ("a fearful road, a road of troubles and of war"). He rides a horse down the black road, cures a drought, and heals the sick in a village. Then he rides the red road with the villagers and has to make four ascents, each representing a generation he will know. He becomes an eagle during the

---

36. *The Sixth Grandfather*, ed. Raymond J. DeMaillie (Lincoln: University of Nebraska Press, 1984), 146.
37. McPherson and Rabb, *Indian from the Inside*, 60.
38. Black Elk's visions were first reported in poet John Neihardt's account of a series of interviews with the healer, *Black Elk Speaks* (Lincoln: University of Nebraska Press, 2004).

second ascent. The ascents get increasingly difficult, suggesting difficult times to come for the people. He transforms back to himself riding on a horse and comes upon a horse needing assistance. Other horses appear and four beautiful virgins encircle the horses and dance while the chief horse sings a song. Accompanied by riders, he proceeds to the top of a mountain, then returns to the Grandfathers who give him sacred gifts. An eagle accompanies him back to his village and he regains consciousness.[39]

Uncertain, Black Elk kept his vision to himself for years. After a second vision when he was nineteen, he accepted that he was a healer and treated people. Ultimately, he seems to have had reservations about how well he fulfilled his purpose because he was not able to do more for his people. However, his vision and his status a holy man continue to be sources of inspiration both to Native Americans and to anyone open to the idea that we can have unique experiences that give us access to other dimensions of reality.

The Challenge of the Native American Perspective

In their respective challenges to the traditional Western perspective, Buddhism and Native American thought share some interesting features. Neither makes a sharp distinction between philosophy and religion. Both suggest that knowledge and understanding come from something more than reason. Buddhism recommends meditation; Native Americans, dreams and visions. Both reject the traditional Western values of rugged individualism and materialism.

Ultimately, however, the combination of the pragmatic character of Native American thought and its respect for the world of nature as a community of living beings makes devastatingly obvious both the moral and practical failings of the culture that tried to eradicate North and South America's original inhabitants. Traditional Western culture regards the world of nature as nothing more than a lifeless commodity to be mined, consumed, and abandoned. It is fixated on amassing short-term gains for a small portion of the global population while it passes the costs to anyone else—even their children's and grandchildren's generations. From a purely practical standpoint, it can be argued that the traditional Western perspective is self-destructive. The price for short-term economic benefits has been, at a minimum: compromises to our health, clean air, clean water, safe soil; a warming planet; and the denial of facts. It can also be argued that the adversarial and competitive nature of capitalism has encouraged antisocial values, empowered authoritarian regimes, and weakened the cause of human rights around the planet.

Sadly, it is plain that the traditional Western outlook does not share the Native American appreciation for *knowledge-how to live successfully in our environment*. The result is an increasingly difficult future. And given this failure, it is important to ask whether embracing other dimensions of a Native American perspective might help reveal a more

---

39. This is an oversimplified and seriously incomplete summary of Black Elk's vision, which takes him nearly seven thousand words to describe. The vision includes many items with symbolic meaning: songs, dances, rainbows, colors, "thunder beings," and so on.

sustainable path—for example, the centrality of responsibility, a respect for the sacred, the importance of generosity, and the value of direct, personal experience in the search for knowledge and understanding.

In that spirit, it seems appropriate to conclude this chapter with one of Black Elk's most famous insights about the benefits that come from properly understanding our relationship with the rest of the universe: "The first peace, which is the most important, is that which comes within the souls of men when they realize their relationship, their oneness, with the universe and all its Powers, and when they realize that at the center of the universe dwells Wakan-Tanka, and that center is really everywhere, it is within each of us. This is the real Peace."[40]

Discussion Questions

1. If you were to interpret your life from a Buddhist point of view, what would you say are the most important challenges to your spiritual development? What kind of karma are you working off from past lives?

2. Have you ever had an experience that is explained best by the idea that you have lived before? What was it?

3. How would you go about decreasing your wants, as Buddhism recommends? What would your life be like? If you succeeded, do you think you would be happier or unhappier?

4. In view of the Buddha's program for achieving enlightenment, do you think that meditation should be as much a part of the curriculum as writing, for instance?

5. As noted in the chapter, "Literature and philosophy, science and religion are all very different branches of knowledge in Western thought. . . . However, in American Indian thought this is not the case. None of these four can really be separated from the others." What do "truth" and "knowledge" look like in a perspective that combines what the West sees as separate?

6. If "the universe is an essentially organic, multifaceted entity," does that imply that it has a consciousness? If so, is this consciousness directing whatever goes on in the universe? What does this imply about "free will"?

7. "Polycentrism" (the idea that "no one perspective can contain the whole truth") is diametrically opposed to a traditional Western philosophical approach to knowledge. In your opinion, which outlook is correct? Does polycentrism even allow us to ask that question?

---

40. *The Sacred Pipe: Black Elk's Account of the Seven Rites of the Oglala Sioux,* recorded and edited by Joseph Epes Brown (Norman: University of Oklahoma Press, 1989), 95.

8. Stories, dreams, and visions occupy a central place in the Native American tradition. As tools for seeking knowledge, wisdom, or understanding, in what way are they better and/or worse than an approach that emphasizes reason, observable evidence, and experimentation?

9. There are a couple of ways that the ideas of feminist philosophers are similar to aspects of Native American thought. What's your reaction to that?

Selected Readings

For the Buddha's teachings, see *The Dhammapada*. For the teachings of two Native American holy men, see John (Fire) Lame Deer and Richard Erdoes, *Lame Deer, Seeker of Visions* (New York: Simon & Schuster, 2000); John G. Neihardt, *Black Elk Speaks: The Complete Edition* (Lincoln: University of Nebraska Press, 2014). Also see *American Indian Thought*, ed. Anne Waters (Oxford: Blackwell Press, 2004).

GLOSSARY

a posteriori: An a posteriori argument draws its conclusion from empirical evidence.

a priori: An a priori argument relies on reason alone.

alienated labor: According to Marx, alienated labor is the type of labor that characterizes capitalism. It has four dimensions: the worker is alienated from the product produced, from the activity of production, from his or her productive nature, and from other people.

analytic statement: An analytic statement attributes a property to something, and that property is already implicit in the definition of that object or concept. For example, "A square has four sides" and "A bachelor is unmarried" are analytic statements.

argument: An argument is a series of statements that you make either orally or in writing, one of which is a claim of some sort, and the rest of which are your reasons for making this claim.

argument from design: The argument from design is an argument for the existence of God that claims that the universe is so intelligently crafted that it must have a creator.

argument from the governance of the world: The argument from the governance of the world claims that the order and intelligence of the activities of nature imply the existence of a being directing them.

behaviorism: Behaviorism is the school of psychology that focuses exclusively on observable behavior and denies free will. Behavior is seen as an organism's "response" to a "stimulus"; the likelihood of a behavior recurring is increased by "positive reinforcement," and it is decreased by "negative reinforcement."

categorical imperative: The categorical imperative is Immanuel Kant's conception of a universal moral law. One formulation of this principle is "Act in such a way that you treat humanity, whether in your own person or in the person of any other, always at the same time as an end and never simply as a means."

conclusion: The technical label for the argument's claim, point, or result, is the conclusion.

consequentialist: A consequentialist approach to ethics claims that the ethical character of an action depends on whether its consequences are positive or negative.

critical thinking: To think critically is to judge whether some claim is believable and convincing, that is, whether it is based on solid facts or good reasons. All intellectual disciplines that deal with evidence and proof are based on critical thinking.

deontological: A deontological theory of ethics argues that actions have a moral character apart from their consequences.

determinism: Determinists deny "free will" and maintain that everything in nature, including human behavior, happens as a result of cause and effect. If every effect already has a cause, then our actions and our choices are simply the result of some preexisting causes that produce them, and they cannot be freely arrived at.

dialectic: Dialectic is Hegel's label for the dynamic and conflict-filled process whereby one force (thesis) collides with its opposite (antithesis) to produce a new state of affairs that combines elements of both (synthesis). Given the primacy of Spirit in Hegel's thinking, Hegel's outlook can be described as "dialectical idealism."

dialectical materialism: Dialectical materialism is Marx's revision of Hegel's dialectical idealism in terms of Marx's belief in the primacy of material, specifically economic, forces. Marx thus sees human history as the clash of opposing economic forces, creating new stages.

empiricism: Empiricism is the philosophical outlook that stresses the importance of basing knowledge on objective, observable facts and physical evidence. Empiricism holds that knowledge and truth are the products of sensory experiences and not of purely mental operations.

epistemology: Epistemology, also called "theory of knowledge," is the part of philosophy concerned with "knowledge" and related concepts.

essence precedes existence: Philosophers have traditionally held that the "nature" of something determines what it is able to do, its limitations, defining characteristics, and the like, that is, its "existence." This position is rejected by the existential belief that our choices determine our nature ("existence precedes essence").

ethical relativism: Ethical relativism denies the existence of universal, objective ethical principles and asserts that ethical judgments are simply an expression of the limited perspective of individuals or societies.

ethics: Ethics, also called "moral philosophy," is the part of philosophy concerned with right, wrong, and other issues related to evaluating human conduct.

existence precedes essence: "Existence precedes essence" is the existentialist rejection of the traditional idea that something's nature determines its abilities and limitations in how it lives. Existentialism maintains instead that our choices ("existence") determine our nature ("essence").

existentialism: Existentialism is a school of thought based on the idea that "existence precedes essence," that is, that our nature is determined by the actions we choose to do. Existentialism argues that freedom is such an unavoidable, and sometimes uncomfortable, characteristic of life that we are "condemned to be free." We are completely free at every moment, absolutely everything about us is a product of our own choices, and we are responsible for each and every detail of our lives.

fallacies: Fallacies are weaknesses or mistakes in argumentation. Fallacies concerned with an argument's "form" or logical structure are formal fallacies. Subject matter fallacies are called informal fallacies.

Forms: The Forms are what Plato calls the nonmaterial, perfect models of everything that exists. They are known only by the mind. The chief Form is the Form of the Good.

free will: Free will claims that we have control over our actions. Our deeds are seen as the product of reflection and choice, not internal or external causal forces.

Freudianism: Freudianism is the largely deterministic, psychological theory developed by Sigmund Freud that claims that the human personality has both conscious and unconscious dimensions. Behavior is ultimately determined by unconscious primal drives, early childhood experience, and the interplay of the three parts of the personality—the id, ego, and superego.

hedonistic calculus: The hedonistic calculus is Jeremy Bentham's system for measuring the amount of pleasure and pain that results from an action. It takes into account seven dimensions of a pleasure or pain: intensity, duration, certainty or uncertainty, propinquity or remoteness, fecundity, purity, and extent.

idealism: In opposition to materialism, idealism maintains that reality is rooted in ideas, not matter. Plato, for example, claims that the Forms are more real and better sources of truth and knowledge than the objects that present themselves to our senses.

indeterminism: Indeterminism is William James's position that in any circumstance we genuinely have more than one option from which to choose. Accordingly, he argues, our actions are not determined.

involuntary: Aristotle labels as "involuntary" actions that result from constraint or ignorance. He does not think we are responsible for involuntary actions.

karma: Karma is a fundamental Buddhist law of the universe. The law of karma holds that all deeds produce positive or negative effects for the one who does them, and these effects extend from one life to the next. Karma is the Eastern equivalent to the Western law of cause and effect, or principle of action and reaction, or balance. It is also described as a law of sowing and reaping.

logic: Logic is the part of philosophy devoted to studying reason itself and the structure of arguments.

materialism: Materialism is a theory about the nature of reality that claims that if something exists, it must be physical and subject to natural laws like cause and effect. Materialism logically implies determinism.

metaphysics: Metaphysics is the part of philosophy concerned with the most basic issues, for example, reality, existence, personhood, and freedom versus determinism. Metaphysics was originally referred to by Aristotle as "first philosophy."

ontological argument: The ontological argument is St. Anselm's argument for the existence of God. It claims that by merely contemplating the notion of God as "something-than-which-nothing-greater-can-be-thought," we become aware that God must exist.

person: A person is a self-conscious, intelligent, living being who can act and communicate. "Human" and "person" are different concepts. Most humans are also persons (someone who is "brain dead" might be an example of a human whose body is alive, but who is no longer a "person"). One does not have to be human to be a person.

philosophy: Philosophy is an active, intellectual enterprise dedicated to exploring the most fundamental questions of life.

political philosophy: Political philosophy is the part of philosophy that addresses the philosophical issues that arise from the fact that we live together in communities. These issues include the nature of political authority, utopias, justice, and the problem of harmonizing freedom and obligation.

polycentric: A polycentric approach to knowledge, characteristic of Native American thought, claims that no one perspective can capture the truth.

pragmatism: Pragmatism is a school of thought that takes a practical and inclusive approach to solving philosophical problems. In connection with the debate between free will and determinism, William James defends free will with the argument that when we take everything into account, "indeterminism" is an explanation that simply "works better" than determinism.

premises: The reasons that allegedly lead to the conclusion of an argument are called premises.

problem of evil: The problem of evil refers to the conflict between the notion of a good God and the existence of evil in the world. This idea is generally used to argue against the existence of God.

rationalism: Rationalism claims that knowledge comes from, or arises in, our minds. Rationalist philosophers argue that the best examples of knowledge are mathematics and logic.

Stoicism: Stoicism is the late ancient school of philosophy that believes that the world is governed by fate. The only thing in our power is our attitudes; happiness is achieved by cultivating a disposition of accepting what is inevitable.

synthetic statement: A synthetic statement attributes a property to something, but that property goes beyond what is contained within the definition of the object or concept involved. For example, "The page is white" is a synthetic statement.

utilitarianism: Utilitarianism is a consequentialist ethical theory advanced by Jeremy Bentham and John Stuart Mill. It uses pleasure and notions like "the greatest good of the greatest number" as standards for judging the morality of actions.

voluntary: Aristotle labels as "voluntary" actions that are under our control. This includes habits or dispositions that seem to be out of our control but nonetheless result from earlier choices made when the matter was in our power. This also includes actions done from culpable ignorance or negligence. Aristotle thinks we are responsible for all voluntary actions.

INDEX

a posteriori argument, 283
a priori argument, 283
absolute space, 247
absolute time, 247
Adversary Method, 40–41, 111, 271–72.
  See also Moulton, Janice
alienated labor, 242–45, 283
allegory of the cave, 148–49
alternate realities, 252–55
American Indian. *See* Native American
  thought
analytic statements, 164–66, 283
animals, nonhuman, 96n6, 183. *See also*
  dolphins and flourishing
Anselm, Saint
  critics of, 200–202
  ontological argument, 197–99
  reply to critics, 202–3
appearance versus reality, 47, 141
Aquinas, Saint Thomas, 191
  argument from governance of the
    world, 192, 283
  Aristotle and, 191
  criticism of Saint Anselm, 201
argumentation, 16–17, 24–28. *See also*
  logic
Aristotle, 11
  Aquinas and, 191
  ethics and, 114
  on action, 70–71
  on character, 71–72
  on freedom, 74
  on logic, 17
  on metaphysics, 10, 10n3
  on responsibility, 72–73
  on virtues, 113–15
Asserting Rule, 29
Augustine, Saint, 194
  on free will, 194
Ayer, A. J., 94n2

bad faith, 86–87
basic human needs, 95–99

behaviorism, 50, 52–56, 283. *See also*
  Skinner, B. F.
  definition of, 52
  freedom and, 53–55
Bentham, Jeremy, 100–102
  empiricism and, 101
  hedonistic calculus, 101–2
  Mill and, 103
  pleasure and, 100–101
  utilitarianism and, 100
Black Elk, 268, 279
British empiricists, 167, 169. *See also*
  empiricism; Hume, David; Locke, John
Buddha, 258–65
Buddhism, 265–68
  compared to Western thought, 265–67
  Dhammapada, 262, 265
  dukkha, 262
  Four Noble Truths, 262–63
  karma, 259–66
  Middle Way, 263–64
  Nirvana, 263–65
  Noble Eightfold Path, 263–64
  origins of, 258
  rebirth, 259
  trishna, 262
  Wheel of Life, 262

capabilities approach, 96
  Martha Nussbaum and, 96
capitalism, 233, 238–46
care, ethic of, 110–15, 278
  emotions, role of in, 112
categorical imperative, the, 109, 283.
  See also Kant, Immanuel
character 71, 120
  Aristotelian view of, 71
  soul and, 120
clarity, 158–59
cogito ergo sum, 158
conclusion, 24, 283
Confucius, 257
conscience, 59, 131. *See also* moral vision

287